Economies in Transition

Economies in Transition: Comparing Asia and Eastern Europe

edited by
Wing Thye Woo,
Stephen Parker, and
Jeffrey D. Sachs

The MIT Press
Cambridge, Massachusetts
London, England

Third printing, 1998

Library of Congress Cataloging-in-Publication Data

Economies in transition: comparing Asia and Eastern Europe / edited by
 Wing Thye Woo, Stephen Parker, and Jeffrey D. Sachs.
    p.   cm.
 This volume is the culmination of a two-year research and policy engage-
ment project undertaken by The Asia Foundation's Center for Asian Pacific
Affairs (CAPA).
 Includes bibliographical references (p.   ) and index.
 ISBN 0-262-23191-3 (hard.: alk. paper).—ISBN 0-262-73120-7 (pbk.: alk.
paper)
    1. Asia—Economic policy. 2. Europe, Eastern—Economic policy—1989–   .
3. Post-communism—Asia. 4. Post-communism—Europe, Eastern. I. Woo,
Wing Thye. II. Parker, Stephen. III. Sachs, Jeffrey. IV. Asia Foundation.
Center for Asian Pacific Affairs.
HC412.E246   1996
338.947—dc21   96-45192
                                                                     CIP

To the children of the world, for whom the transition promises a better future

Contents

Contributors

Leszek Balcerowicz (chapter 5) President, Advisory Council for the Foundation for Economic Education, Warsaw; Chairman, Center for Social and Economic Research, Warsaw; and former Minister of Finance of Poland

Barbara Blaszczyk (chapter 5) Center for Social and Economic Research, Warsaw

Peter Boone (chapters 4 and 6) Lecturer in Economics, London School of Economics (LSE), and Director of the Post-Communist Reform Program, LSE Center for Economic Performance, London

Yuan Zheng Cao (chapter 2) Deputy Director of the Institute for Economic Systems Management, State Commission for Restructuring the Economic Systems (SCRES), Beijing

Bruce Comer (chapter 7) Merrill Lynch, New York City

Marek Dabrowski (chapter 5) Vice Chairman, Center for Social and Economic Research, Warsaw

Daniel C. Esty (chapter 13) Professor, Yale School of Forestry and Environmental Studies, and Director, Yale Center for Environmental Law and Policy, Yale University, New Haven

Gang Fan (chapter 2) Professor of Economics, Graduate School of the Chinese Academy of Social Sciences, and Director of the National Economic Research Institute of the China Reform Foundation, Beijing

Boris Fedorov (chapter 6) Member of Parliament of the Russian Federation, and former Deputy Prime Minister and Minister of Finance

Roman Frydman (chapter 3) Professor of Economics, New York University, and Co-director of the Central European University Privatization Project, Budapest

Carol Graham (chapter 12) Visiting Fellow, Foreign Policy Studies Program, The Brookings Institution, and Adjunct Professor of Government, Georgetown University, Washington, D.C.

Georges de Menil (chapter 10)
Director, Departement et Labora-
toire d'Economique Theorique et
Appliquee (DELTA), and
Professor, Ecoles des Hautes
Etudes en Sciences Sociales, Paris

Stephen Parker (chapter 1)
Chief Economist, The Asia
Foundation, San Francisco

Andrzej Rapaczynski (chapter 3)
Professor, Columbia University
School of Law, and Co-director of
the Central European University
Privatization Project, Budapest

James Riedel (chapter 7)
Professor of International
Economics, The Paul H. Nitze
School of Advanced International
Studies, The Johns Hopkins
University, Baltimore

Jeffrey D. Sachs (chapter 9)
Director, Harvard Institute for
International Development, and
Galen L. Stone Professor of
International Trade, Harvard
University, Cambridge

Baavaa Tarvaa (chapter 4)
Senior Officer of the National
Development Board of the
Government of Mongolia

Vinod Thomas (chapter 8)
Director, Economic Development
Institute (EDI), The World Bank,
Washington, D.C.

Joel Turkewitz (chapter 3)
Central European University
Privatization Project, Budapest

Adiya Tsend (chapter 4)
Rector, Institute of
Administration and Management
Development; Vice President of
the Mongolia Management
Association; and President of the
Mongolian Management
Development Institute,
Ulaanbaatar, Mongolia

Gavin Tritt (chapter 1)
Program Officer, Economics and
Trade, Center for Asian Pacific
Affairs, The Asia Foundation, San
Francisco

Enkhbold Tsendjav (chapter 4)
Professor, Institute of
Administration and Management
Development, and an NGO
leader, Ulaanbaatar, Mongolia

Narantsetseg Unenburen (chapter 4)
Member of Parliament, Mongolia

Yan Wang (chapter 8)
Economist, Office of the Director
of the Economic Development
Institute (EDI), The World Bank,
Washington, D.C.

Wing Thye Woo
(chapters 1, 2, and 11)
Professor of Economics,
Department of Economics,
University of California, Davis

Preface

This volume on "Economies in Transition: Comparing Asia and Eastern Europe" is the culmination of a two-year research and policy engagement project undertaken by The Asia Foundation's Center for Asian Pacific Affairs (CAPA) with the generous support of the Pew Charitable Trusts. The project has taken an explicitly comparative approach to examining Asian and Eastern European transition experiences, with a focus on developing a systematic understanding of the economic and institutional dynamics underlying the transformations from centrally-planned to market economies.

When we started this project in 1994, it was rare for experts and policy makers in the Eastern European and Asian transition economies to meet and discuss common problems and experiences. In fact, we were told that this was a near-impossible task because of the great social, economic, and political differences between the two regions. We were convinced, however, that many elements of the transition process did have general application across economies even with vastly different initial economic and political conditions. Furthermore, we wanted to understand better the interaction of different transition strategies and initial conditions. We designed this project, therefore, to engage leading researchers and policy makers who have been intimately involved with the various transition processes, in most cases from their beginnings. We were also determined to include both a solid research effort as well as meaningful dialogue with key policy makers in the transition economies.

The project's research studies are presented in this volume. Each study has been presented and discussed thoroughly by experts and policy makers in Prague, Ho Chi Minh City, Hanoi, Beijing, Ulaanbaatar, and Washington. The activities in Asia, Eastern Europe, and Washington allowed the project's diverse and multi-talented team to engage in discussions directly with the policy communities in key transition economies, offering insights from research and experience, while in turn getting suggestions to improve the quality and relevance of the project findings. In addition, these policy engagement activities served to expose project participants to new countries, issues, and experiences, which will add to their capacities for further work on these topics.

The first policy conference took place on December 2–3, 1994, and was co-sponsored by the Central European University Privatization Project in Prague, Czech Republic. Then, in late June and early July, 1995, conferences were held in Viet Nam in Ho Chi Minh City and Hanoi, in the People's Republic of China in Beijing, and in Mongolia's capital, Ulaanbaatar. Then, in the spring of 1996, a wrap-up conference was held in Washington, D.C. The conferences in Asia were attended by a wide range of high-ranking government officials, policy analysts, and researchers, and included a number of supplementary activities in each city, such as ministerial roundtables and public lectures, that helped bring the project findings to a broader audience while providing an opportunity for the host-country participants to focus on issues of particular interest and relevance. The project team met as a group with senior government officials in each country, including Deputy Prime Minister Pham Van Kai in Viet Nam, State Councillor Li Tieying in China, and Deputy Prime Minister Enebish in Mongolia.

The challenge of learning from the experiences of other countries, and applying those lessons to policy problems and issues in Asia and the United States, is central to the work of The Asia Foundation. The Asia Foundation is a private, non-profit U.S. organization, with headquarters in San Francisco, 14 field offices in the Asia-Pacific region, and a liaison office in Washington, D.C. Since its creation in 1954, the Foundation has promoted U.S.-Asian understanding and cooperation, and encouraged Asian-Pacific efforts to strengthen representative government, build effective legal systems, foster market economies, increase accountability in the public and private sectors, develop independent and reasonable media, and encourage broad participation in public life.

The Center for Asian Pacific Affairs (CAPA) was created in 1985 as a unit of The Asia Foundation to expand and improve the policy dialogue between Americans and Asians on issues of mutual interest. CAPA's seminars, conferences, and working groups include Asian and American opinion leaders and policy makers. Through its programs, CAPA seeks to identify the nature and direction of political, economic, and security changes in Asia; to explore the impact of these changes on the countries and peoples of the region; and to assess their implications for American and Asian interests and policies.

A project examining such a broad and challenging set of issues involving countries separated by huge distances and, often, cultural differences has posed a real challenge, and has required the energy and commitment of many individuals and institutions. The overall project has been managed by Stephen Parker, Chief Economist for The Asia Foundation, and Gavin Tritt, Economic Program Officer for CAPA. Professor Wing Thye Woo was the project's research advisor. He participated in all aspects of the project and took the lead role in editing this volume. Professor Jeffrey Sachs was closely involved in designing the project, monitoring its progress and offering guidance and his wealth of experience and insights on the transition processes.

Our list of special thanks is long, and we apologize in advance that, for space reasons, we had to leave out the names of many people who made great contributions to the project. The commitment of the research team, which has required not only preparation of papers but also attendance at conferences and policy sessions on three continents, has been incredible. We are very grateful for the generous support of the Prague conference that was provided by the Central European University Privatization Project through the leadership of their Co-directors, Professor Roman Frydman and Professor Andrzej Rapaczynski, and the in-kind support provided by the staff, particularly Joel Turkewitz. We are also very grateful for the support provided by the institutional co-sponsors and hosts of the Asia policy seminar series. In Beijing, we would like to thank The Institute for Economic Systems Management at the State Commission for Restructuring the Economic Systems (SCRES), including Cao Yuan Zheng, Wang Tong, Wang Haijun, and the rest of SCRES, as well as Fan Gang and the Chinese Academy of Social Sciences, who also supported the conference, and the conference participants and discussants. In Mongolia, we would like to express our gratitude to the Institute for Administration and Management Development in Ulaanbaatar, and particularly Adiya Tsend, Enkhbold Tsendjav, and Narantsetseg Unenburen, as well as the many staff members from the IAMD and the Foundation's Mongolia office who worked on the conference, and the participants from government and the private sector who contributed to the discussion. In Hanoi, we would like to thank the Central Institute for Economic Management, including Le Dang Doanh, Nguyen Minh Tu, and Vu Xuan Nguyet Hong; in Ho Chi Minh City we would like to thank the Institute for Economic Research, including Ton Si Kinh, Tran Du Lich, and Bach Van Bay, and the many Vietnamese participants in our conferences and numerous policy roundtables. For the Washington conference, we would like to express our thanks to The Paul H. Nitze School of Advanced International Studies at The Johns Hopkins University, which co-sponsored the public conference, and to its Dean, Ambassador Paul Wolfowitz, Professor James Riedel (Jim was also particularly helpful with all involved in the organization of activities in Viet Nam), and Allison Boyd, as well as the speakers who joined the project team at the conference, including Lawrence Summers, Alan Larson, David Lipton, Susan Schadler, and Michael Walton. Special thanks go to Alan Gelb and the World Bank for hosting a seminar to present the project's findings to staff of the Bank, the IMF, and the IFC.

We need to thank several people who have contributed to the planning process of the project, including with special thanks Kevin F. F. Quigley and Nicholas Lardy, who were indispensable during the early stage of project development, as well as Harry Harding and Alan Gelb for their advice and support. Wing Thye Woo's participation in the project was made easier by the logistical support provided by the Institute of Governmental Affairs at the University of California, Davis, and we would like to thank Alan Olmstead, Director of the Institute, for his overall support of the project. In addition, we would like to thank William P. Fuller, President of The Asia Foundation, Cas Yost and Richard Wilson, former and current Executive Directors of CAPA, Sheldon Severinghaus and the staff of The Asia Foundation program in Mongolia, Allen Choate, the Foundation's Representative for China, Helen Chauncey, The Foundation's Representative for Viet Nam, and the staff of the Foundation's office in Washington. We are also indebted to our indefatigable editor, Catherine Whitney Hoover, without whom this book would not be in existence.

Economies in Transition

I Overview

1

Some Lessons Learned from the Comparison of Transitions in Asia and Eastern Europe

Stephen Parker, Gavin Tritt, and Wing Thye Woo

1.1 Introduction

Nearly two decades have elapsed since Deng Xiaoping and China's reformers announced the Four Modernizations that are transforming China into a new hybrid system—a socialist market economy with Chinese characteristics. Viet Nam followed with a policy of *doi moi* (renovation) in 1986, and this global shift from central planning to market-based economics climaxed with the dramatic economic and political reorientation in Eastern Europe, the former Soviet Union, and Mongolia, beginning in 1990. For the people of these countries, who represent nearly one-third of the world's population, this transition to market-oriented, outward-looking, and private-sector-led economic systems has had a profound impact on economic opportunities, and has created new challenges for everyone—government policy makers, newly liberated entrepreneurs, state-enterprise workers and managers, and the average person facing new incentives on the job and new products on the market.

The process of transition has not been smooth, even for the most successful countries, but there are clear signs that economic strength is returning even to the most troubled transition economies. China, of course, started the process earlier than the rest, and has benefited from over a decade of very rapid growth, averaging 9.4 percent between 1978 and 1995 (World Bank 1996). Although inflation is still a concern, and the paths of private sector development and state enterprise reform still seem a bit unclear, China has made impressive progress in reducing poverty, and its economic future still seems quite bright. Since 1986, Viet Nam has experienced average GDP growth above 7 percent, and seems poised to enter a period of double-digit growth rates, but it also faces the problems of containing inflation and promoting enterprise reform and private sector growth (World Bank 1996).

The economies of most of Eastern Europe and the former Soviet Union, which suffered output collapses following their initial reforms, may have turned the corner. Poland posted better than 5 percent growth in 1994, and this is expected to accelerate. The Czech Republic and Hungary began recording positive GDP growth in 1994 (EBRD 1995, 185). Russia, which experienced the worst output shock of the economies studied in this volume, is forecast to have positive real GDP growth in 1996, with inflation dropping into double digits (Pacific Economic Cooperation Council 1996, 57). These economies still face enormous challenges, including how to reform the system of ownership of property rights, particularly enterprise ownership; stimulate private sector development (which raises political concerns as the state loses control over production); continue stabilizing the macro economy; reform the financial sector; and deal with the social consequences from the fundamental transformation of the economy.

These are all enormous challenges, but we are optimistic about the future for the transition economies in Asia and Eastern Europe. The goal of this volume, and the project that spawned it, is to shed some light on the transition process from a comparative perspective. Clearly there are severe limitations to comparing economies as different as the highly industrialized countries of Eastern Europe and the more agrarian economies of Asia, but much can still be learned for those following in the footsteps of these reformers, such as the economies of Central Asia, and those likely to be faced with the need for radical restructuring in the near future, such as the troubled economies of Africa. In addition, the Asian and European transition economies can likely also learn a great deal from their counterparts, in spite of the substantial differences in their initial conditions and institutional structures, as they face continuing challenges in their transitions.

The transition process usually involves implementation of all or parts of the following reforms. First, macroeconomic stabilization that reduces budget deficits and credit growth is vital to the reform process. Second, transition economies liberalize prices, legalize non-state (i.e., private) enterprises, and end legal discrimination based on type of ownership. Third, external liberalization removes trade and investment barriers and rationalizes the exchange rate regime. Fourth, a transformation of the system of property rights leads to the privatization of state-owned enterprises and new institutional arrangements supporting private ownership.

The transition process is surrounded by myriad issues which would be impossible to document here, much less discuss in detail. However, some of the key questions raised in comparing the transitions of the Asian and Eastern European economies include the following: (1) What is the role of speed in the implementation of the reform package? (2) What is the impact of strategy and policy, and sequencing, as opposed to country-specific initial conditions such as politics, pattern of industrialization, or institutional structure? (3) At what pace, and by what method, are state enterprise reform and privatization needed, and how can the system of property rights and ownership be effectively transformed to create positive incentives? (4) What is the relative impact of liberalization, trade, capital flows, foreign assistance, and integration into the world economy, which bring capital, technology, management know-how, competition, and price pressure that forces domestic producers to be more efficient? Other important issues include the role of legal systems development, particularly in the area of contract law enforcement; and the role of financial sector reforms, particularly in expanding credit more efficiently, and dealing with financial market implications of enterprise reform and privatization, such as the need for a secondary market for tradeable securities under a privatization scheme. The roles of human resource development and social policy also demand exploration.

The papers in this volume explore a series of issues from both a country perspective on transition and a comparative perspective focusing on specific main issues. The country papers take a close look at the transition process in seven key economies in Asia and Eastern Europe— China, Viet Nam, Mongolia, Russia, Poland, Hungary, and the Czech Republic. These country analyses look at the transition to date, from the perspective of the output response to reform as well as the political economy of the process, and then explore some of the near- and long-term policy priorities facing these countries. Six comparative studies then explore some of the key elements of the process, looking for lessons to be gleaned from the experiences of the transition economies to date. This introductory chapter reviews some of the key findings of these chapters, and then explores in greater depth the factors underlying the varied output response to economic reform in the transition economies studied.

1.2 Analysis of East Asian and Eastern European Transitions

China

The paper on "Chinese Economic Reforms: Past Successes and Future Challenges," by Yuan Zheng Cao, Gang Fan, and Wing Thye Woo, describes the "dual-track" transition that has been at the heart of China's reforms. China's initial liberalization created coexisting market and central plan tracks in the price system. A free market was opened while state supply was kept unchanged at the lower plan price. The plan price was adjusted incrementally over time until there was eventual convergence of the plan and market prices. Reform of enterprise ownership structure has followed a similar dual-track plan. Developing alongside the state-owned enterprise structure, a non-state sector made up of private and semi-private enterprises, community-owned rural enterprises, foreign joint-ventures, and individual businesses has driven the high-speed Chinese economy.

China's dual-track reform is geographic as well, with Special Economic Zones granted institutional autonomy that has led to rapid growth in the coastal regions while the interior provinces grew far more slowly. This system has allowed the Chinese reformers to experiment with policy changes on a smaller scale, and has encouraged innovation and investment in the faster-growing regions. However, this disparate development has increased regional income inequality and is unlikely to be politically sustainable in the long term. China has moved to head off this problem by beginning to extend the coastal region liberalization nationally.

The key sources of China's rapid growth and ability to proceed through the transition without a serious output shock, can be found in its economic structure and initial conditions, and its successful integration into the global economy. China entered the reform era as a predominantly agricultural economy with a huge surplus labor force. Low-productivity agricultural labor was able to move into the higher-productivity non-state enterprise activities that blossomed with the ownership reforms. In addition, China's economy was relatively less subject to central planning, and China's reforms, unlike those in Poland and Russia, did not start under the pressure of large macroeconomic imbalances. Liberalization and focus on export production accelerated China's move into higher-productivity manufacturing, provided access to international capital, pulled in modern technology, and raised overall efficiency and innovation by forcing Chinese firms to face world competition and world prices. The key challenge facing China's reformers, according to Cao, Fan, and Woo, is to restructure the state enterprise sector and deal with the clarification of ownership rights in the non-state sector. In addition, market-supporting institutions, such as the legal framework and the tax system, need to be improved.

Viet Nam

As explained in detail in "Transition to a Market Economy in Viet Nam," by James Riedel and Bruce Comer, Viet Nam, like China, moved toward a market economy gradually, starting with limited liberalization of economic activities, especially those in agriculture. While output response was moderate, inflation took hold, rising from 190 percent in 1985 to over 300 percent annually in 1986–88. Viet Nam responded to this macroeconomic crisis decisively in 1989. It liberalized almost all prices, reduced budget subsidies and bank credit to state enterprises, raised interest rates to yield positive real rates, and unified the official exchange rates at the black market level. The economic response was immediate. Inflation was 74 percent in 1989, down from 308 percent in 1988; GDP growth was 8 percent compared to 5 percent; and, most impressively, Viet Nam became a rice exporter after many years of increasing imports of rice. The 1989 program was not unlike what has been described as "shock therapy" in the European transition economies. Two factors explain why Viet Nam, unlike Eastern Europe, experienced growth upon implementation of shock therapy. First, Viet Nam was an overwhelmingly agricultural economy with a large stock of surplus labor—just like China. Agriculture was better placed to respond to incentives created by reform than the industrial sector, which dominated in Eastern Europe and Russia. Second, Viet Nam had the good fortune to discover oil.

Viet Nam has had notable success so far, but further reforms in most sectors are necessary if it is to succeed with an export-oriented liberalization strategy and maintain a growth rate of 8–10 percent over the coming decades. As Riedel and Comer point out, in order to follow this path, Viet Nam will need macroeconomic stability, relatively high rates of savings and investment, and free access for exporters to imported capital goods and intermediate inputs. A key question is whether there is a "critical mass" of private entrepreneurs in Viet Nam, and whether they are in a position to take advantage of continuing reforms. The development strategy recommended by Riedel and Comer is the promotion of a dynamic small- to medium-sized private enterprise sector in manufacturing.

Mongolia

Mongolia lies between China and Russia, and in some ways finds itself between Asia and Eastern Europe in the pattern of its reforms. As described by Peter Boone, Baavaa Tarvaa, Adiya Tsend, Enkhbold Tsendjav, and Narantsetseg Unenburen, in "Mongolia's Transition to a Democratic Market System," the loss of Soviet financing and the collapse of the CMEA constituted a very severe macroeconomic shock that made structural adjustment necessary. It could be argued that Mongolia's isolation, and the severity of the shock to its economy, forced it to implement radical measures, but that does not diminish the import of Mongolia's rapid economic liberalization and move to a democratic system of government. Mongolia still faces enormous economic challenges. On the positive side, it appears to have created a stable political process based on political competition and free speech in political parties.[1]

Russia

"The Ups and Downs of Russian Economic Reforms" by Peter Boone and Boris Fedorov tells a Russian transition story that contrasts quite markedly with the experiences of China and Viet Nam. In the initial stages, Russia's reforms were characterized by rapid political change, but relatively slow economic reform. When economic reform became more serious in 1992, the major impediment was the legacy of past political institutions, the result of flagging political reform. One of the key factors that distinguished Russia from other transition economies was the enormous wealth and income that was to be redistributed after the breakdown of the old system.

Boone and Fedorov conclude that better management of the politics of reform (particularly by the reform team led by Gaidar) and more decisive political reform at the outset would have improved the outcome, but that Russia has made significant progress nonetheless. The Russian people and economy have responded to market reforms as classical economic theory predicts. Although there has been a sharp decline in industrial production, there has been rapid growth in some areas, such as services and trade, that have benefited from the opening to the world economy.

Poland

The discussion in "The Polish Way to a Market Economy 1989–1995," by Leszek Balcerowicz, Barbara Blaszczyk, and Marek Dabrowski, focuses on the importance of politics in the decision-making process. Successful transition in Poland was largely due to the effective use of a political "window of opportunity" by the reformers just after the collapse of the old political system. The first post-communist government in 1989 aimed for a stable, competitive, outward-looking capitalist economy, and moved to implement a stabilization and liberalization program as well as institutional reforms and ownership transformation that allowed the development of the new private sector as Poland's main economic driver.

The authors conclude that radical and comprehensive economic reforms introduced in an initially socialist economy facing severe

---

1. The Parliamentary election of 1996 is an excellent illustration. Much to the surprise of observers, Mongolians turned away from the incumbent (formerly the Communist Party) government and voted in the reformist opposition candidates.

macroeconomic challenges can be successful even in the face of powerful external shocks. The reforms must transform the inherited structures and institutions, be implemented consistently in the face of criticism and pressure, and avoid favoring one sector over another. Another important aspect of the Polish experience described in this paper is the development of the private sector. The stabilization and liberalization program, by enabling the strong growth of a private sector, in some ways, did more to privatize the economy than the actual privatization of state enterprises. The need to continue privatization, which has been proceeding slowly, heads the list of remaining challenges for Polish policy makers. Also demanding attention are inflation and the related budget deficit caused by social policies badly in need of institutional reform, and the need for legal reforms that will protect central bank independence and provide greater security and formal guarantees for private ownership and free economic activity.

The Czech Republic and Hungary

In "Transition to a Private Property Regime in the Czech Republic and Hungary," Roman Frydman, Andrzej Rapaczynski, and Joel Turkewitz focus on why the transition experiences of the Czech Republic and Hungary are so different, especially with respect to the strategies that these countries chose to reform firm governance. The authors identify the key to understanding the different policies and outcomes to be the institutional differences of these countries in the communist period. Prior to 1990, the Czech state had virtually unchallenged control of economic policy, including control over state property and the budget, while the Hungarian state was constrained by non-state interests that had become increasingly powerful during the reforms taken under socialism in the early 1980s.

These inherited institutional structures contributed to different environments for reform. The Czech reformers took advantage of inherited authority and relative autonomy, and the complementary weakness of other civil institutions such as labor unions, local governments, and non-governmental organizations, to foster market institutions through extensive voucher privatization, creation of a stock market, and labor market reform. Hungary was similarly resolute when it came to freeing wages and prices, but it has been less successful in changing corporate governance of the state enterprises. Hungarian reformers chose a privatization policy that emphasized firm-by-firm sale of state assets, that accommodated the interests of enterprise managers and the needs of the state budget in making debt payments. The results were that privatization lagged until what was effectively insider privatization was allowed, and revenue from the sales was too small to help the budget. The story told here elegantly shows the impact of political preconditions, particularly the level of economic autonomy enjoyed by the state firms, on the development of reform policy.

1.3 A Comparative Perspective on Some Key Issues in the Transition Process

One of the key comparative questions raised by close examination of the transition process is how relevant are existing conditions, policy choice, and speed of implementation to the success of economic transformations. In "East Asian Lessons from Economic Reforms," Vinod Thomas and Yan Wang look at the "causes" of economic growth using a global data set. Running a series of regressions of growth rate on variables for policy choices and initial social factors (such as education and income inequality), Thomas and Wang conclude that policies conducive to openness and investment are more significantly related to growth than these initial social factors. Furthermore, they ascribe a key role to government in making markets work, dealing with externalities, and facilitating public investment; Thomas and Wang state that too often "reforms fail not because market liberalization proceeds too quickly, but because supportive, institutional reforms proceed too slowly."

In "An Overview of Stabilization Issues Facing Economies in Transition," Jeffrey Sachs points out that high inflation is almost always the result of fiscal imbalances and low confidence in macroeconomic management, and the most important step in macroeconomic stabilization is fiscal consolidation that usually involves sharp cuts in subsidies and public investment spending. In addition, the government needs to develop new short-term methods for non-monetary financing of budget deficits, such as creating a government Treasury bill market, utilizing foreign borrowing, and perhaps privatizing state assets, which has the added bonus of allowing the government to escape the political obligation to subsidize loss-making state-owned enterprises.

Sachs also points out supplementary policies that will support stabilization, an appropriate and stable exchange rate regime in the short run, and long-term institutional changes that will create an independent central bank that is committed to achieving price stability. In the longer term, fiscal restructuring will especially need to focus on social spending, which is now the main source of budgetary pressures in the advanced economies. Countries in Latin America and East Asia, which now have relatively lower levels of social spending, should try to promote ways to fund pension programs, e.g., the private pension schemes in Chile.

As emphasized by Sachs, one of the chief causes of high inflation is the poor financial performance of state enterprises. The issue of reforming state enterprises is addressed by Wing Thye Woo in "Improving the Performance of Enterprises in Transition Economies." According to Woo, the initial policy response to inefficiency in the state sector was to introduce elements of a market economy within the existing system of centralized property rights. This experimental hybrid has been called "decentralized socialism." Woo concludes that this marketization of state enterprise production without concomitant marketization of property rights increases opportunities for corruption, destabilizes the economy through inflation caused by monetization of rising budget deficits, and leads to few, if any, efficiency gains. He finds that imposing hard budget constraints, while retaining state ownership, causes loss-making SOEs to restructure, but only to the extent necessary to achieve zero profits while maximizing transfers to employees and managers. Unsatisfactory state enterprise performance is thus due not only to the soft budget constraint, but also to the principal–agent problems generated by the system of centralized property rights.

Then the key question is how to go about privatizing these state-owned firms. The experiences in Eastern Europe and the former Soviet Union indicate that it is not easy to establish market institutions, such as secondary securities markets, that enable the efficient functioning of a private property system. In addition, Woo points out that it takes quite a while for the state to remove itself from its controlling role, even when it wants to do so quickly. Woo also concludes that the most effective attack on stagnant enterprise performance is to privatize existing state enterprises to individuals, promote establishment of new private enterprises, and integrate the economy into the global production system.

One of the key ingredients for successful stabilization, and enterprise reform, is opening the economy to world prices and competition. Georges de Menil explores the paths to trade liberalization in his paper on "Trade Policies in Transition Economies: A Comparison of European and Asian Experiences." De Menil shows that large increases in international trade are a central part of successful transition because they help appropriate capitalist efficiency and introduce competition into domestic markets, and ultimately provide access to the consumer goods associated with the standard of living of the advanced industrialized economies.

Looking at the experiences of the six transition economies analyzed in this project, de Menil concludes that the key to the story is liberalization of the trade regime, and that the extent to which trade restrictions were removed largely determined the degree of export growth. He agrees that supportive macroeconomic policies and other factors helped push net exports, but contends that real devaluation and restrictive demand policies also cannot satisfactorily explain the trade performance of the economies included in this study and, most importantly, cannot explain the enormous growth of imports that occurred in the transition. Without these other reforms, trade liberalization might not have been sustainable, but the experiences of the countries studied indicate that extensive trade liberalization is vital to successful trade performance. Most fundamentally, although transition economies clearly faced some amount of protectionism in export markets, trade expansion depended primarily on the supply-side response to the liberalization of the trade regimes which gave domestic producers the incentive to compete in foreign markets.

While stabilizing the macroeconomic situation and restructuring the state sector will, it is hoped, ease the burden on the budget that is created by obligations to grant subsidies to loss-making enterprises, it must be remembered that in many transition economies state enterprises are important providers of social services. In "Strategies for Addressing the Social Costs of Market Reforms," Carol Graham discusses the need for interventions to protect the welfare of poor and vulnerable groups during economic transitions. In the long term, such interventions cannot substitute for basic social services or a consistent macroeconomic framework conducive to poverty reduction. In the short term, however, Graham concludes that for heavily industrialized countries, safety nets can play an important political and social welfare role by protecting large groups of unemployed workers from significant declines in their living standards. In less industrialized developing countries, the most important task is to create viable institutions to provide basic social services and insurance to the majority of the population. Graham points out several important general lessons from the experiences with safety nets in developing countries. Most importantly, social programs that operate transparently and incorporate participation by the poor can reduce poverty and help create political support for sustaining the economic reform process.

In "Environmental Protection During the Transition to a Market Economy" Daniel Esty explores another policy area that often receives far too little attention when economic reformers are formulating strategy. Two vitally important environmental questions arise in the transition process. First, to what extent should countries ignore the environmental degradation wrought by rapid industrialization? That is, should countries clean up as they go along, or try to maximize growth and plan on cleaning up later? A second, related question is how should policy makers manage the stress placed on the environment by growing prosperity that gives rise to new consumer demands?

Esty presents several conclusions from an investigation of environmental policy in a range of transition economies. First, the openness of the political system, perhaps even more than the market orientation of the economy, shapes long-term environmental quality. Second, the most significant factor in the transition process with respect to solving environmental problems is not the attention paid to specific environmental policies; rather, it is how thoroughly and quickly economic reforms are carried out. Esty concludes that market forces are a powerful environmental policy tool, and thus utilization of market incentives that internalize environmental externalities in the decision-making process for producers and consumers should be at the heart of any environmental policy undertaken in the transition. In addition, countries should not delay consideration of environmental impacts and should take advantage of the opportunities provided by "relative backwardness" to learn from the regulatory mistakes of other transition economies. Esty discusses a host of general and specific policy recommendations, such as strengthening the rule of law; aligning market forces with environmental goals; generating popular support, perhaps through encouraging the growth of non-governmental organizations; and decentralizing regulatory authority to some extent.

1.4 The Output Response to Economic Reform—The Role of Pace, Policy, and Preconditions

As we have seen, economic liberalization in transition economies involves implementation of a reform package that includes four components: (1) macroeconomic stabilization; (2) price liberalization; (3) easing trade and investment barriers and rationalization of the exchange rate; and (4) reform of the property ownership regimes, including legalization of private enterprises and privatization of state-owned enterprises. The papers in this volume illuminate a key set of questions: What does the output response to the policy choices made in the transition tell us about the role of speed of liberalization, the importance of initial conditions, and the impact of particular policy choices? That is, how can we, at a very broad level of analysis, generalize about the impact of pace, policy, and preconditions on the success of transition from centrally planned to market-oriented economic systems?

The implementation of the entire policy package within a short time period has been called the "big bang" approach or "shock therapy." Poland implemented all four components on January 1, 1990; Viet Nam implemented the first three components in March 1989; and Russia implemented only the second and fourth component on January 2, 1992. China, where the policy reform process is considered an example of "gradualism," implemented parts of the first three components in 1979. Our analysis of the output response to various combinations of the above components rests on making comparisons that allow isolation of the effects that we wish to study. To determine the impact of speed and broadness of reform on output response, we compare Viet Nam and China, and then compare Poland, Hungary, and Russia. Then, to explore the impact of initial structural conditions on the initial output response, we compare Viet Nam and China as one group with Poland, Hungary, and Russia as a second group.

Rate of Reform versus Rate of Growth

The comparison of Viet Nam and China suggests that there is no relationship between the speed and breadth of economic reforms and the rate of economic growth. When Viet Nam enacted rapid, comprehensive economic liberalization in early 1989, the immediate response was a 3 percentage point jump in the growth rate. The new growth momentum in Viet Nam was able to prevent a recession in 1991 when the precipitous collapse of the CMEA trading bloc delivered negative supply and demand shocks. It must be further noted that the negative CMEA shock was big. Finland, which had close trading ties to the CMEA, saw its average growth rate shrink from 4.2 percent in 1986–89 to 0.4 percent in 1990 and then to –6.5 percent in 1991.

Unlike Viet Nam, China undertook incremental price and sectoral liberalization. The result has been an impressive average annual growth rate of 9.5 percent. The comparison of Viet Nam and China thus indicates that economic liberalization is good for growth, regardless of speed.

This conclusion is reinforced by the comparison of Poland, Hungary, and Russia. The cumulative drop in output upon the implementation of post-1989 reforms was unrelated to the speed and broadness of economic reforms. Output growth in these countries was either stagnant or negative on the eve of their respective reforms, and the cumulative drop in GNP in each case was quite similar, even though Poland had a big-bang reform, Russia had half a big-bang reform, and Hungary had incremental reform. The important observation is that the rapidity and comprehensiveness of the reforms was negatively correlated to the duration of output collapse, and positively correlated to the strength of the output recovery when it occurred. The conclusion here is that in the case of collapsing economies, those that recover quickest and strongest are those that enacted the most radical economic liberalization. We might draw an even more general conclusion—that fast liberalization is better than slow liberalization. After all, China has succeeded best in agriculture, a sector where reform has been comprehensive, and has done badly in the state industrial sector, where reform has been incremental.

The Impact of Initial Structural Conditions and Policy Choice

The comparison between the group of transition economies that had output collapse (Hungary, Poland, and Russia) and the group of transition economies that had output growth (China and Viet Nam) reveals that the difference in output performance likely comes from the difference in initial structural conditions. In both groups, central planning was producing a bundle of goods different than would have been produced by a market economy. Specifically, central planning emphasized heavy industrial producer goods while the market wanted more light industrial consumer goods and service industries. So when economic liberalization occurred, the structure of production had to adjust to match the bundle of goods demanded by the new market economy.

Since Eastern Europe and the former Soviet Union were already industrialized urban societies, with state employment covering 80 percent or more of the labor force, the workers for the new private light industries and new private service industries had to come from the state-owned industrial sector. The output collapse in the state industrial sector and the under-reporting of private sector growth were the primary reasons for the decline in GDP. China and Viet Nam were overwhelmingly subsistence peasant agricultural economies, and less than 20 percent of the labor force was employed by the state sector. The labor demands of the new non-state light industries and new non-state service industries were met by the flow of under-employed labor from the agricultural sector, and hence there was no shrinkage of the state sector. The lesson is that economic reform in Hungary, Poland, and Russia meant inducing structural adjustment, while economic reform in China and Viet Nam meant allowing normal economic development.

1.5 Conclusions

The papers in this volume reveal much about the transition experiences of a broad range of countries. There are no easy answers; both radical reform and gradual incremental reform led to output collapse in some cases and successful transition in others. Initial economic, political, and social conditions are important, but so are the policies liberalizing the economy and initiating transformation of property ownership regimes.

Four lessons stand out. The first lesson is that initial country conditions determine the output response of a centrally planned economy upon its marketization, be it of the all-out or phased-in variety. The existence of surplus agricultural labor in Viet Nam and China, and the over-industrialization of Eastern Europe, are the primary causes of growth in socialist Asia and collapse in post-socialist Eastern Europe.

The second lesson is that it is difficult to persist in economic liberalization without macroeconomic stability; freeing prices without anchoring them with balanced macroeconomic policies produces an economic incoherence that undermines the social consensus for reform. In some cases, budgetary control will be hard to achieve until the loss-making enterprises are taken off the public books by privatization.

The third lesson is that the establishment of effective corporate governance in state enterprises is a long and arduous process, technically challenging and politically difficult. Efficiency improvements in privatized firms have been slow in appearing. This means that the faster an economy can foster the growth of new private firms, the faster the overall production efficiency of the economy would improve.

The fourth lesson is that the chief cause of export growth is trade regime liberalization, with demand and exchange rate policies playing important supplementary roles. This conclusion reinforces the observation from the fast-growing East and Southeast Asian economies that export growth is principally a supply-side response to trade liberalization.

We hope that the experiences of transition described in the following chapters will allow economic reformers to draw specific policy recommendations that are compatible with the economic conditions in their countries. We also hope that the hypotheses and conclusions of these twelve studies will stimulate other researchers to test and modify them, and make them more useful to policy making.

II Country Experiences

2 Chinese Economic Reforms: Past Successes and Future Challenges

Yuan Zheng Cao,
Gang Fan, and
Wing Thye Woo

2.1 Introduction

China has achieved the impressive average annual growth rate of 9.5 percent since economic reform started in 1978. This successful mobilization of the productive forces has transformed the economic structure dramatically. The proportion of the labor force engaged in agriculture dropped from 71 percent in 1978 to 56 percent in 1993, and the proportion of gross industrial output produced by state-owned enterprises (SOEs) declined from 78 percent to 43 percent in the same period. The integration of China into the world economy has been equally dramatic: trade (exports plus imports) rose from 10 percent of GNP in 1978 to 36 percent in 1993, and direct foreign investment was $28 billion in 1993 compared to $2 billion in 1983.

The objectives of this paper are to review the economic policies implemented and to ascertain their effectiveness in promoting growth. The paper is organized as follows. Section 2.2 outlines the gradual (dual-track) reform program that was implemented. Section 2.3 identifies the sources of growth and argues that the impressive economic performance was mainly the result of China being a surplus labor economy. Section 2.4 explains the reasons why gradual instead of radical ("big bang") reforms were adopted. Section 2.5 discusses the consequences of the gradual reform program. Section 2.6 reviews the remaining challenges for economic reform in China.

2.2 The Components of "Dual-Track" Transition

The reform process that started at the end of 1978 can be divided into several stages:

1. From 1978 to 1984, economic reform was centered on the countryside.

2. From 1984 to 1988, reform was extended to the cities at a medium pace.

3. From 1988 to 1992, a macroeconomic stabilization program was implemented and the pace of reform was slowed.

4. From 1992 to the present, a medium pace of reform resumed.

The reform strategy that has been implemented is best described as the dual-track approach: the coexistence of a market track and a plan track. The dual-track approach pervades almost every aspect of policy making: sectoral reform, price deregulation, enterprise restructuring, regional development, trade promotion, foreign exchange management, central–local fiscal arrangements, and domestic currency issuance.

Dual-Track Production and Pricing

The dual-track approach started at the end of 1978 with rapid and comprehensive liberalization of the agricultural sector while the industrial sector remained under traditional central planning management. The agriculture communes were disbanded by distributing the land to the peasants and granting 15-year leases on the land, with the leases being freely tradeable. State procurement prices for agricultural products were raised, and free markets for agricultural products were allowed. Farmers now enjoy a high degree of production freedom: only 5 percent of their production in 1993 was set by the state plan.

In 1984, this dual-track arrangement was extended to industrial goods, with state procurement quotas for consumer goods much lower than for producer goods. The proportion of planned production of total industrial output value has been reduced from over 90 percent in 1978 to 5 percent in 1993 (see table 2.1).

The typical process of dual-price transition is as follows: (1) opening the free market while keeping state supply unchanged at the (lower) plan price; and (2) adjusting the plan price incrementally over time to approach the market price (see table 2.2). Each price increase is usually accompanied by additional consumer subsidies (or tax deductions for enterprises), and the supply offered at the plan price is normally fixed, if not reduced, over time. When the "final punch" for convergence of the two tracks was delivered, the importance of the supply available at the plan price was generally negligible. A good example was the dual-track transition of food prices that began in 1979. By 1992, the supply available at the plan price had decreased to about 20 percent of total food consumption. As a result, no "shock" was observable when "convergence" of food prices took place that year (Cao 1995).

A similar convergence happened in the foreign exchange market. The unification of the official exchange rate and the swap market exchange rate occurred at the end of 1993, when the differential between the two

Table 2.1
Reduction of planned production and sales

	1978	1984	1987	1991	1992	1993
Total planned production (central and provincial)	91	80	—	16.2	12	5
Planned distribution of intermediate goods						
Steel	77.1	—	—	42.2	—	—
Wood	85.0	—	—	22.5	—	—
Cement	35.7	—	—	10.6	—	—
Coal	58.9	—	—	49.7	—	—

Sources: *Growing into the Market: China 1978–1979* (1994), ch. 4, Shanghai United Press; and *Current Reform Policies* (April 1994), State System Restructuring Committee.

Table 2.2
Dual-track transition of pricing system (sales at different prices as percentage of total sales)

	1978	1985	1988	1990	1991	1992	1993
Agricultural goods							
Planned price	94.3	37.0	24.0	31.0	22.2	12.5	10.3
State-guided price[a]	0.0	23.0	19.0	27.0	20.0	n.a.	7.0
Market price	5.6	40.0	57.0	42.0	57.8	n.a.	82.7
Retail sales[b]							
Planned price	97.4	47.0	28.9	30.0	20.9	17.9	12.2
State-guided price	n.a.	19.0	21.8	25.0	10.3	7.1	4.2
Market price	3.0	43.8	49.3	45.0	68.3	75.0	84.6
Intermediate goods							
Planned price	100.0	—	—	44.6	36.0	18.7	12.0
State-guided price	0.0	—	—	19.0	18.3	—	7.0
Market price	0.0	—	—	36.4	45.7	—	81.0

Sources: *China Price Yearbook*, various years; *China Reform and Development Report 1992–1993: The New Progresses and New Challenges* (1994), ch. 3, "Price Reform," China Financial and Economic Press.
a. State-guided price means that the state set an upper limit and a lower limit that the actual price has to fall between.
b. Retail sales refer mostly to sales of consumer goods.

rates was about 50 percent. But at that time, only 20 percent of foreign exchange transactions was still subject to the official exchange rate. In this case, it is noteworthy that the "rationed" component of foreign exchange sales did not decrease in absolute size over time, it only shrank relative to the size of the new track.

By the end of 1993, 45 kinds of goods still remained subject to (state-set) plan prices. Among them were state purchase prices of grain, cotton, and tobacco, and the state sales prices of chemical materials, coal, electricity, oil, natural gas, chemical fertilizers, steel ingot, and cars.

Dual-Track Ownership Structure

The most important dual-track component has been the reform of owner-ship structure. China's rapid economic growth can be mainly attributed to the dynamic development of the "new track non-state sector," which consists of private and semi-private enterprises, community-owned rural industrial enterprises, and foreign joint ventures (see tables 2.3a, 2.3b, and 2.4).

Another important driving force behind the changes in ownership structure is foreign investment, especially overseas Chinese investments. From 1979 to the middle of 1994, $82.3 billion was invested by foreigners in 210,000 projects. Of this, $25.3 billion of foreign direct investment was made in 1993. Of the total foreign direct investment, 67.5 percent is from Hong Kong, Macao, and Taiwan. A considerable portion of the invest-ments from the United States and Japan (which ranked third and fourth, respectively, as sources of foreign investment) are made by Chinese investors from these countries.

The ownership reform started when the collective "commune" system was replaced by household farming (1979–1983). This made a major part of agriculture, which accounted for over 30 percent of GDP at that time, a de facto private economic activity. The agricultural surplus from the resulting agricultural boom, together with the labor released by the rise in agricultural productivity, enabled small private businesses (e.g., in transportation, retailing, and crafts) and community-owned industrial enterprises (i.e., township and village enterprises, TVEs), to develop.

Up until the 1984 relaxation of restrictions on private ownership of enterprises, TVEs were community-owned and their operations were controlled by the local governments. An enterprise could be classified as a TVE only after approval by the local government. A TVE paid (and still pays) lower taxes than a private enterprise. From 1984 onward, the terms of approval and supervision of TVEs have varied greatly across regions.

Table 2.3a
The development of non-state sectors (1980–86)

	1980	1981	1982	1983	1984	1985	1986
Output value of industry (OVI), as % of total OVI	24.0	25.3	25.6	26.6	30.1	35.2	37.7
Employment, as % of total employment	81.1	80.9	80.9	81.1	82.1	82.0	81.8
State budgetary revenue from non-state sectors, as % of total state revenue	18.0	21.2	21.3	22.3	23.0	29.6	25.4
Retail sales, as % of social total	48.6	50.1	51.3	53.0	54.5	59.6	60.6

Source: *China Statistical Yearbook* (1991, 1992, 1993), State Statistical Bureau of the People's Republic of China (English edition).

Table 2.3b
The development of non-state sectors (1987–92)

	1987	1988	1989	1990	1991	1992
Output value of industry (OVI), as % of total OVI	40.3	43.2	43.9	45.4	47.1	51.9
Employment, as % of total employment	81.7	81.6	81.7	81.8	81.7	81.7
State budgetary revenue from non-state sectors, as % of total state revenue	28.6	31.6	33.2	33.6	36.1	—
Retail sales, as % of social total	61.4	60.5	60.9	60.4	59.8	58.7

Source: *China Statistical Yearbook* (1991, 1992, 1993), State Statistical Bureau of the People's Republic of China (English edition).

Table 2.4
Composition of total output value of society (OVS) in 1991 (percentages)

	Total	Agriculture	Industry	Construction	Transpor- tation	Commerce
As total OVS	100.00	18.62	64.49	8.45	3.8	4.64
State- owned enterprises	50.41	2.99	52.94	67.92	81.50[b]	40.20
Non-state- owned enterprises	49.59	97.01	47.06	32.08	18.40	59.8
Collective	—	—	35.70	—	17.80	30.50
Private or individual	—	—	5.70	—	0.80	19.60
Others[a]	—	—	5.66	—	—	9.70[c]

Source: *China Statistical Yearbook* [1990 (English edition), 1991, 1990], State Statistical Bureau of the People's Republic of China.
a. Mainly foreign and joint venture corporations.
b. Based on the volume of freight traffic measured in tons.
c. Retail sales by farmers to urban consumers.

We can classify most TVEs into three categories. The first category is comprised of the TVEs that are actually private in ownership and operation but which registered themselves as collectively owned in order to escape legal discrimination. These are popularly referred to as enterprises "wearing the red cap." With further relaxation of regulations since 1992 on the formation of private enterprises, many TVEs have taken off their red caps.

The second category of TVE refers to those which receive approval from the local authorities in return for a commitment to make an annual contribution to the village funds. In Zhejiang province, the town or village is a shareholder (sometimes, the majority shareholder) in most TVES, but the local government normally refrains from intervening in the investment, dividend, and personnel decisions of the TVEs. This granting of complete operational autonomy to the TVEs has been called the Zhejiang Model. The only tie that these TVEs have to their communities is a financial one, and this financial tie is indistinguishable from the taxes that a private firm is required to pay.

The third category of TVEs is where local authorities exercise tight controls over the TVEs. This tight control over TVEs has come to be known as the Jiangsu Model because of its concentration in Wuxi, Suzhou, and Changzhou, three cities in southern Jiangsu province. In 1985, the Wuxi authorities would confer TVE status on a firm only if its "initial investment was from the savings of a community body," its site belonged to the community, its production equipment was the property of the community, and its distribution of profits complied with the local regulations. The Wuxi authorities protected its TVEs by imposing fines on skilled workers who left for better jobs elsewhere and by limiting the number of partnerships and individual firms that could be set up. Finally, the "average wage rates were not allowed to diverge too much among firms" (Luo 1990, 150).

While the Jiangsu Model is "more highly regarded than ... [the Zhejiang Model because] the former adheres to traditional socialist concepts," it is experiencing financial difficulties in the 1990s. The Jiangsu authorities have attributed the malaise to "the ambiguous property relationship ... [that dampened] the villagers' enthusiasm for township firms,"[1] and:

In the second half of ... [1992, Wuxi, Suzhou, and Changzhou] transferred the operation rights of some deficit ridden small-scale State or publicly-owned enterprises to private businessmen through rental or auction sales.[2]

The above discussion makes it clear that it is hard to be precise about the nature of TVEs. It is primarily because of the vagueness about the ownership and control of TVEs, the great variety of TVEs, and *the evolving nature of TVEs*, that the official statistics on TVEs now cover all non-state enterprises in the rural sector.

The crucial point is the TVEs represent *localized socialism* compared to the centralized socialism embodied by the SOEs. This difference renders SOEs and TVEs fundamentally different in character, even though both are publicly owned in the legal sense and both are subject to government regulations. Three specific differences are as follows:

1. The supervision distance. TVEs operate with shorter supervision distance, i.e., TVEs face less of a principal–agent problem than the SOEs. The direct linkage in TVEs between the local people's working efforts and their economic benefits not only reduces the cost of supervision but also improves the local owners' incentives to monitor the management, exert pressures on managers to improve the business, and complain about managerial appropriation of resources when it occurs excessively.

---

1. "Stuck in an ideological morass," *China Daily*, June 2, 1993.
2. "Successfully combining socialist market theories," *China Daily*, Dec. 15, 1993.

2. TVEs are non-state enterprises. This feature is important in relation to the "softness" of budget constraints. The most important institutional superiority of TVEs over the SOEs is that the former cannot borrow forever to cover their losses. Being a non-state enterprise means that the rescue of a bankrupt TVE is not the state's responsibility. The SOEs, on the other hand, have repeatedly been able to force the state to print more money to bail them out. This institutional feature is the reason why competition does not shut down bad SOEs.

3. Institutional innovation. The institutional evolution of TVEs has been faster because TVEs, unlike SOEs, can implement institutional innovations without central government approval. Recent locally initiated development of a "share-holding collective system" in TVEs and rural community economies shows this feature very well. This freedom of TVEs has enabled them to move closer to best international practices in corporate governance.

In a nutshell, the TVEs, unlike the SOEs, live by the market. During the last economic downturn, the number of industrial TVEs fell from 7.7 million in 1988 to 7.2 million in 1990, while the number of industrial SOEs increased from 99,000 to 104,000.

It must be emphasized that the SOE sector has not been withering away, as suggested in some claims that China has "grown out of the plan." The SOE sector has actually retained its relative standing in employment: 18 percent of the 1978 and 1993 labor force. There were 35 million more SOE workers in 1993 than in 1978.

Dual-Track Regional Development

In 1980, four southern coastal cities (Shantou, Shenzhen, Xiamen, and Zhuhai) were designated "Special Economic Zones" (SEZs). The SEZs were given autonomy to experiment with new institutions and reform; e.g., they were exempted from many of the regulations that govern foreign investment. The resulting phenomenal growth of the SEZs spurred other regions to demand economic liberalization as well. An additional 20 cities were subsequently approved as "economic and technologic development districts" (ETDDs), which had some of the privileges of the SEZs. Hainan province became the fifth SEZ in 1988.

The important impact of the dual-track regional development was that the whole country saw that the high growth in the coastal areas was due to the more rapid development of the non-state sectors (see table 2.5), and not due to state industrial reform.

Table 2.5
Higher growth in coastal regions, 1981–90

	Nation	Guangdong	Fujian	Zhejiang	Jiangsu	Shandong
Average annual growth of GNP	9.3	19.7	17.3	18.9	16.4	16.3
Growth of SOEs	—	10.1	9.5	9.0	9.1	9.2
Growth of TVEs	—	19.5	19.6	24.0	17.8	18.5
Growth of foreign and joint ventures	—	58.6	50.0	38.6	42.3	37.3
Contribution of non-state sectors to GNP growth	—	63.0	60.0	73.0	70.0	63.0

Sources: *Growing into the Market: China 1978–1979* (1994), ch. 3, Shanghai United Press; and *Current Reform Policies* (April 1994), State System Restructuring Committee.

The Decentralization Component

The key institutional innovations of the decentralization reform have been the following:

1. The Budgetary Contracting System (BCS), since 1980 (see Zhong and Hong 1990, and Wong, Heady, and Woo 1995). This was the major device for reshaping central and local fiscal relations.[3] Under the BCS, the central government shares revenues (taxes and profit remittances) with local governments in the following way: (1) the central and the local governments collect revenues on the separate tax bases according to the administrative subordinate relationship (different governments tax different payers); and (2) each provincial government signs a contract with the central government on the amount of revenue remittance for a specified period of time. For the provinces that run budget deficits, the

3. New changes are being attempted in taxation and revenue sharing. These changes include redistributing tax revenues by categories (instead of by taxpayers) between the central and the local governments in order to increase the share of central revenue, rebuilding the revenue transfer mechanism, and redefining the expenditure responsibilities between the central and the local governments.

contract will be on the subsidies from the central to the local government.

2. The Contract Responsibility System (CRS), since 1985, for state enterprises. Under this system, SOEs pay contracted amounts of taxes and profits to the state and retain the rest for themselves. In principle, as long as SOEs can deliver the contracted remittances, the government would not interfere with their operations.

3. Direct borrowing. Since 1985, state grants to local governments and SOEs for operating funds and fixed asset investments were replaced by bank loans. The proportion of SOEs' funds that is raised externally has been increasing dramatically over the years (see Fan, Hai, and Woo, forthcoming). Since 1991, local governments and SOEs are also allowed to borrow directly from workers, households, and other financial institutions. Similarly, the local branches of the central bank and the state specialized banks are also allowed some discretion in formulating their lending policies.[4]

2.3   Sources of Growth

We identify five factors that have been particularly important in generating high growth in China. The first factor behind China's success came from its economic structure and initial conditions. Fan (1993) and Sachs and Woo (1994) have argued that the different fates of gradualism in different countries at various times were actually predetermined by their initial economic structures. Gradualism is more likely to succeed in an underdeveloped (under-industrialized) economy with a huge surplus rural labor force like China than in an "over-industrialized" economy dominated by the state sector, like Poland or Russia.

In aggregate terms, the labor for the new Chinese enterprises came entirely from the agricultural sector, which comprised 71 percent of the labor force in 1978, at the start of the reforms. While individual workers from SOEs did shift to the non-state sector, the aggregate growth of the non-state sector as a share of the labor force is due entirely to the aggregate decline of the share of agricultural workers. Most SOE workers chose not to shift to the non-state enterprises because SOEs were able to offer a more generous package of wages and social protection, largely as a

---

4. The local branches of state banks (the central bank and the state commercial banks) are to a great extent "truly local." The officials of local banks are part of a larger hierarchy, and are usually appointed by higher supervisors within the bank system. In reality, they are directly under the supervision of local authorities and benefit from the local prosperity. They have generally always done their best to meet the loan requests of local officials and local SOEs, although they are somewhat constrained by central regulations (see Woo, forthcoming).

result of the huge subsidies and other benefits that the state continued to bestow on the SOE sector. SOEs provided generous pensions, and heavily subsidized housing, medical coverage, child care, food, and recreational facilities. The Chinese peasants, by contrast, receive none of these benefits and consume only one-third of what urban residents consume. The peasants, therefore, were only too glad to shift out of low-income agricultural activities to the new higher-income jobs in the non-state sector, notably in the TVEs.

This movement of low-productivity agricultural labor into the higher-productivity TVE activities is the primary cause of Chinese growth. Woo (1996) calculated that the reallocation of labor out of agriculture accounted for 1.2 percentage points of the aggregate total factor productivity (TFP) growth rate of 1.5 to 1.8 percent per annum during the 1985–93 period. Another source for the aggregate TFP improvement is simply that TVEs are more efficient than SOEs, most possibly because of the three differences between them discussed earlier.

Besides the existence of surplus agriculture labor, there were two other initial conditions that helped Chinese economic growth. The first supplementary initial condition was that the extent of China's central planning was much smaller than Russia's and Poland's. Qian and Xu (1993) noted that around 25 million commodities entered the Soviet economic plans, while in China only about 1,200 commodities were included. The second supplementary condition was that China's reforms, unlike Polish and Russian reforms, did not start in a situation with large macroeconomic imbalances and a severe external debt crisis that required the implementation of an austerity program. Unlike Poland and Russia, which have been taming inflation and restructuring their fully-employed economies simultaneously, China has been developing its economy by having the TVEs employ the idle agriculture labor.

The second factor behind China's impressive growth is its integration into the global economy. This factor operates through three channels. First, the access to international markets for labor-intensive manufactured goods accelerated the movement of labor out of low-productivity agriculture into high-productivity industry. Second, China could now buy modern technology (some of which was previously denied to China). Third, foreign direct investments increased the capital stock, transferred new technology, made available global distribution networks, and introduced domestic firms to more efficient management techniques.

The third factor behind China's high growth is its saving behavior. China's saving rate is unusually high, even by East Asian standards. Household saving is about 23 percent of disposable income in China versus 21 percent in Japan, 18 percent for Taiwan, 16 percent for Belgium, 13 percent for West Germany, and 8 percent for the United States

(World Bank 1990a, table 4.9). The flow of household savings into the formal financial system (the state banks and rural credit cooperatives) has risen steadily from 3.4 percent of GDP in 1980 to 11.7 percent in 1991. Of the 1991 amount, 3.5 percentage points were extended as loans to collectively owned and individually owned enterprises, and 8.2 percentage points were channeled to SOEs and the government.

It must be pointed out that the high household saving rate reduced inflation in the Chinese economy through two channels. First, the flow of savings through the banks reduced the need to print money to meet the excessive resource demand of the SOE sector. As the official *China Daily* reported:

Loans are continuing to be injected to enterprises which are obviously at the edge of bankruptcy.... Some loans have been used to pay wages, which have a pretty name: "loans to keep social stability." ... According to PBOC [People's Bank of China, the central bank] 46 percent of fresh bank loans last year created unmarketable goods. (*China Daily* February 1, 1993, p. 4)

The above report means that China's high saving rate would have produced growth rates higher than the impressive ones generated so far if so much of the savings had not been used to preserve macroeconomic balance and social stability.

The second channel through which the high saving rate has reduced inflation came from money being (until recently) still the only form of financial saving in China, and the increasing demand for money caused by the high saving rate. The large inflation-damping effect can be seen in the rise of the M2 to GNP ratio from 38 percent in 1979 to 106 percent in 1992. However, this ratio appears to be leveling off as the agricultural economy becomes fully monetized and as new financial instruments appear.

The fourth factor behind China's success in the 1980s was the two disastrous leftist campaigns, the Great Leap Forward (1958–62) and the Cultural Revolution (1966–76), which weakened the administrative capacity of the state and discredited central planning. Fairbank (1987, 320) reported that the Cultural Revolution produced a 60 percent "purge rate among the party officials." The result was that when Deng Xiaoping transferred a significant amount of economic policy-making power to the provinces, the central ministerial and party apparatus were too politically exhausted to resist Deng's decentralization.

The existence of family ties between the mainland Chinese and the overseas Chinese is the fifth factor. The explosive growth of the SEZs in southern China was caused by the wholesale movement of labor-intensive industries from Hong Kong and Taiwan, which were losing their comparative advantage in these industries. China was closer, wages were lower, and language difficulties non-existent compared to the alternative sites in Southeast Asia. (Managers could commute daily from Hong Kong to supervise their factories in Shenzhen.) More importantly, the family connections greatly reduced the transaction costs of the investment by providing reliable local supervisors, inside information on the enforcement of regulations, and contacts with the local authorities.

Of the five factors identified above as important causes of China's achievements in the 1978–94 period, only two factors (China's integration into the global economy sector and its high saving rate) could be considered general lessons for economic reforms. The other three factors (structural features and initial conditions, the Chinese diaspora, and the debilitating mass campaigns) are specific to China's circumstances.

2.4   Reasons for Gradualism

It is important to stress that gradualism was adopted not because there were no proposals for more radical reform programs (see Zhang and Yi 1994). The majority of the society and the leadership in 1978 were not in favor of a radical reform package because the economic situation then was improving rapidly. Following the end of the decade-long Cultural Revolution in 1976, China registered 7.8 percent national income growth in 1977 and 12.3 percent in 1978 (the reform really got going only in 1979). Hence, most ordinary people had not yet totally lost their trust in the old system. It was popularly believed that the economic problems came from the implementation of the "political-struggle-first" doctrine and not from the defects of the central planning system.

The fact is that "gradualism" is less an "adopted approach" or "chosen strategy" but more of an ex post facto description of an unintended evolutionary process. There are two major reasons for this unconscious outcome.

The first reason is that very few people really knew in 1978 what to do. Participants might have known what the first "piece" should be, but might not know what the next piece should be. Indeed the term "piecemeal approach" is a more accurate description than "gradualism." For example, the rural "household contract responsibility system," which later turned out to be the most important step in starting the whole reform process, was banned by the government in 1979 and only "adopted" later after it had become widely practiced by the peasants.

Another example of the lack of a clear perception of the situation and a practical long-term plan is that even to date, some members of the leadership are still convinced that expanding the autonomy of SOEs without changing ownership is the way to solve the current problems in the SOEs. They put their major effort into reforming the state sector and left the non-state sector to "spontaneously" grow by itself. It is therefore ironic that the development of the non-state sector has been regarded by the Chinese policy makers as one of their major achievements.

The second major reason for this unintended evolutionary process has been the absence of a common vision at the elite level. There was disagreement regarding the relative role of planning and markets in resource allocation (see Hamrin 1984, Harding 1986, and Woo 1994). This is the reason why China's gradual reform has been characterized by gradual changing of its reform objectives. China has proceeded through a lengthy path of readjusting its reform objectives, from "a planned economy with some market adjustment," to "a combination of plan and market," and now to "a socialist market economy" (see table 2.6).

The changes in objectives reflect, first, the increasing knowledge in China about the merits of different resource allocation mechanisms and, second, and more fundamentally, the changes in the political balance between various interest groups and the changes in the economic structure resulting from the process of reform and development itself. As the efficiency of the non-state sector was clearly higher than that of the state sector, people became more convinced about the superior efficiency of the market system and offered less resistance to more profound changes.

The "common vision" issue was finally resolved in October 1992 when the leadership formally abandoned central planning in favor of "a socialist market economy with Chinese characteristics." In November 1993, the party agreed not only to accelerate the pace of economic reform (e.g., making the currency convertible for current account transactions as of January 1, 1994) but also to require SOEs to adopt new operating mechanisms:

Large and medium-sized State-owned enterprises are the mainstay of the national economy; ...[for them,] it is useful to experiment with the corporate system. ... As for the small State-owned enterprises, the management of some can be contracted out or leased; others can be shifted to the partnership system in the form of stock sharing, or sold to collectives and individuals.[5]

2.5   The Consequences of Gradual Reform

Convergence of the Two Tracks?

The policy issue is not whether the government should follow a dual-track system, but whether the two tracks should be merged as rapidly as possible. The success of dual-track transition depends mainly on the success of the new track. If the growth rate of the new sector is higher

---

5. "Decision of the CPC Central Committee on issues concerning the establishment of a socialist market economic structure," a document produced as a supplement to *China Daily*, November 17, 1993.

Table 2.6
Official "formula" of reform objectives during different periods since 1978

Period	Objective formula
pre-1975	A planned economy based on the "law of exchange value"
1979–1984.10	A planned economy that is supplemented by market adjustments
1984.10–1987.10	The planned commodity economy
1987.10–1989.6	An economy where the state regulates the market and the market regulates the enterprises
1989.6–1991	An economy with organic integration of planned economy and market regulations
1992–	A socialist market economy

than that of the old sector, then the old sector will continually decline as a proportion of the economy, without explicit reform actions being taken against the old sector.

In practice, the expansion of the old system (in absolute size) has occurred quite frequently. This is because the state has used the revenue from the more productive new sectors not only to cover the losses of the SOEs in the old sector but also to upgrade these SOEs. The result is that the old track has not shrunk proportionately as rapidly as it should have.

From a supply-side perspective, the non-state sector has become the major contributor to China's GDP: 52 percent of industrial output in 1992, and an estimated 57 percent in 1993. In 1991–92, about 80 percent of the increment in GDP was from the non-state sector. From the expenditure side, however, the state sector has remained dominant. In 1992, 79 percent of total bank credits went to the state sector.[6] In 1993, over 70 percent of total social investment in fixed assets was for projects in the state sector. The proportion of the Chinese labor force employed by state-owned units was 18 percent in 1978 and was still 18 percent in 1992. This means that there were actually 32 million more Chinese working in

---

6. It should be noted that, as the bank loans are given to state enterprises at low interest rates (about 10 percent), and the non-state sector is willing to pay higher rates (about 20 percent), some SOEs re-lend part of these credits to non-state firms in the black market and earn interest differentials (that may be higher than their profits). No data is available on the volume of credits which have been "transferred" in this way. But a reasonable estimate is no more than 30 percent of credits to the state sector.

state-owned units in 1992 than in 1978. The state-owned sector is not "withering away."

Corruption is another reason for the survival and expansion of the "old track." For example, in the price reform process, the old track was frequently expanded not only because of pressures from SOEs seeking more resources at low official prices, but also because of rent-seeking by government officials. The higher the share of the production that is designated as "plan sales," the higher will be its market price, and, hence, the greater the amount of resources that can be diverted to the corrupt officials. The result was that for a long time, plan sales were not fixed as they were supposed to be, but increased instead. Sometimes what shrank was the "market track" instead of the "plan track." This is one more reason why the dual-track price system has lasted for so long.

The lesson is clear: the most important challenge in a gradual transition may not be how to speed up the growth of the new track, but how to ensure that the old track does not grow as well. The old track cannot be simply ignored, as many advocates of gradual transition have suggested, because it will not wither away voluntarily. Because of the old track's considerable political clout, it may not only prosper as a parasite of the new track but may also metastasize and crowd out the new track.

"Transitional Corruption" and "Spontaneous Privatization"

Wang and Li (1993) have estimated that, in 1992, official corruption, wage-drift ("wage eats profits and capital"), and stealing have siphoned off at least 100 billion yuan worth of state assets, or about 5 percent of total state assets. A survey done in Shanxi province showed that up to 40 percent of state assets has been dissipated in the past 10 years. Hong Kong banking sources have estimated that about US$10 billion of capital is sent abroad annually. Capital flight from China amounted to one-third of the 1993 gross capital inflow into China. For an economy in which mass privatization with a fairer redistribution of property rights is ruled out, such gradual "spontaneous privatization" seems to be an unavoidable part of the process of moving towards the market.

The Many Disappointments in Chinese Enterprise Reform

Several studies have concluded that total factor productivity (TFP) growth of the Chinese SOE sector has been positive in the reform period, and some of them also indicated that this TFP growth is higher than in the pre-1978 period.[7] But we can regard the Chinese SOEs as having been

---

7. See Woo, Hai, Jin, and Fan (1993) for a critical discussion of some of the key studies.

successfully reformed only if we keep our expectations of SOEs' performance low. Most studies estimate that annual TFP growth in Chinese SOEs is only about half of that in collectively owned enterprises (which include town and village enterprises). This relative inefficiency of the SOE sector is confirmed by Xiao (1991), who found a positive statistical relationship between the TFP growth of a province and its share of industrial output produced by *non-state* enterprises.

Woo, Hai, Jin, and Fan (WHJF 1993) pointed out that the studies of Jefferson, Rawski, and Zheng (1992) and Groves, Hong, McMillan, and Naughton (1995), which found positive TFP growth in industrial SOEs by estimating production functions for the SOE sector, seem to have an important flaw. *The value-added deflators implied in these studies declined during the 1980–89 period*, something which is unlikely to have been the case in view of the average consumer price inflation of 7.5 percent per year. WHJF attributed this anomalous downward trend in the value-added deflators to the studies' use of under-deflated output data and over-deflated input data. In other words, two of the key building blocks of the data appear to be dubious, in a way that likely overstates the real output (and therefore productivity) of the SOE sector.[8]

If we go beyond technical efficiency as the sole criteria of successful reform, and consider the contribution of the SOE sector to macroeconomic stability, then the Chinese SOE reforms look even less successful. Overall profitability of the SOE sector has been declining, and a large proportion of SOEs are still making losses a decade after the start of enterprise reforms. This poor financial performance was most vividly seen in 1992 when output grew 13 percent, and yet two-thirds of Chinese SOEs were running losses in a boom year![9] These enterprise losses cannot be blamed on price controls because the price controls covered only a small proportion of SOEs in 1992. The SOEs may have become technically more efficient but most of them have also become financially less viable. Naughton (1991) has suggested that the primary reason for

---

8. See the exchange on this point between Woo, Fan, Hai, and Jin (1994) and Jefferson, Rawski, and Zheng (1994).

9. *China Daily*, "Budgetary deficit will be cut back in '93," reports on January 26, 1993: "At present, about one-third of State firms are definitely operating at a loss and another one-third suffer hidden losses, according to the State Statistics Bureau." The term "hidden losses" refers to various methods that allow a firm not to show an accounting loss, e.g., the firm is exempted from forwarding sales tax revenue to the state, and a firm's unsold output is valued as income. As long as there is no accounting loss, an SOE can borrow working capital from the banks to pay its employees and supplies.

This two-thirds figure was confirmed by Gao Shangquan, the Deputy Director of the State System Reform Committee of the State Council (the Cabinet) in a speech delivered at the 1992 annual conference of the Chinese Economic Association of the United Kingdom.

the decline in the rate of profitability of the SOEs is the expansion of competition by collectively owned enterprises allowed by the economic reforms. The problem with this explanation is that the fall in SOE profits occurred across the board, even in heavy industries with negligible new entry by non-state firms.

Fan, Hai, and Woo (forthcoming) have suggested that excessive wage increases throughout the SOE sector may have been the more important reason for the decline in profitability. Analyzing a sample of 300 SOEs, they found that the ratio of direct cash income (wages plus bonuses) to net output value rose from 11.6 percent in 1980 to 15.9 percent in 1988, and that indirect income (e.g., housing, in-kind distributions), as proxied by net non-production expenditure, increased more than twice as much as net output value. There was little incentive for the managers to resist wage demands because their future promotion to larger SOEs was determined in part by the increases in workers' welfare during their tenure. The easy availability of loans from the local banks made it possible to increase labor compensation and capital investment at the same time.

Official data on industrial SOEs show that the average annual rate of labor productivity growth and direct real wage growth over the 1978–90 period were 4.4 percent and 4.1 percent, respectively.[10] In a recent study, Zhao (1992) estimated that the indirect real wage grew at an annual average rate of 12.5 percent in the 1978–90 period, raising its share in the total (direct plus indirect) real wage from 15 percent in 1978 to 31 percent in 1990.[11] Incorporating Zhao's finding into the official data, the average annual increase in the real wage was 5.4 percent. This finding supports Fan, Hai, and Woo's (forthcoming) contention that the higher wage growth caused profitability to fall even though technical efficiency might have increased. Another piece of evidence of wage increases being excessive in SOEs is that labor productivity growth in the collective sector is very much greater than the direct real wage growth there: 8.3 percent and 3.6 percent, respectively.

This financial weakness of SOEs destabilized the economy through two channels. The first was through the state budget. Given the dependence of state revenue on income from the SOEs, the budget deficit widened from 2.1 percent of GNP in 1981 to 3.4 percent in 1991, hence contributing to faster monetary growth. The second channel was through the banking system. The bulk of SOE losses were not covered by budget

10. Data are from tables 4.37, 7.1, and 10.16 in *China Statistical Yearbook 1991.* Direct wage is the sum of basic wage and *some* kinds of bonuses and cash subsidies.
11. Table 9 in Zhao (1992). Indirect wage rate growth was computed by assuming that direct wage rate grew 4.1 percent annually. The 12.4 percent figure is the lower-bound estimate because in-kind consumption hidden as production cost is not included in the indirect wage data.

subsidies but by bank loans. Moreover, since the promotion of an SOE manager depended importantly on the expansion of the enterprise under his stewardship, he would continuously pressure the local banks for investment loans. If the firm was not doing well financially, the justification for the investment loan application would be to increase the firm's competitiveness by technical upgrading.

The result of the central bank's accommodation of the requests for loans to cover losses and to finance investments is that the amount of reserve money growth that is unrelated to deficit financing is substantially greater than the deficit itself. Defining the "open deficit" as the government borrowing requirement, the "hidden subsidies" as half of the expansion of reserve money in excess of the amount lent to the government for deficit financing, and the "fiscal imbalance" as the sum of these two items, we found the following data for 1988–1991:[12]

Year	Open deficit (% of GNP)	Hidden subsidies (% of GNP)	Fiscal imbalance (% of GNP)
1988	2.48	2.57	5.05
1989	2.35	2.61	4.96
1990	2.88	3.78	5.66
1991	3.36	3.38	6.74

To summarize, regardless of whether or not the SOEs improved their technical efficiency, they have certainly not improved their financial performance. Just as China did not succeed in producing the new socialist man during the Cultural Revolution despite the hopes of well-wishers, China, like Eastern Europe and Russia, has not succeeded in producing profitable SOEs.

The Rise of the "Revenue-Hiding-in-Local-Economies" Phenomenon

Under the "Contracting Budgetary System" (CBS), the amount of revenue transfer between the local and the central governments is also pre-set by the contracts that were determined by a one-to-one bargaining process between the central and provincial governments. (The provincial governments would then negotiate tax contracts with the lower-down local governments.) As the negotiated amounts are heavily influenced by the tax payments of the previous periods, central revenue growth has not kept up with the growth of the local economies. Moreover, to retain

---

12. The estimate for hidden subsidies is based on the *China Daily* report and Gao's speech (cited in note 9) that one-third of SOEs ran open deficits and that another third would also have been in deficit if not for various subsidies.

more revenues in the local economies, the local governments have increasingly concealed their revenue bases. The local governments would allow local enterprises to under-report their taxable revenues, and in return the enterprises would make contributions to local development projects when the local governments indicate their needs for funds. Such types of concealed-revenue arrangements have played increasingly important roles in the recent development of local economies. According to some surveys, such concealed funds amounted to 40-70 percent of explicit revenue of local governments (Sen and Zhu 1993).[13] If these "out-of-budget" local government revenues were added to the total government revenue, government revenue would not have fallen as much.

The important macroeconomic result is that this hiding of revenue by local governments worsened the budget crisis caused by the dismal financial performance of the SOEs after the decentralization reforms.

2.6   Future Challenges

Two points about China's gradual reform program deserve emphasis. The first point is that the dual-track approach worked in China, but not in Jaruzelski's Poland and Gorbachev's Russia, because there was no surplus agriculture labor in Poland or Russia. The second point is that China's gradualism is an "easy-to-hard" reform sequence. It starts with the easy problems and leaves the hard problems until later. In contrast, the radical approach tackles the hard problems at the beginning.

The major hard-core challenges facing China now are as follows:

1. *Restructuring the SOE sector.* Without this, the financial demands of this sector will always threaten price stability. There are some positive signs, however: the corporatization and management of enterprises through price signals generated by stock markets is becoming a widely accepted idea, and more and more state enterprise are being sold to non-state companies.

2. *Clarification of TVE ownership.* This is necessary if outside capital is to be raised for the expansion of production. Encouragingly, there is now a movement to redefine the property rights of rural industries and redistribute them among members of local communities (see Chen 1994).

3. *Macroeconomic stability.* The recent granting of independence in monetary policy to the central bank will, hopefully, prevent the issuance of easy credits to the SOE sector. It is also necessary that subsidies to SOEs be curbed.

---

13. That is, when the local government collects 100 yuan as "budgetary revenue," it receives another 40 to 70 yuan as the "out-of-budget revenue." They get 140 to 170 yuan in total.

4. *Regional and rural–urban income disparity.* The movement toward giving the backward provinces the same preferential trade and investment enjoyed by the coastal provinces will go a long way in addressing this problem. It is also important that the freeing of agricultural prices and the provision of more social infrastructure in the rural areas be undertaken.

5. *The establishment of market-supporting institutions.* The establishment of a legal framework that facilitates the operations of a market economy should be speeded up. There should also be a tax system that obviates the need for central–local government bargaining and government–enterprise bargaining.

As evident from the above, the overall policy trend gives grounds for optimism. China's market-oriented reform appears to have become irreversible.

3

Transition to a Private Property Regime in the Czech Republic and Hungary

Roman Frydman,
Andrzej Rapaczynski, and
Joel Turkewitz

Reports on the progress of transition in Eastern Europe have tended to assume that the main goals of the process are well known and that the problems are mainly technical: how to control inflation and reverse the output decline, how to introduce clear property rights, and how to transfer state assets into private hands. In fact, however, the picture that emerges from the first few years of transition in Eastern Europe is one in which markets emerge only haltingly, where property rights are often tremendously confused, and where the state's role, as measured by either its share of the GDP or its role as a partial (as opposed to the sole) owner of most larger enterprises, is diminishing slowly.[1] It is of course still rather early to pass any definitive judgments on the success or failure of many policies, and much progress has undoubtedly been made. But the difficulties are also quite considerable, and the tortuous path of the post-communist development is not satisfactorily accounted for by reference to either the inability of the leaders to stick to the right policies or a series of technical and tactical mistakes. More likely, the actual difficulties of the various reform policies have been in fact underestimated and the interconnections among them not sufficiently explored. In particular, the links between the macro and micro reform policies have been, in our opinion, inadequately analyzed, and the interplay between politics and economics has been only very super-ficially examined—mostly as a problem of assuring popular support for certain predetermined economic policies with some purely transitional side effects.

This is obviously not the place to elaborate a more extensive theory of Eastern European transition. But it might be useful to begin this overview of the developments in Hungary and the Czech Republic by focusing briefly on the way we see the main issues defining the transformation process in the region.

---

1. Pistor and Turkewitz (1996).

3.1   The Nature of the Transition Process

The objective of the transition process, all would probably agree, is to set in motion a whole set of mechanisms that would allocate resources more efficiently than they were allocated at the starting point. The initial allocation was excessively administrative and political; the desired allocation would rely much more on markets and individual incentives.

That much is simple. But there are two problems that need to be stressed more than they have been. The point of arrival of the transition process is much less clear than it appears, and the set of allocative mechanisms of a modern capitalist society is much less well understood than most studies of Eastern Europe would lead us to believe. The point is not that markets are not good; it is rather that they are much more complex than their proponents usually consider. The main reasons for this complexity are that most agents in advanced market societies are not individuals but institutions (corporations, unions, banks, pension funds, etc.), and markets themselves are not empty spaces in which agents trade but institutional arrangements of amazing variety. These institutions are not just complex mechanisms; they are also nearly never created by conscious design. Indeed, their very existence is most often tied to the fact that individual agents, under conditions of uncertainty, tend to be guided by various milestones and routines in their environment which are seen as having been helpful in the past. And the reasons certain institutions work are inherently tied to the existence of other institutions in the same environment, with the interconnections among these various systems even more mysterious than the workings of each one of them in isolation. To set the proper direction of post-communist development is not only to eliminate some of the most absurd distortions of the previous regime, but also to foster the establishment of institutions organizing the economic order of the future. However, which institutions are workable in which situation, what are the dangers of degenerative synergies among unknown institutional combinations, and by what means complex institutions get established are questions about which we know much less than would be required to set policies with anything approaching a desirable level of confidence.

Institutions are not only interdependent, historically contingent, and very imperfectly understood; they are also intimately tied with the state. Even in the most liberal societies the state is present as much more than the proverbial umpire; the thousands of volumes of governmental regulations of the most minute aspects of trade, securities markets, banks, insurance, and all levels of industrial production can hardly be viewed (as they often tend to be) as merely setting the "rules of the game" played by non-state actors. The state is not only a very powerful player;

the boundaries between the state and the non-state actors are constantly contested, redrawn, and redefined.

This is not to say that the distinction between the state and non-state parties does not make sense or that the success of a market economy does not depend on where the line between the two is drawn. On the contrary, the fundamental meaning of the transition process is tied precisely to this question. But what it means for the state to redefine its role in the economic system and how it should redraw its activities are questions that are much more difficult than has been admitted. In every society, a large portion of available resources is politically or administratively allocated: in the advanced Western countries the share of state expenses in the gross national product ranges between one-third and one-half (with a few states, such as Sweden and Denmark, approaching 60 percent), and even this figure does not include the impact of state regulation on the reallocation of resources on the private market. The redefinition of the state's role in Eastern Europe is thus only very imperfectly captured by the metaphor of "withdrawal"; while shrinkage is clearly in order, what is even more needed is a reorientation of state activity that creates a *new mode of interaction*, a balance of power between the state and non-state actors which we have called elsewhere the "private property regime." [2] What this regime is and how it affects overall efficiency of resource allocation is far from being as clear as the term "market economy" may suggest.

The second problem that needs to be stressed, if the simplistic assumptions about the transition process are to be corrected, is that the institutional setup of the past is as important for the understanding of the process as the estimated point of arrival. In the 1950s, an attempt was made to subject all parts of the Soviet empire to an essentially unitary policy dealing with the most minute aspects of socioeconomic organization. As a result, the countries of Eastern Europe were molded largely in the same image and began to exhibit a very high degree of uniformity in their economic systems. But even then, countries such as Hungary and Czechoslovakia had quite different prewar traditions which were embodied deeply enough in their industrial and institutional structure not to be eliminated within a few years—which is how long the Stalinist regime was in force. As soon as the Soviet system's ambition to clone itself in every detail throughout the whole empire relaxed somewhat after 1956, the centrifugal forces operating on the frontiers became quite considerable. While both Hungary and the Czech Republic very painfully learned the limits of creating their own versions of the communist regime, the developmental paths of the two countries sometimes revealed

2. Chapter VI in Frydman and Rapaczynski (1994).

very considerable differences in the way their economic life was organized. Even more importantly, the economic divergences were accompanied by the development of very different political forces which shaped the configuration of interests at the start of the post-communist transition.

The importance of the institutional setup at the starting point of the transition is directly related to the issue we have discussed previously, concerning the interdependence of institutional development. Reform policies are often regarded as a more or less standard package of measures such as price liberalization, elimination of subsidies, privatization, etc. Although some general lines of necessary policies are applicable to most countries, the level of generality at which such policies appear similar is too high to be genuinely informative, since the details, the combination, and the impact of particular measures will be quite different in different environments. The idea of a standard package ignores the fact that the way in which complementary policies interact cannot be thought of in terms of a standard general procedure.

Consider the case of a stabilization program. Very similar sets of stabilization policies could have very different social costs, depending on the speed with which the existing microeconomic structures are capable of responding to the general change of environment in which they operate. Thus, even in countries with similar industrial structures, in which the costs of transition in terms of the necessary shrinkage of heavy industry and intersectoral reallocation of resources may be similar, the effect of an attempt to harden the budget constraints of firms will be very different if managers are generally in control of the enterprises than if the enterprises are controlled by workers or private owners. The reason for this is that the payoffs expected by different actors from the success or failure of government policy are quite different, and this affects both the type and the speed of adjustment on the firm level, as well as the overall cost of transition. Thus, for example, the private owner of a firm that relied completely upon subsidies from the state, might react to a cut in state support by selling the firm's assets (including perhaps valuable real estate) and deploying his capital elsewhere; while in the same situation a manager in control, whose human capital is specifically invested in the particular type of enterprise, will attempt to improve its performance without engaging in more radical restructuring. If such lesser adjustment is not viable and the pressure of budget constraints persists, the firm may ultimately go into bankruptcy and the more radical restructuring will occur, although at a much higher transition cost. But if the lesser restructuring is sufficient to permit survival, the suboptimal situation will persist indefinitely. On a broader, macroeconomic level, the stabilization policy may produce a low inflation level, but also a very low rate of growth.

An expected answer to this may be that macroeconomic stabilization is insufficient and should be accompanied by microeconomic reform, such as privatization. But if the privatization policy introduces an even greater pressure on the managers in control of much of the productive resources in a given economy, the resistance to *both* microeconomic and macroeconomic reforms is apt to grow to a level at which the government policy simply loses its credibility. The managers might respond to the standard package of reforms not by cutting costs but by increasing interenterprise credit, failing to pay taxes or repay loans to state banks, and mobilizing their economic power for political purposes. It does not help much to say that if the government sticks to its guns, the economic agents will have to change their behavior. The point is that the government cannot stick to its guns: the cost of this path of transition is simply too high. A better method might be to adopt a privatization policy that converts the managers' hold on the enterprises into a more formal title, so as to lower their resistance to reforms. But this has its price as well: managerial privatization may be very hard to sustain politically in the Eastern European environment and, if extended to a larger constituency that includes the workers, tends to limit the insider-controlled firms' access to capital and significantly slow the pace of restructuring.[3] And this in turn might yield, in a slightly longer term, similar pressures to those generated by the more radical policies.

What we have said so far should not be understood as implying an extreme form of path dependence that would amount to historical determinism. The contingent system of institutional arrangements characteristic of each country does not determine any unique set of policies that may be successfully pursued, any more than a single "package" of reform measures is applicable to all the countries in transition. But the status quo does limit the policy makers' flexibility, and the deep interconnectedness of the various policies requires that the reform process be much more tailored to individual situations than is usually admitted. As we shall see, what the Czech Republic did in the last few years would not have been possible in Hungary, and to attempt to do it would probably have resulted in consequences that would not bear any recognizable similarities to the Czech reform process.

Our analysis of the changes in Hungary and the Czech Republic after 1989 will focus on the interaction among the main actors in the transition process: the state enterprise sector, the state itself, the privatized sector, and the new private businesses. This interaction takes place along several dimensions of the reform process, corresponding to the basic sets of institutional arrangements indispensable for a proper functioning of

---

3. Chapters IV and VI in Frydman and Rapaczynski (1994).

what is usually referred to as the "market economy." The term "market economy" is to a certain extent unfortunate, since many observers tend to associate it too exclusively with a system of free prices and a few simple legal norms establishing basic property rights. In fact, as we have stressed, the term hides a great variety of complex institutional arrangements, all of which have to be configured in a way which is only very imperfectly understood, but which engenders what we have called "the private property regime." For the purpose of the present discussion, we shall focus on two main dimensions of the transition process to the private property regime and the reform policies associated with them: marketization, and the reform of firm governance. The third important dimension, the reform of the state, requires a separate treatment, which we leave for another occasion.[4]

3.2   Historical Background

General Comparisons: The Role of the Past

In 1990, in the wake of the communist collapse, the Czech Lands were still a part of Czechoslovakia. But considered separately from its Slovak partners, the Czech Republic was, on the surface at least, surprisingly similar to Hungary. Both were relatively small countries—the area of Hungary was 93,033 square km, that of the Czech Lands 78,645 square miles—with nearly identical population—10.4 million. Their GDP was also very close—Hungary's was $33.05 billion and the Czech Republic's was $31.6 billion—although, for reasons to be discussed later, their industrial structures were rather different (see table 3.1).

The two countries also shared significant portions of their historical experience. For a long time both countries were part of the Hapsburg empire; both experienced a nationalist rebirth in the nineteenth century; and both fell under the sway of Soviet communism after World War II. Finally, both rebelled against their Soviet masters and suffered a humiliating invasion: Hungary in 1956, Czechoslovakia in 1968.

But there were significant differences as well. Before World War II, the Czech Republic was one of the richest countries of Europe—the GDP per capita of Czechoslovakia in 1937 was 90 percent that of Austria and 70 percent of France.[5] The Czech lands were by far richer than the poor

---

4. For a discussion of the implications of continued high levels of state ownership in Eastern Europe on the reform of the state, see Pistor and Turkewitz (1996).

5. Kaser and Radice (1985), and Begg (1991, 245–46). For an overview of the structure of the Czechoslovak economy during the inter-war period, see Teichova (1974, 1988). For a similar treatment of the Hungarian economy, see Berend and Ranki (1985).

Table 3.1
Basic comparisons in 1990

	Czech Republic	Hungary
Population	10,364 million	10,374 million
Area	78,645 square km	93,032 square km
GDP (in US$)	31.6 billion	33.05 billion
Percent of GDP (in US$) contributed by:		
Industry	50%	27%
Agriculture	7%	12%
Services	32%[a]	31%[b]
Other[c]	11%	30%

Source: PlanEcon.
Note: For Hungary, various sources give different numbers for the share of services in the GDP.
a. Includes trade, services, and depreciation (which was reported together with services).
b. Includes trade and services.
c. Includes construction, transport, and communications.

and mostly rural Slovakia, which had in fact been a part of Hungary until 1918. Hungary, by contrast, with a GDP of $120 (in constant prices) per person (barely over 60 percent of Czechoslovakia as a whole), was at the time a poor country, with over 50 percent of the population employed in agriculture and only 23 percent in industry.[6] Czechoslovakia was a stable democracy prior to its occupation by Nazi Germany; Hungary was an authoritarian state dominated by the nationalist right.

Much is often made of the difference in the economic history of the two countries, and especially of the importance of the capitalist and democratic traditions of the Czech Republic, which is believed to continue to influence the behavior of present-day Czechs and account in part for the relatively smooth transition process in the Czech Republic. The relative ease with which the Czech industry is adapting to the Western markets,[7] the low unemployment rate, and the political acceptance of the transition are all sometimes traced to the historical traditions.

6. Enyedi (1976, 19) and Begg (1991, 245).
7. For an argument that even in the face of the Council for Mutual Economic Assistance (CMEA) collapse, Hungarian industry did not successfully adapt to Western markets in 1991, see Rodrik (1994a, 332). But trade data are generally in

What is more striking than these "soft" hypotheses is some solid evidence of the superiority of the Czech industry, as compared to that of Hungary, just before the fall of the old regime. Hare and Hughes (1992) compared the value added (in world prices) in different industries in three Eastern European countries, and argued that the percentage of the Czechoslovak manufacturing output for which the country had a comparable advantage at world prices (27 percent) was over three times as large as in Hungary (7 percent). When the Czechoslovak figure is considered in light of the very different performance of industries in the Czech and Slovak parts of the country, the disparity between the Czech Lands and Hungary is bound to be even more striking. The share of "value subtractors" in the Czechoslovak economy (19 percent) was also smaller than in Hungary (24 percent), and most of that was presumably in Slovakia as well.

Given the fact that Hungary was the most "reformed" socialist country and Czechoslovakia was among the most hidebound, conservative ones until the very end of the communist regime, this apparent superiority of the Czech industry is rather surprising—some might even be tempted to look at it as evidence of the superiority of central planning over socialist market reforms. But in fact, the explanation may have something to do with the old industrial traditions in the Czech Republic, together with a feature of the communist planning system that is usually ignored.

The so-called "central planning" of the communist countries in fact involved very little genuine planning. What fitted this description best were a few prestige projects, mostly in heavy industry, often with military significance. Such projects had absolute priority with respect to access to scarce materials and human capital, consumed an inordinate share of the planners' attention, and drained resources from much of the rest of the economy. The ability to concentrate on narrowly defined, high-prestige tasks, requiring high-level, short-term mobilization of resources from several disparate areas was in fact a hallmark of the communist regime, especially in its heroic Stalinist version, which relied on a hierarchical command structure and military-like obedience from an army of compliant apparatchiks.[8] But once one moved from the highly visible, grand industrial projects to the mundane tasks of making

dispute because of discrepancies between payments accounts and custom statistics [see Organization of Economic Cooperation and Development (OECD) 1993], and OECD (1993a) data show a significant reorientation of trade in 1992, with a weakening in 1993 and 1994 (*New York Times* October 26, 1994).

8. Communism may have shared this feature with other totalitarian regimes. Gross (1979) observes that Blitzkrieg was not accidentally associated with the Nazi regime.

sure that the required amount of fabric was available for a clothing manufacturing plant or that the lack of a replacement part did not stop an entire assembly line producing important consumer goods, the idea of central planning all but disappeared. The planners could not possibly keep abreast of the information required to coordinate the enormous variety of activities going on even in a moderately complex society, and their subordinates had every incentive to withhold that information from those who used it to make ever greater demands on their efforts. What took the place of planning in such a situation was a mechanical system of targets arrived at by a slight increase "from the achieved level," followed by a process of constant, ad hoc renegotiation between the enterprises and the organs above them.[9] At this level, the central "plan" was in fact nothing more than a constant effort to keep production going, put out the biggest fires, ameliorate the worst shortages, and, above all, correct the gross macroeconomic imbalances between production and consumption. The planners were simply reacting to the imperfect signals they received from below and striving to keep their heads above water.

It was this curious planning system, probably more than any internalized norms of the pre-communist society, that most likely served as a lifebelt for the preservation of the industrial tradition of the Czech Republic. For ideological reasons, the grand socialist construction projects centered on the previously rural Slovakia, a paradigm of the much-vaunted communist industrial development. In the Czech Lands, on the other hand, the communists found a relatively well-functioning portion of the Czechoslovak economy. They naturally failed to modernize this reservoir of wealth in line with the developments in the West. Indeed, by most calculations, the experience of the Czech Republic was a showcase of the destruction that communism could wreck upon an advanced European country: between 1937 and 1990, the per capita GDP of the Czech Republic fell from a level significantly higher than Austria's to barely 16 percent of the Austrian level.[10] However, because of the planning "from the achieved level," the basic prewar industrial structure of the Czech Republic was probably preserved to a significant extent, together with some basic technical skills and organization. While the essentially new Slovak industry was much more tightly fitted to the CMEA market and the military requirements of the Warsaw Pact, and thus much more subject to the post-communist shock, the Czech industry could more easily adapt to new conditions. Even by comparison with Hungary's relatively reformed system, the Czech Republic's ability to

9. For a description of this system of planning, see Birman (1978).
10. The Czech Republic data for 1990 comes from PlanEcon; the data for Austria is from OECD (1993a).

reorient its industrial production to Western requirements was probably significantly superior.

The Nature of Industrial Organization: The Capital Stock and the Problems of Intersectoral Reallocation

The path of communist development in Eastern Europe is to a large extent embodied in the capital stock of its industries and the way most resources are allocated. Consequently, much of the costs of moving to a new property regime are related to the transaction costs of correcting these aspects of industrial organization. Because a good part of the old industrial structure includes a configuration of durable goods used in providing a very substantial portion of employment, any changes in this configuration are likely to involve serious social as well as material costs, and pose significant political problems.

The special nature of the Eastern European transition, as opposed to the post-communist development in the less industrialized and more agricultural countries of Asia, is the hypertrophy of its industrial development and its very peculiar structural characteristics. Thus, while the Asian countries may perhaps ignore their white elephant projects, and move ahead with the creation of the new private sector, the weight of the past bears much more heavily on Eastern Europe. The existing inefficient industries, which constitute a very substantial portion of the industrial sector and employ a very large proportion of the workforce, will be a crushing burden on the rest of the economy unless they are radically shrunk, restructured, and modernized. Indeed, the whole importance of privatization in the region is related to this issue.[11]

While the information concerning the nature of the capital stock in both countries is necessarily sketchy, the differences in this respect are potentially of great importance in the transition process. We have explained already why, for historical reasons, the structure of industry may be more rational in the Czech Republic than in Hungary. On the other hand, given the large influx of foreign debt capital in the 1970s, the capital stock of the Hungarian industry was probably less obsolete at the start of the transition process.[12]

The more important difference between the two countries lies in a significantly different allocation of resources among the various sectors of the economy (table 3.1), with industry constituting nearly twice as great a share of GDP in the Czech Republic as in Hungary. This is due to

---

11. Chapter 1 in Frydman and Rapaczynski (1994), and Sachs and Woo (1994).
12. Still, one-third of the existing capacity in the food industry and one-half in the engineering industry in Hungary should reportedly be replaced in order to bring them up to Western standards (OECD 1993a).

two factors. First, the Czech Republic has traditionally been a very heavily industrialized country; the proportion of industry simply did not go down since the war, as it did in most advanced Western economies, but the proportion of the entirely dysfunctional communist projects was probably smaller than in the other countries of the region. Second, after a period of intense industrialization in the first two decades, since 1968 the reform-minded Hungarian leaders did not put the same emphasis on industrial expansion, paying more attention to the development of services and the improvement of agriculture. While both Hungary and the Czech Republic have thus entered the post-communist period with their share of inefficient industries in need of serious restructuring, the problem in each country was probably less serious than in many other Eastern European countries, where the industry was both too large and very irrationally configured.

In terms of the development of services, at the beginning of 1990 both countries seriously lagged behind the Western economies, with services responsible for 37 percent of employment in Hungary and 36 percent in the Czech Republic, as opposed to 55 percent in Austria and 64 percent in France.[13] Moreover, the quality of the service sector was notoriously poor, especially in the Czech Republic, where virtually no private ownership of service outlets was allowed. In Hungary, by contrast, a significant private sector of small businessmen, primarily in the trade and service sectors, had been growing since 1968, particularly in the 1980s.[14]

The Effects of Socialist Reforms: The New Interest Politics

Perhaps the most important difference between the starting points of the Czech Republic and Hungary resulted from the economic policies of the communist regime in the last two decades of its existence. While quite similar in many other respects, the two countries stood at the opposite extremes in the (admittedly rather narrow) spectrum of the communist ideology. After a short period of political thaw during the Prague Spring of 1968, a rule of strict communist orthodoxy was reimposed on Czechoslovakia by the Warsaw Pact invasion of 1968, and the restored

---

13. Official data on the size of the service economy in Hungary significantly underrepresent the actual number of individuals involved in the provision of services, given the existence of an extensive gray or black economy. In the mid-1980s, for example, official statistics indicated that approximately 4 percent of the workforce was employed by the private sector. Time allocation studies conducted during the same period found that almost 33 percent of all active time was spent in activity in the second economy. See Blanchard, Commander, and Coricelli (1995, 312).

14. For data on the development of the new private sector, see Earle, Frydman, Rapaczynski, and Turkewitz (1994) and below.

hard-liners definitively rejected any attempts to introduce either political or economic reforms. Consequently, the structure of the classical command economy was restored and maintained until the very collapse of the communist regime. By contrast, the response of the Hungarian communists to the Soviet invasion of 1956, after a rather brief reign of terror, was to engage in a series of economic reforms and attempt to buy political and social peace in exchange for a measure of economic flexibility.

Because we believe that, contrary to widespread belief, the Hungarian economic reforms have, on the whole, placed the country in a less advantageous position than the more orthodox policies of Czechoslovakia, and that, as a result, the Czechs have in fact enjoyed, to borrow Gershenkron's phrase, an "advantage of backwardness,"[15] it is important for us to explain the legacy of the Hungarian reforms, as we understand it.

A significant break with the classical economic command system in Hungary was first made by the so-called "New Economic Mechanism" (NEM), introduced in 1968. The NEM replaced the system of compulsory plans and direct administrative control over the enterprises with indirect controls, based on financial indicators and incentives. Although the center retained control over key aspects of the economic activities of state enterprises, the system came to be based on the principle of at least limited enterprise autonomy. The reforms came to a halt in the 1970s, but resumed with renewed vigor in the 1980s.

The economic benefits of the Hungarian reforms prior to 1989 were not overwhelming. A combination of greater attention to agriculture, a modest freeing of private initiative in trade and services, somewhat more consumer-oriented production, and a large influx of imports paid for with foreign loans allowed the authorities for some time to offer the limited prosperity of the "goulash communism." There was also some improvement in the pricing system, partly as a result of the relaxation of some controls, but mainly as a result of greater export orientation of the Hungarian economy. Modest steps were taken on the way to banking reform, and the tax system was partially modernized in the last years of the communist rule. All of these changes may have allowed for a somewhat more gradual pace of reform after 1989. From the point of view of the post-communist period, however, the greatest benefits of the communist reforms were probably reputational: the Hungarian economy was believed by many to be by far the best placed for the future, and this allowed Hungary to attract the greatest amounts of foreign investment in the first few years after the demise of the communist regime.[16]

---

15. Gershenkron (1962).
16. In 1991, for example, foreign direct investment in Hungary amounted to US$1,462 million. By comparison, the combined total foreign direct investment in Czechoslovakia, Poland, and Romania was US$987 million (Kogut 1996).

Despite these improvements, the Hungarian reforms had a very clearly delimited plateau of achievement, and the economy pretty quickly hit on hard times again, especially when the influx of foreign loans dried up in the 1980s. The market elements of socialist Hungary were always quite limited, with the state continuously intervening to subsidize failing enterprises, redistribute revenues from one sector to another, fix prices of most strategic commodities, and protect the inefficient state enterprise from foreign and domestic competition.[17]

What the reforms unambiguously accomplished was an increase in the power of state enterprise managers, who became the most powerful economic, and gradually political, force in the country. The main result of the early NEM reforms was to give the managers a more significant voice, relative to other organs of state administration, concerning the running of their enterprises. A further strengthening of the position of Hungarian managers took place in 1984, with the creation of so-called Enterprise Councils and a conferral of "self-management" rights on a large group of enterprises. As pointed out by knowledgeable observers,[18] the managers in fact controlled most Enterprise Councils, and their power only increased over time, as they lobbied the state for additional subsidies and concessions.

What began as a devolution of managerial control culminated in the state's loss of ownership rights. The most important milestones in this progression took the form of two laws which went into effect in 1989 and allowed state enterprises to spin off a portion of their assets into subsidiaries organized as commercial companies, as well as to convert whole enterprises into separate joint-stock and limited-liability companies.[19] This led to a widespread transformation of socialized enterprises into mere holding companies, "owning" a portion of the shares of new companies created out of their assets, with another portion partially owned by the managers and partially enmeshed in a maze of cross-ownership arrangements which effectively insulated the insiders from any external control.

The importance of this process lies in the fact that the state never recovered its control over the previously socialized assets. The creation of a special State Property Agency, for the purpose of reasserting the state's rights over its holdings, at most managed to introduce one more player into the complicated game centered around Hungarian companies. As debts were dumped into dummy corporations, assets were leased through a series of subsidiaries, departments were reorganized as

---

17. Kornai (1992).
18. See, e.g., Voszka (1993).
19. For the description of this corporatization process, see Hankiss (1990), Stark (1990), and Frydman, Rapaczynski, and Earle et al. (1993).

separate legal entities, and ever more complicated deals were entered into by the managers, bankers, foreign investors, and the state, the organizational structure of the Hungarian economy came to be more and more an artifact of various hedging strategies, tax policies, and state bailouts rather than an arrangement designed to assure economic efficiency. The subsequent choice and outcomes of Hungarian privatization policies, and indeed the whole progress of post-communist reform, can hardly be understood except against the background of this convoluted state of ownership relations (referred to by one expert as "recombinant property" [20]) and the political consequences that inevitably flowed from it.

In no other communist country was the situation as different from Hungary as in Czechoslovakia, where the balance of power remained much more favorable to the state, with its highly centralized institutions. To be sure, as the Czechoslovak economy gradually degenerated in the last years of the communist rule, the managers of very large industrial enterprises also gained considerable influence over the planning process and were able to steer toward their empires a significant portion of the resources administered through the political system. But until the very end, the Czechoslovak communist authorities steadfastly refused to relax much of their hold over the economy, and the enterprise managers never succeeded in converting their influence within the state administrative structure into quasi-formal entitlements, much less the full property rights enjoyed by many of their Hungarian counterparts. Consequently, when the first post-communist government in Czechoslovakia announced its determination to carry out a large-scale reform program, which granted comparatively few privileges to enterprise insiders, the managers were not in a position to offer effective resistance or assure their control over the transformation process.[21]

As we shall see, the Czech "advantage of backwardness" was very much related to the preservation of the strong state and the weakness of the special interests unleashed by the communist reform process in such countries as Hungary or Poland. We have noted already that the embodiment of the old system in the considerable durable assets of the Eastern European economies does not permit the countries of the region to proceed with their reforms in a piecemeal manner, simply removing the old restraints on private initiative and releasing the energies of the

---

20. Stark (1996).
21. Although the Parliament refused to grant enterprise insiders any formal preferences in the Czech privatization program, the specific mode of the program's implementation did in fact give them certain advantages. Also, the centralized process of reform resulted in a great concentration of power in the Czech banking sector. The Czech privatization program is described in section 3.4.

new private sector. Instead, the reform process requires a very costly and complicated transition in which the dysfunctional structures erected by the old regime are sufficiently reformed not to choke off the rest of the economy. This means, above all, that some external ownership control must be injected into the organizational structure of the state sector, so that the incentives of the most important actors—managers and workers—are brought into line with the long-term interests of the whole community. This process of reform is naturally painful, as state enterprises, with their bloated employment, must be shrunk or liquidated, and the old power structure must be thoroughly revamped. A task of this kind, in which a global, system-wide restructuring probably must precede the possibility of marginal improvements, cannot be successfully accomplished without an expedient use of state power. It is precisely here that the socialist reforms potentially weakened the ability of such countries as Hungary to effect the necessary initial changes, since they organized and empowered the very special interests that have the most to lose from a speedy transformation of the state sector.

The Foreign Debt and Fiscal Discipline

Related to the already discussed weakening of the state vis-à-vis the new special interests is the different attitude of the state toward fiscal responsibility in Hungary and the Czech Republic.

The classical model of socialism had a relatively effective way of avoiding inflationary pressures. Although the system was endemically incapable of ensuring that shortages of particular commodities did not arise, it had sufficient tools to control the aggregate balance of supply and demand. In the producer goods sectors, prices were essentially irrelevant, since the allocation of goods was mostly done through a centralized distribution system. In the consumer sector the balance was maintained by controlling wages and trying to synchronize the aggregate levels of consumer goods production with the overall levels of demand. Although imbalances occasionally occurred, prices were rarely adjusted upwards (usually under the cover of quality improvements), and imports were used to relieve particularly acute deficiencies.[22]

While the Czech Republic was, in a way, a model of socialist fiscal discipline, with inflation between 2 and 5 percent and budget deficits always under 1 percent of GDP, the Hungarian difficulties in controlling inflation antedate the post-communist reforms: inflation averaged 7 percent

---

22. For the way in which a "global" supply and demand equilibrium was maintained in Czechoslovakia, see Earle, Frydman, Rapaczynski, and Turkewitz (1994).

Table 3.2
Debt indicators in 1990

	Czechoslovakia	Hungary
Debt (in US$ millions)	5,390	21,396
Debt/GDP	17%	65%
Debt/exports[a]	85%	269%
Total debt service/exports	13%[b]	53%

Sources: Dervis and Condon (1994), Institute of International Finance (1994a, 1994b).
a. Debt stock, service, and export figures are in convertible currency only.
b. For the Czech Republic in 1991.

in 1985, 9 percent in 1987, and 17 percent in 1989.[23] While this is not a bad record as compared to, say, Poland, the growing lack of discipline was clearly one of the effects of the state's losing its power vis-à-vis the enterprises, which clamored more successfully for new subsidies and a relaxation of wage restraints.

But the most important difference in terms of the budget, also traceable to the divergent characters of the communist regime in the two countries, concerned the external debt levels with which the Czech Republic and Hungary entered the post-communist period (table 3.2). Here again, the austere nature of the Czech orthodoxy, with its worse access to the capital markets in the wake of the Soviet invasion and the mistrustful attitude of the communist leaders toward dependence on foreign bankers, created another "advantage of backwardness" on which the later reformers could capitalize. The Hungarian leaders, by contrast, confident in the ability of market socialism to compete in the world markets, went on a borrowing spree in the 1970s from which the country never fully recovered. The borrowed money was ultimately very inefficiently invested (much of it was in fact consumed). The debt burden thus did not produce the expected returns and not only continues to weigh heavily on the Hungarian budget, but also influences other reform policies, such as privatization, where the government's constant expectation of additional revenues for the servicing of the debt stands in the way of an effective disengagement of the state.

---

23. Dervis and Condon (1994).

3.3 Marketization

The aspect of the transition process to which we refer as "marketization" comprises a set of polices aimed at perfecting those markets[24] (primarily the product and labor markets) which already existed, albeit in a restricted and distorted form, at the beginning of the reform process, and the creation of new markets, such as those for capital and corporate control, for which there was no room under the old regime. The set of policies pursued within the framework of marketization includes price liberalization, reduction of subsidies, import liberalization, inflation control, introduction of convertible currency, antimonopoly measures, establishment of stock exchanges and bond markets, banking reform, modernization of commercial and securities legislation, and other measures facilitating the development of market exchanges of all kinds.

Although there is some disagreement as to the best way in which marketization reforms should proceed, and particularly whether they should be introduced in one fell swoop or more gradually, there is no significant disagreement as to their general desirability: in the long run, the policies we have listed are generally thought to be necessary for the creation of a market economy. What is somewhat less clear is what exactly can be accomplished through marketization policies alone. Most observers agree, at least by now, that something more is needed for the reconstruction of the Eastern European economies; privatization is often believed to be necessary as well. But marketization, by itself, is said to create significant pressures toward a more rational allocation of resources, and recent studies have argued that the environment introduced by marketization policies leads to a significant restructuring of the state sector, even without ownership reforms.[25]

It is our view that the primary effect of Eastern European marketization is the creation and development of a new private sector, and only secondarily a rationalization of the remaining state sector. We need not deny, of course, that state enterprises do react to the hardening of the budget constraints, and that they are forced to rationalize certain aspects of their operations. But without other, structural reforms, the direct effect of marketization on the state sector is relatively limited. Indeed, if the socialist reformers had been less timid or less constrained in their pursuit of market-oriented policies, they would also have put through most of the measures involved in a standard marketization

---

24. By using this term we in no way intend to imply that the markets in question are anywhere near perfect in any economy, to say nothing of the countries of Eastern Europe, even after the basic reforms are put in place.
25. Pinto, Belka, and Krajewski (1993).

package of a post-communist reform. But in the absence of new entrants into the market, either in the form of new domestic businesses or foreign competition, the marketization reforms would have been unlikely to make the socialist economy truly viable.

The main effect of post-communist marketization policies, then, is the creation of a space in which private agents are able, often for the first time, to deploy the resources at their disposal outside of the sphere dominated by the political allocation process. These resources, be they at first only labor and very modest capital derived from family savings, can now be used without the crippling restrictions typical of even the most liberal communist regimes, and the resulting explosion of private entre-preneurship is the most visible direct effect of marketization. In fact, perhaps the main contribution of the squeeze imposed on the state sector by the hardening of the budget constraints was that many state enterprises were forced to sell a part of their assets to cut costs and gain additional revenues, and a supply of trucks, machines, and equipment found its way into the new private sector.

Once the role of the private sector is growing, and once foreign com-petition is brought in by the reduction of import restrictions, market-ization begins to have an *indirect*, secondary effect on state enterprises, which must, if they want to survive, go beyond slothful forms of intra-sectoral rivalry or simple retrenchment. Even then, it is extremely unlikely that purely competitive pressures, without an effective ownership reform, can make the state sector perform sufficiently well to allow for its long-term survival.[26] Indeed, even after its privatization, the former state sector might be too set in its inefficient ways to be able to restructure effectively without constant pressure from growing new private businesses.

Perfecting the Product Markets

Rationalizing the price system and bringing relative prices in line with world prices and real domestic costs was one of the most urgent prior-ities for all the post-communist countries that took reforms seriously. Given the different starting points, Hungary proceeded more gradually than the then Czechoslovakia, which adopted a "big bang" version of price liberalization.

---

26. While the world-wide experience with poorly performing state enterprises strongly supports this conclusion, specific data regarding the performance of state enterprises in Eastern Europe and Russia relative to comparable private companies is just now becoming available. See Carlin, Van Reenen, and Wolfe (1994) for broad case study data indicating that most state firms in the region responded to changing conditions through basically passive strategies that were focused, even in the best cases, on loss minimization.

Prior to 1990, only 15 percent of prices had been set administratively in Hungary, while 100 percent were so fixed in the former Czechoslovakia.[27] The idea, however, that 85 percent of Hungarian prices were set by the market must be viewed with a certain degree of caution, since the practice of decentralized price setting always lagged behind theory. The Hungarian economy was among the most concentrated in the world, so that genuine price liberalization, without serious competition from abroad, would have resulted in a monopolistic price system. Moreover, the absence of a coherent firm governance structure meant that even a rational system of monopoly pricing could not have been expected. Instead, enterprise management was likely to cater to various special interests, both within and without the enterprise (to say nothing of personal enrichment), rather than to minimize costs and maximize profits. Not surprisingly, therefore, in the absence of property reforms allowing the entry of new firms and the exit of non-performing firms, the communist marketization policies were necessarily halting and incomplete: the way in which enterprises were supposed to set prices was regulated by strict rules concerning the relation of prices to costs, as well as several laws against "unfair profits." [28] Enterprises also had to clear their prices in advance with the central price office, which could decide to intervene at any point for reasons such as paternalism, welfare considerations, protection of domestic production, export incentives, price stability, and periodic re-adjustments of subsidies.[29] As a result, the formally "free" prices were quite far from their proper level, although the distortions might have been significantly smaller than in the other communist countries.

Be that as it may, the new, post-communist Hungarian authorities felt they could build on the prior reforms. Except for residential rents, price subsidies on most consumer products, such as household energy, meat products, pharmaceuticals, etc., were gradually eliminated during 1991 and 1992; informal controls were largely lifted; and the remaining administrative prices were considerably readjusted. Exchange rates were unified and the forint was pegged to a basket of Western currencies (DM and US$). A few quantitative restrictions on exports and imports have remained, but generally trade has been quite free, with the nominal average tariff at 13 percent in 1991.[30]

In the Czech Republic (then still a part of Czechoslovakia), the transition was much more dramatic, but the general outcomes were quite

---

27. Bruno (1994).
28. Kornai (1990a).
29. Kornai (1990a, 80–85). See also Swaan (1990).
30. OECD (1993a), Balcerowicz and Gelb (1994), European Bank for Reconstruction and Development (EBRD) (1993b), and Rodrik (1994a). There were also additional charges on imports which amounted to ca. 5 percent.

similar. The government introduced a package of reforms effective as of January 1, 1991. Prices of fuels and energy, apartment rents, transport, and selected agricultural products continued to be regulated, but most others were rapidly decontrolled (table 3.3). A unified exchange rate for the koruna was tied to a basket of five Western currencies, with the initial exchange rate fixed significantly below the previous level. Tariffs were set lower than in Hungary (averaging about 5 percent), with a temporarily higher tariff on consumer goods (20 percent, later in the year reduced to 15 percent), and no quantitative restrictions.[31]

The price rationalizing measures necessarily had an effect on inflationary pressures in the economy. We have seen already that price increases became quite significant in Hungary in the last years of the old regime, while the Czech Republic had no inflation problem prior to 1990. But since relative price adjustments are generally upwards, liberalization could easily have led to a heating-up of inflation, unless accompanied by strict monetary and other measures. Given its big bang policy, the threat was particularly obvious in the Czech Republic, where producer prices shot up by 47 percent in the first two months of the program (January and February 1991), only to stabilize at very low inflation levels afterwards. Consumer prices also rose very rapidly (47 percent in the first quarter), and the rate of increases came down a bit more slowly, but was quite low by mid-1991. The Czech Republic was thus extremely successful, indeed the most successful among the countries in transition, in controlling inflationary pressures in the wake of reforms, although inflation accelerated somewhat in 1993 and has not been fully suppressed (table 3.4). The Czech Republic was also very successful in maintaining effective wage controls, which were reimposed in 1993 to contain an increase in inflation and maintain competitiveness abroad.[32]

Hungary, with its more gradual policies, never experienced the sudden burst of inflation characteristic of the aftermath of "shock therapy," but inflation has been a persistent problem. While the continuous process of price adjustment may be a factor in this inflationary pressure (which in turn makes relative price adjustments more difficult), much of it is probably due to other factors, primarily budget deficits, where the pressure on the Hungarian government, with its large foreign debt and huge transfer payments, is much more severe than in the Czech Republic.[33]

The element that needs to be stressed in the context of price rationalization and the creation of an effective product market is the paramount importance of foreign trade. We have argued already that state enterprises, given their governance and monopolistic structure, react in

---

31. OECD (1994), Rodrik (1994a).
32. OECD (1994a).
33. For a comparison of the two countries' budgets, see OECD (1993a, 1994a).

Table 3.3
Price liberalization in the Czech Republic 1990–1992

	1990	1991	1992
Percent of GDP comprising goods with state-regulated prices	85	18	6

Source: (OECD 1994a).

Table 3.4
Inflation rates, consumer price index, 1990–1993

	1990	1991	1992	1993
Czech Republic	9.7	56.6	11.1	20.8
Hungary	28.9	34.8	22.8	22.5

Source: Dyba and Svejnar (1994).

only a limited way to price liberalization, and that the entry of new competition is a key to changes in their behavior. The new private sector in all countries in transition is largely concentrated in trade and services, with very little resulting competition for the large state manufacturing empires. While all countries try to increase competition in the state sector by various demonopolization measures—Hungary has been trying to break up some of the large empires since the 1980s—the effect of such measures is rather limited, given the structure of the capital stock of Eastern Europe and the degree of regulatory ability required by anti-trust policy in general. In this situation, pressure from foreign competition is absolutely crucial, not only for the restructuring impulse that it gives to the sluggish domestic producers, but also as a means to "import" the relative price structure of the more advanced economies.

Perfecting the Labor Markets

There was a time in the development of the Soviet form of socialism when non-market allocation determined a significant and growing portion of all labor utilization. A system of internal passports and residence permits, which in fact tied a large proportion of rural and small-town population to their employment, was a growing aspect of the Stalinist economic order. Among the more educated, urban population, a system of employment assignments for university and professional school graduates eliminated all choice for a substantial portion of entrants into the labor force. Campaigns urging masses to "volunteer" for work on large construction projects forced people to accept employment in unattractive locations. Extensive use of army recruits, especially in seasonal work in agriculture, further added to the proportion of administratively allocated labor. Finally, an archipelago of forced labor camps was an indispensable element of much of the communist development in its "classical" period.

Although the system of administrative allocation of labor never became as widespread in Hungary and the Czech Republic as it was in the Soviet Union, labor mobility was restricted in a number of ways in these countries as well. To the extent that coercive allocation did not replace more traditional ways in which individuals disposed of their labor, some elements of a labor market were, of course, present throughout the communist years. But even if the more explicitly coercive forms of labor assignment came to play only a minor role in the last years of communism in Central Europe, the state attempted, until the very end, to regiment both the supply and the demand side of the labor market. The authorities pursued a policy of maintaining full employment, regardless of the productivity losses that such a policy entailed. Enterprises could always pass on their labor costs to their customers, and there was practically no pressure to reduce employment. Indeed, given the full employment policies and the difficulty of attracting new employees through higher wages (because of wage controls), there was a chronic shortage of labor and hoarding was a universal response. The full employment policy, in turn, gave the state no choice but to control wages in order to counter inflationary pressures. The Czechoslovak authorities were much more successful in this than the Hungarian ones, who lost much of their control over special interest pressures, but both countries had rigid wage control systems. In addition, the fully administrative allocation of housing and internal mobility restrictions (one could not ordinarily receive employment in desirable locations, such as the capitals, without a residential permit, which in turn depended on securing employment) further prevented spontaneous geographical reallocations. Finally, the possibility of self-employment was nearly non-existent in Czechoslovakia, although in Hungary the restrictions on small private entrepreneurship were becoming increasingly less burdensome.[34]

---

34. A rough estimate of the number of self-employed persons prior to 1990 can be derived from the number of unincorporated businesses, of which approximately 70,000 existed in Czechoslovakia in 1989 (primarily in the service and crafts sectors). At the same time, Hungary had over 320,000 registered entrepreneurs.

The creation of better functioning labor markets was—and largely remains—a primary requirement of a successful transition. The distortions created by years of regimentation made a reallocation of labor to more productive employment as important as the reallocation of any other resources. The bloated employment in state enterprises has to be reduced, a large amount of retraining and job–employee matching has to be accomplished, and large masses of people have to be moved across different sectors of the economy: from the state to the private sector, from heavy industry into services, and from company towns and industrial regions to the rest of the country.

As the enterprises face hardening budget constraints and falling demand, they respond by cutting production and, somewhat more slowly, employment. In itself, this shedding is a positive sign of restructuring. But the reabsorption of the released capital and human assets into more productive uses is a slow process, limited by the absence of appropriate (capital and labor) markets and the lag in the growth of the private sector. The special problem of the reallocation of labor is that, unlike in the case of useless capital assets, labor is not easily retired or kept idle at low cost. High unemployment imposes serious financial burdens on the state (which maintains the social safety net) and, indirectly, on the whole economy. Even more importantly, unemployment creates social dissatisfaction which poses the most immediate threat to the sustainability of the whole reform policy. The main question concerning labor market reforms, then, is how quickly the obstacles to full marketization should be removed without endangering the reform process, and what is the price of maintaining certain forms of government intervention.

Government policies regulating the labor market fall into three broad categories: the regulation of supply, the regulation of demand, and the facilitation of market transactions concerning employment. Hungary and the Czech Republic differ quite substantially along most of these dimensions. While both governments have intervened to ease the strains that the transition puts on the labor force, the Czech government did so more on the side of stimulating demand, while the Hungarian authorities have been more active in limiting supply. Also, the two countries have used significantly different methods to smooth the functioning of their labor markets.

The primary tool of the Czech labor policy has been the control of wages to slow down the growth of unemployment and maintain competitiveness abroad. The government's ability to keep down the nominal growth of wages significantly below inflation, so as to produce a much greater fall in real wages since 1989 than in Hungary (see table 3.5), is probably another effect of the inherited strength of the state with which Czechoslovakia entered the reform period. The government conducts its wage policy through a tripartite council, which it has been able to dominate, and a series of tax regulations imposing severe penalties on wage increases in excess of the agreed norms. In the early stages of the reforms, the excess wage taxes could be as high as 750 percent (for raises over 5 percent above the norm), while more recently the maximum tax was 300 percent. Controls were abandoned briefly in the first half of 1993 but were reimposed in July of that year, when the wage growth turned out to be too high.[35]

Hungary, by contrast, has been much less successful in controlling the growth of wages. An excess wage tax was also in operation until the end of 1992, but a number of exemptions made the tax ineffective, especially in the last year of its operation. The exemption for small companies apparently led to a widespread splitting up of state companies,[36] and another one excluded joint ventures with foreign participation.

Although it is impossible to assess definitively the effect of wage policies on the levels of unemployment, given the existence of other important factors, unemployment has been markedly lower in the Czech Republic than in Hungary (table 3.6); indeed, the Czech Republic is unique among the post-communist countries in this respect, as in the (probably not unconnected) levels of political stability and support for the policies of marketization.

Has the price for the strict wage controls, in terms of its effect on the extent of restructuring, also been high? The answer to this question cannot be given with complete certainty. But there is no evidence that the Czech enterprises are not restructuring, since the levels of layoffs have been quite high in some areas.[37] Also a relatively high proportion of

---

35. Freeman (1994), OECD (1994a), and Dyba and Svejnar (1994).

36. OECD (1993a). The exemption was for companies with wage bills under HUF 20 million, or some $270,000. Given Hungarian wage levels, this amounted to employment above some 120 persons. This was significantly higher than in the Czech Republic, where companies with fewer than 25 employees were exempted. Given the freedom of Hungarian state companies to create subsidiaries, the exemption made it possible for a large number of state firms to avoid all wage controls. In the Czech Republic, by contrast, the exemption in practice applied only to new private businesses in which other, market-based restraints were operating as well.

37. From 1990 to 1991, employment in the state sector in Czechoslovakia declined by over 1,000,000 (20 percent), and the following year witnessed an additional reduction of the workforce by over 650,000 (approximately 17 percent) (Ham, Svejnar, and Terrell 1995). The decline in employment cannot be satisfactorily explained by privatization, because privatization of the industrial sector only began in late 1992. Research by Boeri suggests that the active labor policy of firms played an increasing role in the cutback of employment in the 1990–92 period. While purely involuntary layoffs accounted for only 17.9 percent of the 1990–91 decline, they were responsible for 24.8 percent of the 1991–92 reduction. (Boeri 1993, 1995.)

Table 3.5
Real wages, annual percentage change, 1990–1993

	1990	1991	1992	1993
Czech Republic[a]	−6.3	−40	11.1	−3
Hungary[b]	−2.4	−0.6	1.7	−0.5

Source: EBRD (1994).
a. Annual percentage change in the average wage in industry minus percentage change in the annual average of consumer prices.
b. Annual percentage change in gross earnings per employee minus percentage change in the annual average of consumer prices.

Table 3.6
Unemployment rate (percent), 1990–1993

	1990	1991	1992	1993
Czech Republic	0.8	4.1	2.6	3.5
Hungary	1.5	7.5	12.3	12.1

Sources: Commander et al. (1995); Ham, Svejnar, and Terrell (1995).
Note: Unemployment rate calculated as of December 31.

the laid-off workers find new employment, and a significant number is probably working in the unrecorded private sector, thus indicating that an intersectoral reallocation is taking place as well (table 3.7). The figures comparing intersectoral reallocation in the two countries also point to relatively minor differences, mostly due to the greater movement away from (more overstaffed) agriculture in Hungary (table 3.8).

The reason why a wage policy in the period of transition may be less harmful than in the more stable economies may be related to the fact that wages play a relatively minor role in the process of labor reallocation in transition. Wage data from most countries in Eastern Europe reveal little difference between salary levels in the private and state sectors, and when the entire wage package is considered, private sector employees, on average, do worse than state sector workers. The primary force that makes people look for new employment in countries like Hungary and the Czech Republic is the pressure on state sector firms to reduce their bloated employment levels.

Table 3.7
Unemployment inflow and outflow rates, 1992 averages

Country	Unemployment rate	Inflow rate	Outflow rate	Outflow to jobs
Czech Republic	3.1	0.6	25.8	18.0
Hungary	11.7	0.5	7.0	3.0
Poland	14.9	0.7	4.0	2.3

Source: Blanchard, Commander, and Coricelli (1995).
Note: Inflow rate is expressed as a proportion of the labor force; outflow rate is expressed as a proportion of unemployment.

Table 3.8
Sectoral shares of labor, 1989–1992 (percent)

	Czech Republic		Hungary	
	1989	1992	1989	1992
Agriculture	11	8	18	10
Industry	47	44	40	37
Services	42	48	42	53

Source: Burda (1994).

Moreover, much of the reallocation of labor is to small private firms which either are exempt from wage controls or find it relatively easy to keep their employment "unofficial" and evade the new taxes. Where the controls are most effective is in the state sector and the still unmonitored privatized sector, and this is where, given the failures in the corporate governance arrangements, they are most needed.

The process of reallocation may also be assisted by various state policies facilitating the matching of workers to new employers. Here also the labor market policies of the Czech Republic and Hungary differ quite substantially. While Hungary invests rather heavily in retraining programs of rather dubious value, the Czech Republic relies more on an extensive system of providing information about new vacancies, together with quite ungenerous unemployment benefits. The Czech labor offices are indeed the only ones in Eastern Europe to be staffed at levels similar to those in the West (30:1), resulting in better job intermediation and more effective supervision. Where employment is subsidized, the subsidy is usually direct: before the breakup of Czechoslovakia (when much higher levels of unemployment in Slovakia required a more aggressive policy), the state devoted 70 percent of its active labor market policy expenditures to job creation through public works programs, rather than through a much more dangerous subsidization of existing employment (as may be increasingly the practice in Hungary).[38]

A very important aspect of the development of the labor markets in the transition economies is related to the housing policy. Under communism, housing in both Hungary and the Czech Republic was extremely heavily subsidized, with the resulting severe shortages and an administrative system of allocation. Although the introduction of a more unrestricted housing market is among the primary prerequisites of labor mobility, especially when unemployment is likely to be heavily concentrated in certain parts of the country, all the post-communist countries continue the policy of heavy rent subsidization. While we do not have the data comparing mobility in the two countries, the Czech Republic may be further advanced on the road toward a freer housing market as a result of its extensive program of housing restitution. What is the present effect of this on the development of the labor market, however, cannot be told with any degree of precision.

We have mentioned already that the Hungarian government has been more active than the Czech government in regulating the supply side of the labor markets. A policy of early retirement was not very successful, but generous unemployment benefits took off some pressure from the labor market.[39] The Czech Republic, by contrast, where unemployment is often viewed as the fault of the individual rather than of the state,[40] has the most ungenerous and decreasing benefits in all of Eastern Europe, despite its being the richest country of the region. As a result, the proportion of people losing or quitting their jobs who ended up receiving unemployment in 1991 and 1992 was much lower in the Czech Republic than in Hungary. In addition to people finding new employment in the official and unofficial economy, a significant proportion of the Czechs are thought to be finding new jobs in the neighboring countries (Germany and Austria), and many (especially women) seem

38. Burda (1994).
39. For a comparison of levels of unemployment compensation in Eastern Europe, see Burda (1994).
40. Freeman (1994) citing a study by the Czech Academy of Sciences in the second half of 1991.

to be leaving the labor market altogether.[41] In Hungary, by contrast, unemployment seems a more attractive option.

Development of Capital Markets and Financial Institutions

Equity Markets

Unlike the product and labor markets, the capital market did not exist at all under the old regime. The only exception was a rudimentary bond market established in Hungary in the 1980s, which allowed a number of firms to issue debt securities, mostly to individual savers. Since 1988 secondary trading was channeled through a pilot exchange, and the state began to issue Treasury bills, but the Hungarian bond market was always more of a curiosity than a truly significant exception to the communist rule. In the classical model of the communist economy, all long-term external enterprise financing was done by allocations from the state budget, channeled through the central "monobank" or a special investment bank. As the regime enacted some reforms, the credit system was somewhat decentralized, especially in Hungary, where, as early as 1987, the monobank was split up into a central bank and five separate commercial banks, but the allocation of credit never ceased to be very tightly controlled. Indeed, decentralization of investment always lagged behind the reforms of the production and distribution systems. Even the allocation of short-term credit had little or nothing to do with standard creditworthiness evaluation.

A switch to a new mode of financing was, then, a necessity, not just to harden the budget constraint of the enterprises, but also—indeed, primarily—to effect a change in the objective function of enterprise management. The interests of capital had to be properly asserted, and the creation of a new financing system, together with privatization and corporate governance reform, was among the main tools of inducing the required structural adjustments on the level of individual firms and across the different sectors of the economy. As in any capitalist society, the flows of capital were expected to assure that firms restructured (or simply retrenched) their operations, that resources would move from the overbuilt industry to the underdeveloped trade and service sectors, and that savings would in the future be directed to the uses promising the highest returns.

While banks were likely to remain important, perhaps dominant, institutions of external financing in post-communist Central Europe,

---

41. The participation levels among women (generally very high in Eastern Europe) in Czechoslovakia went down by 10.9 percent between 1989 and 1992. It stayed the same in Hungary during the same period. The participation of men declined by 7 percent in Hungary and by only 1.3 percent in Czechoslovakia.

especially given the proximity and influence of Germany, the banking system needed to be fundamentally reformed to be able to perform the tasks given to it under the new conditions. Even in a bank-dominated system, equity and bond markets, as well as non-bank types of institutional investors, would have to develop. In particular, although public equity markets could not have been expected to become a very important source of corporate financing in the near future, their speedy establishment was viewed as very important in a number of countries, and nowhere more so, perhaps, than in Hungary, where a formal stock exchange was inaugurated in Budapest as early as June 1990. Stocks of ten companies were floated at the time, with six of them listed (i.e., satisfying the more stringent conditions set up by the exchange), and a number trading in parallel on the Vienna stock exchange (to lessen the price distortions due to low levels of capitalization in Budapest).[42]

In the most advanced economies, equity markets do not play a very significant role in the provision of new financing for the corporate sector: in the U.S., new stock issues accounted for a mere 2 to 3 percent of total financing between 1960 and 1980.[43] But equity may play a more important role in Eastern Europe, with its inflationary and highly uncertain environment making risk and inflation premiums on debt too high for most enterprises. How much of this new financing may be expected to flow through the public equity markets (rather than controlling investments by strategic trade investors) is a matter of some debate; however, the liquidity and confidence levels afforded by well-functioning stock exchanges might be among the factors making foreign portfolio investment more likely. Even more importantly, the development of equity markets may have a significant impact on the way Eastern European firms are managed and monitored. To be sure, proxy fights and takeovers are not likely to play a major role with respect to most corporations, but the informational aspect of public equity trading may be an important element in the process by which management performance is monitored and evaluated.

The post-communist reformers have faced the following questions: Under what conditions can effective equity markets be created, and how can their functioning be assured? The Hungarian answer was that the standards set up by the exchange had to be very high, even if this meant that initially only very few companies could be listed or even traded without formal listing. Also, the Hungarians were of the opinion that companies should be floated on the exchange through IPOs, in which shares of privatized companies (for only previously state-owned

---

42. For the description of the early functioning of the Budapest Stock Exchange, see Mészáros (1993).
43. Grosfeld (1994).

companies were of sufficient size to be publicly traded) were sold for cash to the public.

The Czech approach was very different. The idea here was that an effective exchange presupposed relatively large capitalizations, thus creating conditions for robust trading and high degrees of liquidity. The Prague exchange did not open until 1993, when the first wave of Czech mass privatization was completed, transferring for nominal charges a very substantial proportion of shares of all Czech enterprises to private individuals and special investment privatization funds.[44] Together with the Prague Stock Exchange, another, less formalized over-the-counter exchange, known as RM, was introduced on the basis of the computerized system prepared for the processing of vouchers which the Czech citizens used to obtain their shares in the privatization process. Consequently, over 600 companies are traded on the main Prague exchange alone,[45] and its capitalization is almost twice that of the Budapest Stock Exchange (table 3.9). The disparity becomes more pronounced when debt securities are excluded: capitalization of the Prague Stock Exchange alone is more than eight times greater than that of Budapest, and equals a hefty 42 percent of the Czech GDP.[46]

But capitalization figures are not everything: dumping a lot of shares on the exchange does not ensure any particular level of activity, nor does it say much about the levels and quality of monitoring that goes on. It is clear that the Hungarian exchange is simply too small to make much of a difference, and it is not clear whether it is likely to grow in the near future. But can the Czech exchange do significantly better?

The jury is still out on this question. The overwhelming majority of companies traded on the Prague exchange are unlisted and most of them are not actively traded. The turnover is still rather small, and prices, which quadrupled between August 1993 and March 1994, tumbled shortly afterwards. Moreover, a few very large players (the privatization investment funds) own large stakes in most companies, and much of the trading among these holders takes the form of private barter (which may lead to still further concentrations). The presence of very large holders makes the markets less liquid, and the informational disparities between the few insider holders and the large number of potential outsider investors may make the large holdings still more illiquid.[47] Free

---

44. For a description of the Czech privatization program, see section 3.4.
45. Institute of International Finance (1994a).
46. For comparison, the capitalization of the exchanges in Germany is 21 percent; in the U.S. it is 58 percent. See Newman, Milgate, and Eatwell (1992).
47. The presence of a large institutional investor may increase the levels of public confidence in the company and raise the price of the remaining shares. But when the large investor wants to exit, the corresponding fears among outsider investors may lead to very steep discounts.

riding on the research and monitoring of the large investors also diminishes the incentive for the other market participants to allocate significant resources for this purpose, further eroding the governance impact of public trading. Finally, large concentrations of holdings make it unlikely that a market for corporate control will develop alongside the market for minority investment.

There are also some positive signs indicating that the Czech experiment may be succeeding. Foreign portfolio investment on the Prague exchange was US$300 million in the fourth quarter of 1993 alone,[48] and it is likely to grow in the future. It is also likely that the existence of the investment intermediaries created by the privatization program, some of which have a foreign component, is an important factor, since they provide a monitoring service and indirectly raise the confidence levels that foreign portfolio investors need in order to invest in the unfamiliar environment of Central Europe.

It is this element of effective intermediation that creates the institutional backbone of the public trading system, and it is much more likely to come into being through the incentives of a mass privatization program, such as the Czech one, rather than through the undoubtedly careful establishment of stock exchanges, such as those in Budapest or Warsaw, the trading on which is necessarily hampered by the meager supply of companies and the shortage of core (trade) investors that seem to be needed in most cases before a company can be successfully floated.

Bond Markets
Although the development of bond markets in the two countries proceeds in parallel to the establishment of equity markets, the significance of the two is quite different. Bond markets do not provide a significant source of funding for the enterprise sector in either country. But while debt securities remain relatively a minor phenomenon in the Czech Republic and are resorted to on an almost equal basis by the government and private corporations, the debt market in Hungary is the almost exclusive province of the state and is one of the primary mechanisms by which the state raises its revenues.

Hungary, with its very heavy foreign debt burden and very large transfer payments, is the prime example of a country in which the borrowing needs of the state overwhelm the credit market, as well as dry up most of the domestic funds that could otherwise go to the equity market. Indeed, the state has only a limited interest in the real development of financial markets, since they may provide competition

---

48. Institute of International Finance (1994a). Due to the decline of the Prague Stock Exchange for most of 1994, the rate of foreign portfolio investment slumped, but still reached an estimated US$819.3 million.

that could significantly raise the cost of borrowing for the state. The Hungarian government's access to international financial markets is limited; although the government has been very firm in its insistence on meeting all its debt obligations, the sheer size of its indebtedness makes it impossible for Hungary to achieve an investment grade rating for its bonds. Consequently, the absorption of domestic savings is very important for the state's ability to sustain its spending. At the same time, the population has very few other avenues of investment for its savings: given capital controls and the minuscule size of the public equity market, government securities and bank deposits are the only opportunities other than direct investment in one's own business. By putting otherwise laudable pressure on banks to improve the quality of their portfolios, the state is in fact putting pressure on them to invest more and more of their capital in state obligations. As a result, the proportion of savings absorbed by the government is extremely high (see table 3.11), as is the share of turnover in government obligations on the Budapest Stock Exchange (see tables 3.9 and 3.10).

The situation is much more favorable in the Czech Republic, which has inherited a much lower level of foreign debt and has been able to hold the line against large social transfer expenditures. The government's share of GDP in the Czech Republic is about 60 percent of that in Hungary, and the government has been able to keep the budget balanced. Consequently, its borrowing needs are much smaller and its access to finance, including the international markets, where Czech bonds have investment grade ratings, is much greater.[49] Although private sector borrowing is still limited, there are some signs that the situation may be changing, with several "firsts" in recent months. The most remarkable among them was the recent issue of the Ceskoslovenska Obchodni Banka, which was oversubscribed at just 70 basis points above the Libor rate.[50]

Banking Reform
We have said already that the banking sector is likely to remain the main source of enterprise financing in Eastern Europe in the foreseeable future. But due to the peculiar perversions of the past, the reform of the banking sector presents some of the thorniest problems of the transition.

---

49. The City of Prague bond issue in March 1994 had a spread of 120 points above the comparable U.S. Treasuries (*Financial Times*, October 14, 1994).
50. *Financial Times*, October 14, 1994. It should be noted that, given the practice of the international rating agencies of never rating private issuers higher than the government of the state in which they are located, Czech firms have an advantage over those from the other post-communist countries.

Table 3.9
Bond and equity markets

	Budapest Stock Exchange	Prague Stock Exchange
Daily turnover	HUF 838.2 million (approx. $8.38 million)[a]	CzK 200 billion[b] (approx. $7.14 billion)
Market capitalization	HUF 883.8 billion (approx. $8.8 billion) (shares HUF 181.5 billion)	CzK 435.9 billion (approx. $16.6 billion) (shares CzK 410.4 billion)
Structure of turnover		
Shares	27%	50.1%[c]
Bonds and bills	64%	49.9%
Compensation vouchers	9%	n.a.

Sources: ING Securities (1994), Standard and Poor (1994), and Budapest Stock Exchange reports (1994).
n.a.: not applicable.
a. Average in 1994.
b. Average in July 1994.
c. Includes listed and unlisted shares.

Table 3.10
Hungarian and Czech debt securities on the Budapest Stock Exchange and the Prague Stock Exchange, 1991–1994 (in billions)

	31 Dec. 1991	31 Dec. 1992	31 Dec. 1993	31 Dec. 1994
Hungary (in bln forints)				
Government bonds and Treasury bills	15.0	139.3	313.9	704.3
Corporate bonds	0.1	1.8	9.3	44.4
Czech Republic (in bln CzK)				
Government bonds and Treasury bills	n.a.	n.a.	10.6	25.9
Corporate bonds	n.a	n.a	4.5	21.6

Sources: Havas (1995) and Prague Stock Exchange (1995).
Note: The Prague Stock Exchange (and securities trading) opened in 1993.

Table 3.11
Government use of savings

| | Credit to government (as percent of total domestic credit) | | |
	1990	1991	1992
Czechoslovakia	8.5	6.6	2.9
Hungary	42.4	41.7	47.1

Source: Dittus (1993).

Several factors created a permanent excess of demand over supply and determined a non-market system of credit allocation under the old regime. First, official interest rates were centrally set and reflected the planners' growth priorities rather than the availability of funds. Interest rates were very low; once inflation accelerated, the real interest rate stayed negative for extended periods of time. Second, even in the more reformed systems, the ability of enterprises to raise prices as a result of a rise in costs made them willing to borrow without much concern for the effect this might have on profitability. (Indeed, since profit was calculated as a percentage of total cost, large financing costs might simply increase it.) Finally, poor performance was often rewarded with additional state subsidies, and the soft budget constraint made enterprises have few second thoughts about taking on additional loans.

As long as the regime lasted, the banks did not respond to the excessive demand for credit with an increased interest rate; such a policy would have contradicted the planners' priorities. Instead, credit was rationed in accordance with various regulations, which opened its availability to bargaining and political influence. Even non-performance rarely triggered a negative reply to a credit request. Except for the last couple of years of the regime in Hungary, the banks had to inform the appropriate ministry about reasons for their refusal of credit to state enterprises.[51]

The consequences of this system persisted beyond the fall of the regime. First, after years of lending in which creditworthiness, in the normal sense of the word, did not really play any role, the assets of the banks consisted of a large portfolio of loans of extremely doubtful validity. The quality of the banks' portfolios deteriorated even further

---

51. Zwass (1984).

when most enterprises lost their captive markets and faced the falling demand of the post-communist environment.

Second, the banks never developed any expertise in real practices of finance. In this respect, it might be said that they were further from being real banks than the communist enterprises were from being real firms. The latter at least produced some goods, and although they sorely lacked managerial and financial expertise, they did possess some engineering skills and experience. The banks, by contrast, having functioned for many years as mere instruments of bureaucratic control, lacked the most elementary skills in evaluating creditworthiness in a market economy; even the system of accounting did not correspond to the basic standards used in the capitalist system.

Third, the banks had developed all kinds of links to their borrowers that made them at least as dependent on the enterprises' continued existence as the enterprises were dependent on the flow of credits. The communist system had not required banks to write off bad loans. In the new situation, a sudden write-off would make the banks immediately insolvent, and therefore they continued to lend to the non-performing enterprises after the beginning of the transition. In addition, in Hungary at least, as a result of the 1987 banking reorganization, enterprises acquired equity stakes in the banks and thus significantly strengthened their bargaining position.

Fourth, the efforts to harden the budget constraint of the enterprises have paradoxically introduced another complication into the banks' portfolios. The first serious curtailment of credit coincided with another change which allowed enterprises to go around the banking system and extend credit to each other.[52] The practice, known as "interfirm credit," was not voluntary; it was forced on the enterprises by the nonpayment by their own customers, and it spread as a chain reaction. This new source of "soft budget constraint," which caused a great piling up of new debts of unknown quality, made it that much more difficult to judge the financial soundness of the banks as well, since their own assets consisted of loans to the same enterprises.

The problem of missing skills and the wherewithal of modern banking (a simple transfer could take weeks) would be bad enough. But the deeper problem of modifying the banks' behavior was in the basic structure of their incentives. To stop chasing good money after bad, the

---

52. During most of the communist regime, enterprises were strictly prohibited to engage in any financial transactions bypassing the banks (which enforced state controls). But decentralization in Hungary relaxed this requirement in the 1980s, and the change in Czechoslovakia came in 1990. The credit crunch that resulted in the rise of interenterprise indebtedness occurred in Hungary in the wake of IMF intervention in 1987; in Czechoslovakia, it came after 1989.

banks would have to be put in a position of not going down with the loss-making enterprises to which they refused to lend. This spoke for a recapitalization program that would make the banks solvent. But a recapitalization may also have the opposite effect. It diminishes the credibility of the state's claim that the banks must face a hard budget constraint; a massive infusion of capital from the state budget engenders precisely the opposite expectation—another bailout. This impression is only strengthened by the fact that a true withdrawal of further credits to enterprises might result in massive bankruptcies, which, coming on top of the already painful retrenchment, no Eastern European government thinks it can really afford.

The story of Hungarian efforts to make the banks solvent is a lesson in precisely this political exercise. The post-communist recapitalization schemes began in 1992, with a large-scale swap of bad loans (which were consolidated in a specially formed new fund) for government securities. In this first round, the government exchanged 20-year bonds with the value of some HUF 80 billion (approx. $1.1 billion) for HUF 102 billion of bad loans, but the banking practices hardly changed and the banks' portfolios (partly as a result of reclassification of the "doubtful" loans into the "bad" category in expectation of a new bailout[53]) further deteriorated.[54] The expected efforts to work out the consolidated bad loans did not materialize either. The government responded with another scheme in 1993, this time recapitalizing the banks to the tune of HUF 114 billion in exchange for their agreement to work out the bad loans. Another "tranche" of the recapitalization program came in 1994, with a further HUF 17 billion. Enterprises are said to have scrambled to be included in the program, with the effect that many apparently slackened in their restructuring efforts.[55] All the while, the cost to the government was roughly equivalent to 6 percent of GNP in 1993, a lion's share of the budget deficit.[56]

The Czech experience is only a little more reassuring. At the beginning of the reform period, the credit extended by the banks to enterprises was much larger than in Hungary—it amounted to some 74 percent of GDP in the old Czechoslovakia. According to national sources, the percentage of bad loans in this portfolio may have been significantly smaller than in Hungary: 20 percent instead of 29 percent,

---

53. There were also tax incentives for such a reclassification (Bonin and Schaffer 1994).

54. The value of bad loans increased between September 1992 and September 1993 (Bonin and Schaffer 1994).

55. Bonin and Schaffer (1994).

56. If the bailout of cooperative banks is included, the figure grows to 9 percent of GDP (Bonin and Schaffer 1994).

but IMF estimates indicate that the difference was exaggerated.[57] To deal with the problem, in 1991 the government also consolidated CzK 110 billion ($3.6 billion) worth of bad loans and removed them from the banks' assets, but instead of infusing new capital into the banking system, the scheme simply shrank the state banks by relieving them of an equivalent amount of liabilities to the National Bank and the savings banks.[58] While the first scheme concerned special low-interest revolving credits that the banks had been forced to extend under state order, the next rescue plan provided the banks with state bonds to the tune of CzK 50 billion ($1.67 million). Of this amount CzK 12 billion was a straightforward capital contribution, and CzK 38 billion was a form of swap in which the banks were supposed to write off the debts of otherwise viable enterprises and exchange their debt for equity within five years (i.e., after privatization). A further bailout cleaned up the books of the Obchodni Banka (the Bank of Foreign Trade).

The effectiveness of the various recapitalization schemes has been the subject of much debate. The banks are clearly somewhat more solvent after the massive infusion of capital, but they continue to be inefficient and their future is uncertain. To the extent that they became more prudent, they have relied less on sounder lending policies, and more on holding large amounts of state bonds, with a resulting curtailment of lending to the productive sector. They have also relied on short-term lending and large interest rate spreads, thereby further crowding out firms that can turn for credit elsewhere (foreign banks, above all) and thus increasing the proportion of credit risk in their portfolio.

The answer universally recommended for reversing the spiral of recapitalizations is bank privatization. On this score, the effect of the Hungarian schemes has been a progressive *increase* in the state's equity share in the major banks, with the last round bringing state ownership back to levels above 90 percent. This is not necessarily a negative phenomenon: the non-state share of bank ownership was mainly in the form of cross-ownership, which meant that the banks' customers among the enterprises often were able to use their leverage as owners to influence the banks' policies. But the efforts to sell the shares of the banks have been very slow to produce significant results. The only potential customers are foreign parties, and this creates a series of political and other obstacles, because banks have used the specter of foreign control to preserve their management's entrenched position, and politicians have been unwilling to take the risk of defying them.

---

57. Dittus (1993). But the proportion of bad loans in Slovakia was probably much higher than in the Czech Republic.
58. European Bank for Reconstruction and Development (1993b).

The Czech Republic has gone much further than Hungary in the privatization of the banking sector, as indeed in privatization in general, although the methods used there may bring new types of dangers. The role of banks in the Czech privatization will be discussed in more detail in the next section. But the main problem inherent in the Czech mass privatization scheme was that the banks were allowed to control privatization investment funds, which came to control a very substantial portion of privatized assets. To ensure that the voucher scheme would not amount to a mere transfer of ownership from one state hand to another (state-owned banks), the banks themselves were partially privatized in the same process. Not surprisingly, as the banks came to control most of the important investment funds, the funds in turn focused heavily on acquiring shares of the banks themselves. As a result, banks became large shareholders of each other through the medium of investment funds, as they simultaneously came to own most of the Czech non-banking enterprises. (Table 3.12 shows two examples of bank ownership structure in the wake of the first wave of voucher privatization.) Indeed, the degree of "self-ownership" is also high: one bank, Investnicni Banka, is 17 percent owned by the funds it controls.

Table 3.12
Bank cross-ownership in the ownership structure of two Czech banks

Ceska Sporitelna Bank	
Fund of National Property	40.0%
Investment funds associated with Investnicni Banka	8.8%
Investment funds associated with Komercni Banka	3.9%
Investment funds associated with Vseobecna Uverova Banka[a]	1.6%
Komercni Bank	
Fund of National Property	44.0%
Investment funds associated with Investnicni Banka	10.8%
Investment funds associated with Ceska Sporitelna Banka	4.9%
Investment funds associated with Vseobecna Uverova Banka	4.3%
Investment funds associated with Komercni Banka	3.4%

Source: 1993 Fund of National Property Database.
a. Vseobecna Uverova Banka is a bank created and owned by the Czech and Slovak National Banks, and other state financial institutions.

Whether this banking structure will lead to a German type of arrangement, in which banks relatively effectively monitor corporate performance, or whether the Czech form of bank cross-ownership will allow the banks to avoid any effective external control, in order to resist genuine restructuring and sit parasitically on top of the productive sector, is a question that is still impossible to answer. The fact that many Czech banks are now planning to increase their equity by new share issues to the public is a sign that the closure of the system may not be permanent.[59] On the other hand, the high remaining share of state ownership and the symbiotic relation between the state and the banking sector may lead to renewed bailouts and dependence, especially if the political leadership devolves to a less market-oriented team.

The Growth of the Private Sector
We have argued above that the main effect of marketization policies is the creation of the new private sector in the transition economies. If the growth of this sector is to be viewed as the measure of the success of marketization policies, the Czech Republic and Hungary have achieved remarkable progress since 1989.

It is difficult to measure the precise growth of the new private sector, as opposed to the private sector as a whole (including privatized firms). The most easily available figures concern new business entities and registered entrepreneurs (table 3.13). Although many of these businesses arose in connection with privatization of state assets, most of them can be safely classified as new, since only with respect to relatively large enterprises (most of the private sector businesses are very small) does it make sense to make a strong distinction between privatized and new private businesses. In the case of stores, service outlets, and many other small businesses, the main asset obtained from the state was the real estate on which the business is located: the value of most other assets (inventory, furniture, machines, goodwill, etc.), even if included in privatization, was essentially negligible.[60]

Viewed in this light, the numerical growth of new private businesses in both countries has been extremely impressive. It is especially striking in the Czech Republic, which entered the post-communist period with a

---

59. For the plans of the Czech banks to raise equity through public issues, see Institute of International Finance (1994a).
60. For a full argument concerning this (as well an analysis of small privatization in the Czech Republic and Hungary), see Earle, Frydman, Rapaczynski, and Turkewitz (1994).

negligible number of small businesses, and by 1994 had a ratio of approximately one registered economic entity for every 10 citizens.[61]

It is more difficult to use the figures for the whole private sector to estimate the new businesses' contribution to GDP, both because of the inclusion of large (partially or totally) privatized firms and because a significant portion of new private businesses operate on the black and gray markets. (A recent report estimated that the value of unregistered Czech trade in 1994 was between 100 and 140 billion CzK, i.e., approximately 10–15 percent of GDP,[62] and knowledgeable analysts estimate the value of transactions on the Hungarian black market at 25–30 percent of GDP.)

As might be expected, new entrants, especially the newly registered entrepreneurs, have been disproportionately active in the less capital-intensive sectors, such as retail trade, services, and construction, leading to a rapid domination of these areas by private businesses. This shift has been particularly dramatic in the previously thoroughly nationalized Czech Republic, where 75 percent of retail trade revenues in 1993 flowed to private establishments, whereas just two years earlier the same figure was a mere 11.4 percent.[63] Moreover, by all indications, the new private sector is significantly more efficient than the old firms, state or privatized. (See table 3.15.)

Both countries have pursued various policies designed to assist private businesses, especially through the creation of special loan facilities to ensure a flow of affordable credit. It is doubtful, however, that these programs have had a significant effect on the growth of the private sector. Of more importance probably was a system of employment subsidies provided by the Czech government as part of its policy of encouraging the absorption of workers laid off from the state sector. By the end of 1992, the Socially Purposeful Jobs (SPJ) program was credited with assisting the creation of almost 105,000 new jobs, over 80 percent of which were in the private sector.[64]

---

61. Some of the numbers in table 3.13 must be treated with caution. Significant downward adjustment is necessary, for example, to correct for businesses that are registered but essentially inactive: one-third of Czech private entrepreneurships were found to be inactive in 1994. Estimates of the proportion of entrepreneurs engaged *full time* in running their businesses range from 10 to 30 percent (Frydman, Rapaczynski, Earle, et al. 1993, 66). On the other hand, the registered entities do not include those operating in the sizable gray and black economies in each country.

62. Kadera, *Hospodarske trendy* Komercni banky no. 4/95.

63. Creditanstalt Securities (1994).

64. OECD (1994a).

Table 3.13
Number of registered business organizations in the Czech Republic and
Hungary by selected legal form

Period	Total business organizations[a]	Private entrepreneurs, non-agricultural[b]	Shared or limited liability firms[c]	Joint-stock companies (at end of period)
Czech Republic				
1989	18,837	—	•	43
1990	178,993	124,455	3,034	658
1991	955,647	891,872	23,112	2,541
1992	1,118,637	982,075	39,495	4,076
1993	1,250,216	995,054[e]	60,376	4,813
1994[d]	1,064,850	804,784	82,279	5,763
Hungary				
1989	391,099	320,619	5,086	307
1990	495,250	393,450	25,407	646
1991	652,230	507,655	65,906	1,027
1992	785,925	602,423	101,537	1,712
1993	925,863	677,264	145,210	2,375
1994	1,001,973	755,543	183,246	2,896

Sources: Czech Statistical Office (1993, 1994); Central Statistical Office of Hungary,
National Bank of Hungary (1994).
Note: Czech Statistical Office symbols: (•) indicates data not available; (—)
indicates phenomenon did not occur.
a. This figure includes, in addition to data shown in table, cooperatives,
independent farmers, budgetary, and contribution-based organizations.
b. In the Czech Republic, "private entrepreneurs, non-agricultural," refers to
the entrepreneurs registered under Law on Private Business passed in April
1990 (No. 105/1990). Prior to 1990, about 1 percent of the employed population
(70,000 people) were private entrepreneurs, usually small craftsmen.
c. "Shared or limited liability firms" include general and limited partnerships,
limited liability companies, and joint-stock companies.
d. Third quarter 1994.
e. Third quarter 1993.

Table 3.14
GDP contribution of private and state sectors (percent at end of year)

	1989	1990	1991	1992	1993	1994
Czech Republic						
State sector	89	88	83	72	52	30
Private sector	11	12	17	28	48	70
Hungary[a]						
State sector	87	80	75	67	55–60	50
Private sector	13	20	25	33	40–45	50

Sources: Czech Statistical Office (1994); National Bank of Hungary *Annual Report* (1994).
a. The Hungarian data is based on estimates by the National Bank of Hungary (ownership statistics are not officially collected).

Table 3.15
Comparison of new start-up firms with incumbent firms, 1991–1993

	Change during 1991–1993 (in percent)	
	New start-up firms	Incumbent firms
Sales	+22	−1
Profits	+14	−64
Average number of employees	+23	−32
Inventories	−32	−24
Average salary	+34	31

Source: Zemplinerova et al. (1994).

Small businesses are notoriously difficult for governments to aid and, for the most part, government policy toward them should be deemed a success if it does not impede their development through ruinous taxation or excessive regulation. Although both Hungary and the Czech Republic enacted a set of tax breaks for new businesses[65] and gave small

---

65. In Hungary, from 1991 to 1993 a total tax holiday was granted to private enterprises founded by domestic parties in the first year of their operation, and only 50 percent of their profits were subjected to taxation in the following two years. The Czech Republic granted similar tax preferences for private firms formed between 1990 and 1992.

businesses preferential wage and social security tax treatment,[66] of most importance was probably the simple inability of the governments to collect taxes from the new private sector. Many small businesses used the mismatch between their operations and an antiquated tax system designed for large enterprises to hide a large portion of their revenues, and many others, operating within the unofficial economy, have simply avoided paying taxes altogether. Next to the inherent flexibility of small businesses and a huge under-supply of services at the beginning of the transition period, this "comparative advantage" of the small businesses may have been among the main reasons why they took such a decisive advantage of the opening provided by the various marketization policies.

3.4 The Reform of Firm Governance Arrangements

We have stressed already (in section 3.2) what may be the most distinctive characteristic of the starting point of the Eastern European transition: the fact of the material embodiment of the huge misallocations of the communist period in the capital stock of the post-communist economies, and in the overexpanded industrial state sector in particular. This hypertrophy of the dysfunctional state sector makes the future economic development of Eastern Europe more "path dependent" than that of the less industrialized socialist countries of East Asia that are now embarking on a new course of market reforms. The reason for this is that the state sector in Eastern Europe is too big to be "left alone" while a new, dynamic private sector takes off. Unless dealt with in a comprehensive manner, the state sector is likely to become a political and economic time bomb that will undermine the whole reform process. In particular, as long as the incentives of the main actors in the state sector (managers, workers, and bureaucrats) are not modified through a thorough-going reform of the governance institutions, the state firms, even if they are forced to change somewhat their *modus operandi*, will not respond properly to market signals and undergo sufficient restructuring to make them viable in a genuine market environment. This very strong agency problem, combined with the political power which the state sector possesses to extract rents from the state, means that without a strategy of comprehensive governance reform (of which privatization is a necessary component), the state sector will constitute a permanent drain on the resources of the state, which ultimately may make the marketization reforms not sustainable.

---

66. In Hungary, the wage tax levied on sole proprietors ranged from 5 to 10 percent, compared with an average wage tax of about 35 percent. Wage tax preferences of similar magnitude existed in the Czech Republic.

This point is not universally understood, since some distinguished analysts have argued that privatization was a misguided policy detracting attention from the development of the new private sector.[67] In essence, the "evolutionists" believe that the post-communist state sector is so deeply dysfunctional that any attempt at improving it is likely to be more costly than building from scratch. Although some fixed capital might perhaps be used by private entrepreneurs, its privatization should be attempted only if it can be extracted from the organizational framework of the state enterprises within which it is embedded. Insofar as most of the state sector is concerned, it should simply be allowed to die its natural death, and leave room for new and better organizations of the capitalist economy. The only reason for not closing down the state sector right away is that a move of this kind would lead to too many social dislocations. With time, when new businesses are able to absorb the labor force now employed by the state, the state sector will simply shrink and wither away.

The problem with this view is not in its assumptions. Although the quality of the capital stock of the various post-communist economies differs considerably from country to country—and both Hungary and the Czech Republic are at the most viable end of the spectrum—a successful transition is only possible if many of the old white elephants are simply closed down, rather than restructured and refitted for a new existence. Also, the evolutionists are probably right that even if some of the state sector firms can be restructured to make them viable, the cost of this may often exceed what it would take to build *ab ovo*, either because the restructuring itself is very costly or because the firm, even after restructuring, will be less dynamic than a greenfield project would be. But this is precisely the problem of path dependence: the embodiment of the past in the durable assets of the present raises the transaction costs of transition and may perhaps force a solution that would not be optimal if one were to start from scratch.

The problem with evolutionism is in its conclusion that an ownership reform of the state sector should not be attempted, or at most relegated to a secondary objective. The evolutionists recognize that an abrupt liquidation of most of the state sector is politically impossible; it may also be economically wasteful, since the extent of dislocation is likely to be greater than necessary. The conclusion, however, seems to be that the state sector should be kept in some sort of transitional limbo, which may last for many years, during which state control may in fact have to be increased, so as to ensure that the old enterprises do not continue to waste an inordinate share of scarce resources.

---

67. The first to take this position was Kornai (1990b), whose position was developed in the context of a discussion about the future of Hungary.

The idea that government policy might lead to a slow strangulation of the state sector is entirely unrealistic and flies in the face of everything we know about the behavior of states around the world. Governments do not kill state industries when they are inefficient. They subsidize them, "modernize" them, "preserve jobs" in them, protect them from "unfair competition," assure their "fair profits"—in a word, nurse them rather than kill them. The likely result of the evolutionist policy, therefore, is a prolonged period of *increasing* subsidization of the state sector. The resulting drain on the budget will have to be covered either through increased taxation of the new private sector, or through deficit financing, either of which will choke off the development of the private sector and undermine the whole reform process.[68]

There is therefore no alternative to a serious reform of the state sector, although the exact shape which such reforms might take cannot be prescribed independently of the special situation in each country. The observation that perhaps the greatest threat from the continued presence of the state sector is its political hold over the state, which can neither close it down nor resist its demands for subsidization, also points to the primary function of the reform: to decrease the *political* power of the state sector. Whatever else privatization is supposed to accomplish, it will fail unless it succeeds in this objective.

The state's ability to achieve this objective, as well as its choice of an appropriate enterprise reform strategy, depends to a large extent on the quality of the capital stock inherited from the communist regime. We have indicated already that this quality differs from country to country. Where the possibility of restructuring state sector firms into viable (even if not exactly the most dynamic) entities is unlikely to succeed with respect to a very substantial portion of the state sector, the real objective of structural reform, including privatization, is to attempt a change in the configuration of political power of the various interest groups such that the process of retiring the state sector does not destroy the remaining reforms. A mere change in ownership is unlikely to constitute a sufficient barrier between the state and the enterprises so as to make the state's commitment to hard budget constraints credible; only a form of ownership change that increases the collective action costs of the relevant pressure groups can have some effect.[69] But when a significant portion of the state sector is potentially viable, then a privatization

---

68. It is also unlikely that a healthy private sector can develop alongside a large state sector. For an argument that the state sector has a corrupting influence on the incentives and objectives of private entrepreneurs, see chapter VI in Frydman and Rapaczynski (1994), and Pistor and Turkewitz (1996).

69. For a further discussion of this issue, see chapter VI in Frydman and Rapaczynski (1994).

policy, by changing the governance system of firms and refashioning the incentives of the parties in control of corporate decision making, can redirect the behavior of that same portion of the former state sector away from dependence on state handouts and toward market-oriented objectives. Even if the viability of some of the privatized firms is relatively short-lived, so that the restructured portion of the state sector will not survive in the long run, the resulting relaxation of political pressures may create a window of opportunity for the development of the new private sector which will sustain the reform policies in the future.

The political significance of privatization has not escaped the attention of the Czech reformers; there is evidence that they considered it to be the single most important aspect of their strategy with respect to the state sector. The whole thrust of the Czech policy was to privatize as quickly as possible, without any concern for the financial advantages of the state, and with the primary objective of creating a large class of people and interests with significant stakes in the economic viability of the former state sector. The relatively well-configured capital stock of the Czech economy, the strength of the Czech state, and the low level of organization of special interests tied to the state sector combined together to make this strategy uniquely realistic.

The capital stock of Hungary was, as we have seen, also among the best in the communist world, although the number of nonviable enterprises with potentially great political power (due to their size and location) may have been greater than in the Czech Republic. The level of special-interest organization and the lack of clarity about the role and objectives of privatization among the Hungarian leaders was also much greater than in the Czech Republic, and this may have made the Hungarian policy much less effective.

This is not to say that the privatization process in Hungary was not driven by political considerations. But whereas the Czech leadership was essentially proactive—attempting to *create* a constituency for its policies—the Hungarian government was much more reactive: its privatization policies were driven by the existing set of attitudes among the electorate and the necessity of accommodating the state enterprise managers, party cadres, and political supporters. At the same time, the apparent success of the gradualist transition strategy, especially as measured by the ability of Hungary to attract foreign investment in the first years after the collapse of the old regime,[70] convinced the Hungarian leadership that speed was not among the most important factors

---

70. The net inflow of foreign direct investment into Hungary during 1989–93 was US$6,009 million. The Czech Republic received $2,414 million over the same time period, and Poland received a roughly similar amount. See Kogut (1996).

in the privatization efforts.[71] Instead, the Hungarian leadership stressed the need for privatization based on "real owners" rather than artificial recipients of state assets, and the need to use privatization as a means of raising revenues for the state budget, saddled as it was with huge foreign debt obligations. As a result, the role of ownership change in the restructuring process was viewed by the policy makers as merely one among many aspects of a broader transformation process in which state officials would be responsible for supervising pre-privatization reorganization as well as assuring a proper post-privatization ownership structure.

These very diverse backgrounds and assumptions concerning the purposes of privatization account in large part for the nearly diametrically different policies adopted in Hungary and the Czech Republic. The Czech privatization was largely based on a free distribution of assets to the population at large, with a minimum degree of state engineering and maximum reliance on non-state parties and the market to determine the post-privatization structure of ownership and operations. The Hungarians, by contrast, have relied nearly exclusively on sales of enterprises, with a lengthy process of valuation and preparation, as well as negotiations among a number of parties interested in shaping the post-privatization reality. Although the future of the privatized firms in the Czech Republic is still by far not assured, the flow of assets from the state to the private sector has been extremely rapid, and a potentially critical mass of private firms was created by the program. The Hungarian sales programs, on the other hand, have been bogged down in delays and bureaucratic wrangling, with the state sector remaining very large, increasingly dependent on the state, and increasingly less likely to be ultimately privatized. Finally, as we have already explained (in section 3.3, under "Equity Markets"), the Czech program has led to more robust secondary capital markets, including growing foreign portfolio investment, so in the long run the original giveaway may have contributed more to bringing in foreign capital than the painstakingly designed Hungarian sales programs.

Privatization in the Czech Republic

Although the Czech Republic is now identified as the most resolute bastion of free market ideas in Eastern Europe, the commitment to the free market position was not a foregone conclusion at the time of the Velvet Revolution of 1989. The government which took over upon the demise of the last communist regime had strong social democratic

---

71. The influence of the evolutionist point of view, represented by widely respected Janos Kornai, might have played some role in this as well.

leanings and was inclined to revive many of the socialist reforms popular in 1968. These reformist sensibilities were apparent in the passage of a new law on state enterprises,[72] which placed emphasis not on privatization but on improving the performance of the state sector. Only in the long run would state enterprises be privatized through a sales method. The long transition period was explicitly expressed in the opening sentence of the official commentary that "the new law is to ensure the prerequisites for the optimal operation of enterprises during the next few years."

But the ascendancy of the reformist socialist line (and the enterprise managers who backed it) was short-lived. The June 1990 election victory of Civic Forum signaled popular support for a more market-oriented reform program and broke the stalemate that had developed concerning the appropriate economic policy for the transition period.

The new government moved immediately toward a commitment to privatizing the greatest number of assets at the fastest possible pace. Privatization, as we have noted, was primarily a political objective; powered ahead by dynamic leaders, the Czech efforts have been tremendously successful in eliminating direct state ownership in large portions of the economy. At the same time, the commitment to privatization has been pursued with sufficient pragmatism and a readiness to adapt and modify the initial strategic approach to changing conditions.

Although free distribution of state assets constituted the core of the program and received most international attention, a significant part of the program was a sale of stores and other small businesses inaugurated in 1991 and completed soon afterwards. In other ways, however, Czech small privatization was as remarkable as its other privatization programs, since it relied almost exclusively on public auctions and gave no preferences to the employees or managers of the privatized businesses. Again, the unique strength of the Czech state may have made it possible for the reformers to proceed in an extremely centralized fashion and hold the line against concessions to insiders. The program wound down by the beginning of 1993 after having sold off almost 22,000 units and generating CzK 30 billion (US$1 billion) in proceeds.[73] The program created a large class of new small businessmen, firmly committed to a new regime.

Another large portion of the Czech privatization strategy was an extensive program of restitution. It began in 1990 with measures to return physical assets confiscated from religious orders and private persons by the communist regime and proceeded to restitute real estate, businesses, and land to former owners, as well as to compensate victims

---

72. Law no. 111/1990.
73. For a detailed treatment of the Czech small privatization program, see Earle, Frydman, Rapaczynski, and Turkewitz (1994).

of the communist repression.[74] To date, an estimated CzK 150–200 billion (US$5–7 billion) worth of property has been returned to former owners. Also in 1991, the central government began to transfer housing and municipal service industries, such as sewage and water treatment facilities, back to the municipalities. This effort resulted in the shift of assets worth some CzK 350 billion (US$12 billion).

The preceding programs all represent notable achievements in their own right but they left basically untouched the large state enterprises that made up the core of the Czech economy. The first tentative step to develop a privatization strategy for these industrial enterprises occurred in 1991 with the passage of the Large Scale Privatization Law.[75] Extraordinary skills of divination would have been required to foretell the course that large-scale privatization would take in Czechoslovakia from the vague provisions of the law, which was a compromise document permitting the use of a wide range of mechanisms, including direct sales and tenders, as well as new and untested techniques of free distribution. The fact that Czech privatization soon came to be dominated by the giveaway component was, therefore, not a feature mandated by legislation, but rather the result of discretion given to a dynamic group of reformers centered around the Federal Ministry of Finance and the person of Vaclav Klaus.

Although the reformers around Klaus initially argued that free distribution should be the exclusive privatization mechanism, the need to gain support of parties that could threaten the success of the program, especially managers, led to the adoption of a set of rules that gave a degree of continued involvement to government ministries and enterprise insiders. Quite interestingly, the process was defined loosely enough to encourage most of these insiders to believe that they could turn it to their advantage. But the insistence on the great speed with which the program was to be executed ensured that the various interest groups had little time to organize and change course once the true outcome of the process was becoming clear.

The basic structure of the program was relatively simple. A list of enterprises to be privatized was compiled in July 1991, including roughly 70 percent of all firms in Czechoslovakia, with the total value estimated at CzK 1,200 billion (US$40 billion). The firms were then divided into two groups to be privatized in two successive "waves." [76]

---

74. For a discussion of the major restitution laws, see Frydman, Rapaczynski, Earle, et al. (1993).
75. The Act on the Conditions and Terms Governing the Transfer of State Property to Other Persons, Act No. 92/1992.
76. Since the second wave is still in progress, our analyses are based primarily on the results of the first wave.

At the same time, every citizen of the country was entitled to purchase for a nominal sum of CzK 1,000 a book of vouchers for which a portion of the shares of the privatized enterprises would be exchanged at special, centralized auctions.[77] The vouchers had no denomination[78] and were nontransferable, except to special privatization funds which could exchange them for their own shares.

The managers of the enterprises to be included in the first wave were required to submit plans by October 31, 1991 for the privatization of their firms.[79] Although not required to include any particular privatization mechanism in their proposals, managers soon learned that proposals calling for firms to be sold directly to themselves and their employees would be rejected by the authorities which had to approve them. Instead, they were encouraged to submit plans that called for most, if not all, of the equity of their firms to be privatized through voucher auctions. The managers hoped that the free distribution scheme would result in a dispersed ownership structure that would leave them firmly in control.

An ingenious, and uniquely Czechoslovak, feature of the plan, which significantly limited the managers' ability to sabotage the program, was the fact that, in addition to the required manager plan, any individual could submit, until the middle of January 1992, an alternative project for the privatization of all or part of any enterprise in the program. After the "founding organs" of the enterprises (i.e., the branch ministries), which were in this way co-opted to participate in the program, reviewed all the plans and passed on their recommendations, the Minister of Privatization, in close consultation with the Minister of Finance, was in charge of approving a privatization plan for each enterprise.

The efforts to encourage the greatest possible use of free distribution proved to be quite successful. Approved privatization plans called for over 60 percent of the total value of the firms to be privatized in the first wave to be distributed via the voucher program, with 417 firms to be privatized exclusively through vouchers.[80] Quite remarkably, the

---

77. The technical challenge of organizing both the distribution of vouchers and the nation-wide multiple-round auctions were enormous. For a description of the mechanics, see Frydman, Rapaczynski, Earle, et al. (1993).

78. Strangely enough, the Czech plan was the only one which resisted the temptation to put a monetary denomination on the vouchers, even though again and again the vouchers ended up trading at huge discounts.

79. Managers of enterprises scheduled for the second wave were required to submit similar proposals by August 16, 1992.

80. Slightly smaller numbers were actually privatized (see table 3.16). The other components included proposed sales to foreign or domestic investors, as well as some sales to enterprise insiders. In certain cases (above all, those of the banks), the state retained a large portion of the equity. Three percent of

competing projects submitted by non-insiders were also accepted in high numbers: in cases in which the plans directly competed against each other (and these cases were likely to involve the most desirable assets), the outsider projects were in fact chosen more often than the managerial plans.[81]

While the promise of a vast number of tiny shareholders had been important in winning managerial acceptance of the mass privatization program, it is likely that an actual fragmentation of ownership on the firm level would have had disastrous consequences, leaving managers basically unmonitored and free to pursue their interests, free of both state or private control. The innovative solution to the problem of dispersed ownership was the creation of privatization investment funds, i.e., financial intermediaries which concentrated the holdings of the population and managed them on its behalf. Although there was some doubt whether this strategy would be effective, relying as it did on uncoordinated participation of the voucher holders, in the end, partly as a result of advertisements promising very high rates of return, the investment funds flooded into the market and proved to be enormously successful both in attracting interest in the voucher program and in convincing individuals to utilize their services. Three-quarters of the adult population elected to participate in the first wave, and investment funds managed to obtain 71.5 percent of all the voucher points available in the first round.[82] The overall results of the first wave privatization and the role of voucher auctions are shown in tables 3.16 and 3.17.

Most of the 423 investment funds which competed for the vouchers managed to attract only a small number of points (in which the vouchers were denominated). But a few funds amassed huge pools of vouchers; the top seven funds came to control 44.5 percent of all voucher points, and the 13 largest funds collected 55 percent of all points (see table 3.18). The level of ownership concentration achieved by the top few investment funds radically changed the expected outcome of the whole voucher program, with concerns about potential over-concentration replacing the previous worries about excessive dispersal of ownership.

---

the shares of each firm was also retained for purposes of compensation for persons subject to expropriation or persecution. In the event, 90 percent of assets that were actually privatized were sold through vouchers (which probably means that many proposed cash sales were delayed or did not take place).

81. See Kotrba (1994). This feature of the program has not been noted by most commentators, who frequently have pointed to the overall success rate of the managerial plans (approx. 60 percent, as opposed to 17.3 percent for the competing projects) as a proof that the managers dominated the decisions concerning future ownership structure.

82. Levels of participation in the second wave were roughly similar. However, the percentage of voucher points contributed to investment funds slipped to 64 percent.

Table 3.16
Extent of privatization of first wave firms, August 1994

Percentage of shares privatized	Number of firms
0–20	268
20.1–50	75
50.1–70	130
70.1–90	334
90.1–100	463

Source: Fund of National Property (FNP) Database, August 1994.

Table 3.17
Importance of the voucher mechanism in the privatization of first wave firms, August 1994

Percentage of shares privatized using voucher auctions	Number of firms
0–20	339
20.1–50	93
50.1–70	117
70.1–90	383
90.1–100	352

Source: FNP Database, August 1994.

These concerns are quite understandable, especially when viewed in light of the already noted connection between the privatization funds and the post-communist banking system, as well as the levels of cross-ownership among the banks (see "Banking Reform" in section 3.3). Indeed, five of the seven largest funds are controlled by domestic financial institutions, which were only partially privatized in the same wave. Even without this complication, the prospect of a bank-controlled economy might raise serious concerns, despite the success of the German model, since the inherently conservative nature of bank ownership may not be suitable for an economy in need of radical restructuring. The barely commenced restructuring process within the banking system, and the effective insulation of the banks from private control which their cross-ownership may provide, raises a concern that the party put in charge of monitoring the restructuring of the Czech economy may not be up to the job.

Table 3.18
Holdings of seven largest investment funds in the first wave of voucher privatization

Investment group	Number of points (in millions)	Number of shares obtained
Ceska Sporitelna	950,432,200	21,376,611
Investnicni Banka group	724,123,600	13,594,068
Harvard group	638,548,000	15,225,108
Vseobecna Uverova	500,587,700	11,985,444
Komercni Banka	465,530,300	11,931,808
Ceska Pojistovna	334,040,900	7,623,311
Slovenska Investicie	187,917,000	4,432,770
Total for top seven IPFs	3,801,179,700	86,169,120
Total in first wave	8,541,000,000	277,800,000

Sources: Privatization Ministry and Mladek (1994).

Table 3.19
Ownership of financial institutions associated with major investment fund groups

Financial institution	Total property (in billion CzK)	Voucher share	Foreign investment	Fund of National Property (state)	Other
Ceska Sporitelna	5.6	37%	0%	40%	23%
Investnicni Banka group	1.0	52%	0%	45%	3%
Vseobecna Uverova	2.04	52%	0%	45%	3%
Komercni Banka	4.56	53%	0%	44%	3%
Ceska Pojistovna	0.38	65%	0%	0%	35%[a]

Source: Mladek (1994).
a. Although the FNP does not own equity in Ceska Pojistovna, the 35 percent listed as "other" is held by a group of state institutions.

An additional level of concern comes from the fact that the only significant outside owner of Czech banks is the state, which retained a large stake in each institution (see table 3.19). The very high levels of state control cast some cloud over the whole ownership pyramid created by the privatization process, with non-financial companies at the bottom, the bank-controlled funds in the middle, and the state at the top, retaining a high degree of control of the banks themselves. Which parties will thus ultimately emerge as de facto controlling the Czech economy, and how able they will be to exercise the necessary monitoring and supervision of the restructuring process, is still somewhat of an open question. The economic vitality and public support generated by the privatization program warrant some confidence in the future, although the prospect of a government less committed to market reforms than the present one in control of the Czech state makes one equally apprehensive.

Privatization in Hungary

We have seen that Hungary entered the post-communist reform period with much less of a clean slate than the Czech Republic. In particular, the Hungarian privatization process has been unfolding against the background of pre-1990 ownership transformations, including the massive redrawing of boundaries of state firms and the managerial "spontaneous privatization" of a significant portion of state assets. The clouding of titles resulting from this process, through which the managers tried to insulate themselves from any external control, has never been reversed, and the state has never been able to resolve the fundamental conflict between the interest of the managerial class and the state's own claim to ownership and control. The state's inability to come up with an effective privatization strategy is a consequence of this history.

It is possible, of course, to overstate the independence of enterprise managers or the degree to which state actors were peripheral to the operation of Hungarian firms in the last years of communism. Branch ministries continued to supervise directly at least one-third of all enterprises, and the state's indirect presence was felt in the self-managed firms as well. Rather than freeing enterprise managers from dealing with the state, the communist reforms gave them a new bargaining power vis-à-vis state officials. As a result, each side had to accommodate the other, and informal relations between them, as well as among the managers themselves, acquired a very special significance, as both sides attempted to shore up their positions through personal bonds and coalitions networks that outlasted the old regime.

The real and perceived abuses of spontaneous privatization produced a sharp reaction among the electorate, which in 1990 brought to power

the first freely elected government, led by Jozsef Antall. The new authorities responded to the popular clamor against the unrestrained activities
of enterprise managers by promising to subject the process of transformation to the control of the newly created State Property Agency
(SPA). The SPA became the official holder of most state assets and took
over the supervision of 1,848 out of the approximately 2,000 state enterprises in existence. Far from being charged with a speedy privatization
of the Hungarian state sector, the SPA's mandate was primarily to stop
the uncontrolled privatization process and restore state control.

Prevention of further abuses did not, however, amount to a coherent
strategy for the privatization of the remaining state property. For the
most part, the Antall government proved to be incapable of formulating
such a strategy or managing the actual task of transferring the state
holdings into private hands. Throughout the four years of its existence,
the government's policy shifted from one ill-conceived program to
another, without producing significant results. Although the SPA has
been able to curtail the most blatant abuses of the pre-1990 period, its
lack of direction and the inability to overcome the resistance of
managerial interests led to a paralysis of Hungarian privatization, with
managers and the state each capable of blocking further progress, but
incapable to move it forward. The lack of a sense of urgency of the privatization effort only confounded the picture. The Hungarian officials
contemptuously dismissed free distribution schemes as dangerous
experiments, incapable of producing "real owners." Viewing their role
as Eastern European counterparts of Western investment bankers, the
officials insisted on careful preparation of each privatization transaction
and hoped to find foreign "core investors" for each enterprise.

The early SPA privatization effort, the First Privatization Program,
reflected fully the illusions of the new bureaucracy.[83] It was a completely
centralized program in which 20 enterprises were selected on the basis
of their presumed attractiveness for foreign investors. SPA officials
commissioned a series of expensive studies, planned every detail of
post-privatization ownership structure, and asked prospective investors
to commit to specific business strategies and employment levels.
Coupled with managerial resistance and unrealistic expectations concerning sale proceeds, the program dragged on as the chosen firms
languished in limbo and their financial position deteriorated in the face
of changing business conditions. In the end, not one of the firms was
sold as expected, and the First Privatization Program came to be
acknowledged as a wholesale failure.

---

83. For an overview of the First Privatization Program, see Frydman, Rapaczynski,
Earle, et al. (1993).

Somewhat more successful was the other early SPA program, known as Preprivatization, which was intended to sell off retail trade businesses and service outlets.[84] The program ended up selling 7,016 shops and service outlets, primarily through public auctions held from 1991 to 1994. But the SPA was generally unsuccessful in meeting either its budgetary goals or in prying away the most valuable stores from the entrenched managers of large state retail empires. As a result, the percentage of retail trade units privatized in Hungary was a fraction of that tranferred in either Poland or the Czech Republic.

In hindsight, the failures of the early SPA programs, especially with respect to the privatization of larger firms, were predictable. In attempting to arrange elaborately structured tenders of prime state assets, the SPA technocrats created a situation which allowed for only two, equally unpalatable, outcomes: either the assets would be purchased by foreigners (the only parties with sufficient resources to make large bids) and the government would be criticized for selling off the nation's crown jewels, or the sales would fail and the government would be criticized for being incompetent. As fate would have it, the Agency managed to fall into both traps: it was able, between 1990 and 1992, to privatize just enough property to be castigated for selling off to foreigners, but not enough to contribute much to reducing the state deficit or to avoid accusations of incompetence.

Politically damaged by its unpopular privatization strategies, the Forum government moved, in the later years, to increase its direct control over the process. Thus, while the SPA was initially set up to be an independent agency, subject to annual guidelines passed by Parliament and controlled by a Board of Directors made up of 11 members, by 1993 a Minister without Portfolio (usually referred to as the Minister of Privatization) was put in control of the Agency and has operated with few policy restrictions (since the practice of passing the annual guidelines was allowed to lapse).

A still greater degree of governmental control, as well as an explicit retreat from even the theoretical commitment to privatization, came in 1992, with the formation of the State Holding Company (known as "Av Rt"). Firms directly owned by the state were from then on divided into two groups: those to be privatized in the near future, and those which for political or economic reasons were to be retained, at least in part, by the state. The Av Rt was designated as the body responsible for the long-term holdings, and although the SPA retained a greater number of state companies, the value of the 169 firms shifted to the Av Rt (HUF 1,303 billion in 1994) dwarfed the value of SPA holdings (HUF 396.3 billion).

---

84. For a detailed accounts of Preprivatization, see Earle, Frydman, Rapaczynski, and Turkewitz (1994).

Table 3.20
Revenues of the State Property Agency (in HUF billion)

	1990	1991	1992	1993	September 1994
Total revenues	0.67	31.38	74.56	77.90	54.56
Cash revenues					
Hard currency sales	0.53	24.61	40.98	25.50	4.54
Forint sales	0.14	4.82	17.51	15.30	10.11
Dividend and other income	0.00	0.94	4.74	2.40	1.84
Total cash revenues	0.67	30.37	62.23	43.20	16.49
Non-cash revenues					
Credit	0.00	1.10	9.07	21.70	23.40
Compensation note sales	0.00	0.00	2.26	13.00	14.67
Total non-cash revenues	0.00	1.01	11.33	34.70	38.07

Source: State Property Agency, *Privatization Monitor*, various issues, 1992–94, Budapest.

The changes in the management structure of state assets were accompanied by a change in the government's approach to privatization as well. Becoming aware of the lack of constituency supporting the sales of state assets to foreign purchasers and of the potential of privatization with respect to buying political support of selected interest groups, the Forum government used its increased control of the privatization process to reorient the transfer and sale programs to further more political objectives. Thus, legislation passed in February 1992 mandated a transfer of HUF 300 billion worth of shares to the newly capitalized Social Security and Health Care Funds, managed by groups associated with labor unions. Another law provided for the emission of compensation notes worth over HUF 220 billion, to be used by victims of communist expropriations. The run-up to the 1994 national election witnessed the birth of yet another transfer scheme, known as Small Investor Program, designed to provide subsidized loans to purchasers of state assets. This shift toward selective giveaways or subsidized sales to domestic beneficiaries is clearly revealed in the recent data concerning property transfers by the SPA, which show the decreasing importance of sales to foreigners and the explosive growth of preferential sales programs since 1992. In fact, by 1994, the "revenues" from non-cash payments to the SPA were more than twice as large as those brought in by cash sales (see table 3.20). Although such selective giveaways may be politically expedient, they create significant resentment among the bypassed groups and are much less able to legitimize the privatization process in the eyes of the wider public.

Concurrent with the changes in the methods of payment has been a change in the structure of privatization efforts. By the middle of 1991, the Antall government had both tired of fighting the enterprise managers and succeeded in replacing a fair number of communist-era managers with Forum loyalists. Its opposition to insider privatization thus slackened, as did its commitment to centralized privatization programs. The so-called Self-Privatization program, inaugurated in the middle of 1991, was an outcome of this change of attitude. The program aimed at decentralizing the sale of a large number of small and medium-sized firms, giving the managers and private consultants a measure of freedom in designing and implementing privatization sales.[85] Since the SPA was also more willing to sell small firms to managers and other domestic parties, the Self-Privatization program, despite remaining bureaucratic obstacles, produced a more significant rate of success than any previous attempts. Under this program 392 firms have been sold, wholly or in part, as of April 1994, accounting for almost one-half of the 835 sales contracts signed by the SPA since its inception.

A measure of decentralization has also been introduced into the privatization of larger firms. Although no specific programs exist to structure these proceedings, the SPA has become more open to increased managerial involvement. At the same time, the growing importance of a number of subsidized transfer mechanisms, such as Employee Stock Option Plans[86] and leasing leasing contracts, which allowed the insiders to purchase their firms on preferential terms, gave the insiders the means to participate in the more expensive transactions. (The growing importance of the subsidized transfer methods is illustrated in table 3.21.) Such sales are still very tightly controlled by the SPA, however, and their numbers are relatively small.

---

85. For an analysis of the Self-Privatization program as it related to the trade and service sector, see Earle, Frydman, Rapaczynski, and Turkewitz (1994).

86. Employee Stock Ownership Plans (ESOPs), in which privatization occurs through the purchase of an enterprise by an employee organization, was accepted as a method of privatization by the 1992 Law on Employee Stock Ownership Program. ESOPs, which usually are made up of managers and employees, have been formally granted preferential treatment in tender offers and access to loans.

Table 3.21
State-supported methods for domestic sales

	1991	1992	1993	1994 Sept.	Total
Employee stock ownership plans[a]					
Number of cases	1	8	123	51	184
Face value (HUF bln)	0.03	1.80	22.49	11.84	36.22
Leasing					
Number of cases	0	0	9	15	24
Face value (HUF bln)	0	0	2.99	3.10	6.09
E-credit[b]					
Value (HUF bln)	1.01	9.07	21.70	23.40	55.18
Compensation notes[c]					
Value (HUF bln)	0	2.2	13.00	14.67	29.87

Source: State Property Agency, *Privatization Monitor*, September 1994, Budapest.
a. For a description of employee stock ownership plans, see footnote 86.
b. E-credits are heavily subsidized government loans available to assist in the purchase of state property. Since 1993, the annual interest cost to borrowers was 7 percent, significantly below inflation.
c. For a description of compensation notes, see text below.

Table 3.22
Incidence of state ownership in Hungary, December 1992

Percentage of state ownership	Number of firms	As a percentage of large firms in Hungary
100	1,564	16.6
75–99.9	626	6.7
50–74.9	285	3.0
25–49.9	340	3.6
0.01–24.9	406	4.3
Total	3,221	34.2

Source: 1992 Hungarian Tax Database.

Despite the recent changes, the Hungarian privatization process has remained sluggish. Although the SPA boasts of greater than 50 percent reduction in the number of firms under state control, a closer examination reveals that the value of state holdings sold to date has been estimated to be as low as 11 percent of the total.[87] Interestingly, an almost equal proportion of state assets has been removed from SPA's jurisdiction through bankruptcy or liquidation, which are reported to have been increasingly due less to real insolvency than to the manipulation of the rules by the managers who bring the firm into bankruptcy in order to acquire its assets without SPA's control.

As important as the failure of the state to sell a significant proportion of its portfolio has been its inability to untangle the web of property relations dating back to the communist transformations of the 1980s. A large mass of the Hungarian economy is still linked together by cross-ownership ties that ultimately lead back to a single common owner—the state. (An examination of a non-representative group of Av Rt firms showed that an average firm held shares in ten other companies.) Property links forged by commercialized state companies have proven to be remarkably resistant to attack, and the tax data for 1992 (presented in table 3.22) show that the state is a significant indirect owner in many more firms than officially listed in the SPA's and Av Rt's portfolios. A dramatic indication of the government's failure to gain control over its property is thus its inability, to this day, to quantify with any degree of accuracy the assets of the firms it owns.

3.5   Concluding Remarks

The Czech Republic shares with Hungary a common experience of monopoly state ownership of the means of production, and a corresponding material legacy embedded in distorted patterns and distribution of industrial production. However, historical commonality should not be understood as synonymous with identity. As we have stressed, the Czech Republic and Hungary emerged from their communist periods with important differences in institutional and asset endowments. Chief among these was the extent to which the Czech state had managed throughout the communist period to retain unchallenged dominance in economic matters, including control over state property and the budget. A much greater degree of power sharing had evolved in Hungary, due in large measure to the considerable efforts of the Hungarian communist authorities to put through internal economic reforms. As a result, the Hungarian government's ability to conduct economic

---

87. See Pistor and Turkewitz (1996).

policy was effectively constrained by powerful non-state interests endowed with various formal and informal entitlements conferred in the process of reforms.

Post-communist Czech officials have made extensive use of their inherited state authority to foster market institutions, as evidenced by their forceful and centralized approach to privatization and the creation of a stock market, or their wage and labor policies. The flip side of the strength of the Czech state is that it partially reflects the weakness of other civil institutions, such as labor unions, local governments, or various private bodies. The absence of strong non-state parties has complicated the readjustment of power between state and non-state forces, and brought to prominence a novel group of financial intermediaries which, while formally private, retain significant links to state institutions. The objectives of these owners and their competence remain subjects of debate. The future development of the Czech economy thus depends in part—a greater part than one might wish—on the likelihood that the government will continue to be led by individuals with an ideological commitment to removing the state from day-to-day economic decision making.

In contrast to the high degree of consistency in the economic strategies followed by their Czech counterparts, Hungarian officials have pursued relatively diverse approaches to macroeconomic and microeconomic reforms. At the macroeconomic level, the government has been resolute in freeing prices and wages, but much less reliance has been placed on market forces at the microeconomic level. From a labor policy emphasizing state-sponsored training of employees and entrepreneurs, to a restrictive approach regarding the creation of financial markets and an extremely complex program of privatization, Hungarian authorities have elected institutional reform strategies that require continuous administrative intervention and conserve the limited power of the state apparatus. These disparate reform tactics have been shaped by the pressure on the government to generate large amounts of hard currency to service foreign debt, as well as by the political interests of various groups seeking to shape economic policy on behalf of their special constituencies. Given the high cost of these pressures, future Hungarian economic development will depend on the ability of the government to deal effectively with the stubborn remnants of goulash socialism—the enormous internal and external payment obligations, and the Gorgon's knot of confused ownership rights over industrial assets.

4 Mongolia's Transition to a Democratic Market System

Peter Boone, Baavaa Tarvaa, Adiya Tsend, Enkhbold Tsendjav, and Narantsetseg Unenburen

4.1 Introduction

Mongolia was the second-longest communist-ruled country after the Soviet Union. Being landlocked between China and Russia, and having no open border with China for much of this period, its economic and political system became inextricably linked with Russia and the countries of the Council for Mutual Economic Assistance (CMEA) for almost six decades. These links suddenly broke on January 1, 1991. Soviet credits to Mongolia, which averaged 37 percent of GDP annually, were abruptly stopped, and trade volumes with the CMEA countries fell sharply. The economic collapse that ensued was possibly the greatest of all the (peaceful) formerly socialist countries. As shown in table 4.1, the decline in domestic absorption equaled approximately 62 percent of GNP, much more than the decline experienced in Eastern European countries or during wartime destruction. Mongolia's political leaders responded to civil protests by calling elections in early 1990, and Mongolia's first elected Parliament met in October 1990.

The elections in 1990 led to the creation of a coalition government that was dominated by the Mongolian People's Revolutionary Party (MPRP) but included several highly placed members of the new opposition. During 1991 there was a clear cleavage in policy making. Some officials wanted to delay policy actions until the political outcome in Russia was obvious, and others called for immediate radical reform to a market system similar to Poland's. The outcome was a mixture of both approaches. Some prices were freed; some trade was liberalized; the banking system was deregulated; and, most surprisingly, the world's first voucher privatization program was begun.

But these initial steps in the reform process were only partial. The government maintained strong controls on external trade, foreign exchange, and many prices, and it continued to intervene directly in resource allocation. There was also considerable leeway for local governments and

Table 4.1
Comparisons of the decline in national purchasing power during economic transformation, the Great Depression, and wartime (percentage of GDP)

		Current account	Real GNP	Terms of trade	Total
Formerly socialist					
Mongolia	(1989–91)	–37.1	–18.0	–6.6	–61.7
Czechoslovakia	(1989–91)	0.0	–18.6	–5.4	–24.0
Hungary	(1989–91)	0.0	–11.2	–3.7	–14.9
Poland	(1989–91)	0.0	–19.9	–2.9	–22.8
Great Depression					
France	(1929–32)	1.1	–14.6	n.a.	–13.5
Germany	(1929–32)	1.3	–19.1	n.a.	–17.8
United Kingdom	(1929–32)	–4.3	–17.8	n.a.	–22.1
United States	(1929–33)	0.0	–32.6	n.a.	–32.6
Wartime					
Austria	(1937–46)	n.a.	–36.0	n.a.	–36.0
Italy	(1938–46)	n.a.	–49.7	n.a.	–49.7
Japan	(1938–46)	n.a.	–50.5	n.a.	–50.5
Spain: Civil War	(1935–40)	n.a.	–25.7	n.a.	–25.7
USSR	(1938–46)	n.a.	–8.3	n.a.	–8.3

Sources: For Eastern Europe, Rodrik (1992); for Mongolia, author's own calculations; all others from *Historical Statistics for Europe*, various editions.
Notes: 1. The change in external financing was calculated as the nominal decline in the current account balance during the period divided by the initial level of nominal GDP (measured in dollars) for the country at the start of the period. These balances include any foreign assistance granted to offset the initial external shock.
2. The periods are chosen to capture the decline from peak to trough for the relevant episode.

police to restrict trade and control prices in many regions. The size of the initial collapse, the diffuse nature of decision making, and the partial policy measures contributed to the loss of monetary control in 1991 and 1992.

The Mongolian example of reform is interesting because in many ways it has been highly successful, despite the fact that neither the government nor the population was prepared for such abrupt change. It also provides lessons and warnings as one of the most rapidly reforming countries among the so-called second wave reformers. The surprising outcome is that Mongolian policy reforms have brought it further towards a democratic market system than any country in the Commonwealth of Independent States (CIS), and possibly on par with the fastest reformers of Eastern Europe. There are several reasons for this progress.

First, the early alliance with the former USSR was not founded in a people's revolution in favor of a socialist system; rather, it reflected a need to carve out and protect Mongolia's independence from China. This made it much easier for the country, and particularly for the younger generation (over half the population is under 18 years of age), to accept and support radical change. There have been few protests against reform measures, and there is a broad social consensus today that Mongolia should maintain a liberal democratic market system.

Second, the early parliamentary elections proved instrumental in ensuring macroeconomic reforms. In a wave of euphoria after the elections, the new Parliament passed a long list of laws guaranteeing property rights, allowing free trade, and generally providing the legal basis for reforms and sending a clear signal that market reforms had begun. The number of private businesses skyrocketed in 1991 and 1992; many of these were small traders and commercial businesses. These businesses played the important role of arbitrating prices and providing an outlet other than the state system for sales of agricultural and manufactured products. As the number of traders grew, the state's ability to control prices and enforce state orders declined accordingly. To some extent, the gradual pattern of reform reflects a de facto loss of the officials' ability to enforce regulations. Without strict control on trading and private activities in place, the Mongolian example suggests that large-scale reform becomes inevitable.

Mongolia was the first country to introduce a voucher privatization program, and now has the greatest share ownership per capita of any country in the world. All retail trade, small enterprises, virtually all livestock, and more than 50 percent of large enterprises have been sold via auctions or insider buyouts for vouchers. Large enterprises were auctioned in a central stock exchange through brokers linked by computer to district offices. There were several technical flaws in this program, the most serious of which was that the vouchers were non-tradeable. This resulted in a diffused ownership pattern. However, the process was an important step in establishing enterprise autonomy and the first step to better corporate governance. The privatization program has also proven to be politically popular.

Problems in the financial sector and macroeconomic stability are closely linked. One of the first liberalization steps was to allow new private commercial banks to form before any regulations, such as reserve requirements, or bank supervision were in place. Of course, this was a recipe for inflation, and the money supply rose sharply as these banks grew in 1990 and 1991. A reorganization of the central bank in mid-1991 brought this process under control, but new problems are now being encountered.

One of the most sensitive political issues today is how to handle Mongolia's external debt with Russia. The outstanding debt amounts to 10 billion rubles, or at the old official exchange rate 16 billion dollars, which is 32 times the Mongolian GDP. With such large numbers, any negotiations over debt reduction become purely political. Mongolia is in a weak bargaining position because its whole economic infrastructure is highly dependent on Russia. This is one area where international coordination, possibly through the IMF or Paris Club, could prove extremely helpful for Mongolia and other countries in a similar situation.

This chapter is organized as follows. Section 4.2 begins with a brief historical background to political change and a discussion of recent government policy. Section 4.3 examines financial sector reforms and monetary policy. Section 4.4 discusses enterprise privatization, and section 4.5 outlines price liberalization. Agricultural reform and foreign trade policy are covered in sections 4.6 and 4.7. Section 4.8 summarizes our conclusions.

4.2   Government Policy and Democracy during Transition

There is a Mongolian saying that "Mongolia exists because Russia and China exist." Landlocked between two great neighbors, and apart from her own brief supremacy under Ghenghis Khan, Mongolia's independence has always been limited by the need to balance external relations with her neighbors. After three centuries of rule by Manchuria, Mongolia gained independence in 1921 under the leadership of Sukhbaatar. The revolutionary leaders immediately turned to Russia for support, and in 1924 they created the Mongolian People's Revolutionary Party. During the next six decades both economic development and politics mirrored a Soviet program.

There is no question that this brought development. Table 4.2 summarizes the main economic indicators. By 1990 Mongolia's manufacturing sector contributed 36 percent of national income. The main industries included copper mining, light food products, textiles and clothing, and other agriculture-related products. Agricultural production was arranged in a system of state-owned farms and cooperatives that produced grain but were dominated by approximately 25 million livestock. There was a well-developed social infrastructure. Nearly 100 percent of the population is literate, and indicators of health care, sanitation, and housing are extremely high compared to countries at a similar income level and given the harsh climate.

Table 4.2
Basic facts about Mongolia

Population (millions)	2.1
Under 19 years (%)	49
Under 35 years (%)	75
GNP per capita (US$)	500
Division of GNP in 1990 (%)	
Agriculture	19
Manufacturing	36
Services and other	46
Real GNP and industrial production growth	
GNP growth (1990–95)	–16
Industrial production (1990–95)	–34
Livestock (millions) in 1995	27
Sheep	15
Other	12
Livestock privately held in 1995 (%)	93
Livestock privately held in 1990 (%)	21
Exports in 1995 (US$ million)	512
Copper (estimate)	240
Other (estimate)	282
Growth rate in 1992–95 (%)	39
Imports in 1995 (US$ million))	389
Energy	120
Other	269
Growth rate in 1990–95 (%)	–3
Current account balance in 1995 (US$ million)	123
1995 (% GNP)	11.5
1990 (% GNP)	–33.0
Division of trade (% of total volume)	
Russia in 1995	32
China in 1995	12
Other in 1995	56
Russia in 1990	82
China in 1990	10
Other in 1990	7
Broad money supply as % of GNP in 1995	24.8
CPI inflation (1995 monthly average %)	2.5
Fiscal indicators (% GNP)	
Current government revenue	27.2
Current government spending	29.4
Net credit financing (– = surplus)	–2.2

Sources: *Bank of Mongolia Statistical Bulletin, State Statistical Bulletin* (various issues).

Table 4.3
Major political and economic events from 1990 to 1995

1990	
March	Hunger strikes lead to decision by politburo to call elections
April	Constitutional reform ensures property rights and allows private trade
June	Elections to Bhaga Khural (Parliament). The MPRP wins 59 percent of the vote and seats in Parliament; six opposition parties win remaining 41 percent of votes and seats
October	Mongolia's first elected Parliament meets
October	Prime Minister Byambasuren is appointed by Parliament, and a coalition government is formed
1991	
January 1	CMEA trade regime ends and all credits from the USSR are abruptly ended
January 16	Resolution 20 permitting partial price liberalization is issued by the government
April	Mongolia receives emergency aid from the United States and Japan, and joins the IMF and World Bank
May	Parliament appoints a new central bank governor who subsequently devalues the tugrik from 7 to 40 tugrik/dollar
June	Mongolia enters into negotiations for an IMF standby arrangement and reaches agreement at the end of July
August	Privatization vouchers are distributed
September	Second major set of price liberalization measures
October	Mongolian congress meets to decide a new constitution; meetings are prolonged by several weeks and the government offers to resign
1992	
January	Congress agrees on a new constitution with a single parliament and a weak president. Elections are called for June 1990
February	Mongolian stock exchange auctions first large enterprise
March	Third set of price liberalization measures prior to a donor's conference
May	New central bank governor is appointed after former governor resigns when large foreign exchange losses occurring between 1986 and 1991 are revealed
June	IMF ESAF program is terminated after failure to meet program targets
June	Elections give 57 percent of the vote to MPRP and 43 percent to opposition parties; MPRP gains 70 out of 75 seats in Parliament as a result

Table 4.3 continued

July	New MPRP government under Prime Minister Jasrai is appointed
October	New three-year IMF agreement is reached
1993	
March	Exchange rate is unified and last major price and trade liberalization measures are taken
June	Opposition party candidate, President Ochirbat, is reelected president

Both politics and economics depended heavily on the former Soviet Union. The major political events discussed in this paper are summarized in table 4.3. With the arrival of glasnost in the USSR, a reform movement surfaced in Mongolia. After hunger strikes in spring 1990, the Mongolian Politburo began political reforms. The constitution was amended to legalize private enterprises, and parliamentary elections were called. Six opposition parties, all with a similar radical reform agenda, competed with the MPRP in the elections. The opposition parties performed strongly in the large cities but not in the rural regions. The outcome was that the MPRP won 59 percent of the vote and seats in the Parliament.

In a demonstration of national unity, in autumn 1990 a coalition government was formed with four opposition party members, including the First Deputy Prime Minister in charge of the economy, and nine MPRP members. Parliament met in October 1990, and in the following nine months it passed or presented 27 laws to transform the economy to a market system (see table 4.4). This was a period of euphoria, when all radical changes seemed able to pass through Parliament without substantial scrutiny. While the laws played an extremely important role in signaling the extent of change in the country, actual implementation and interpretation of the changes fell far behind the laws' intent.

The government faced a very difficult economic environment. On January 1, 1991 all foreign credits from the USSR were suddenly stopped. This shock coincided with the collapse of the CMEA, which brought trade volumes down sharply. Rough estimates of the size of the negative CMEA shock have placed it on par with wartime destruction, and well above the negative shocks of the other formerly socialist economies (see table 4.1).

Table 4.4
Laws passed, under revision, or presented before Parliament during the first nine months of democratic Parliament

1	Tax Law	Passed
2	Banking Law	Passed
3	Privatization Law	Passed
4	Pension Law	Passed
5	Labor Law	Passed
6	Customs Law	Passed
7	Trade Unions Law	Passed
8	Property Ownership (amendments to the civil code)	Passed
9	Criminal Law (amendments to laws on crimes against property)	Passed
10	Law Defining the Role of the President	Passed
11	Law Defining the Role of the Parliament	Passed
12	Law Defining the Role of the Government	Passed
13	Social Security Law	Passed
14	Company Law	Passed
15	Law Permitting Membership in the IMF	Passed
16	Amendments to Laws Concerning Political Parties	Passed
17	Social Insurance Law	Passed
18	Immigration Law	Under Revision
19	Law for Non-Profit Organizations	Under Revision
20	Education Law	Before Parliament
21	Land Law	Before Parliament
22	Religion Law	Before Parliament
23	Statistical Office Law	Before Parliament
24	Consumer's Law	Before Parliament
25	Anti-Monopoly Law	Before Parliament
26	Budget Law	Before Parliament
27	Bankruptcy Law	Before Parliament
28	Constitution	Before Parliament

Source: Unpublished records from the Mongolian Parliament.

In response to the impending crisis, on January 16 the government passed Resolution 20, which liberalized many prices.[1] The resolution left many areas of the economy still under control. State orders remained for most agricultural products, and for industrial products for external trade. Foreign exchange controls persisted, and the official exchange rate was 10 percent of the parallel rate.

During the first stage of crisis, when it was still unclear what would happen in the Soviet Union, the government received vigorous support from Western governments. The United States and Japan provided emergency credits, and in July 1991 the government signed its first standby agreement with the IMF. Western aid in 1991 equaled 8 percent of GNP, partially making up for the loss of Soviet financing. The agreement with the IMF led to further price liberalization in 1991, but exchange controls and state orders persisted.

The next major political reform came in October 1991, when a new constitution was approved and a single parliamentary system was created. The constitution created a strong parliamentary democracy with a relatively weak president as the head of state. New elections were called for June 1992.

The end of the parliamentary session in June 1991, and the decision to call new elections for 1992, marked the end of the period of rapid reform. Parties began positioning themselves for the upcoming elections, and many reforms agreed to in the IMF program were never implemented. As quickly as Mongolia had become a favorite of the international community, it now lost favor, and the political events in Russia meant that it permanently lost its international political importance.

The June 1992 elections gave the MPRP almost complete control of the Parliament. The elections were well contested, with serious campaigning and public interest. But because the opposition parties were divided among six groups, and they still did not manage to penetrate the rural vote, the MPRP won 70 of the 75 seats in Parliament. It should be noted that the electoral laws in these elections were based on the "first past post" rule, a formula agreed to by all parties in advance of the elections. The MPRP had obtained only about 57 percent of all votes cast.

In July 1992 the president nominated Prime Minister Jasrai, who formed a cabinet from MPRP members. The new cabinet presented a reform program calling for completion of most economic liberalization measures in a step-by-step program. As described below, the government

---

1. The remaining price controls were for most basic food products and some industrial goods. The decree also called for the doubling of all bank deposits and wages. Only cash money and some enterprise deposits were not doubled. The near-immediate result was a doubling of most prices, including the parallel market exchange rate.

has now completed most price liberalization measures, and has completely liberalized trade and the foreign exchange market. It has also passed new taxation laws, a budget law, a law to promote foreign investment, and a securities law.

While the competition for votes had at times slowed reform during this period, the development of a democratic process may in time prove to be Mongolia's greatest strength. The last few years have allowed the political system to develop a process for coordination of powers across the various actors, and have ingrained the right of political competition and free speech in political parties, particularly in urban areas. It appears that a stable political process has been created.

4.3 Financial Reforms and Monetary Policy in 1990–1995

In this section we first describe the formation of the two-tier banking system and current problems in the financial sector. We then outline monetary policy, and the relation between banking structure and the growth of monetary aggregates. One lesson from Mongolian financial reform is that clear, credible monetary policies are needed to ensure a stable commercial banking structure.

Establishment of a Two-Tier Banking System

Prior to the reforms, Mongolia had a monobanking system common to centrally planned economies. The State Bank operated some 400 branches throughout the country. It acted as an agent of the government; its role was to allocate credits as needed to meet official production targets. Interest rates were kept low, and the exchange rate was fixed. Money and capital markets did not exist.

The first commercial banks were opened before measures were taken to establish bank regulation, create instruments of monetary control, and ensure adequate corporate governance. In mid-1990 the first three commercial banks (Co-operative Bank, Bank of Investment and Technological Innovation, and Trade and Development Bank) were formed by allocating each bank a fraction of the assets and liabilities of the State Bank.

It was not until May 1991 that the new Banking Law was passed, formally recognizing a two-tier banking structure. The old central bank was renamed the Bank of Mongolia, and it was given the task of creating a banking system consistent with the development of a market economy. Under this law the Bank of Mongolia was formally made independent of the government. The Governor is appointed by Parliament

Table 4.5
Ownership structure and paid-in capital of commercial banks (end of March 1994)

	Paid-in capital, in thousand dollars (US$1 = 400tg)	Share of ownership by owner category[a] (%)				
		G	SE	PR	CO	PI
Agricultural Bank	375	7.6	0.0	41.3	50.6	0.5
Autoroad Bank	152	76.5	0.0	23.5	0.0	0.0
Bayanbogd Bank	183	0.0	0.0	0.0	0.0	100.0
Business Bank	260	0.0	0.0	85.6	0.0	14.4
Central Asian Bank	290	0.0	0.0	80.5	0.0	19.5
Cooperative Bank	430	33.9	26.7	36.3	1.5	1.7
Industrial Bank	1,300	0.0	2.0	69.7	2.0	26.3
Insurance Bank	790	70.0	26.3	0.1	0.8	2.9
Investment BITI	3,000	78.8	0.0	21.0	0.0	0.2
Mercury Bank	480	11.0	0.0	79.7	0.9	8.4
Peoples' Bank	2,518	9.0	0.3	90.6	0.0	0.1
Post Bank	850	11.6	0.0	58.5	0.0	29.9
Selenge Bank	320	58.2	0.0	41.8	0.0	0.0
Trade and Development	700	100.0	0.0	0.0	0.0	0.0
Ulaanbaatar	230	0.0	0.0	28.6	0.0	71.4

a. G = government, SE = state enterprises, PR = private and privatized enterprises, CO = cooperatives, and PI = private individual.

for five-year terms, and is solely responsible to Parliament.[2] The law also called for all commercial banks to meet capital adequacy requirements and reserve ratios. This latter measure gave the Bank of Mongolia more control over the money supply.

Mongolia's experience shows that the commercial banking system can develop extremely rapidly to meet the needs of its clients. There are now fifteen commercial banks, and the Bank of Mongolia has transferred all its commercial activities to these banks. Table 4.5 lists the banks and shows their current ownership structure. They have 600 branches and

2. The Bank of Mongolia is responsible for currency issue, inter-bank settlements, supervision and prudential guidelines of commercial banks, ensuring soundness of the banking system, and management of foreign reserves.

employ 500 personnel. Nine of the commercial banks are licensed for foreign exchange transactions and they maintain correspondence accounts with 90 commercial banks abroad. This compares to no commercial banks and no foreign correspondence accounts prior to 1990.

Problems in the Banking System

While the banking system has had many positive developments, there are also serious problems on the horizon.

First, the ownership structure of these banks presents a real risk to financial sector solvency. Some large state-owned enterprises capitalized banks in order to secure credits through insider lending. These banks are dependent on a few enterprises for a substantial fraction of their assets, and these enterprises are often within the same industry.[3]

The second problem is the legacy of inherited debts, which are approximately equal to the paid-in capital of the banking system. The government has continued to order banks to provide credits to the agricultural sector and some enterprises at below market interest rates. The agricultural credits reflect the continued centralized procurement of flour, grain, and some meats.

The third major problem is the existence of interenterprise arrears. In Mongolia these take a rather extreme form, with a chain linking the Erdenet copper mine, the power system, the petroleum importing company, and local governments. These debts reflect continued soft budget constraints in enterprises and local governments. Many local governments do not pay energy bills and wait for the central government to bail them out.

Finally, the problems in the banking system have been aggravated by the financial stabilization program. The Bank of Mongolia has pursued a tight monetary policy since late 1992. The ex-post real interest rate on loans currently averages 5–10 percent per month, and this is likely to cause loan defaults and liquidity crises in some of the commercial banks in the near future.

Monetary and Banking Policy

After decades of price stability, the early reform period was characterized by high inflation and lack of monetary control. Until 1991 the government received approximately 25 percent of its revenues as direct financing from the Soviet Union; in addition, it earned approximately 12

---

3. For example, the Agricultural Bank is concentrated in agriculture, the Industrial Bank serves light industry, and the Insurance Bank serves the meat industry.

percent of GNP, or one-third of budget revenues, through trade and trade-related taxes. The government responded to the drop in revenue caused by the CMEA collapse by printing money to finance its expenditure. The results were inflation rates of 154 percent in 1991, 321 percent in 1992, and 183 percent in 1993.

A second cause of price inflation was the decentralization of the banking system. Beginning in mid-1990, the new commercial banks, in the absence of adequate supervision, issued credits liberally. As there was little monetary overhang prior to 1990, this expansion of the money supply contributed to higher inflation during the January price liberalization.

Monetary control was achieved after the elections in June 1992 and the appointment of a new central bank governor in May 1992. Beginning September 1992, as part of a program with the IMF, the Bank of Mongolia kept the money supply constant for the remainder of the year. Since then, seasonal credit issues in the spring and autumn, and the continued price and exchange rate liberalization, have contributed to mild inflation. As of 1995, CPI inflation has fallen to 2 percent per month. The exchange rate has been roughly stable for well over a year.

The new Banking Law has allowed the Bank of Mongolia to use reserve requirements to limit commercial credit issue. Difficulties came when the Bank of Mongolia issued base money to finance agricultural procurement. To regain control over the money supply, the Bank of Mongolia now places loan ceilings on each of the commercial banks, and banks face penalties if they exceed their targets. From November 1993 onward, the Bank of Mongolia has used open-market operations to supplement its efforts to control the money supply.

The Bank of Mongolia has taken the IMF advice of setting minimum deposit interest rates. These averaged 7 percent per month during 1994, providing a real return in dollars of approximately 6 percent per month. In March 1996 the floor was at 4 percent per month. The IMF's rationale was that there was insufficient competition in the commercial banking system, and without deposit floors, low deposit rates would limit savings in the banking system. The IMF argued that the reduced money demand would have jeopardized financial stabilization.

The tugrik is now convertible for current account purposes, and an active parallel market has effectively made it a fully convertible currency. Exchange rate unification was completed gradually, with an initial depreciation from 7 to 40 tugrik per dollar in June 1991, followed by successive depreciation until full unification in March 1992.

The Bank of Mongolia has also improved the payments system. There is a new clearing system for the commercial banks, and nine commercial banks are licensed to have correspondent accounts with foreign banks.

The bank has also authorized enterprises and commercial banks to deal in bills of exchange and promissory notes.

The Bank of Mongolia now needs to prevent further insider lending, to delineate carefully governance and ownership, and to provide funding for recapitalization of banks that are deemed viable for future operations. Furthermore, it is important that the Bank of Mongolia consistently implement a clear monetary stabilization program. If commercial banks have faith in perpetual central bank bailouts, they are likely to continue offering unsustainable deposit rates and making loans that will likely end in default. The bank should provide clear information on its future monetary policy, e.g., by announcing publicly the reserves it has built up and its future targets for inflation and the exchange rate.

4.4   Restructuring Enterprise Management

Mongolia implemented a nationwide voucher privatization program in the summer of 1991. The Privatization Law had passed Parliament by a 51 percent to 49 percent vote in May 1991. By May 1992, virtually all retail shops and small enterprises had been auctioned or sold to insiders for vouchers. Today, the majority of industry has been corporatized and sold through centralized share auctions, and approximately 90 percent of livestock is now in private hands. The remaining enterprises and state-owned shares will be sold through cash sales at the Mongolian Stock Exchange. Land ownership is still under discussion.

Details of the Privatization Program

Privatization was a cornerstone of the reform program. The goal of the reformers was to reduce the role of the state in the economy, and permanently change the balance of political power. A voucher scheme was chosen because of the low level of savings, the absence of the private property, and a desire to allow the whole population to participate in the process.

Every citizen born before May 31, 1991 was given three red vouchers and one blue voucher which could be used to buy small assets (retail shops, trucks, etc.) and large assets (mainly shares in enterprises), respectively. Distribution of these coupons started in July 1991. The privatization law created an independent State Privatization Commission and local privatization commissions to implement the program.

The Mongolian Stock Exchange was established and stockbrokers were located throughout the country. Some 300 brokers were trained and licensed in Ulaanbaatar, and then given financial incentives based on their ability to attract business from the population. Every province has several competing brokers, and there was a mass media campaign to promote the program and educate the public.

Under the Privatization Program, all small businesses, all livestock, all agricultural enterprises and cooperative farms, and 340 large state enterprises were to be privatized. However, Government Resolution No. 170, issued on June 7, 1991, restricted privatization in some of the large enterprises to no more than 50 percent of share capital, and excluded state-owned enterprises in mining, energy, transportation, communications, and water supply from the privatization scheme.

Share auctions for the large-enterprise privatization began in February 1992 at the Mongolian Stock Exchange (MSE). Workers were given a preferential right to use their voucher, at a face value of 10,000 tugrik, to buy shares of enterprises at the listed book value. This was a very modest benefit, giving workers the ability to purchase directly between 5 and 10 percent of enterprise shares.

The auctions occurred weekly at the MSE. During the week, brokers in regional offices would collect vouchers and share orders from households. Each household specified a share price and the number of shares they wished to purchase. Brokers then compiled these into block orders and bid for lots offered at the stock exchange. Representatives at the Mongolian Stock Exchange would communicate with their regional brokers by modem during the auction to determine what price to bid.

Enterprise Management Reforms: First Results and Lessons

The legal reforms, pricing reforms, institutional changes, and other macroeconomic reforms described above radically changed the environment for enterprise managers and employees. After a lifetime of state control, virtually all state regulation was withdrawn, and enterprise managers gained autonomy in almost every decision they made. They gained the right to hire and fire employees, set wages and prices, sell goods internally or externally, and generally conduct business activities as they deemed best.

Table 4.6 shows the extent and speed of these changes by using the results of a small survey of enterprise directors conducted in mid-1992. The interesting result was that enterprise directors, regardless of form of ownership, believed they have the right to make all operational decisions except not to pay taxes. Twenty out of 21 enterprise directors reported that the government was intervening less in management of the enterprise than in 1990. Roughly three-quarters of all enterprise directors believed they have the right to set prices independently and to

Table 4.6
Results from a survey of 21 enterprise directors in Mongolia

	Yes	No
1. Is the government intervening less in the management of your enterprise than it did in 1990?	20	1
2. Do you believe the management of a *private* enterprise has the right		
(a) to set its own price without any control from any government ministries or agencies?	16	5
(b) to refuse to carry out state orders for goods if the enterprise so chooses, and instead sell goods to a different purchaser?	17	4
(c) to hire and fire employees as it chooses?	18	3
(d) to refuse to pay taxes?	1	20
3. Do you believe the management of a *state* enterprise has the right		
(a) to set its own price without any control from any government ministries or agencies?	15	6
(b) to refuse to carry out state orders for goods if the enterprise so chooses, and instead sell goods to a different purchaser?	14	7
(c) to hire and fire employees as it chooses?	15	6
(d) to refuse to pay taxes?	1	20
4. In general, does the government have the right		
(a) to hire and fire the director of a *private* enterprise?	1	20
(b) to hire and fire the director of a *state* enterprise?	12	9
(c) to order *private* enterprises to sell goods at below market prices to other enterprises?	1	20
(d) to order *state* enterprises to sell goods at below market prices to other enterprises?	1	20
(e) to demand additional tax payments above the taxes specified in the tax law from *private* enterprises?	2	19
(f) to demand additional tax payments above the taxes specified in tax laws from *state* enterprise?	2	19
5. Would/has the voucher privatization program reduced the ability of the government to intervene in operations of your enterprise?	17	3
6. Would/has privatization made it easier to receive credits from commercial banks?	8	8

Table 4.6 continued

7. Do privatized enterprises have the right to retain more foreign exchange from their exports than state enterprises?	15	4

Note: The survey was conducted by the Market Research Institute, Ulaanbaatar in April 1993. The twenty-one enterprises were chosen as representative of major enterprises in Mongolia. Sixteen of the twenty-one enterprises are participants in the voucher privatization program. Eleven of the enterprises are currently private, and ten are more than 50 percent state-owned. Several respondents could not provide answers to questions 5, 6, and 7.

refuse to carry out state orders. This was at a time when some price controls were still in place, and many of these enterprises were legally required to fulfill state orders. The fact that they believed they were not obliged to carry these out shows not only the extent of changes in enterprise autonomy over this period, but also the reason why the government eventually was forced to abolish many price controls and state orders. The growth of enterprise autonomy, and the ability of private traders to conduct trade with these enterprises, provided an alternative channel to the state order system which effectively weakened the power of the ministries to enforce their controls. The responses also show that there is no difference in the general attitude of directors as to the rights of private or state-owned firms.

Table 4.6 also shows that the privatization program may have played a role in granting more autonomy to enterprises. Twenty out of twenty-one directors said the state does not have the right to fire a director of a private enterprise, but only nine out of twenty-one believed the state cannot fire the director of a state enterprise. Furthermore, seventeen out of twenty respondents reported that the privatization program has reduced the ability of the government to intervene in operations of their enterprises. Since most enterprises were scheduled to be privatized, it may be that the privatization program played an important role in signaling managers' new autonomy—and reinforcing other legislation described above.

Problems of corporate management remain severe in state enterprises. Until 1990 a large part of industry was dependent on Soviet advisors. There were reportedly 50,000 resident Soviet advisors in the mid-1980s, mostly engineers and other technical specialists, but almost all of these people had gone by 1991. With the assistance of the United Nations Development Program, the Institute of Administration and Management Development was launched in 1991 to help retrain managers.

There has been substantial progress towards creating a national accounting system consistent with international standards. In early 1992 the Ministry of Finance introduced a regulation defining the new accounting standards, and in 1993 Parliament adopted a Law on the Accounting System. This law implements international accounting standards and auditing regulations consistent with a market system. The Economic College in Ulaanbaatar was established at the start of the reforms to train students in accounting, business, and economics.

4.5   Price Liberalization

Price liberalization was the first major step in economic reform. The official price structure in Mongolia was highly distorted, particularly due to the low prices of transportation and energy under the Soviet system. This was an important factor in ensuring the solvency of many industrial enterprises that ship goods and receive supplies by rail across Siberia. But with the breakdown of the CMEA system, and the movement to world prices for all goods and services, many enterprises have become insolvent.

Price Liberalization during the Reform Period

The major steps in price reform are outlined in table 4.7. The first serious price deregulation occurred immediately after the CMEA crisis in January 1991. However, there were still maximum prices for various goods, two-tier pricing once state orders were met, and a (variable) surrender requirement for export earnings. A ration system was also introduced for basic food items.

The next major step was on October 17, 1991, when as part of an IMF agreement the government cut the number of goods subject to retail price control from 35 to 17. The share of controlled prices in consumer baskets fell from 40 percent of urban household budgets to 20 percent as a result of this measure.

This pattern of gradual price liberalization and abolishment of state orders in part reflected the loss of control of government officials at all levels of government. The legal reforms in 1990 resulted in rapid growth of private traders throughout 1991 and 1992. By mid-1992 some 2,000 new private businesses, mostly in the trade sector, had been created. These traders were able to arbitrage prices and get around state regulations so that the state order system gradually broke down. Enterprise directors, with their much greater autonomy, became more bold in choosing not to fulfill state orders. The end result was that state retail shops became more and more empty, and the state order system broke

Table 4.7
Major price, state order, and exchange rate reform measures

Price measures	
1986	Increase in wholesale prices
1988	Introduction of limited two-tier pricing for agricultural products
1989	Increases in selected retail prices, and some easing of foreign exchange restrictions
January 16, 1991	Resolution 20
	– all retail prices freed excluding 35 categories of goods (approximately 50% of CPI freed)
	– other state prices doubled
	– wages and household deposits doubled
October 1991	Number of controlled prices cut from 35 to 17
March 1992	All remaining retail prices except flour, bread, and vodka under rationing. Energy and communications are freed. Farm gate prices are also freed, although grain is effectively controlled due to the monopoly of the flour mills
State orders	
1991–1993	Gradually eliminated by the end of 1993
Exchange rate reform	
June 1991	Official exchange rate devalued from 7.1 to 50 tugrik/dollar. Barter rate kept at 15 tugrik/dollar. Parallel rate is approximately 80 tugrik/dollar.
May 1992	Barter rate devalued to equal official rate at 40 tugrik/dollar. Parallel rate at 250 tugrik/dollar.
May 1993	Exchange rate unified at approximately 400 tugrik/dollar.

down. This had a disruptive effect on industrial production since many state enterprises waited for promised supplies of goods which never materialized.

Figure 4.1 shows evidence of gradual price reform in terms of the pattern of real money balances during 1990–95. Those countries that had "big bang" price liberalization generally experienced a steep drop in the real money balance at the time of liberalization, followed by a gradual increase later on as households and enterprises built up deposits and cash

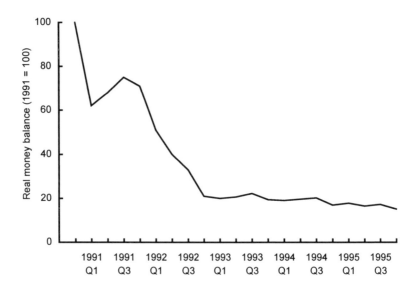

Figure 4.1
Real money balances in Mongolia during 1991–1995 (1991 = 100). Source: Bank of Mongolia.

balances. In Mongolia, however, there was a gradual erosion of the real money balance until 1993. The initial price liberalization in January 1991 only took the economy part way to liberalization. But as the private economy grew, and both the national and local governments lost their ability to control prices, inflation continued to outpace money growth. More or less complete price liberalization was finally achieved in March 1993 when the final major step, unification of the exchange rate, was taken.

4.6   Agricultural Reforms

Mongolia has always been heavily dependent on agriculture. The agricultural sector employs 30 percent of the workforce, with livestock taking up 73 percent of gross agricultural output. A substantial fraction of industry also depends on wool, leather, and cashmere as basic inputs.

In the early 1960s all livestock became part of agricultural cooperatives. By 1990 there were two types of agricultural enterprises: state enterprises (*sangiin aj ahui*) and agricultural cooperatives (*hegdel*). State enterprises were owned by the state, while agricultural cooperatives were in theory owned by their members. In practice, the operations of both types of enterprises were directed by the state. An average state farm had 23,000 hectares of arable land and over 500 employees; a typical cooperative had 400,000 hectares of pasture, 65,000 livestock, and over 400 employees.

The main issue that has dominated agricultural reform is privatization. The three major sets of actors were the Union of Agricultural Cooperatives (which represented the directors of cooperatives), the Union of Individual Herdsmen, and the Privatization Commission. Each group proposed a different privatization plan, and there was substantial debate over procedures and the politics of alternative choices. Not surprisingly, the debate over how to privatize the cooperatives polarized very quickly. The existing cooperative directors wanted to maintain the joint-stock companies as large farms, while the Privatization Commission and the Union of Individual Farmers wanted to fully privatize the livestock and assets of the cooperatives. In the end, the individual farmers won the debate, and agricultural cooperatives have now been completely eliminated. Over 90 percent of livestock is now under private ownership, and the assets of most cooperatives have been distributed to members.

However, some serious side effects have occurred. Some animal shelters, veterinary services, and organized fodder services have not been maintained, in part because privatization programs often did not sufficiently take into account how to organize these services in a market system. Because families are no longer organized into a central unit with publicly provided schooling and health programs, primary school enrollment in rural areas has dropped sharply.

To increase competition and improve distribution, agricultural commodity exchanges were organized in 1991, with branches in every province and community. These exchanges buy raw materials from individual herdsmen and sell them to industrial enterprises and foreign companies. The rapid growth of private traders has gradually strengthened the bargaining position of herdsmen in the new system.

The Current Situation in Non-Livestock Sectors

There are much greater difficulties with grain and dairy processing. The large state farms are highly mechanized and land quality is low. It is not clear that they will be viable when fertilizer, energy, and spare parts must be paid for at world prices. So far the government has no coherent plan to deal with state farms. The state farms have been partially privatized, but 51 percent of shares remain in state hands. To maintain price controls on bread, the government set low prices for flour, and this meant that state farms did not receive sufficient revenues from grain sales. The government has been forced to provide low-interest credits at harvest time to the flour mills to procure harvest, and these credits in turn have threatened financial stability. Further reform of the state farms will be necessary in the near future.

4.7   Foreign Trade Policy

Under central planning, Mongolia's exports and imports were handled predominantly through barter arrangements with CMEA countries by seven state foreign trade corporations (FTCs).

Mongolia was extremely dependent on the CMEA for trade, and on a small category of export goods for export earnings. Over 80 percent of trade volume was with the former Soviet Union, and over 90 percent was with the CMEA. In 1988 and 1989, minerals (mainly copper and fluorite) and other non-food raw materials (cashmere, wool, camel hair, and hides) accounted for over 70 percent of exports.

The biggest external shock was the loss of Soviet financing: this equaled approximately 37 percent of GNP prior to the reforms (see table 4.1). There are some difficulties converting ruble trade to dollar trade, but the magnitude of the collapse is similar under alternative reasonable definitions (see Appendix 4). In 1991 exports fell by 40 percent and imports fell by approximately 50 percent. The loss of trade destroyed the industrial base, which was heavily reliant on Soviet technology and customers. It also caused power shortages and fuel shortages, because all energy imports and mining and power-generation equipment were supplied and supported by the USSR.

Reforms and Adjustment to the Shock

In early 1991, virtually all exports required licenses, and the licensing process proved a real hindrance to private sector trade. The categories of goods requiring licenses was reduced to 13 in mid-1992, and then to 11 at the start of 1993. By the end of May 1993, all quantitative export and import controls were eliminated.

Mongolia's foreign trade is quickly reorienting towards non-CMEA countries. Trade with China now equals 12 percent of total trade, compared to nearly zero in the late 1980s. Mongolia's trade with Russia fell from 82 percent of total trade in 1990 to 32 percent in 1995. The main shift is towards trade with G-7 countries, which now equals 24 percent of trade volume, compared with only 3 percent in 1990.

Mongolia has reached several international trade agreements. The government has negotiated most-favored-nation (MFN) status with Japan, the United States, and the Republic of Korea; has applied to join the General Agreement on Trade and Tariffs (GATT); and has signed a cooperative agreement with the European Economic Community (EEC). There is also a five-year agreement with the European Community guaranteeing access to the European cashmere market.

Foreign Financial Flows

In 1991, Mongolia lost access to commercial borrowing as external credit lines were cut and arrears increased. External assistance from donor countries and international institutions has played a crucial role in overcoming the crisis. During the first two years of reform, Mongolia received approximately $125 million in foreign aid. This is equivalent to 12 percent of GNP on an annual basis. Most of this was in the form of short-term balance-of-payments support in grants or highly concessionary loans.

Tight macroeconomic policies have also helped the Bank of Mongolia to recover its reserve position. After having literally no gross reserves in June 1991, by 1995 the Bank of Mongolia had rebuilt gross reserves to $65 million, which is roughly six weeks of imports.

One of the most sensitive outstanding issues is how to handle Mongolia's long-term debt to Russia, which equals 10.5 billion transferable rubles. Payments so far have been suspended by mutual agreement, but Russia is now requesting that Mongolia enter into negotiations and begin servicing this debt. At the old official exchange rate of 0.6 rubles/dollar, the total debt would be over thirty times Mongolian GDP. This is an area where the international community could play an important role in assisting Mongolia to achieve a fair outcome. Given the importance of Western financial assistance to both Russia and Mongolia, it makes sense to deal with outstanding Russian debts in a multilateral framework rather than arranging separate bilateral negotiations for each type of debt and credit.

Until 1991 all foreign investment was from the CMEA countries. These were often "turnkey" projects: the Soviet builders fully constructed the enterprise, and Soviet advisors stayed behind to assist in daily operations. To promote foreign investment the government passed a foreign investment law in 1990 which allowed for unrestricted capital repatriation and profit remittance. This was revised in 1993 to include tax holidays for joint ventures. So far, foreign investment has not played an important role in the transition. As of August 31, 1994, there were 343 foreign joint ventures, and most of these are small.

4.8   Conclusion

Communists who believed we could completely alter the economic form of society in three years were visionaries, I say it will take at least a century. (Vladimir Ilyich Lenin, *Observer, Sayings of the Week*, 1921)

The real lesson from Mongolia's reform is that extremely rapid change is possible even in the most isolated countries. There were three important factors that forced change in Mongolia. First, the size of the CMEA shock made reform inevitable; the only real question was the pattern and speed of adjustment. Second, the move to a democratic system set in motion a set of reforms which allowed the creation of thousands of private traders and gave operational autonomy to the enterprises. These changes made it impossible for all levels of government to maintain strong controls and regulations that limit prices and trade. This same sequence of events is occurring in other countries such as Russia, Ukraine, and Kyrgyzstan, and the result is a gradual decline in the role of the state, and rapid growth of an unregulated private sector. Third, the role of Western financial support in smaller countries can be extremely important. Mongolia continues to receive substantial Western aid in the range of 8–10 percent of GNP annually. The government has taken full advantage of IMF technical assistance in designing its reform program. International donors can potentially play a similarly important role in other CIS countries.

Mongolia is now in a very promising situation. GNP is projected to grow by 4 percent in 1996 after rising by 2 percent in 1995. Dollar exports rose by 58 percent in 1995, and domestic investment is now increasing. While many institutional reforms remain, there are now clear signs that the most difficult period of crisis has ended. Perhaps the most promising aspect of the current reform is the creation of a stable democratic political system.

Appendix 4   Measuring the External Shock and the Importance of Trade

To measure the magnitude of the external shock, it is necessary to develop time series showing the share of trade in GDP and the absolute level of external financing. In doing so we run into the usual problems of converting ruble figures to dollar values.

The IMF reports that GDP per capita in Mongolia is approximately $558 in 1989, and the World Bank estimates $360 in 1990. Using (1) the Soviet estimate that Mongolian GDP per capita is 32 percent of Soviet GDP, and (2) that Russian GDP is $1,738 per capita, we estimate Mongolian GDP per capita to be $638. Based on these three estimates, we assume that Mongolian GDP per capita is $500 in 1991.

There are several possible methodologies to measure the trade–GDP ratio, and each has very different implications for the size of the external shock. The first is to convert all ruble trade at the official exchange rate of approximately 0.6 rubles/dollar, and then express it as a percentage of the assumed GDP. The second is to convert ruble trade to tugrik at the official rate of 4.4 tugrik/dollar (or approximately 5.6 tugrik/dollar if we adjust for the effective devaluation brought on by gross subsidies on exports financed by import taxes), and then compare the tugrik value of trade to the official tugrik value of GDP. The third method, which we use in the text, is to make assumptions concerning the dollar value of various categories of ruble trade, and then compare these with the dollar value of GDP.

The results of using these variations are shown in Table 4A.1. In the first section of the table, we use the official exchange rate. The share of imports is more than 100 percent of GDP. External financial assistance falls from 70 percent of GDP to 15 percent of GDP, for a net decline of 55 percent of GDP. This clearly overstates the value of turnkey projects and equipment and machinery, which form a substantial share of Mongolian imports.

The second method shows much lower shares of imports and exports, and a much smaller amount of net financing as a share of GDP. This method captures the true cost of these goods, relative to other goods, at domestic prices in the economy. In our opinion, this method gives estimates of the domestic share of exports and imports which are too low. Our reasoning is based on comparing the 1991 ratios with the earlier ratios. In 1991 the share of exports in GDP is approximately 35 percent, and this second method puts it at 25 percent in 1990. Trade volumes for virtually every major item of exports declined by 20–50 percent during 1991, and by a faster rate than GDP.

Table 4A.1
Comparisons of the size of the external shock using alternative methods to value ruble trade (percent of GDP)

	1986	1987	1988	1989	1990	1991
Method 1[a]						
Exports	89.3	85.0	83.0	78.9	70.3	35.1
Imports	160.7	143.4	146.4	153.5	115.2	43.2
Turnkey	62.1	49.6	39.4	37.4	41.2	7.6
Net services	4.2	2.1	−1.5	−12.0	−11.4	0.0
Current balance	−129.3	−105.9	−104.3	−124.0	−97.6	−15.7
Method 2[b]						
Exports	31.7	29.2	27.2	26.2	24.6	35.1
Imports	56.1	49.2	48.0	51.2	40.2	43.2
Turnkey	21.2	17.0	13.0	12.5	14.3	7.6
Net services	1.9	0.7	−0.6	−4.1	−3.9	0.0
Current balance	−43.7	−36.4	−34.4	−41.6	−33.9	−15.7
Method 3[c]						
Exports	55.1	52.3	52.6	50.7	44.2	35.1
Imports	85.5	77.0	83.5	88.2	68.6	43.2
Turnkey	20.7	16.5	13.1	12.5	13.7	7.6
Net services	2.8	2.2	0.7	−2.8	−3.0	0.0
Current balance	−48.3	−39.1	−43.3	−52.8	−41.1	−15.7

Source: authors' own calculations based on IMF and government data.
a. Method 1 converts ruble trade at the official exchange rate of 0.6 ruble/dollar. Dollar trade and clearing trade are added at dollar value. The dollar value of GDP was calculated based on the estimate that GDP was $600 per capita in 1989 and adjusted for IMF estimates of real GDP growth and official population surveys for other years.
b. Method 2 converts ruble trade and dollar trade to tugrik at the official exchange rate adjusted for the effective depreciation of the exchange rate through export subsidies and import taxes. Gross export subsidies equaled approximately 25 percent of total exports during the period. The ruble/tugrik exchange rate was adjusted upward accordingly, resulting in a rate of approximately 5.6 tugrik/dollar. The dollar rate used for clearing and Western trade was the official rate (approximately 3 tugrik/dollar during the period). The total tugrik value of trade was then divided by the tugrik measure of GDP. In 1991, dollar trade and the dollar value of GDP, as calculated in method 1, are used.
c. Method 3 converts ruble trade to dollars using the official exchange rate (0.6 rubles/dollar) for the trade category comprising fuels, mineral raw materials, and metals. All other trade is converted at one-third the official rate (1.8 rubles/dollar). For 1989 and 1990 the share of trade by category of good was extrapolated from 1988 data. Dollar GDP was calculated using the same formula as method 1.

Thus the share of exports in GDP should have fallen from 1990 to 1991 and not increased.[4] This is also true for import-GDP shares in 1990–91.

The third method is based on explicit relative pricing of the exports and imports. In particular, copper, oil, and raw materials were priced close to world prices, based on an exchange rate of 0.6 rubles to the dollar in 1989 and 1990 (for example, oil was priced at approximately 70 rubles per ton, which is 112 dollars per ton at the official exchange rate). But it is clear that other exports and imports, including foodstuffs, machinery, and equipment, were well overpriced. Mongolian meat exports were contracted at the equivalent of $2.35 per kilogram, while the border prices were approximately 40 percent of this. Machinery and equipment imported by Mongolia and turnkey projects were also considered to be too highly priced. To roughly capture this pricing difference, in our third method, we calculate trade values based on the following exchange rates:

Fuel, minerals, and metals: 1 dollar = 0.6 rubles

All other: 1 dollar = 1.8 rubles

In short, the official exchange rate was devalued by 200 percent for imports that were not basic raw materials. For Mongolia, the latter is mostly trade in copper and oil, which has continued at sharply lower volumes in 1991. These adjustments, as shown in table 4A.1, give a much more credible pattern for the movements of the share of exports and imports in GDP during 1990 and 1991. Based on these estimates, the net change in external financing from 1989 to 1991 was 37 percent of GDP at world prices. Since the actual domestic opportunity cost of these goods was well below their dollar value, the true impact on the economy of the shock should be less than this measure.

---

4. This is true since we are using a measure of GDP per capita in dollars which effectively allows for no adjustment in the real exchange rate. Given the balance-of-payments crisis, a sharp devaluation of the exchange rate could result in a rise in the share of exports in GDP because the dollar value of GDP falls while the dollar value of exports falls by less.

5

The Polish Way to the Market Economy 1989–1995

Leszek Balcerowicz,
Barbara Blaszczyk, and
Marek Dabrowski

5.1 Introduction

In 1989, before the start of the radical economic stabilization and transformation program, the Polish economy was suffering from two main "disorders." The first was structural, manifested by the low and decreasing effectiveness of management, which led in turn to low standards of living. The basic reason for this structural disorder was a defective economic system: Poland's economy was dominated by the state, closed to the outside world, equipped with false prices, and deprived of both internal and external competition. This sort of structural disorder was common to all the post-socialist countries.

The second disorder traumatizing the Polish economy in 1989 was near-hyperinflation and massive shortages of goods. In the second half of 1989, prices rose by more than 20 percent monthly, and foreign currency reserves were approaching a critically low level. Compared with the dramatic situation in Poland, the economies of Czechoslovakia and Hungary at that time were far more stable.

Six years later, Poland is seen by most analysts and commentators as a success story: growth is high, inflation is falling, and most of the economy is privately owned. We personally participated in the implementation of the Polish transition. In this paper we wish to shed more light on both the initial conditions and the conceptual dilemmas that Poland's authorities faced in 1990 and 1991. We will also discuss the main outcomes of Poland's transformation, its future prospects, and lessons for other transition countries.

The structure of this paper is as follows. In section 5.2 we give a historical overview of the pre-transition period. In section 5.3 we discuss

We are very grateful to Andrzej S. Bratkowski for allowing us to use macroeconomic data prepared by him. Of course, we take exclusive responsibility for the quality of this paper and the conclusions it presents.

the policy options and dilemmas that opened up before the first democratic government of Poland in September 1989. Section 5.4 is devoted to the stabilization and liberalization program of 1990 and its continuation in the following years. Section 5.5 contains a general overview of the institutional reforms, section 5.6 describes the privatization process and development of the new private sector, and section 5.7 discusses the reconstruction of the banking sector. In section 5.8 we summarize the results of the Polish transition and propose some general lessons for other transition countries. Finally, in section 5.9 we specify the remaining agenda for Poland's transition.

The main finding of this paper is that the successful transition in Poland (despite unfavorable initial conditions) was mainly due to the effective use of a political window of opportunity which the reform team faced just after the collapse of the old political system. More generally, this factor plays a crucial role in explaining why some countries (e.g., Czechoslovakia, Estonia, and Latvia) have been successful in their transition efforts, while others (such as Belarus, Ukraine, Russia, and Romania) have not.

5.2 Historical Background of Poland's Transition

Poland in the late 1980s belonged to the same category of reformed planned economy as Yugoslavia and Hungary, although Poland was less advanced in terms of economic liberalization. The economic system was partly centrally planned and partly market governed, with very ineffective macroeconomic control and with enterprises not guided by profit maximization. The foundations of this non-plan and non-market system (using Tamas Bauer's terminology) were created mainly in 1981–1982 by the big economic reform debate in 1980–1981,[1] and the Martial Law political conditions of 1982.

The most important elements of the 1981–1982 reforms were

1. conferring limited autonomy to state-owned enterprises (SOEs), e.g., wage setting, and partially eliminating some intermediate organs and organizations;

2. abolishing the traditional central plan targets and replacing them with the so-called "operational programs" and "government orders" for selected groups of products (but central allocation of selected basic raw materials, semi-products, and foreign currencies was maintained);

3. partially liberalizing domestic prices;

---

1. We presented the most market-oriented proposals in these debates. See Balcerowicz et al. (1981).

4. partially demonopolizing foreign trade and introducing a system of retention quotas for foreign exchange earnings;

5. allowing some degree of private sector activities and small-scale foreign investments.

Although many minor modifications were adopted in the next five years, the general logic of that economic system remained unchanged until 1987.

Serious macroeconomic imbalances in Poland had their origins in the early 1970s, when Edward Gierek, First Secretary of the Polish United Workers' Party, and Prime Minister Piotr Jaroszewicz financed an ambitious modernization of Polish industry and a consumption boom through large-scale foreign borrowing. The result was a severe balance-of-payments crisis at the end of the decade. During this period the basic elements of a very extensive and expensive system of social protection were created. The explosion of wages after the August 1980 strikes (that gave birth to the Solidarity movement), combined with continued price control, completely devastated the state budget and macroeconomic stability. The authorities responded with wide-scale rationing of basic food, and industrial and consumer products.

The subsequent history was characterized by policy cycles. Shortages and budget crises were addressed by administrative price increases, but then wage explosions and expansionary fiscal policy would follow and create once again the shortages, inflation, and budget crisis. In the last communist government, Prime Minister Mieczyslaw Rakowski attempted some fundamental systemic reforms. He undertook significant de-regulation of private economic activities (Law on Economic Activity, December 23, 1988), foreign trade, and foreign direct investment, and attempted to start a privatization program. However, the rules governing privatization were unclear, and in the resulting confusion, nomenklatura privatization was the norm (Blaszczyk and Dabrowski 1993).

Expansionary macroeconomic policies were the weakest link in Rakowski's economic program. The government's decision of April 17, 1989 regarding the increase of the minimum procurement prices of agricultural products was influenced by the forthcoming election campaign and contributed to the final collapse of the state budget in mid-1989. The National Bank of Poland (NBP) played at this time an absolutely passive role, financing the budget deficit through an unlimited and interest-free credit to the government. The price and wage freeze introduced in July 1989 only strengthened the market panic.

In this situation the "marketization of the food economy," i.e., the freeing of prices and elimination of the rationing system, was undertaken by the Rakowski government on August 1, 1989. The decision was

Table 5.1
Characteristics of Poland's initial conditions in comparison with other Central and Eastern European countries

Positive elements	Negative elements
Much higher share of market regulation than in the other countries (except Hungary)	Huge monetary overhang which resulted in open and hidden inflation
Agriculture dominated by private owners	Large foreign debt (almost $50 billion)
Easier and more liberal private contacts with the West	Critical situation of the state budget
The pre-war legal framework (commercial code and other regulations) was not damaged	Very strong organized workforce without organized counterpart
Much more independent state enterprises and therefore better management and human capital	Agreements made by negotiations between the government and the opposition (1989), which could not have been kept (for example on extensive wage indexation)
In the late 1980s the last communist regime launched some reforms that liberalized small private business activity, joint-venture law, and foreign trade and investment. Introduced the first stage of banking reform	The law from 1989 failed to prevent uncontrolled privatization and asset stripping by the former members of the managerial staff (so-called "nomenklatura privatization")

absolutely necessary. However, it came a few months too late and was accompanied by pro-inflationary monetary, fiscal, and wage policies. All employees and pensioners received 100 percent income compensation for inflation. The minimum procurement prices increased once again. Inflation jumped to 39.5 percent in August and 54.8 percent in October 1989.

Table 5.1 presents some of the initial conditions of Poland's transformation in comparison with other transition countries of Central and Eastern Europe.

5.3   The Choice of the Transition Strategy

The first post-communist government in Poland, headed by Tadeusz Mazowiecki, was appointed on September 12, 1989. The new government had a clear vision of the type of economy it wanted at the end of reforms: a stable, competitive, outward-looking capitalist economy. This differed in a fundamental way from the previous reform attempts, in which some type of socialist market economy was usually the most ambitious target.[2] Creating the necessary new economic order involved two basic moves: (1) the liberalization of prices and foreign trade; and (2) a comprehensive institutional transformation of enterprises (privatization), the banking sector, local government, and the tax system, as well as the creation of completely new institutions, e.g., a stock exchange.

Because of the very difficult initial situation, the choice of available economic strategy was more dramatic in Poland than, for example, in Hungary. None of the policy options were free of risk. On one hand, there was the radical option: swift stabilization, fast liberalization, and deep institutional transformation of the economy. Because transforming institutions (e.g., privatization) is necessarily a protracted process, the stabilization and liberalization package would have to be introduced within an as yet non-capitalist economy. The response of the system might be more unpredictable and worse than the reaction of an economy dominated by private business, such as, for example, in Germany after 1948.

However, this risk had to be measured against the dangers inherent in the alternative option of gradual reforms. Postponing the fight against high inflation until a time when the economy has basically been privatized would be like abandoning a fire to try and rebuild a house while it was still burning inside. Similarly, attempting to eliminate galloping inflation gradually would be like trying to put the fire out slowly. Gradually liberalizing prices and access to international trade would preclude swift elimination of massive shortages and fail to produce a definite improvement in the price structure. It would simply mean repeating the same old partial reforms, all of which had ended in failure.

Gradual reform would also mean wasting political capital demonstrated by the public's willingness to accept difficult, radical economic steps. This sort of political capital is a typical benefit of any large-scale political breakthrough, but it quickly vanishes, giving way instead to "normal" politics conducted by political parties, a game of special interests. Finally, social psychology tells us that people are more prone to adjust their attitudes to the surrounding environment when this environment has just undergone radical change than when it is going through gradual change.

---

2. At that time, ideas of "the socialist market economy" or another "third way" were popular, especially among the left wing of the Solidarity movement. It complicated the political debate on the transition process, especially with respect to privatization issues.

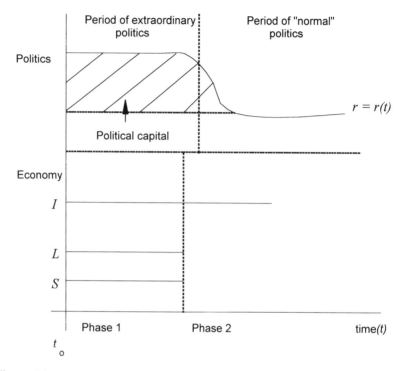

Figure 5.1
Political and economic dynamics of the transition process

For all these reasons Poland opted for a radical economic program. Figure 5.1 illustrates the essence of this program, the components of which are radical macroeconomic stabilization (S), radical liberalization (L), and comprehensive institutional transformation (I).

The lower part of figure 5.1 illustrates a radical economic strategy, as symbolized by the length of lines S, L, and I (see Balcerowicz 1995). Alternative strategies would have longer lines, or would be shifted to the right; e.g., S shifted to the right would symbolize a delay in stabilization, as in the former Soviet Union. The upper part of the diagram illustrates the political scene, as characterized by the function $r = r(t)$, which expresses the level of public readiness to accept radical economic measures, starting at the moment t_0, which is close to a great political breakthrough. It is based on the assumption that major discontinuities in a country's history, i.e., liberation from external dependence and a change of regime, produce a special state of mass psychology and a corresponding state of political system which are reflected in an abnormally high level of r; this can only be maintained for a relatively short time. This period of "extraordinary" politics gives way to "normal" politics, as described by the public choice theory of James Buchanan and others, when r is much lower. The surplus of r over this "normal" level is the *political capital*. It can be regarded as a precious resource which is gradually depleted by time. It is probably a non-renewable resource, granted by history.

Concentrating radical and drastic measures in the period shortly after a great change in a country's history enables one to tap a precious reserve of political capital. In contrast, delaying these measures by applying "milder" economic strategies involves a much lower probability of eventually getting them accepted or, conversely, a much higher risk of social protest, as the level of r is lower during periods of "normal" politics.

Figure 5.1 also shows that one can distinguish two phases of radical economic transformation. Phase 1 is dominated by the effects of those measures which work faster, i.e., S and L, and of faster institutional changes, e.g., the privatization of shops, restaurants, road transport, etc. If all these measures are undertaken shortly after a great political breakthrough, then phase 1 largely coincides with the period of extraordinary politics. Phase 2 consists of slower institutional reforms, e.g., privatization of larger enterprises, and has to be carried out during the period of "normal" politics. This partly explains why they usually meet with more political resistance than the drastic measures of the first phase.

5.4 Implementation Process: Macroeconomic Stabilization and Liberalization

In the last quarter of 1989, preparations were made to introduce a stabilization and liberalization (S and L) program, which was enacted on January 1, 1990. In the meantime, some temporary emergency measures were taken. From October 1, 1989, most of the subsidies for food products and some intermediate inputs were eliminated. Starting in September 1989, the NBP began to tighten the money supply, increase the nominal interest rate, and depreciate the exchange rate against the U.S. dollar both in nominal and real terms. This policy allowed an almost complete elimination of the huge gap between the official and the free-market exchange rate by the end of 1989. In October 1989 wage indexation in the enterprise sphere was limited.

The S and L program, introduced on January 1, 1990 and drawn up in consultation with the International Monetary Fund, consisted of the following five major components.

1. Restrictive monetary policy, most clearly expressed by a drastic reduction in the money supply and the establishment of a high interest rate (exceeding inflation in real terms from March 1990). This move was accompanied by a law regulating credit operations by introducing interest rate adjustments in all credit agreements that were made in the past. The law also restricted the so-called "preferential credit."

2. Elimination of the budget deficit, predominantly through further drastic reductions in subsidies for food, raw materials, production input, and energy carriers, as well as the removal of tax exemptions. A substantial budget surplus was achieved in the first three quarters of 1990.

3. Further liberalization of prices (since January 1990, ca. 90 percent of prices were determined by the market) as well as a significant increase of prices that were still under administrative control, for example, fuels and energy, transportation tariffs, housing rents, and pharmaceuticals. Some other price deregulation steps were taken during 1990 (e.g., a liberalization of coal prices from July 1, 1990). Housing rents were partly deregulated only in 1994.

4. The Polish currency, the zloty, was made convertible for transactions at a single exchange rate. The exchange rate was stabilized at 9,500 zlotys per 1 U.S. dollar as a nominal anchor.[3] There was also liberalization of foreign trade (elimination of import quotas and most export quotas, and unification and reduction of tariffs).[4]

5. Restrictive income policy, manifested mainly by the elimination, at the end of 1989, of general wage indexation in the state enterprise sector which was introduced in July 1989. In addition, severe tax penalties on wage increases in the state sector (so-called *popiwek*) were introduced.[5] This policy allowed only a modest growth of wages with respect to price increases. (The index ratios were as follows: 0.3 in January 1990, 0.2 from February to April, 0.6 in May and June, 1.0 in July, and 0.6 since August.) During the following years, excess wage taxation was gradually relaxed

3. It was kept at this level until the devaluation in mid-May 1991. From October 1991 the pre-announced scrawling peg formula was adopted, which worked until May 1995.

4. At the end of 1990 strong political pressure to return to trade protectionism arose first from the agricultural lobby, and later came from the industrial lobby. In spring 1991, several custom rates for agricultural products were increased. From August 1, 1991 all custom tariffs were doubled. After the Association Agreement with the EEC was signed by the Polish government in December 1991 (followed by the free-trade agreement with EFTA and the creation of CEFTA), import tariff policy became more stable.

5. *Popiwek* was introduced in 1982 and existed during the 1980s, although the detailed construction of this instrument and even the formal name of the tax were changed almost every year.

(especially after December 1992) and finally was abandoned at the end of 1994.[6]

The architects of the 1990 S and L policy expected a rather moderate output decline and believed that recovery could likely begin in the second half of 1990. Although this forecasting mistake did not have any direct influence on the effectiveness of S and L, it created a nervous political atmosphere around the government program. When output decline at the beginning of 1990 was higher than forecast and the expected recovery did not come, pressure started increasing on the government and the NBP, which resulted in a search for possible ways of reactivating the national economy. Politicians and economists did not realize then that output decline is not only a Polish phenomenon but a common feature for all the transition economies. Moreover, in retrospect it is now clear that output decline in Poland was the smallest among the economies in transition.

Furthermore, an additional note of caution regarding statistical data seems appropriate. The inherited statistical system is not capable of giving an accurate description of the economy as it undergoes dramatic change. It focuses on the shrinking public sector and is not capable of reflecting fully the fast-growing private sector, at least in those countries which have introduced a radical economic strategy. As a result, the official data tend to overstate the decline in GDP during the first stage of economic transition. (There were also other methodological shortcomings; see Bratkowski 1993.) As a result, the official data for Poland for 1990–91 registered a decline of about 18 percent in GDP, while estimates carried out at the Research Institute of the Main Statistical Office in Poland put that decline at 5–10 percent (Rajewski 1993). One should remember that these estimates do not capture the benefits of radically eliminating shortages and improving the range and quality of goods.

Unfortunately, this knowledge was not available in mid-1990. As a result of the intellectual confusion around the supposed deep output declines, the end of the second quarter of 1990 brought a general relaxation of the macroeconomic policy. (Monetary policy was relaxed even earlier, in April 1990.) This relaxation gave an inflationary impulse in the second half of 1990 and a rather limited boost to output. Rising inflationary pressure induced the NBP to start a monetary contraction. The adopted measures included three substantial increases of the discount rate from October 1990 to January 1991, an increase in the level

---

6. Many technical aspects of this tax were changed permanently. The most important change was connected with moving from controlling the total wage bill of enterprises to controlling the average wage (it took effect from January 1, 1991).

Table 5.2
Fiscal performance, 1989–1995 (in percent of GDP)

	1989	1990	1991	1992	1993	1994	1995
Total revenues	**34.4**	**47.3**	**42.6**	**45.1**	**47.6**	**48.3**	**47.2**
I. Current revenues	34.1	47.0	42.1	44.7	46.8	47.2	46.1
A. Tax revenues	30.5	41.6	35.6	38.1	40.7	40.7	40.4
1. Corporate income tax	8.1	15.2	6.9	4.5	4.2	3.4	3.1
2. Personal income tax	4.2	4.8	5.8	8.9	9.7	9.9	9.7
3. Social security contribution	8.7	11.4	10.5	11.4	11.0	10.7	11.1
4. Turnover tax/VAT	7.2	6.7	7.6	9.0	11.4	12.8	12.9
5. Trade taxes	0.0	0.7	2.1	2.3	2.8	2.3	2.0
6. Other domestic taxes	2.3	2.9	2.8	2.0	1.6	1.5	1.5
B. Non-tax revenues	3.5	5.4	6.4	6.6	6.1	6.5	5.7
1. Profit from NBP	1.5	1.8	0.8	1.1	0.9	1.1	1.1
II. Capital revenues	0.3	0.3	0.5	0.4	0.8	1.1	1.1
Total expenditures	**39.9**	**43.6**	**48.9**	**51.8**	**49.9**	**50.5**	**49.8**
I. Current expenditures	36.4	39.7	45.7	48.4	46.7	47.4	47.2
1. Wages and salaries	4.2	4.4	6.2	8.1	7.9	10.0	8.5
2. Goods and services	2.5	4.8	7.8	6.2	4.4	3.3	6.4
3. Total interest payments	0.0	0.4	1.6	3.1	3.8	4.4	5.3
a. domestic	0.0	0.4	0.7	2.1	3.0	3.5	4.0
b. foreign	0.0	0.0	0.9	1.0	0.8	0.9	1.3
4. Subsidies	10.6	7.7	5.1	3.3	3.9	4.1	1.8
5. Transfers	16.3	18.9	20.7	19.9	20.6	21.6	21.0
II. Capital expenditures	3.4	3.9	3.2	3.4	3.3	3.1	—
General government balance	**-6.0**	**3.7**	**-6.7**	**-6.7**	**-2.3**	**-2.2**	**-2.6**
I. Domestic financing	6.3	-3.0	6.8	6.9	2.7	4.1	2.4
II. External financing	-0.2	-0.7	-0.1	-0.3	-0.4	-1.9	0.2

Source: Database of the World Bank.

Table 5.3
Basic monetary statistics, 1989–1995

	1989	1990	1991	1992	1993	1994	1995
Broad money, including foreign exchange deposits; previous year = 100	—	198.9	133.4	159.9	136.0	138.2	134.8
Domestic broad money (M2); previous year = 100	—	496.2	147.4	160.4	128.8	138.7	150.2
Share of domestic M2 in the total M2, in %	27.5	68.6	75.0	75.2	71.2	71.5	79.6
Total domestic credit; previous year = 100	—	335.6	230.6	161.0	138.9	129.7	119.6
Credit to government; previous year = 100	—	160.5	843.8	205.0	144.6	134.8	103.5
Credit to non-government; previous year = 100	—	385.4	157.9	133.2	133.4	125.2	135.3
Domestic M2: GDP, in %	22.3	23.3	23.8	26.8	25.6	25.4	—
Nominal interest rate of 6-month deposits, avg., in %	—	56.4	55.0	39.8	31.1	29.3	—
NBP rediscount rate, avg., in %	—	48.0	47.4	34.0	29.4	28.3	26.0

Source: Database of the World Bank.

of required minimum reserves, and credit rationing for the state-owned enterprises. This drastic package helped to stop inflation again.

In early 1991 Poland was faced with new challenges for macro-economic policy connected with the collapse of CMEA trade, the second wave of output decline, and the post-stabilization fiscal crisis. The high profitability of enterprises quickly declined as very high inflation was stopped, energy prices were adjusted, and competitive pressure increased. As a result, revenue from corporate income taxation (the main source of budget revenue in 1990) collapsed dramatically. On the expenditure side, social expenditure exploded, particularly for pension programs, which were over-generously indexed (see table 5.2).[7] Subsidies to the social security funds increased from 4 percent of total budgetary expenditure in 1988 to almost 24 percent in 1992.

For the next three years, fiscal policy became the central issue of stabilization attempts. Every budget law, budget provisorium, or budget adjustment until the first half of 1993 (i.e., September 1991, December 1991, February 1992, June 1992, November 1992, and February 1993) was connected with the drastic adjustment measures related mainly to unemployment benefits, pension benefits, subsidies, tax and import tariff exemptions, improving tax collection, housing programs, and so forth.

The economic recovery and tax reform, especially the introduction of a value-added tax (VAT), improved the fiscal situation by the end of 1993 and in 1994 (see table 5.2). This development contributed to the weakening of political interest in further fiscal discipline in 1994 (especially in the social policy sphere) and even to the reversal of some earlier decisions. For example, from January 1, 1994 the minimum pensions were increased from 35 percent to 39 percent of the average wage in the enterprise sector.

Monetary policy has also not been consistent enough. NBP has constantly had problems with controlling the money supply (see table 5.3). From 1991 to 1994 monetization of the budget deficit was the main reason for the excessive money supply. From mid-1994, rapidly growing international reserves became the main source of money expansion. (See table 5.4.)

The fluctuations of fiscal and monetary policies had negative impacts on stabilization. As we mentioned earlier, the first stage of stabilization effort in the beginning of 1990 was quite successful in bringing monthly inflation of 30–50 percent down to 3–5 percent. Unfortunately, due to the political instability and premature loosening of monetary and fiscal policies, the disinflation process in subsequent years was rather slow. The annual inflation rate was 60 percent in 1991, 44 percent in 1992, 38 percent in 1993, and 30 percent in 1994. In 1995 it was 27 percent.

Macroeconomic policy is not the only sphere to experience some setbacks during 1994–1995. The Pawlak and Oleksy governments have also made several decisions that have resulted in de facto attempts to reverse previous reforms in economic freedom and policy regarding competition.

---

7. For a more detailed analysis of the post-stabilization fiscal crisis in Poland, see Bratkowski et al. (1995).

Table 5.4
Poland 1988–1995: Basic macroeconomic indicators

	1988	1989	1990	1991	1992	1993	1994	Q1 1995[a]
	(corresponding period of previous year = 100)							
Real GDP	104.1	100.2	88.4	92.4	102.6	103.8	105.2	107
Real consumption	102.7	98.7	88.3	103.3	103.5	105.1	103.9	103
Real gross investment outlays for fixed capital	105.4	97.6	89.9	95.9	100.7	102.2	108.2	120
Real industrial output	105.3	99.5	75.8	88.1	103.9	107.3	111.9	109.4
Real wages and salaries	114.4	109	75.6	99.7	97.3	97.1	100.0	104.5
Inflation (CPI), end of period	173.9	739.6	349.3	160.4	144.3	137.6	129.5	121.6
Dollar exchange rate (end of period)	502.55	6,500	9,500	11,072	15,449	21,079	24,312	25,098
Rediscount interest rate	6.0%	61.3%	84.1%	47.8%	39.0%	35.4%	28.3%	27.4%
	(in US$ millions)							
Exports	8,311	7,575	10,863	12,760	13,977	13,585	16,950	22,878
Imports	7,302	7,335	8,649	12,709	13,485	15,878	17,786	24,705
Trade balance	1,009	240	2,214	51	492	–2,293	–836	–1,827
Current account balance (payment base)	–107	–1,419	716	–1,359	–269	–2,329	–944	–2,299
Capital account balance (commitment base)	–3,195	–2,722	–6,893	–5,627	–1,554	713	974	10,210
Foreign investment	—	—	10	117	284	580	542	1,134
Gross foreign reserves of the NBP	n.a.	2,503	4,674	3,800	4,287	4,281	6,029	14,964
Net foreign reserves of the banking system	3,024	3,380	7,822	6,505	8,120	8,755	13,607	20,436

Sources: Blaszczyk, Bratkowski, and Dabrowski (1995); Database of the World Bank.

The creation of a sugar cartel, the concentration of cooperative banks, massive intervention in agriculture (for instance, introduction of compensation payments), reduction of the rate of privatization, consolidation of the monopoly of Polish Telecommunication, and the reintroduction of licensing for many kinds of economic activity are only few examples of policies undertaken by the Pawlak and Oleksy governments which can seriously threaten the future of the Polish transition.

5.5   Overview of the Basic Institutional Reforms

The transition program has not been limited to stabilization and liberalization; it also has included many important institutional and social reforms. Among the most important are the following:

1. Creation of a uniform tax policy for all ownership sectors of the economy; removal of a significant number of allowances, exemptions, and special benefits from the tax system; and reduction of top bracket tax rates for direct taxes. The second stage of the tax reforms included the introduction of the personal income tax from January 1, 1992, the new law on corporate income tax (March 1992), and the value-added tax from July 5, 1993.

2. Introduction of a customs law corresponding to EEC standards (from 1990).

3. Extensive public finance reform, including the abolition of almost all extra-budgetary funds and the introduction of the new budgetary law (from 1991).

4. Acceptance of new anti-monopoly legislation (March 1990), creation of an anti-monopoly office (April 1990), and the break-up of state-owned enterprises in several industries.

5. Update of the Civil Code, Civil Behavioral Code, and legislation governing land use (autumn 1990). Among others, these changes accelerated the formation of a real estate market, helped to develop collateral lending, improved the execution of civil contracts, and removed unequal treatment of state and private contractors. Together with the updated state enterprise law, the changes allowed SOEs to sell out or rent redundant assets, which contributed to speeding up small privatization and to restructuring many SOEs.

6. Speeding up the reorganization of the banking sector and updating the banking law. It was done in several steps. The most significant changes to the banking law—introducing Western European norms of bank behavior and accounting—started to work from March 1992. Many new privately owned banks were formed in 1989–1991, including some with foreign investment.

7. Strengthening the independent position of the NBP. The NBP is still not fully independent from Sejm; Sejm must approve the monetary program each year and may set an upper or lower limit on central bank financing of the budget deficit.

8. Speeding up of "small" privatization, i.e., firms in wholesale trade, road transport, construction, and services. Essentially, this process was completed by the end of 1991.

9. Creation of a legal and institutional basis for "large" privatization (1990).

10. Acceptance of the Law on Securities Market and Mutual Funds (March 1991); opening of the Warsaw Stock Exchange in April 1991.

11. Acceptance of the new Foreign Investment Law that eliminated most licensing and allowed the free repatriation of profit and invested capital (July 1991).

12. Implementation of the system of local self-government and the re-introduction of municipal ownership, which was abolished in 1950 (May 1990).

13. A new Employment Law (December 1989) creating a network of employment offices, and the introduction of unemployment benefits.

14. Reform of the pension system, implemented in several stages. The Law on Pension Revalorization (October 1991) was the most important step in this process. Unfortunately, the final outcome of pension reform was not prudent and this has created an enormous financial burden on the budget. Automatic adjustment of pension benefits to wages in the enterprise sector was one fundamental mistake. Furthermore, the Parliament has continued to make it easy for people to qualify for the pension system, especially for disability pensions and farmer's pensions (which are funded almost entirely, 95 percent, by the state budget). Several drastic and politically unpopular adjustment steps were taken in 1992 and 1993 (see section 5.4) to slow down the pace of indexation.

15. The introduction of the decentralized system of social aid for the poor, starting January 1991.

The institutional transition to a market economy is not yet complete. Particularly, the list of urgent social policy reforms waiting for elaboration and implementation is still very long. It includes some further adjustment measures (e.g., changing the indexation of pensions from being wage-related to price-related, and increasing the retirement age for women) and more fundamental systemic reforms, such as general pension reform, introducing health insurance, and changing the labor law.

Table 5.5
Processes of ownership transformation of state enterprises. Number of enterprises in the process of transformation

			In liquidation			
Date	Total	Transformed into State Treasury companies	Total	Under the Law on State Enterprises	Under the Law on the Privatization of State Enterprises	Transformed under the Law on Agricultural Property of the State Treasury
12-31-90	130	58	72	28	44	—
12-31-91	1,258	308	950	534	416	—
12-31-92	2,478	480	1,459	797	662	539
12-31-93	3,934	636	1,956	1,091	865	1,342
12-31-94	4,597	713	2,289	1,248	1,041	1,595
12-31-95	5,119	958	2,507	1,358	1,149	1,654

Sources: *Privatization of State Enterprises in 1994* (1995), Chief Statistical Office, Warsaw; *Dynamika Prywatyzacji* (1996).

5.6 Privatization and the Growth of the New Private Sector

"Large" Privatization

At the starting point (December 1990) there existed 8,441 SOEs. Up to December 1995 the privatization process has covered 5,119 SOEs, of which 1,610 have been privatized. Table 5.5 shows the pace of ownership changes for the main privatization paths during the last six years (1990–95).

Most of the enterprises that changed ownership were small companies employing fewer than 200 persons. Only the group of 958 enterprises initially transformed into State Treasury companies (commercialized) was an exception; these enterprises generally employed more than 500 people.

The distribution of enterprises between different privatization paths was as follows: 958 SOEs were transformed into companies solely owned by the State Treasury, 1,149 were assigned for direct privatization through liquidation, 1,358 were assigned for real liquidation under the state enterprise law, and 1,654 were transferred to the State Treasury Agricultural Agency. Of the 3,465 non-agricultural enterprises that entered the privatization process, 1,610 enterprises have been privatized (160 through the capital track, 1,054 through direct privatization, and 396 using the real liquidation procedure). (*Dynamika Prywatyzacji* 1996.)

In addition, 263 state enterprises were communalized and 118 enterprises were transformed into 58 companies of the State Treasury under the February 5, 1993 Law on the Transformation of Enterprises of Special Importance to the State (they are temporarily not subject to privatization). More than 400 SOEs were liquidated under the bankruptcy procedure. Up to the end of 1995, 5,943 SOEs were subject to different ownership transformations (see table 5.6).

Of the 160 privatized large enterprises, 22 were privatized through initial public offerings; their shares are traded on the Warsaw Stock Exchange. The direct sale of shares of privatized companies to individual investors (foreign or domestic) was generally more prevalent than privatization through initial public offerings. In many cases, a mixed privatization scheme was used that combined private sale and public offerings. More than half of capital privatization projects were executed with the engagement of foreign capital. An important new element of capital privatization in 1993–1995 was the privatization of four large state-owned banks (see section 5.7).

Although the 160 large privatization cases involved only 10 percent of all completed privatization projects (1,610), these enterprises are much bigger than the others and represent an important part of the former state-owned sector. One should add that most enterprises privatized on the capital track, especially through foreign equity investment, show very good economic performance, and in many of them an in-depth restructuring process has been launched (Dabrowski 1994, Blaszczyk 1994).

Direct privatization through liquidation, which was designed for small and medium-sized enterprises, was undertaken for 1,149 SOEs and was completed in 1,054 cases (91 percent). Of the whole group of privatized enterprises, this group comprises 65.4 percent. These numbers show that this is the quickest, efficient, and most popular way for property rights transfer in Poland. Three basic types of procedures (or combinations of procedures) are possible in liquidation under the privatization law: the sale of an enterprise's assets, leasing, or entering the assets as a contribution in kind into new companies. In fact, however, in the vast majority of completed cases (68.6 percent), liquidated enterprises were leased to companies formed by the employees of the former enterprises. The price for such a lease is subject to negotiations, without public bidding, and the payments are made in installments.

148   Leszek Balerowicz, Barbara Blaszczyk, and Marek Dabrowski

Table 5.6
Number of state enterprises subjected to ownership transformations by legal path, December 31, 1995

	Number of state enterprises	As percent of enterprises existing on 12-31-90	Comments
Existing on 12-31-90	8,441	100	—
Transformed into commercial companies under the Law on Privatization of State Enterprises	958	11.3	135 of them have been privatized
Liquidated under the Law on Privatization of State Enterprises (direct privatization)	1,149	13.6	897 projects completed
Liquidated under the Law on State Enterprises (liquidation)	1,358	16.0	293 projects completed; 365 went into bankruptcy procedures
Taken over by the State Treasury Agricultural Agency	1,654	19.5	—
Liquidated under the Bankruptcy Law	449[a]	5.3	—
Handed over to local governments under the Law on Communalization	263	3.1	May undergo further transformations
Transformed into companies under the Law on Ownership Transformations of Enterprises of Special Importance	118	1.4	Temporarily not subject to privatization
Total number of enterprises undergoing ownership transformations, including:	5,943	70.4	—
Privatization completed	1,610	19.1	—

Source: *Dynamika Prywatyzacji* (1996).
a. Data are for December 31, 1994.

Foreign investors may use several ways to set up business in Poland. The first is to establish a joint venture with a Polish private or state-owned company. The second is to purchase a majority share holding or portfolio investment in a privatized or private company, and the third is a greenfield investment. By the end of 1995 some 24,000 enterprises with foreign investments were active in Poland, but only in 360 of them was the value of foreign equity higher than $1 million. The entire value of foreign investments in larger enterprises was $6.8 billion at that time; additional investment commitments have been valued at $5.2 billion. The value of smaller investments was estimated at $1.8 billion. Altogether, the value of the invested capital was $8.5 billion in December 1995 and has shown a cumulative growth (Agency of Foreign Investment). The main legal barrier remaining for foreign investors has been the restriction on the purchase of land.

The Law on State Enterprises regulates, among other processes, the restructuring and liquidation procedures of enterprises which are in poor financial condition. The assets of these enterprises are sold by the liquidator to third parties in a public bidding by auction, and the proceeds go to pay off the creditors. Liquidation under this scheme supports privatization processes on a significant scale. It allows small private firms to acquire assets of liquidated state enterprises relatively cheaply. Up to December 1995, decisions about liquidation of SOEs were taken in 1,358 cases, but only 396 liquidations have been completed. The remaining 900 liquidations are not finished yet. The 440 liquidation projects commenced under the enterprise law ended up as bankruptcy procedures (*Dynamika Prywatyzacji* 1996).

Ownership changes in the economy have also included bankruptcies. In 1990–94, 814 SOEs were involved in bankruptcy procedures. In several insolvency cases, creditors decided to take over the enterprises and became the new owners.

Additionally, in 1993 and 1994, under the new Law on Financial Restructuring of Enterprises and Banks, in 190 cases banks started composition agreement procedures in relation to indebted enterprises. More than 70 percent of these cases are SOEs or state trading companies (STCs). The average employment in these enterprises was 1,300 employees. For these enterprises the law provided restructuring procedures such as banking conciliation agreements, public sale of bank debts, debt-for-equity swaps, and liquidation or bankruptcy. These procedures will lead, in many cases, to the privatization of the enterprises concerned.

There still exist some 4,300 firms in the legal form of state-owned enterprises, and of these, some 3,600 enterprises can be potentially privatized. However, this number can be misleading for the assessment of ownership transformation because it includes also the effects of the deconcentration and demonopolization process, which split some 300 large state-owned enterprises into more than 1,000 smaller independent firms.

By December 1995, within the group of 3,615 state-owned enterprises, some 329 were in bankruptcy procedures, more than 280 were restructuring under a commissioner, 65 were under banking composition procedures, and more than 600 were in preparatory stages for privatization or liquidation (*Dynamika Prywatyzacji* 1996). Still, some 2,000 state-owned enterprises were lacking any legal or organizational steps leading to privatization.

"Small" Privatization

The privatization of the retail, catering, and service sectors is the most successful part of ownership transformation in Poland. This process was completed during three years (1990–92) and resulted in privatization of about 97 percent of all retail shops, outlets, restaurants, and small service shops (Earle et al. 1994).

There was no special government program or law on small privatization. Instead, the government concentrated on the transfer of real estate on which these businesses operated. A restoration of ownership rights of local governments and housing cooperatives to this real estate resulted in breaking contracts with state retail trade organizations and establishing new contracts with private users, mostly former employees of the local units. Thus the prevailing form of ownership transfer of retail shops, crafts, premises, and industrial objects was through renting them.

The result of small privatization during 1990–1992 was the transfer of ownership of 31,662 retail shops, 19,690 service and craftsmen shops, 1,186 small industrial firms, 54,591 pieces of real estate, and 67,151 apartments.

As a consequence of small-scale privatization, more than 90 percent of the people employed in domestic trade worked in private enterprises by the end of 1992. Small communal premises and units are to a large extent currently in private hands, but in most cases the real estate is still owned by local authorities (*Informacja...* 1993).

The Growing Share of the Private Sector in the Economy

The explosive development of the new private sector appears to be the main driving force of ownership transformation of the economy and at the same time the unquestionable *differentia specifica* of the Polish privatization.

Table 5.7
Number of economic units in public and private sectors on December 31, 1989
and December 1, 1995

Ownership form	1989	1995
State enterprises	7,337	4,357
Municipal enterprises	—	482
Commercial code companies with state majority	1,224	2,023
Domestic commercial code companies (private)	15,252	90,843
Joint ventures	429	24,086
Businesses owned by individuals	813,145	1,693,427
Cooperatives (with cooperative banks)	16,691	19,822

Sources: *Rocznik Statystyczny* (*Statistical Yearbook*) (1991), GUS, Warsaw; and
Zmiany strukturalne... (1996).

Table 5.8
Employment in the national economy by sector as of December 1989 and
December 1994 (in millions)

Sectors		1989	1994
Private sector	Agricultural	4.0	3.9
	Non-agricultural	1.8	4.5
	Total private sector	5.8	8.4
Cooperatives		2.2	0.7
Other socialized entities		0.2	—
	Total non-public sector	8.2	9.1
Public sector		9.3	5.8
Total employment in the national economy		17.5	14.9

Sources: *Rocznik Statystyczny* (*Statistical Yearbook*) (1991), GUS, Warsaw; *Small
Statistical Yearbook* (1995), GUS, Warsaw; and *Biuletyn Statystyczny* (*Statistical
Bulletin*) (September 1994), GUS, Warsaw.
Note: The gray area on the right side shows the private sector after the 1991
changes in statistical classification, and the gray field on the left side shows the
previous private sector.

As a result of very liberal regulations affecting the establishment of new businesses, a significant group of new entrepreneurs were able to launch their businesses using very little start-up capital. One should also note the importance of the relatively liberal regulations allowing state enterprises to sell or lease their physical assets. The availability of cheap assets from this source helped new businesses to compensate for the shortage of private capital and the limited access to bank credits.

Table 5.7 shows the number of private businesses in the Polish economy that have been established over the last four years and the shrinking number of public enterprises. There was a more than sixfold increase in the number of domestic commercial law companies and partnerships, and an explosive 46-fold increase in the number of joint ventures.

Table 5.8 shows the changes of employment in the private and public sectors. By the pre-1991 definition, the number of private sector workers grew from 5.8 million in 1989 to 8.4 million in 1994. However, the nature of cooperatives changed from public to private over this period. So by the 1991 definition, the number of private sector workers was 9.1 million in 1994. The share of the private sector in the total employment in the economy amounted to 60.6 percent in December 1994. But the share of employment in enterprises having initiated privatization in the total workforce was 10.5 percent, and only 5.5 percent of the total workforce was employed in privatized enterprises.[8]

5.7 The Reconstruction of the Banking Sector

At the beginning of 1989, prior to the fall of communism, a new banking law was introduced. At the same time, local branches of the National Bank of Poland were transformed into nine state-owned commercial banks. In 1991 these nine commercial banks were transformed into joint-stock companies of the State Treasury, and the new banking law allowed for a rapid creation of new banks. Although the number of private banks exceed the number of state-controlled banks, the private banks are usually small in their financial operations and capital base. Some 80 percent of bank equity is owned by the state and is concentrated in the 50 biggest Polish banks. The ownership structure of banks at the end of 1993 is shown in table 5.9.

Speeding up the reorganization of the banking sector and updating the banking law was done in several steps. The banking law was amended in March 1992 to strengthen supervision over banking. The

---

8. *Small Statistical Yearbook* (1995), GUS, Warsaw.

Table 5.9
Number of banks by form of ownership at the end of 1993

Type of ownership	Number of banks
State banks	2
Property of NBP	2
State cooperative bank	1
Joint-stock company of the State Treasury	8
Joint-stock company with a majority of capital from state-owned entities	20
Banks with shares held by state foundations or funds[a]	5
Banks with shares held by local authorities	6
Banks–joint-stock companies with a majority of private capital	28
Banks with shares held by foreign capital	10
Banks with all shares held by foreign capital	5
Banks–joint-stock companies with a majority of cooperative banks or cooperatives	4
Cooperative banks[b]	1,800

Sources: *The Banking System in Poland, Almanac of Polish Banks,* and own estimates.
a. These banks are as follows: Bank Incjatyw Spoleczno-Ekonomicznych: 62.68 percent owned by the Employment Fund, and 19.18 percent owned by the Agency for Industrial Development. Bank Ochrony Srodowiska: 44 percent owned by the National Fund for the Protection of the Environment and Water Management. Gecobank: 79.8 percent owned by the Foundation for Polish Science. Sopot Bank: 11 percent owned by Agencja Morska. Polski Bank Rozwoju: 6.35 percent owned by the Agency for Industrial Development.
b. Most of the cooperative banks act as branches of the Bank Gospodarki Zywnosci. In nine banks the co-owners were other Polish banks (not counting the NBP, cooperative banks, and foreign banks).

adopted measures included more restrictive criteria for licensing new banks, maximum limits on credit exposure to individual clients, an obligation to create reserves against non-performing assets, and a minimal risk-related capital adequacy ratio on the level of 8 percent. In 1993 foreign exchange position limits were introduced, and in 1995 the accounting system of the banks was made compatible with that of the EU banks.

The Law on Financial Restructuring of Enterprises and Banks adopted in February 1993 opened a decentralized process of debt renegotiation, debt trading, debt-to-equity conversion, and bank recapitalization. It was aimed at decreasing the portfolio of bad credits in banks and unblocking the so-called payment arrears between enterprises. This would be accomplished by recapitalization of the commercial banks so that they could carry the burden of financial restructuring of indebted enterprises, which in most cases implied reduction of debt. The nine commercial banks that were separated from the NBP inherited the burden of those bad loans. This put their financial standing and the whole banking system in serious jeopardy. At the end of 1991 the share of bad loans in the banks' portfolios amounted to 34.8 percent.

To be eligible for recapitalization the banks had to accomplish the following: (1) commission an experienced accounting firm to prepare financial reports that analyze the bank's loan portfolio quality, (2) separately identify low-quality loans, (3) form a separate organizational unit to manage low-quality loans, and (4) produce loan portfolio restructuring plans.

Recapitalized banks could no longer grant or underwrite loans to bad debtors, excluding cases where the new funds result from the bank conciliation agreement.

Recapitalization was obtained by transferring 15-year State Treasury bonds to the banks. The bonds would initially be serviced by the State Treasury. Once a bank is privatized, the Fund for Privatization of Polish Banks takes over the burden of servicing bonds transferred to this bank.

The total value of bonds distributed between the seven commercial banks amounted to 11 trillion old zlotys (ca. US$600 million). Two state-owned banks (PKO BP and BGZ) were also supported by the State Treasury with the bonds. In December 1993 BGZ was supported with 4.27 trillion old zlotys (ca. US$200 million). In November 1994 BGZ was again supported with 12 trillion old zlotys (ca. US$ 500 million), and regional agricultural banks received 3.3 trillion (ca. US$140 million). This operation was related to the change in structure of BGZ, which was transformed into a joint-stock company, the owners of which are four regional banks, incorporating over 1,000 cooperative banks (see above). Finally, PKO S.A. was recapitalized with a bond value of 3.7 trillion old zlotys (ca. US$150 million).

The seven commercial banks were required to sell by March 31, 1994 any bad debts that were not covered by another restructuring procedure at this date. For BGZ and PKO BP, these deadlines were set by the Ministry of Finance at September 30, 1994.

The law provided for the following financial restructuring procedures: banking conciliation agreements, public sale of bank debts, debt-for-equity swaps, and liquidation or bankruptcy. According to data from the Council of Ownership Transformation, by February 15, 1995 some 400 banking conciliation procedures were started concerning debts worth 17 trillion zlotys (US$750 million). Out of these 400 cases, 224 were settled and they covered 10 trillion zlotys worth of debt (US$450 million). In 399 cases, banks applied for bankruptcy of their debtors, which covered 3 trillion zlotys worth of debt (US$130 million). Only in 28 cases were debts swapped for equity, which covered 1.2 trillion zlotys (US$53 million) of debt. Finally, 2,000 debt titles, with face value amounting to 3.2 trillion zlotys (US$140 million) were sold for 675 billion zlotys (US$30 million); thus, the average price was 21 percent of the face value of the debt.

It is too early to evaluate fully the impact of the Law on Financial Restructuring of Enterprises and Banks on the Polish banking system. The first experiences with the execution of the law indicate that the share of bad loans in bank portfolios has decreased from 34.8 percent of total loans at the end of 1991 to 32 percent at the end of 1993. The banks themselves predicted that this ratio could further decrease to 22.8 percent at the end of 1994 and 7.8 percent (which is about the ratio for banks in developed economies) at the end of 1996. This is a result of not only the restructuring of old debts but also of the tougher criteria for granting new loans, criteria which have been enforced by the NBP for banks that had been recapitalized. The banks also predict a noticeable improvement of financial conditions of those enterprises that underwent financial restructuring, so that shares taken over by the banks in debt-for-equity swaps can be sold with a good profit within two or three years.

The process of privatizing the nine commercial banks, which were separated from the NBP in 1989, began in 1993. In April 1993 Wielkopolski Bank Kredytowy (WBK) was privatized, and in late 1993/early 1994 Bank Slaski (BSK) was privatized. In both cases the Ministry of Finance searched for a strategic investor. With WBK the strategic investor became the European Bank for Reconstruction and Development (28.5 percent), and in the case of BSK it was the Dutch bank ING (25 percent). The State Treasury retained a large number of shares, which were gradually sold after introduction on the stock market. In January 1995 Bank Przemyslowo-Handlowy (BPH) was privatized by public offer. The State Treasury (represented by the Minister of Finance) also left a dominant package for itself with the intention of selling it either to a strategic investor or on the stock market after privatization. The privatization of Bank Gdanski was launched at the end of 1995.

Apart from the group of nine, other state-owned commercial banks have been privatized on an individual basis. For example, Bank

Inicjatyw Gospodarczych (BIG) was privatized in 1990 by issuing new shares, which were bought by private owners. Bank Rozwoju Eksportu (BRE) was privatized in 1992 by the same method. Both became listed on the Warsaw Stock Exchange, which allowed them to increase their capital several times.

The banking law states that a bank can allocate 25 percent of its own capital to shares of other companies. This limit has to be observed by a bank even if it acquires securities in fulfilling an issue underwriting contract. In some instances it is possible to raise that limit up to 50 percent with the consent of the Chairman of the NBP. In 1992–94, 47 banks were permitted to exceed the 25 percent limit (11 commercial banks and 36 cooperative banks). Some other banks were refused such consent.

5.8   The Results of the Transition Process and Lessons for Other Transition Countries

The main accomplishments of the Polish transformation can be summarized as follows.

1. *Hyperinflation was quickly eliminated,* but the inflation rate is still too high (although the pace of disinflation has been faster than, for example, in Chile in the second half of the 1970s).

2. *Shortages and queues were quickly eradicated.* At the same time, there was an improvement in the range and quality of goods. To begin with, this improvement was mainly due to imports, but in time it resulted from the increasing availability of domestic products. Such decisive elimination of shortages was primarily a result of the radical S and L program, combined with rapid privatization in the distribution sphere (shops, wholesale, road transport, etc.), and with the very fast growth of the private sector.

3. *The role of money as a medium of exchange increased radically,* as the Polish zloty became freely convertible into goods and other currencies. The reduction in inflation and a sharp increase in real interest rates also radically increased the role of the Polish zloty as a medium for savings.

4. *The private sector has been growing extremely fast, especially in the form of newly established small and medium-sized firms* (see table 5.10). The Polish economy is already predominantly private. However, the current state of the Polish privatization process is not entirely satisfactory because of the uneven pace of privatization in different sectors, the high number of remaining state-owned enterprises, and the high value of resources remaining in the public sector.

5. One of the outcomes of the tough stabilization and liberalization package was *the increasing number of state enterprises that started to restructure* and adjust to the rules of a market economy.

6. Along with changes in ownership and organizational structures within the economy, *output is being substantially restructured*. The overgrown industrial sector has fallen from 52.3 percent of GDP in 1989 to 46.6 percent in 1991, and the previously neglected service sector has increased in the same period from 34.8 to 46 percent of GDP (*Rocznik Statystyczny* 1993).

7. There has been *rapid technological modernization of production capacity*. The purchase of investment goods from the OECD rose by over 150 percent in 1990–92, and overall investment in machinery and equipment also increased significantly (Bratkowski 1993).

8. *Profound changes have occurred in foreign trade and investment.* Thanks to S and L, Poland has made a radical shift from a defensive import substitution strategy to outward-looking growth, and foreign investment has increased considerably (see table 5.4). However, this is still too little in comparison with, for example, Hungary and the Czech Republic.

9. The changes in the structure of output and the increase in overall economic efficiency have had *beneficial ecological effects*. In most parts of Poland environmental pollution has stopped worsening, and in some regions the environmental quality has actually improved.

The general lesson is that a radical and comprehensive economic program, introduced in an initially socialist economy under extremely difficult macroeconomic conditions, can be successful in spite of powerful external shocks.[9] One can see three main reasons for this. First, being comprehensive and radical, the program was able to break down the inertia and structures of the inherited economic system and could benefit from the political capital which emerged in the wake of the great political breakthrough of 1989. Second, the program was, on the whole, implemented consistently in spite of growing criticism and pressure, especially in 1991. And third, one of the basic rules in devising and implementing the program was to avoid favoring one sector over another or, even worse, one enterprise over another. Introducing the new

---

9. It must be mentioned that the profound institutional and economic transformation, implemented at a time when the country was affected by some powerful external shocks, has brought about open unemployment, which now stands at around 15 percent. However, some one-third of the registered unemployed are de facto illegally employed in the "gray" sector. The unemployment reflects not only the painful process of economic restructuring but also many rigidities of Poland's labor market (especially those associated with the aggressive trade unions) and deficiencies of employment legislation.

Table 5.10
Dynamics and share of the private sector

Year	1990	1991	1992	1993	1994 (estimates)
Share of the private sector in GDP (%)	30.9	42.1	47.3	51.5	55.6
GDP dynamics in the private sector (%)	−4.5	+26.7	+15.3	+13.0	+7.0
GDP dynamics in the state sector (%)	−14.4	−22.1	−6.6	−6.6	+2.8
GDP dynamics in the entire economy (%)	−11.6	−7.0	+2.6	+2.6	+5.0

Source: Blaszczyk, Bratkowski, and Dabrowski (1995).

general rules was absolutely essential to creating a transparent legal framework, improving efficiency, and avoiding pervasive rent-seeking by various interest groups.[10]

It is in these last two features in particular that the Polish economic reform strongly differs, in our opinion, from that in Russia and most other Eastern European countries. Another important difference is that in Poland the decisive stabilization effort came at the very beginning of the economic transformation process. In Russia stabilization came later, to be interrupted after only a couple of months in the middle of 1992; and in Ukraine stabilization has been delayed almost three years.

Other more specific economic lessons to be learned from Poland's experience are as follows:

1. The spontaneous and extremely rapid development of the private sector has turned out to be a more important way of privatizing the economy than the privatization of state enterprises. However, things would have been even better if the latter had happened more rapidly too.

2. The radical S and L forced many state enterprises to sell or lease part of their assets to private firms. In this way, S and L contributed to the growth of the private sector and thus to the privatization of the entire economy.

---

10. After taking government control in October 1993, the left-wing coalition has been trying to return to more differentiation in economic policy, and more subsidies, tax exemptions, and discretionary licensing. Fortunately, a solid legal and institutional framework created during the first two years of transition inhibits this process.

3. The Polish economic program showed that it is possible to abolish massive shortages in a couple of weeks and to increase drastically the range of goods available to consumers and producers in the course of one or two years.

4. The radical S and L induced many state enterprises to adjust to the more demanding, but also potentially more rewarding, conditions of the market economy. However, an even larger increase in their overall economic performance could be achieved, on average, if they were privatized.

5. Finally, the Polish example shows that it is possible to introduce current account convertibility in one step, instead of doing it gradually over a couple of years, as was the case in Western Europe in the 1950s.

Turning to the *social processes*, one should note that successful economic reform gives rise to two strongly opposing tendencies. One is the tendency towards social stability and satisfaction, arising from the elimination of shortages and from the great increase in general economic opportunities. This satisfaction is felt by those who can make direct use of these economic opportunities, e.g., new entrepreneurs, bankers, accountants, management consultants, and the many employees in the growing private sector. However, *successful* economic reform also gives rise to discontent, felt and often manifested by those who fear unemployment or are actually unemployed, and who are unable to make direct use of the greater economic freedom, or whose *relative* pay or prestige has declined (this is true, for example, of many of those employed in mining or heavy industry).

These two tendencies are used and sometimes exaggerated in the political process by opposing political groups or parties. The pro-reform parties try to appeal to those who are interested in the continuation of reforms, while the anti-reform parties try to identify with the malcontents. The direction of economic policies is largely determined by the clash of these two types of political organizations.

5.9 Remaining Agenda

The parliamentary elections in September 1993 were won by the moderately anti-reform parties.[11] A similar political phenomenon had occurred (or would occur) in almost all of Eastern Europe (Lithuania, Slovakia, Russia, Hungary, Bulgaria, partly in Estonia and Slovenia). Many observers were surprised that the left-wing coalition which has

---

11. Pro-reform parties achieved unsatisfactory results while the extreme anti-reform, populist parties failed completely. Most of the latter did not get the 5 percent minimum which allowed them to be represented in Parliament.

controlled the Polish government since October 1993 is continuing some reforms, for example in the housing sector. The pension and social welfare reforms have proceeded very slowly because of resistance inside the ruling coalition, and from the previous president, Lech Walesa.

As a result, starting from autumn 1993 the transition process in Poland was slowed down significantly. Inflation is still relatively high in comparison with not only the developed countries but also with the Czech Republic, Slovenia, and Slovakia. Privatization of the largest industrial enterprises is proceeding slowly. The budget situation, although improved in 1993–1994, is not viewed as sustainable in the long run because of the delay of serious institutional reform in social policy, the pension system, health care, and education. Thus, the remaining economic agenda in Poland involves further reducing inflation, completing the privatization of large-scale enterprises, and reforming the social security system and the health services.

The transition of the political system is also not completed. The Constitution and laws do not sufficiently protect the independence of the central bank and the stability of public finances. In addition, private ownership and the freedom of economic activity require greater constitutional security and legal guarantees than are supplied by the current system.

In this situation there is a need to plan a comprehensive program of the next stage of the economic and political transition in Poland. Otherwise, Poland's achievements so far could be lost.

6   The Ups and Downs of Russian Economic Reforms

Peter Boone and
Boris Fedorov

6.1 Introduction

Most people forget that reforms began in 1985 when Gorbachev came to power, not in 1991 or 1992. His early reforms set the course for Russia's changes. This first stage of Russia's reforms was characterized by rapid political change but (too) slow economic reform. When economic reforms finally began for serious in early 1992, the situation was quickly reversed: the main impediment to professional economic reform was the legacy of past political institutions and (too) slow political reform. There is no doubt that things could have been done much better.

Gorbachev's political reforms opened the Communist Party and the existing system to widespread criticism. The election of the Congress of People's Deputies for the USSR, and subsequent similar elections for a Congress in Russia in 1990, were key events that changed the nature of economic and political debate. However, in 1992 this same Russian Congress provided the rallying point for those opposing economic reform.

When serious change did start, the government was attacked from all sides. It was soon clear that political reform lagged behind economic change. There was a brief moment in early 1992 when comprehensive reform could have been introduced, but within weeks this opportunity was lost due to poor political management and the enormous pressures against clear reform measures.

In this paper we argue that one of the key factors that made Russia different from other countries with respect to its reform pattern was the enormous wealth and income that was to be redistributed after the breakdown of the old system. The assets that were up for grabs included the revenues from seigniorage (amounting to 32.7 percent of GNP), at least $10 billion in rents from natural resource extraction, another $12.5 billion from resources financed by bilateral credits, and around $600 billion from property to be redistributed.

The scope for gain undoubtedly played an important role in the subsequent pattern and politics of reform, and the cards were stacked against reformers from the start because they lacked clear legitimate authority and political skills. However, better management of the politics of reform, more decisive measures at the start, and more political reform at the beginning certainly could have improved the outcome.

Even with all the mistakes, and the lack of political certainty and clarity of direction, Russia has achieved much progress and the economic reforms have brought enormous change. As shown in table 6.1, the economic decline has been severe, but it has been roughly similar to the declines in the other large countries of the former Soviet Union (FSU). While industrial production has declined, banking services have expanded, equity and bond markets have developed, and a large new service sector has appeared. Most Russian enterprises are now privately owned.

After 10 years it is high time to examine the mistakes and successes of Russian reforms and to consider the lessons from Russia's experience. Section 6.2 outlines the main political changes that guided reform. Section 6.3 discusses specific components of Russia's reform program and the problems that were encountered. Section 6.4 presents outcomes and lessons from the Russian experience.

6.2 Historical Background

The reform era can be divided into four sub-periods. (1) The early Gorbachev years, beginning in March 1985, marked the start of reforms. (2) A major break occurred in August 1989, when Ryzhkov's government was appointed after the first elections for the Congress of People's Deputies were held in the USSR. (3) The next break occurred in November 1991, when Yegor Gaidar was appointed deputy prime minister by Yeltsin and he was given the mandate to implement radical reforms. (4) The final period began in January 1994 after the first elections for a new Duma.

March 1985 to August 1989

The initial Gorbachev years were full of optimistic expectations but there was very little progress towards reforms. Gorbachev attempted to create a socialist market economy by embarking on gradual reforms. Since Gorbachev aimed to reform the planned economy, rather than introduce anything like a market system, it is no surprise that there were no milestones that make this era stand out, such as price liberalization, foreign trade liberalization, privatization, and establishment of new market institutions.

Table 6.1
Main indicators of the Russian economy

	1990	1991	1992	1993	1994	1995
Real GDP (% change)	−4	−13	−19	−12	−15	−3
Industrial production (% change)	−0.1	−8.0	−18.8	−16.0	−21	0.0
Retail prices (% change)	5.6	92.7	1,354	896	302	205
Exchange rate (rubles per US$ at year end)	1.7	1.7	415	1,247	3,550	4,650
Dollar GNP per capita at market exchange rate (fourth quarter)	—	—	550	1,750	2,100	—
Unemployment rate (mid-year)	—	—	—	5.3	6.3	7.7
Gross external debt in convertible currencies	61.1	67.0	78.2	86.8	92.8	—
Population (millions)	148.3	148.9	148.6	148.3	148.2	148
Real GDP growth in other CIS and Baltic countries:						
Kazakhstan	0	−13	−13	−12	−25	−12
Ukraine	−3	−12	−17	−17	−23	−5
Estonia	−8	−11	−14	−7	6	6

Sources: EBRD, *Transition Report* (1995) and *Russian Economic Trends* (1995).

Perhaps the biggest achievement during this period was the introduction of the Law on Cooperatives. This law had nothing to do with
cooperatives—it effectively legalized primitive private enterprise—but it
did provide the first chance for many individuals to enter into small
business. To this day businessmen remember this first opportunity for
entrepreneurship as a golden bonanza. It was easy to start new companies in trade, services, and small-scale production, and this new segment

of the economy flourished in what was effectively a tax-free environment. A second breakthrough during this era was the creation of the first commercial banks in 1988.

However, the majority of economic reforms up to 1989 should be categorized as experimentation within a socialist market framework rather than as serious reforms of the system. Some measures were taken to elect managers in state enterprises, and there was much discussion of price reform and ways to provide greater incentives to managers, but none of these actions were effective.

In many instances these mistakes backfired and set the course for future changes. Gorbachev's anti-alcohol campaign is infamous for creating a large budget deficit as tax revenues from alcohol dried up. The government embarked on an external borrowing spree while at the same time spending foreign exchange and gold reserves. By allowing regional experiments with decentralization and greater autonomy, the government threatened dissolution of the state by bringing the separatists' demands to the foreground.

Furthermore, despite the reform-inspired discussions (e.g., convertibility of the ruble was first officially mentioned in June 1987), this period helped little in educating officials in the operations of a market economy. This was an era marked by very tiresome and painstaking hits and (mostly) misses. Apart from the creation of thousands of small cooperatives, few clear benefits could be identified by 1989. The economic debate during this time was often very far from the reality of a market system, and it proved to be a costly period for which Russian taxpayers today and in the future must pay.

August 1989 to November 1991

It was Gorbachev's political reforms, and mistakes in his economic policies up to 1989, that provided the main impetus for reforms. The growing shortage of basic goods, the separatist trends in the union republics, the gradual breakdown of interenterprise relations, declining discipline and morale of government staff, and lack of definite progress in most areas of economic policy pushed Gorbachev to take more active steps.

This was a period when political reforms far outpaced economic reforms. With the growing tension between a highly controlled economic regime and a more liberal political environment, it was becoming clear that either political reforms would have to be stopped or economic reforms would have to accelerate.

In March 1989 the first elections for the Congress of People's Deputies were held in the USSR.[1] While the elections were controlled to restrict the types and number of candidates, it was a God-sent miracle in this situation. The new Congress led to the formation of the first Soviet government, and the new government was somewhat reform-oriented. The academician L. Abalkin became head of the reform commission and deputy prime minister.

In late 1989 Abalkin's reform program was officially announced and adopted. It was a gradualist strategy and contained many of the important measures needed to update the Soviet economy and start market-oriented reforms. His program was clearly a step upwards, albeit a small one, in the quality of reform ideas that penetrated high circles.

Abalkin's approach accomplished little because it was unsuited for the economic and political situation in the country. It underestimated the importance of rapid change in the price and trade systems, the role of the central bank, and fiscal reform and privatization. The reform strategy was so gradual in design that it was doomed from the moment it was conceived.

The other reason for the imminent failure of the program was the weakening position of Moscow vis-à-vis the union republics. The loss of central control meant that economic policy actions taken in Moscow would have little impact on the country.

The problems facing the central government and the failure of current measures became so apparent that more accelerated reforms came on the agenda. For example, in March 1990 N. Petrakov, one of Gorbachev's assistants, convened a meeting of economists to try to devise an alternative program. When this plan was completed, Gorbachev welcomed the ideas but never attempted to implement them or use them in a practical manner.[2]

---

1. The Congress of People's Deputies was elected in March 1989 with subsequent runoffs lasting until May. It met in June and the proceedings were televised throughout the country. The Congress elected the Supreme Soviet, which then approved nominees for the Council of Ministers. The debates in each of these forums were surprisingly open and included harsh criticisms of economic policies.

A similar Russian Congress of People's Deputies was elected in March 1990, and it was responsible for choosing the Russian Supreme Soviet (or Parliament). Since in 1990 the Russian Congress seemed inconsequential, and most prominent Russian politicians preferred to stand as candidates for the Soviet Congress. It was this Congress and the Parliament chosen by it that Yeltsin dealt with until its dissolution in September 1993 prior to the December 1993 elections.

Rules for candidacy in each of the elections ensured that the majority of candidates were predisposed towards the Communist Party. Officially there was no party structure in either Congress.

2. Boris Fedorov, one of the authors, took part in these meetings.

The situation changed dramatically when Boris Yeltsin became head of the Russian Parliament, which swiftly declared Russian sovereignty. This was the turning point when the internal debate became so highly politicized that issues related to economic reforms faded into the background. From here on, major discussion of economic reforms came about only in response to dire political need.

An attempt to save the situation was undertaken in August–September 1990, when an advisory team, which included G. Yavlinsky, N. Petrakov, S. Shatalin, and B. Fedorov, designed the famous "500-day Program." This advisory team was formed under a joint ordinance by Gorbachev and Yeltsin. (Abalkin was invited to join the team but refused to participate.)

The "500-day Program" was a major step forward in the economic reform debate. It called for rapid reform of virtually all sectors of the Soviet economy, including price liberalization and privatization. The program failed to be implemented because none of the highest politicians seriously wanted it. At this time, the Russian and Soviet governments were living in two separate worlds; they hardly cooperated on any issue and each side was waiting for some resolution of the crisis. The actions they did take were out of desperation, such as the Pavlov-Gerashchenko confiscatory monetary reform in 1991.[3] Such types of desperate measures led to chaos and loss of credibility of the authorities, with no tangible positive results.

The impasse was broken with the abortive August 1991 coup d'état when the Russian government became the political master of its own territory. As the republics gained power relative to the center, they withheld revenue transfers; in addition, their own central banks started issuing ruble credits without authorization from Gosbank, the central bank of Russia.

The last months of 1991 were characterized by record food shortages, price increases, uncertainties, and total paralysis of the authorities. The growing crisis played one clear and positive role: it emphasized to the Russian leadership that urgent economic reforms were needed and that the old economic system had irreversibly broken down.

November 1991 to January 1994

The growing crisis in late 1991 clearly required the acceleration of economic reforms. However, with very little progress made after the abortive coup, it was not clear that anything was actually going to be done. This changed suddenly when Yeltsin unexpectedly asked Yegor Gaidar to head an economic team to design Russia's reforms. Gaidar's

---

3. In January 1991 Prime Minister Pavlov and Viktor Gerashchenko, Chairman of Gosbank, announced a surprise currency reform canceling 50 and 100 ruble notes.

appointment was largely due to strong support from Yeltsin's political advisor and later first deputy prime minister, Gennady Burbulis. Nobody had predicted that Gaidar would be named deputy prime minister in charge of economic policy.

But this miracle happened out of desperation, and Gaidar was given enormous authority to conduct economic policy.[4] This was the breakthrough that the Russian reform process needed. In a few months Russia was transformed into a new country by measures that included the following.

- near complete price liberalization,
- liberalization of foreign trade,
- freedom to conduct economic activity,
- unified and convertible foreign exchange,
- start of a mass privatization program, and
- attempts at financial stabilization.

The problem in this first stage of real reforms was that the members of the Gaidar team remained isolated within a small part of the bureaucracy and they never received sufficient support from the political elite.[5] While Yeltsin backed the reformers strongly at the start, over time presidential support appeared to wane.[6] By early spring, Gennady Burbulis, who had been the main supporter of Gaidar on Yeltsin's team, was being attacked by the Parliament and was beginning to lose favor with Yeltsin.[7] During this period Yeltsin surrounded himself with much less reform-minded advisors. Gaidar never developed a strong rapport with Yeltsin; their policy meetings were irregular and infrequent.

The government was attacked from all sides from the very beginning. In December 1991, then Vice President Aleksander Rutskoi labeled the Gaidar team "small boys in pink shorts with yellow boots," and in January 1992 the Speaker of the Parliament, Ruslan Khasbulatov, was

---

4. Former Prime Minister Silaev was sent to Brussels as ambassador to the European Community (EC).

5. The Gaidar team included A. Chubais, head of the privatization ministry; A. Nechaer, minister of the economy; P. Aren and S. Glazier, minister and deputy minister of foreign trade; L. Grigoriev, foreign investment committee chief; A. Shokin, originally the deputy prime minister in charge of social affairs; and other advisors, such as S. Vasiliev and K. Kazalovsky.

6. Yeltsin initially appointed himself prime minister in order to avoid an early confrontation with the Parliament over the choice of prime minister.

7. Burbulis was Yeltsin's most important political strategist and advisor during autumn 1991 and spring 1992. He was strongly supportive of the Gaidar team, and it was largely due to his influence that Yeltsin chose Gaidar to lead the reforms (see Yeltsin 1994, 150–2).

calling for their resignation. During the crucial time in November 1991 when the Gaidar team needed to ensure sound monetary policy, the Parliament refused to relinquish control or replace the central bank chairman with a reform-oriented leader.[8]

The Gaidar team had no experience and few of the skills needed to deal with the executive and legislative branches. Rather than attempt to build support in other branches of power, they isolated themselves within the government, and even there their power was gradually eroded as some ministers resisted reforms and as bureaucrats prevented changes. In his autobiography,[9] Yeltsin writes "... by sophisticatedly refusing to 'dirty their hands with politics' and leaving all political initiative to [Burbulis], the Gaidar team made a tactical error that cost us all a great deal."

This inexperience led to the eventual downfall of the team. Gaidar responded to attacks by making too many compromises and he tended to trust "old specialists" who eventually outwitted and ousted him. While he brought some excellent economists to the government, he also kept for no apparent reason anti-reform personnel such as Vasily Barchuk in the powerful position of Minister of Finance. One of his greatest mistakes was to support the former head of Gosbank, Viktor Gerashchenko, to become head of the Russian Central Bank in July 1992. Gerashchenko immediately expanded monetary growth, ending any hope that Russia could stabilize in 1992.

By April 1992 there was not much fighting spirit left in the reformers. The government narrowly survived an April meeting of the Congress of People's Deputies after they submitted their resignation as the Congress began. One demoralizing moment came when Vladimir Lopukhin, one of the members of the Gaidar team, was abruptly dismissed by Yeltsin in May 1992 and replaced by Viktor Chernomyrdin, the former director of Gazprom (the gas company). This was the first in a string of cabinet changes that would weaken the Gaidar team and raise the power of the industrial lobby.

The end of the Gaidar era came on December 12, 1992, when the Congress of People's Deputies rejected Gaidar for the position of prime minister. He was replaced by Viktor Chernomyrdin. Chernomyrdin's appointment did not turn out to be a decisive turning point against reforms that so many commentators at the time predicted. Chernomyrdin proved to be a very able and tough leader. His experience in Gazprom and as minister of energy from May 1992 gave him the ability to deal with old Soviet directors and bureaucrats, and he was able to preserve a balance between reform measures and the anti-reform actions demanded by the industrial lobbies.

8. Aslund (1995, 97).
9. Yeltsin (1995, 159).

Table 6.2
Party factions in the state Duma (December 1993 elections)

	Number of deputies	Share of vote (%)
Russia's Choice (liberal)	74	16.5
December 12 Union (liberal)	32	7.1
Yabloko (liberal)	29	6.5
PRES (centrist)	31	6.9
New Regional Policy (centrist)	60	13.4
Russia's Women (centrist)	23	5.1
Democratic Party of Russia (centrist)	15	3.3
Agrarian Party (communist)	55	12.3
Communist Party (communist)	45	10.0
Russian Way (nationalist)	13	2.9
Liberal Democratic Party (nationalist)	64	14.3
Independent	7	1.6
Total	448	100.0

Source: Aslund (1995, 201).

Chernomyrdin's government kept key members of the Gaidar team in power. Most importantly, the head of the State Committee for Privatization, Anatoli Chubais, remained. He has proven to be one of the most skillful politicians amongst Gaidar's initial appointees. He designed and implemented the mass privatization program.

Yeltsin also brought Boris Fedorov, a professor of economics and previously the Russian Minister of Finance in 1990, into his government as Minister of Finance. Fedorov had the reputation of being a sound macroeconomist and a strong political fighter. Fedorov renewed efforts to coordinate monetary policy and prevent a threatening hyperinflation by reinstituting a credit committee that was responsible for coordinating all decisions over new credits. He also eliminated import subsidies, raised energy prices, abolished subsidized government credits to agriculture and northern territories, and introduced government bonds.

However, in this period political debate again interfered and prevented full stabilization and rapid reform. The Supreme Soviet and the Congress of People's Deputies became more aggressive—instead of just attacking the government they now opposed the president outright. This conflict increasingly led to a stalemate.

The culmination of this stalemate came on September 21, 1993, when Yeltsin dissolved the Supreme Soviet and Congress of People's Deputies and called for new elections and a referendum on a new constitution. The violent response of the Congress led to its abolition, and this ended the immediate political uncertainty and gave voters a chance to show their assessment of economic and political changes.

The December 1993 election results were negative, if not disastrous, for the reformers (table 6.2). Yegor Gaidar's party, "Russia's Choice," received only 15 percent of the vote. The combined vote for the liberal parties was only 30 percent, while the nationalists, under Vladimir Zhironovsky, gained 23 percent. The Communist Party gained 12 percent of the vote. When individual seats and party lists representatives were combined, the end result was a Parliament that was roughly equally divided between liberals, centrists, and a third grouping of communists and nationalists (the so-called "red-brown coalition").

The election results forced changes in the government. Chernomyrdin, who had dissociated himself from the election campaign, was able to stay on as prime minister by playing the role of a technocrat with substantial appeal to the centrists. Yegor Gaidar, who had been brought back into the government briefly as a deputy prime minister from September 1993, resigned on January 16. Boris Fedorov resigned on January 20. Chernomyrdin called for new "non-monetary measures" to control inflation, and he defended Gerashchenko's stewardship of the central bank. The most prominent reformist left in the cabinet was A. Chubais, who continued in his original assignment of privatizing the state sector.

January 1994 to end of 1995

In the December 1993 elections, voters also approved a new constitution that gave substantial economic and political powers to the president.[10]

10. Under the new constitution there are two chambers. The lower house, the Duma, has 450 members elected via party lists and single candidate ridings. The upper house, called the Federation Council, has two members chosen from each of 89 regions, and members were originally elected alongside with the Duma. The president nominates the prime minister and the Duma must then approve the nomination by a majority vote. If the Duma rejects three nominees, then the president can dissolve the Duma and call new elections. Also, if the Duma passes a no-confidence motion in the government, then the president can ask for the resignation of the government, or instead ignore the motion. If the Duma passes a second no-confidence motion within three months of the first motion, the president must either change the government or dissolve the Duma and call new elections. Most laws must be passed by both the Duma and the Federation Council with a majority. If the president vetoes the legislation, then the Duma can overturn the veto with a two-thirds majority.

Thus, while the government faced a relatively hostile Parliament, the new constitution ensured that the president held the main power over the direction of economic policy.

The December 1993 elections did not prove decisive in redirecting economic reforms in any particular way. Instead, the subsequent period was characterized by gradual improvements but lack of serious reforms in many key areas.

Most of 1994 was wasted in terms of reform efforts. Not a single economic measure of any serious importance was implemented during this period. The government tried to stabilize the economy in early 1994, and the monthly inflation rate fell to 4 percent in August. However, stabilization was abandoned when the central bank and ministers caved in to pressures for agricultural credits and subsidies to northern territories in the summer and the fall. By December 1994, inflation was back to a monthly rate of 17 percent. The softened policy stance was foreseen in financial markets and led to a 27 percent depreciation of the ruble on October 11, 1994, as investors lost confidence in the government. This has been immortalized as "Black Tuesday," but it marks a positive step forward in the policy-making environment. Government and central bank officials now recognize that financial markets can and will abruptly penalize unsound credit policies.

The results in 1995 have been more positive. In January 1995 Chubais was appointed first deputy prime minister in charge of economic affairs, and he implemented a stabilization program. The initial results of this program are promising, but it is too early to judge its success or failure; much will depend on the results of upcoming parliamentary and presidential elections. The government avoided pressures to loosen policies in the autumn as they did in 1994, and by November 1995 the monthly inflation rate had fallen to 4.5 percent.

One of the more surprising results has been the gradual normalization and improvement of macroeconomic policy making and the parliamentary process. A new central bank law was passed by the Duma which gave substantial independence to the central bank chairman. The new president of the central bank, Sergei Dubinin, is pro-stabilization and was approved by a wide margin in the Parliament. In addition, for the first time since 1991 a budget has been passed prior to the start of the new fiscal year (1996).

6.3 Components of Economic Reforms

The former nomenklatura, the old political elite, and overly sympathetic observers have combined to criticize Russia's reforms as having too much shock and too little therapy. But such diagnoses ignore the realities of reform. In many areas reforms have been far too slow and very incomplete. To draw lessons from Russia's reforms, it is worthwhile to highlight major achievements and failures of the various components of economic reform.

Price Liberalization

This major step was made on January 2, 1992, but unfortunately price liberalization was stretched over too long a period. Price liberalization was simply a necessity in January 1992. In 1991 the government had begun a set of haphazard price reforms, first partially liberalizing producer prices in 1991 and then raising consumer prices to limit enterprise losses and shortages. A small private market for goods was permitted to flourish, and here prices rose well above official prices due to the exploding monetary overhang.[11] The 1991 price reforms merely reflected the turmoil and there was no clear plan or program. By the end of 1991 goods had almost completely disappeared from state shops, and the state price system had completely broken down.

On January 2, 1992, most prices were freed. Price controls were maintained for energy and transportation, and there were controls on some key consumer goods, including certain types of bread, milk, medicine, rent, and public utilities. Local governments also kept the right to control prices of basic foodstuffs and to limit markups in retail stores.

The Gaidar team had hoped that the reforms would lead to a rapid improvement in the availability of goods, but the situation improved over a much longer period of time than anticipated. For example, Goskomstat data showed that meat was available in only 27 percent of towns by December 1992, up from 14 percent in March 1992.

Lack of more rapid progress was due in part to continued controls; in part, to the poor nature of the national distribution system; in part, to the monopolies that some local entities continued to have over distribution. High inflation and low interest rates also encouraged enterprises and households to hoard goods. There is no doubt that price reforms were needed and that they helped, but more needed to be done to increase the supply of goods.

---

11. We can define the monetary overhang as the excess of money supply over money demand at official prices. There were two sources of the increasing monetary overhang. The first was the rapid growth of the money supply due to the budget deficit and loss of control over the issuance of ruble credits after the breakup of the USSR. The second was a sharp decline in the demand for rubles as expected inflation caused a flight to alternative assets. The latter was underestimated at the start of the reforms, and was the main reason why the government and the IMF expected far lower price increases than actually occurred in January 1992.

It is worthwhile to evaluate some of the arguments advanced at that time in favor of price controls. Some argued that because Russian industry was overly energy intensive, it needed a respite to restructure and reduce energy dependence. Although there may be some truth to this argument, it is only true for a subset of enterprises, and it is really a question of weighing the political and economic costs against the benefits of maintaining controls. The most intensive energy users are very often exporters (such as metallurgy). These exporters made substantial profits from trade liberalization, and energy price controls merely raised their profits. The less intensive users could adjust wages and product prices to compensate for the higher costs. On the budgetary side, the higher energy tax revenues from the liberalized prices would have reduced the budget deficit significantly.

Another argument for price controls was that price liberalization would paralyze industries due to endemic monopolies. But in fact, as a study by Brown, Ickes, and Ryterman (1994) has shown, Russian industry is no more monopolized than in the West. They found that only 43 out of 21,391 civilian manufacturing enterprises constituted monopolies at the national level, and enterprises with 35 percent of market share accounted for only 4 percent of all employment.

In retrospect most key participants agree it was a clear mistake to take three years to reach the present degree of price liberalization. There is a case to be made for maintaining controls on rents and utilities to households (as part of the social safety net), but the costs of not fully liberalizing other prices were a loss of tax revenues, corruption, and energies wasted on political infighting generated by the remaining price controls.

Trade Liberalization

The main part of trade liberalization occurred at the start of 1992. Most state orders were effectively abolished, thus fully liberalizing domestic trade. Thousands of private trading companies quickly appeared. There was, however, only partial liberalization of foreign trade.

The most important remaining restrictions on foreign trade were the export licenses and quotas established on energy and raw materials that make up to 50 percent of Russian exports. The export quotas and licenses served as a royalty system to claw back some of the large expected profits in the natural resource sectors. The initial plan was to auction the quotas so that the government could raise revenue for the budget. In 1992 these exports amounted to $22 billion (table 6.3). Approximately $10 billion of this amount was to be collected via export taxes and sales of quotas.

The idea was that by limiting the export of raw materials one could avoid a sudden collapse in domestic availability of these resources (or

Table 6.3
Foreign trade and balance of payments (CIS and non-CIS countries, $ bln)

	1991	1992	1993	1994	1995[a]
Exports	53.9	41.1	43.9	50.0	75.0
Energy and minerals	26.3	21.7	22.2	—	—
Imports	−45.1	−36.9	−27.1	−36.8	−51.0
Energy and minerals	1.3	1.0	0.9	—	—
Net services plus grants	−5.7	−5.5	−5.7	−8.7	−12.0
Current account balance	4.1	−1.3	11.1	4.1	12.0
Long- and short-term capital	0.4	−3.7	−13.0	−12.5	—
Errors and omissions	−1.9	−7.6	−12.7	1.5	—
Capital account	−1.5	−11.3	−25.7	−13.0	—
Overall balance	2.6	−12.6	−14.6	−7.5	—
Net international reserves (− = increase)	0.6	−1.3	−3.3	3.9	—
Arrears on debt service and deferrals	1.7	13.9	18.3	3.6	—

Source: *Russian Economic Trends*, various issues.
a. Projections based on data from first three quarters of 1995.

equivalently, a sudden rise to world prices) which could harm domestic industry, while at the same time raise revenues for the budget through the resource taxes and sales of export licenses. The truth is that it would have made more sense to subsidize industry directly. The procedures and rules of the quotas and licenses were wide open to corruption, causing federal revenues to be almost nil. To some extent, when exporters could not obtain a license they found ways to smuggle their goods through the porous borders with the other countries of the Commonwealth of Independent States (CIS).[12]

12. According to *Russian Economic Trends* (1995, vol. 2, no. 1, table 11), the revenues to the budget from foreign activity taxes were approximately $1.5 billion in 1992. Very rough calculations show how far this was from potential revenues under the announced regulations. The domestic price of oil in 1992 was roughly $30 per ton, and this compared to a price of $115 for Russian oil on world markets. Allowing for transport costs of $15 per ton, a competitive scheme should have netted the government the difference between the world price net of transport costs and the domestic price, or $70 per ton. Sixty-six million tons of

In the late 1980s there was still much discussion over how quickly the ruble could be made convertible. Analysts often made the mistake of likening Russia's situation to post-war Europe, and argued that Russia should follow Europe's example of gradual introduction of convertibility over a period of 10 to 20 years. This would have merely led to continued inefficient allocation of foreign exchange. The central bank and the government were in no position to choose who should receive foreign exchange, and exporting enterprises had too many means to avoid surrender. The result of a new official exchange rate different from the market rate would only have been evasion of surrender requirements.[13]

Convertibility on the current account came into practice in July 1992. This was preceded by a sharp devaluation of the ruble at the start of the reform, and pressure from the IMF forced through unification of the exchange rate in July 1992.

One of the most important and striking reforms during the period was in local commerce. Millions of Russian citizens went into the streets to trade just about everything. This explosion of trade occurred after Gaidar pushed through a decree in January which explicitly stated that enterprises and households were permitted to trade anything, at any price, and anywhere they chose. This decree broke the early resistance of the police and local governments to free domestic trade.

Budget and Monetary Policies

The lack of coherence in trade and price liberalization mirrors the failure of policies aimed at macroeconomic stabilization. In order to understand the failure to stabilize the economy and to conduct coherent reforms, we need to remember that few of the political elite supported such measures. At any time only a handful of people in the government were truly in favor of economic reform, and they rarely had the support of Prime Minister Chernomyrdin, President Yeltsin, or Parliament.

This problem was most readily seen with the budget. The Gaidar plan for 1992 called for an annual budget deficit of 1 percent of GDP. During the first quarter of 1992 the cash budget surplus turned out at 0.9 percent of GNP compared with a deficit of over 25 percent of GNP in 1991.

---

oil were exported to non-CIS countries in 1992, so this could have raised $4.6 billion. In addition, natural gas exports and other mineral exports, according to tax laws, should have raised substantially more than this amount. The $10 billion figure quoted in the paper is a rough estimate of potential revenues.

13. The practical importance of the official exchange rate was actually related to the pricing of imported goods distributed through government channels. This was particularly important for imports resulting from disbursements of official bilateral credits. Once these credits were reduced, and due to pressure from the IMF to unify the exchange rate, the political balance shifted in favor of unification.

Table 6.4
Government fiscal indicators and deficit financing (percent of GNP)

	1992	1993	1994	1995
General government [a]				
Revenues	33.1	25.7	27.3	—
Expenditures	37.2	35.3	37.3	—
Deficit	4.1	9.6	10.0	—
Federal deficit [b]	—	10.4	10.4	3.2
Sources of financing federal deficit				
Monetary	—	—	7.0	0.3
External finance	—	—	0.8	0.7
Bonds	—	—	2.0	2.1
Other non-monetary	—	—	0.6	0.0

Source: *Russian Economic Trends* (1995).
a. General government includes federal, local, and extra-budgetary funds, expenditures, and revenues.
b. The federal deficit refers to the federal budget only.

But then things fell apart. Revenues from foreign trade failed to materialize, (because of the corruption endemic to the export quota system), and President Yeltsin granted tax exemptions to regions and enterprises. One saving measure would have been to tax domestic energy and raise energy prices, but there was no political support for such measures at that time. Yeltsin fired the energy minister, Vladimir Lopukhin, in April 1992 precisely because he proposed such measures.[14]

The opposition to Gaidar's policies got stronger over time. By June, Yeltsin had re-shuffled the cabinet to include three industrialists, and the government effectively had given up on monetary and credit control. The governor of the central bank at that time, Georgy Mathyukin, while not a member of the Gaidar team, was increasingly being forced into their camp as the Parliament attacked him for raising refinance rates and rationing credits. Instead of supporting Mathyukin in his fight with the Parliament, the government ousted him. In retrospect, monetary policy was perhaps the weakest link in the stabilization program.

---

14. In his autobiography, Yeltsin writes, "There was a very concrete reason for Lopukhin's dismissal. Using him as a battering ram, Gaidar was putting pressure on me to release prices on energy resources simultaneously with other prices without any restrictions." (Yeltsin 1994, 167.)

Table 6.5
Monetary aggregates and the allocation of seigniorage

	1991	1992	1993	1994	1995H1
M2 money (rbs bln)[a]	1.0	7.1	36.7	104.7	156.8
Average monthly M2 increase (%)[b]	7.0	18.2	14.7	9.1	7.5
Velocity (GNP/M2) [a]	1.9	5.4	10.0	10.0	7.5
Seigniorage (percent GNP) [c, e] (via credit issue only) of which allocated to: [a]	—	32.7	13.3	9.8	1.3
Commercial banks	—	13.7	4.8	1.8	0.4
Government	—	10.5	5.9	7.9	0.9
Other FSU	—	8.5	2.6	0.1	0.0
Monthly nominal interest rates on central bank loans [d]	—	7.5	11.7	14.2	15.0
Inflation (CPI) [b]	8.3	31.2	20.5	10.0	10.7

Source: *Russian Economic Trends* and author's calculations.
a. Value in December.
b. Geometric average annual increase.
c. Arithmetic average of monthly values.
d. Monthly interest rate of the CBR at mid-year.
e. This is calculated as the monthly change in net credits issued by the CBR divided by monthly GNP and then averaged over the 12 months of each year. Note that in 1995 M2 money growth has largely been due to accumulation of foreign reserves at the central bank along with a rising money multiplier.

The July appointment of Viktor Gerashchenko as head of the central bank came just two weeks after Russia signed its first standby agreement with the IMF, and ironically it marked the start of a near-hyperinflationary period. Gerashchenko immediately responded to enterprise demands for credits. With interest rates controlled at low levels, the demands for credits were enormous. At the same time Gaidar made compromises with the industrialists and the fiscal budget was loosened, with large credits directed to agriculture, industry, and the northern territories. These became known as the "Gaidar credits," and Gaidar justified them as the only means to maintain the privatization program:

We were losing contact with all of the industrial structures. We could not even count any longer on unlimited support from the President ... it was evident that policy would have to change, leaving us with two options: either accept the change of economic policy ... or resign immediately.   (Gaidar and Pohl 1995, 37)

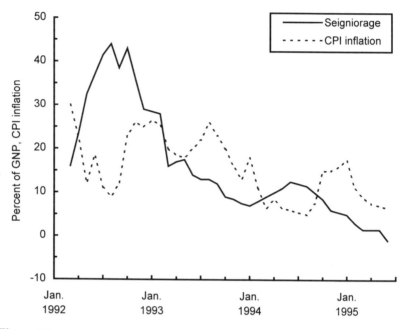

Figure 6.1
Seigniorage and CPI inflation (January 1992 to June 1995)

The other real problem for policy making at this time was the ruble. There was never a clear plan for dealing with the ruble, and so long as the Central Bank of Russia (CBR) honored the credits of other republics, they effectively had license to print money at Russia's expense. By June 1992 these credits already amounted to 8.5 percent of GNP in 1992 (see table 6.5) and were a major source of inflationary money.

Russia very much needed to take control of her domestic currency and to prohibit other countries from issuing rubles, but this required political decisiveness which no one was prepared to undertake. The issue was complicated by the IMF when, in a May 1992 meeting of CIS officials in Tashkent, they proposed and actively promoted an unworkable program to maintain a ruble zone throughout the CIS. This would have required voluntary and unverifiable constraints on credit issue at every central bank—this of course was impossible in the existing political situation.

The sheer size of credit issue in Russia reached proportions that were unheard of in other high-inflation countries, and this undoubtedly explains why it was so difficult to stop the process in those early months and years. In 1992, seigniorage to the central bank from credit issue equaled 32.7 percent of GNP (table 6.5) and was primarily directed to enterprises and other republics. These levels of seigniorage could only be supported while the payments system remained inflexible and enterprises did not conserve on money balances to avoid the inflation tax.

But over the next few years both these factors changed. As enterprises and households stopped saving in rubles and began holding spare cash balances in other currencies, the demand for rubles fell and inflation rose. In 1993 and 1994 while seigniorage fell, inflation remained high for precisely this reason (figure 6.1). With the relaxation of monetary and fiscal policy in the summer, the ruble–dollar exchange rate collapsed by 27 percent on October 11, 1994. This brought home once and for all the message that the days when the central bank could issue large credits without causing hyperinflation were over.

Tax Reform

One of the biggest failures of Russian economic reforms is in the area of tax collection and tax reform. Before 1991 the Soviet Union and Russia had no real tax collection system, and it had to be developed hastily in order to avoid financial collapse in 1991 and 1992. This is why so little thought was given to details and the overall efficiency of the system. Under the current rules there is too heavy a reliance on corporate taxes and little attention to individual taxes. The array of taxes on businesses have cumulated into excessively high marginal tax rates on corporate income.

It is already clear that the tax system needs a major overhaul. The government has planned to undertake major tax reform only in 1997. This delay will undoubtedly slow the development of private business. Listed below are several basic measures which need to be taken as part of any tax reform.

- abolishing the excessive wage tax;
- redefining the concepts of income, costs, and profits;
- phasing out double taxation and lowering value-added tax (VAT);
- increasing property taxes;
- phasing out export duties and many import tariffs; and
- introducing accelerated depreciation.

Privatization and Enterprise Reform

Privatization is hailed as a major success in the Russian reform program. The voucher program, designed and carried through by Anatoli Chubais, has been a major success when measured by the number of enterprises that have ultimately been privatized. The speed and scale of privatization in Russia has far outpaced every other formerly socialist country: as of April 1995, three-quarters of Russian industry was privately owned.[15]

The program has had great impact on the political debate within Russia. By divesting assets from the state, the government has reduced the overall ability of line ministries to interfere in the activities of enterprises. Further, by transferring these assets to private individuals, the program has created a large number of shareholders with a vested interest in maintaining enterprise autonomy and ensuring rapid development of property rights. These benefits are most clearly seen in the December 1995 election campaign: while all the parties have criticized the details of the program, not even the communists are calling for a serious reversal.

The economic impact of voucher privatization is less clear. Early empirical evidence based on survey data by Earle, Estrin, and Leshchenko (1995) shows that privatized companies do not perform or behave differently from state-owned enterprises. This is a common finding in other Eastern European countries also, and it appears that only the de novo private sector really acts and operates as we would expect market-based private enterprise to operate. Privatization may still promote the de novo sector, since it permits state enterprises to divest assets legally, but the direct impact on state enterprises does not appear large, at least in these initial years.

The weak performance of these privatized enterprises is less surprising when we examine ownership structure. The voucher privatization program offered two main alternatives to enterprises. The workers and managers could maintain 51 percent control of the enterprise by purchasing shares at inflation-eroded book value prices, or they could receive 25 percent of shares free and then be able to purchase another 10 percent of shares at a discounted price.[16] The remaining shares were to be held by the state property fund and sold in auctions for vouchers.

Boycko, Shleifer, and Vishny (1995) point out that the major reason this set of options was chosen was political. Enterprise managers and workers already had a de facto claim on enterprises because they controlled daily operations, and through strikes and non-cooperation they could have jeopardized any program that threatened their control. The government's options were either to wait until it became strong enough to fight off these interests (if it ever did) or to move ahead with a program to create clear ownership rights and control. Survey evidence

---

15. As of April 1995, 73.7 percent of industrial enterprises have been privatized and these accounted for 84.6 percent of total industry output.
16. There was a third option that was not used. See Boycko, Shleifer, and Vishny (1995) for a discussion.

reported in Earle, Estrin, and Leschenko (1995) suggests that workers or managers are the dominant owners of 55 percent of privatized state enterprises, while the state remains the dominant owner in 34 percent, and outside owners are dominant in only 11 percent.[17]

In theory, insider control should not be so serious a problem. Once property rights are defined, enterprise managers and workers can always sell their shares on open markets or to bidders that wish to gain control of an enterprise in order to restructure it. For these equity markets to operate, however, there must be clear rules and procedures.

There are several incentives operating today that suggest insider owners may still wait before they restructure enterprises or divest assets. When there are outstanding shares held by the state, or by workers with weak control rights, it is only normal that a director would want to take actions to limit the market value of these shares so that management or friendly entities can buy up the remaining outstanding shares at low prices.

Thus a serious problem arises because the incentives of enterprise owners clash with the government's desire to create well-functioning property rights. There are many examples of enterprises restricting access to shareholder registrars, limiting published information on their firms, and hiding or underestimating profits. The legislation guiding shareholder rights is only now being established by the Duma, but it will still take several years for these measures to be effectively enforced. In the meantime, a handful of enterprises, such as the oil producer LUKoil and the large utility company Mosenergo, are creating their own security registrars operated by independent authorities. These companies choose this approach because they want to raise money in equity markets. However, for the vast bulk of firms that could not raise external financing, or for those firms whose managers and workers still hope to buy up shares at low prices, there are few incentives to create effective ownership rights.

The impact of these issues on the prices of energy stocks can be seen in table 6.6. Share prices have collapsed after initial euphoric rises in early 1994. Today Russian shares sell at the lowest price/earnings ratios found in any nation in the world. The market value of enterprises such as Mosenergo, the main electricity generator for Moscow, today equals roughly 18 months' earnings, i.e., the value of P/E is 1.5. This compares with a typical price of ten times earnings for electricity generators in Eastern Europe, and fifteen times earnings in the United States. The market values of oil and gas producers, as shown in table 6.6, are similarly

---

17. These estimates are based on results from their random sample of 325 privatized enterprises.

low when measured by market capitalization relative to known reserves, and by market capitalization relative to production.[18]

Table 6.6 shows that at current market prices the top ten oil producers in Russia are worth only 0.6 percent of GNP, but if property markets develop and risk is reduced then they could be expected (based on conservative comparisons with Western standards) to rise closer to 15 percent of GNP. Political uncertainty and vague shareholder rights are believed to be the two most important concerns that keep share prices low.

The size of the wealth distribution underlying the privatization program is unprecedented anywhere in the world. Enterprise profits of former state enterprises in the national accounts are roughly 20 percent of GNP, [19] so at a P/E ratio of 1.5, these assets are worth 30 percent of GNP ($90 billion). But if P/E ratios rise to more reasonable levels, e.g., as in Poland, where they are around 10, then the assets would be valued at 200 percent of GNP ($600 billion).

The current low valuation of assets means that part of this redistribution is still to come—i.e., once asset prices rise. But low equity prices pose a serious problem for the government in its next stage of the privatization program. In most cases, authorities do not even try to enhance the value of companies by inviting independent organizers of auctions and allowing foreigners to participate. The goal now is to raise revenue for the budget by selling remaining shares in state enterprises for cash. With the top ten oil companies valued at only 0.6 percent of GNP, government leaders can only expect modest revenues and they are certain to be criticized for selling assets at too low a price.

There has been much less progress in private land ownership. Boris Yeltsin first advocated private land ownership five years ago, and various decrees on the issue have been published since then, but the problem is still unresolved. Indeed the Duma recently adopted a land code that in effect precludes privatization of land. The opposition to land

---

18. There are obvious difficulties with measurement of profits due to inflation accounting, and oil reserves in the West and Russia are measured differently. But whether using P/E ratios or measures of asset valuation based on real assets, such as cost per telephone line in the telecommunications sector or cost per megawatt of power generation capacity, all calculations suggest the prices of assets in Russia today are extremely low. The total market capitalization of the Russian market is estimated at only US$ 20–25 billion; this demonstrates the degree of distortion.

19. This is a very rough estimate based on the Goskomstat official statistics showing total profits of enterprises. The actual figure may be higher due to underreporting and unrecorded enterprises. The official data on wages, profits, indirect taxes, subsidies, etc. do not come close to adding up to total GNP. See *Russian Economic Trends* for a discussion of these issues.

Table 6.6
Market values of Russian oil producers

	Daily production (M bbl)	Reserves (M bbl)	MCap at Feb. 1995 stock market value (US$ billion)	MCap based on typical Western MCap/production ratios (US$ billion)
Surgutneftgaz	250	10,880	0.6	10.0
Yuganskneftgaz	209	11,680	0.4	8.4
LUKoil-Kogalymneftgaz	185	7,860	0.1	7.4
Noyabskneftgaz	165	4,650	0.2	6.6
LUKoil-Langepasneftegaz	108	4,530	0.1	4.3
Megionneftgaz	96	2,100	0.1	3.8
Tomskneft	82	3,500	0.1	3.3
Permneft	65	n.a.	0.1	2.6
Purneftgaz	60	6,090	0.2	2.4
Orenburgneft	54	2,164	0.1	2.2
Total	1,274	53,454	2.0	50.9
(Total, as % GNP)	—	—	0.6	15.5

Source: *Russian Economic Trends* and Brunswick Brokerage.
Note: A typical western ratio of market capitalization in million dollars per thousands daily production is 39. An alternative would be to calculate market value based on known reserves. This would lead to even higher estimated values for Russian producers (approximately three times the reported value in the fourth column of this table).

reform comes from the groups that are most threatened by it—namely, the leaders and managers of the collective farms who are represented by the left-wing Agrarian Party. They continue to do everything in their power to limit disintegration of collectivist agriculture.

In this environment reform and change in the agricultural sector has proceeded at a snail's pace. State and collective farms continue to operate in the same inefficient manner and are supported through import tariffs and regular subsidies. The first wave of private farmers has met so many difficulties, in part due to non-cooperation from the state sector, that the number of private farms has stopped growing. With the growing political power of the leaders and managers of collective farms in the form of the Agrarian and Communist Parties, it is possible that agriculture will continue to stagnate and be sheltered for years to come.

Legislative Process

The reforms in Russia began to a large extent with destruction of political and legal process. This left many people with the erroneous view that Russia lacked the legal infrastructure needed to support reforms; hence they argued that this was a major handicap to implementing reform measures.

But in fact Russia's problem was in many ways the opposite. There were enormous numbers of reform-oriented laws adopted between 1990 and 1995, but at the same time there was widespread disregard for the law at every level of decision making. Often the groups passing laws and signing decrees knew they were in conflict with other legislation, and they used the resulting confusion to frustrate attempts by others to introduce (or limit) reforms. The legal process became another weapon in the battle between the various groups, and each group paid little regard to the costs and final outcome. One major conclusion from this is that we cannot expect reforms to flourish until authorities at all levels develop greater respect for law and legal process.

The second problem is inherited from the Soviet era, namely, the practice of purposely writing vague laws in order to allow discretion when implementing governmental and ministerial instructions. The legal process would be better served if direct action laws were established so as to make clear rules of the game.

The third major problem with the legal system is the appalling lack of punishment for noncompliance with laws. The Russian system requires that all sanctions be included in the criminal code, and this means that many specific laws often cannot be enforced.

Foreign Assistance, External Debt, and Reserves

Gorbachev handed over a bankrupt state to Yeltsin. From 1986 to 1991 the Gorbachev regime tried to hold the state together by financing consumption through foreign loans, sales of gold, and foreign reserves. By August 1991 foreign reserves had been almost completely depleted; Vnesheconomnank, the main bank responsible for foreign transactions in the former USSR, was bankrupt; and external debt had grown to $67 billion.

The debate over foreign assistance to Russia began early and has changed significantly since the start of reforms. There is no doubt that foreign assistance could have benefited the reform efforts early on. For example, if small amounts of assistance were directed to the budget, and ideally if this assistance was in the form of grants rather than credit, then it might have strengthened the hands of the reformers to fight off pressures from the groups fighting against reform. But this could only have played a small role in the political battle, and it would not have dealt with many of the other problems plaguing the Gaidar team, such as the rapid alienation of the Parliament. These benefits must be contrasted with the Russian reality that very often foreign assistance has slowed reforms—because it allowed Gorbachev, and sometimes Yeltsin, to temporarily postpone making needed policy changes.

On balance, the outcome of the early debate over foreign assistance was probably harmful rather than helpful to reform. Gorbachev, Yeltsin, Yavlinsky, and Gaidar all helped encourage public expectations that foreign assistance could solve Russia's economic problems. They played this card continually and helped create an expectation that large-scale Western assistance was just around the corner. The pinnacle was reached when the G-7 announced a $24 billion package to support Russia in April 1992. This came at a critical moment prior to a meeting of the Congress of People's Deputies, which was threatening to fire the government. In his autobiography, Yeltsin remarks that in April "The mood in the government was one of concern, if not depression. The only reassuring note was the promise of the Group of Seven to rapidly provide major financial aid." [20] But apart from this moment, the history of foreign aid to Russia is riddled with mismanagement on both sides and enormous false hopes.

On the Russian government side, the real tragedy was that foreign assistance continued to be misused and wasted under the new regime just as it was in the past. In 1992 the major part of assistance came in the form of $12.5 billion of bilateral credits from donor countries. A large part of these credits financed equipment and machinery which was shipped directly to the purchasing enterprises. But the government took on the bill for these goods, and while in theory enterprises were required to pay the government in return, in practice either most of the funds simply disappeared or the ruble payments were only a tiny fraction of the true cost of the goods.

Western governments and international agencies also played a negative role. Instead of meeting with the new Gaidar government to work out serious forms of assistance, the first step the West took after Gaidar was appointed was to demand that Russia be prepared to repay eventually all Soviet debt under the "joint and several" agreement with

---

20. Yeltsin (1994, 165).

other FSU countries. After this meeting many promises of assistance were made, and symbolic gestures such as airlifting EU beef and food into Russia were begun, but these efforts only had a minor impact on economic change, and they did little but raise false expectations among the population and politicians.

Today assistance from the IMF does play an important role in the stabilization program. The IMF program has conditionality on monthly monetary and budget targets, and this no doubt plays a key role in maintaining coordination between fiscal and monetary policies. But such assistance also means that Russia's public external debts continue to increase (the IMF promised $6 billion in 1995), and it relieves pressure on the government to cut wasteful expenditures. It would be even better if the government and the Central Bank of Russia took on the discipline of self-reliance as part of the stabilization program.

There is one clear area where foreign assistance is essential. This is to reschedule external debt obligations which can no longer be rolled over in private markets. Many of the debts taken on by the Gorbachev regime were short-term loans which are now due for repayment. These payments are due from the federal budget, but they must be rescheduled over a sufficiently long term in order to be repaid. This is one area where Western assistance could have been helpful early on, but both the London Club and Paris Club were reluctant to make agreements.

Corruption

One of the most compelling arguments in favor of clear, rapid, and principled reform measures is the need to limit corruption. There is no doubt that the gradual and unclear pace of Russia's reforms contributed to, and were often motivated by, corruption at the highest levels. The step-by-step elimination of trade restrictions, gradual removal of price controls, large-scale subsidies issued by the central bank, unclear laws and enforcement procedures, and general lack of due process have been important sources and causes of the growth of corruption at every level of government.

There are few studies or reports that empirically measure these problems. In an interesting econometric study of the allocation of credit by the Moscow local government, Treisman (1995) found that a variable capturing whether an enterprise director had "connections with city officials" was the only variable that robustly explained who got credits. Variables that referred to official explanations for soft credits, such as whether an enterprise provided foods needed for Moscow city, had no explanatory power. Handelman (1994) provides a detailed discussion of profits gained from regional banks' issues of fraudulent promissory notes which probably required duplicity on the part of central bank officials.

Undoubtedly the evolution of the rents to be gained from corruption will be an important factor determining the future pace of reform in Russia. We have identified four broad areas where rent-seeking and corruption gave prime incentives to distort macroeconomic policies and legal change in 1992. These were the large revenues from seigniorage, revenues from controls on exports of natural resources, the potential gains from property redistribution, and the distribution of bilateral credits.

There is good reason to believe that the scope for rent-seeking and asset-grabbing has now been sharply reduced. Enterprise shares and privatization provide the last broad area where large gains can still be made. One reason for the success of the current stabilization program is that potential revenues from seigniorage are now much lower, given the new financial instruments produced by the now more developed financial system (see figure 6.1). Likewise, the supply of bilateral credits has been cut, and the government has instituted a process where the budget prices foreign exchange at market rates. The (real) appreciation of the ruble has reduced the profitability of natural resource exports, and the new owners are demanding price liberalization, so there are fewer rents in this sector to be appropriated.

6.4 Outcomes and Lessons from the Reforms

It is very difficult to give recommendations to other countries based on the specific Russian reform experience; nonetheless, there are several important points.

The first absolutely clear point is that the Russian people and economy have responded to the introduction of market reforms in exactly the way that economic theory predicted. Under Soviet rule the economy was highly industrialized, with a strong military orientation, and it lacked sufficient services and consumer products. While there has been a sharp decline in industrial production, we do see rapid growth in some areas of services and trade that reflects restructuring. The sectors which are declining most quickly, such as textiles and light industry, are those that face the greatest world competition and suffer from the lowest productivity. Recent indicators show the industrial decline has stopped, and growth will probably resume in 1996 or 1997 (table 6.1).

Early fears that unemployment would explode and labor markets would not function have also been proven wrong. There is an active labor market in Russia, with levels of employee turnover (both hirings and firings) that match the most active labor markets in the West (Layard and Richter 1994). While the older generation has had more difficulty adjusting than the younger generation, the early view by some commentators that workers were unreformable was obviously unfounded.

The second lesson is that the debate over shock therapy versus gradualism and the discussion of optimal sequencing of reforms is simply uninteresting in the Russian case. There are economic arguments in favor of both rapid reform and gradual reform (see Blanchard, forthcoming) but these do not lead to clear conclusions. In Russia the choice was more straightforward and political.

Russian reforms began because Gorbachev launched the country into political reforms that were deeply inconsistent with the old economic system. The breakup of the Soviet Union and collapse of the planned system gave Yeltsin and Gaidar the first real chance to carry out economic reform. But within months of starting the reforms, the opponents to change were able to organize and rebel through the Congress of People's Deputies.

After those first few months, reforms have proceeded haltingly and at far too slow a pace. In 1992 there were enormous resources to be divided amongst the winners. These included rents from natural resource exports amounting to $25 billion per year, monetary seigniorage equal to 32.7 percent of GNP for a period of time, bilateral credits of $12.5 billion, and some $600 billion of property to be distributed. It is no wonder that the political system became corrupted and deadlocked and macroeconomic policies took second place.

It may have been possible to avoid some of this disruption through more transparent rules and policy making. In retrospect it was clearly a mistake to delay introducing financial stabilization, full price and trade liberalization, full currency convertibility, and a national currency during that brief period in late 1991 when reforms were most possible. Many of these measures could have reduced the amount of resources "up for grabs" by limiting the future debate over the scope of further reform.

The irony of Russian reforms is that they began because political change outpaced economic change, but having begun, political reform soon lagged behind economic change. The Gaidar team never tried to build a working relationship with the Supreme Soviet or Congress of People's Deputies, and hence from the start the reformers were politically isolated and dependent on Yeltsin. Yeltsin could and probably should have called for greater political reform right from the start. If the Constitution had been revised in autumn 1991 and spring 1992, and if elections for a new Parliament were called early on, then it might have been possible to build greater consensus at the start of the program. This would have given the government a longer respite and a clear mandate to complete the reform process.

7 Transition to a Market Economy in Viet Nam

James Riedel and
Bruce Comer

7.1 Introduction

Viet Nam is in transition to a market economy, but this transition is just a means to a greater end, which is to make the economy prosperous and dynamic. The leadership of Viet Nam did not decide to "go market" because of any kind of ideological conversion from Marxism-Leninism to capitalism; instead, it discovered the hard way that the alternative to a market economy does not work. In addition, there was ample evidence from other countries in the region, in particular from Viet Nam's ideological soul-mate, China, that the market system can work. The initiation of a far-reaching reform program in 1986, under the banner *doi moi* (renovation), was a bold political move, but an obvious economic one.

The advantages of a market economy were not oversold in Viet Nam. On the contrary, the success of the *doi moi* program has undoubtedly exceeded anything imagined by those who coined the slogan. When the program was initiated, the economy was in decline, inflation was soaring, and many were fleeing the country by whatever means possible. Less than a decade later, Viet Nam had recorded five consecutive years of GDP growth at an average annual rate of 8 percent, had brought down inflation from triple to single digits, and had attracted foreign capital from both public and private sources.

How did Viet Nam do it? Why was it apparently so much more successful than most other countries in transition to a market economy? Are Viet Nam's past successes sustainable over the long run? If not, what

This paper was written in collaboration with Dr. Le Dang Doanh and Dr. Nguyen Minh Tu of the Central Institute for Economic Management in Hanoi and Mr. Tran Du Lich of the Institute for Economic Research in Ho Chi Minh City. We are indebted to Dr. Roger Leeds, Dr. Morris Morkre, and Professor Wing Thye Woo for helpful comments and suggestions. We are grateful to The Asia Foundation, in particular Mr. Stephen Parker and Mr. Gavin Tritt, for encouragement and support throughout the project.

are the missing ingredients of a successful long-run growth strategy? Viet Nam has created a market economy, but is it an efficient, dynamic one?

7.2 Socialist Transformation: 1975 to 1986

Economic Reunification: 1975 to 1980

With the political reunification of Viet Nam in 1975 came the question of how rapidly the economies of North and South should be reunified. The decision to proceed as rapidly as possible was reached at the Fourth Congress of the Communist Party of Viet Nam, in December 1976. The vehicle for economic reunification was to be the Second Five-Year Plan (1976–1980), the goals of which had been laid down since the Third Party Congress in the 1960s and had been aimed mainly at achieving a socialist transformation of Vietnamese society (Duiker 1989, 27). As in other socialist countries, this meant public ownership of the means of production, which took the form of state ownership of industry, collectivization of the agricultural and handicraft sectors, and a state monopoly on foreign trade. The central plan was to be the principal device for allocating inputs and outputs, with prices fixed and regulated. The plan was to be used mainly for accounting purposes.

Economic reunification of the two regions of Viet Nam proved difficult. Strenuous efforts in 1976 and 1977 to collectivize agriculture in the South were largely unsuccessful, mainly because of the resistance of farmers (Nguyen and Bandara 1993, 6). Consequently, during the Second Five-Year Plan (1976–1980), agricultural output grew only 1.9 percent per year, well below the population growth rate of 2.3 percent and far behind the planned target growth rate for agriculture of 8–10 percent per year.

Nationalization of industry and commerce in the South proved no more successful. By the end of 1977, there were still about 400 private factories and nearly 15,000 small businesses and handicraft shops under private ownership in the Saigon area (Duiker 1989, 44). Party leaders, apparently convinced that the failure to collectivize the countryside was due in part to failure to nationalize industry and commerce, launched in early 1978 a massive effort to eradicate private industry and commerce in the South. Within days of a decree prohibiting "bourgeois elements" from engaging in commerce, more than 30,000 private businesses closed their doors (Duiker 1989, 48). Not surprisingly, these measures had a disastrous impact on industrial output and overall economic activity. Thus, in spite of the Second Five-Year Plan's emphasis on industrialization, industrial output over the plan period hardly grew at all (table 7.1).

Table 7.1
Growth rates by sector during the Second Five-Year Plan (1976–80)

	Target growth rate (%)	Actual growth rate (%)
National income	13–14	0.4
Agriculture	8–10	1.9
Industry	16–18	0.6

Source: Doanh (1994, 3).

The disastrous effects of attempting to collectivize agriculture and nationalize industry and commerce were further compounded by the failure of promised foreign assistance from Western countries and China to materialize, following Viet Nam's invasion of Cambodia in 1978. Thus, just five years after the communists' stunning victory and political reunification of the country, the socialist economy of Viet Nam was at the brink of disaster, with real per capita income falling from an already intolerably low level.

Repairing Socialism: 1980 to 1985

With the approach of the Sixth Plenum of the Fourth Party Congress, in September 1979, it was apparent that something had to be done to repair the economy. This gave the upper hand to those favoring economic reform. The goal of complete socialist transformation of the economy was retained, but a more gradual approach to it was adopted. In addition to slowing the rate of socialist transformation, the Sixth Plenum adopted two market-oriented reforms, although because of an apparent struggle between the "reformers" and the "hardliners," the implementation of these reforms was delayed until January 1981 (Nguyen and Bandara 1993, 10).

The first of the two major reforms was the initiation of a "contract" system in agriculture, which set quotas for household units rather than for entire cooperatives and allowed households to retain and trade any output in excess of their quota. In effect, the cooperatives were reduced to a subsidiary role of allocating land, supplying inputs, and providing technical assistance (Nguyen and Bandara 1993, 8). As table 7.2 shows, the response to this reform was a remarkable acceleration in agricultural output, albeit a short-lived one, as quotas were successively raised in succeeding years.

Table 7.2
Growth and inflation rates (1980–86)

	1980	1981	1982	1983	1984	1985	1986
Real GDP growth (%)	−3.7	5.1	8.2	7.1	8.4	5.6	3.4
Agricultural growth (%)	6.8	5.8	3.2	8.1	8.0	4.2	1.5
Industrial growth (%)	−9.6	12.5	13.9	6.7	6.7	13.2	4.6
Inflation rate (%)	125.1	169.5	195.5	149.5	164.9	191.6	487.3

Sources: Nguyen and Bandara (1993, 9, 14) and World Bank (1994b, 128).

The second major reform was directed at industry and became known as the "three-plan system." Under this system, state-owned enterprises were subject to three plans. Under Plan One, the enterprises were provided with the inputs at subsidized prices and in turn were required to supply set quantities of goods to the state. Under Plan Two, the enterprises could produce beyond the amount specified in Plan One and use revenues to purchase additional inputs. Plan Three gave enterprises the right to engage in sideline activities more or less on a free market basis, which became known as the "fence-breaking" (*xe rao*) movement. In industry, also, the introduction of even a limited amount of economic freedom had a tremendous effect, with industrial growth rising from an average of 0.6 percent in the Second Five-Year Plan to about 7 percent in the Third Five-Year Plan.

In spite of the positive responses to economic liberalization in industry and agriculture, the influence of the "hardliners" in the Communist Party was restored by the mid-1980s, intensifying the pressure to force collectivization of agriculture in the South. What undermined the reformers more than anything else was the emergence, in the early 1980s, of severe macroeconomic imbalances, reflected in high and rising inflation. Inflation undermined the reform movement not only because it was a symptom of the failure of the reforms, but also because it reduced the real wages of civil servants, creating dissatisfaction in their ranks (Haughton 1994, 7).

The source of rising inflation in the early 1980s was the budget deficits of state-owned enterprises which, under the central planning system, were automatically financed by central bank credits. It is important to note that while financial deficits were inherent in the command economy system, the piecemeal market-oriented reforms only served to exacerbate the financial problems of state-owned enterprises. The diversion of resources into sideline ("fence-breaking") activities, while no doubt encouraging firms to respond to market signals they would otherwise have ignored, increased the operating deficits of state enterprises under Plan One and allowed them to borrow more from the central bank than they would have otherwise. Thus, by 1986, after five years of piecemeal economic reform, combined with a more gradual approach to socialist transformation, Viet Nam again found itself facing an economic crisis.

7.3 Embracing the Market

A Gradual Beginning: 1986 to 1988

In 1986, as the Sixth Party Congress was preparing to meet, the authorities in Viet Nam faced two realities: (1) the all-out approach to socialist transformation of the economy did not work; and (2) the gradual approach, tempered with market-like reforms, was also seriously flawed. The decision taken in December 1986 to change course and transform Viet Nam into a market economy, albeit one with a "socialist orientation," was a bold political step but an obvious economic one, especially in light of the successes of neighboring market economies, in particular in China.

The slogan for the economic reform program adopted by the Sixth Congress was *doi moi* (renovation), which suggests anything but a full-scale conversion from socialism to capitalism. It suggests instead a cautious acceptance of the market as a means for achieving growth and, thereby, preserving and strengthening the party's political and economic control. Thus, the goal was to transform the country gradually into a "socialist market economy" through step-by-step reforms.

In agriculture, the reforms went beyond the contract system to confirm the household as the basic production unit and to further limit the role of cooperatives. Farmers were no longer required to sell contracted amounts of output to the state, but instead could sell off their product in the market after paying taxes and commissions (Nguyen and Bandara 1993, 12). In addition, in 1988, households were given land tenure for at least 15 years, and land was made transferable under certain circumstances. Thus, for all intents and purposes, the dominant sector of the Vietnamese economy was effectively privatized.

The socialist orientation of the market economy that Viet Nam was trying to create required that industry would remain state-owned; thus,

Table 7.3
Growth rates by sector (1986–88)

	1986	1987	1988
GDP (%)	3.4	4.0	5.2
Agriculture (%)	1.5	–3.5	5.9
Industry (%)	4.6	11.4	3.9
Services (%)	—	5.6	8.9

Source: Nguyen and Bandara (1993, 14).

measures to reduce the direct control of the central and provincial governments over the state-owned enterprises were not immediately forthcoming. Private economic activity did, however, blossom in the informal commercial sector immediately after *doi moi*, as doors of restaurants and shops opened almost as fast as they had closed during the purge of the private sector in 1978.

Another early and important step in the *doi moi* program was the elimination of the state monopoly of foreign trade in 1988, allowing the establishment of Foreign Trade Organizations (FTOs) and permitting some firms to engage directly in international trade outside the FTOs. Following the Law on Export and Import Duties on Commercial Goods, promulgated in December 1987, most quotas were eliminated and replaced by import duties, with rates initially ranging from 5 to 50 percent (UNDP/World Bank 1994b, 48). In addition to freeing up international trade, another early step was a new law permitting and even encouraging foreign direct investment, by providing tax holidays, guaranteeing against expropriation, and allowing full repatriation of profits.

The outcome of Viet Nam's gradual approach to transition to a market economy in the second half of the 1980s interestingly parallels very closely the outcome of its gradual approach to transition to a socialist economy in the first half of the decade. As table 7.3 indicates, substantial increases in growth rates were recorded in the service sector and in the industrial sector. Poor harvests resulted from bad weather in 1987, but agricultural output rebounded in 1988. However, the generally strong growth performance in 1987 and 1988 was, as in the early 1980s, accompanied by severe macroeconomic imbalances, reflected in high and rising inflation and a mounting balance-of-payments crisis.

As in the earlier period, the source of the macroeconomic imbalance was public sector deficits, which as before were financed by borrowing from the central bank and, until 1990, from the Soviet Union (table 7.4).

Table 7.4
Macroeconomic indicators from 1986 to 1988 (percentages)

	1986	1987	1988
Government budget/GDP (%)			
Revenue	13.2	12.2	10.4
Current expenditure	13.4	12.7	13.6
Government saving	−0.2	−0.5	−3.2
Capital expenditure	5.6	3.9	3.8
Overall deficit	−5.8	−4.4	−7.0
Foreign loans	2.2	1.4	2.3
Central bank credit	3.6	2.9	2.9
Domestic credit growth rate (%)	—	324.6	394.9
Inflation rate (%)	487.3	301.3	393.8
Official exchange rate (dong/US$)	18	225	900
Parallel rate (dong/US$)	425	1,270	5,000

Source: Riedel (1993).

Having retained the planning apparatus and dual (official vs. market) price system in industry, macroeconomic imbalances under the *doi moi* program were inevitable. Furthermore, the longer the imbalances persisted, the more difficult they became, as inflation undermined the demand for real money balances, which in turn increased the inflationary effect of any given expansion of central bank credit.

A second vicious circle propelling the country toward a macroeconomic crisis operated through the effect of inflation on the real exchange rate, the outcome of which was a serious overvaluation of the dong and a consequent deterioration of international competitiveness. An indication of the extent of currency overvaluation is given in table 7.4, which compares the official and parallel (or black market) exchange rates.

Full Speed Ahead: 1989 to 1991

In early 1989, Viet Nam faced a macroeconomic crisis not unlike the one it encountered in 1986, with inflation running at an annual rate of about 400 percent. In addition, Viet Nam's current account deficit, which had risen to about 10 percent of GDP, was largely financed by aid from the Soviet Union, aid which Vietnamese authorities were well aware would no longer be forthcoming. Under the pressure of an imminent crisis, the authorities boldly decided to accelerate the process of transition to a market economy with a combination of structural reforms and stabilization measures.

The principal structural reform, adopted in early 1989, was the liberalization of prices and the elimination of the system of state procurement. One cannot overstate the importance of these measures. The dual pricing system, by forcing producers to sell to the state at artificially low prices, and then financing their resulting losses through government subsidies financed by the borrowing from the central bank, destroyed efficiency and stability simultaneously. The problem was especially severe in the case of rice, for which the official price in 1988 (50 dong/kg) was only one-ninth of the free market price (450 dong/kg). With the rise in the official price of rice to the market level, rice production in 1989 increased 12 percent over the 1988 level. In one year, following price liberalization, Viet Nam was transformed from a rice importer to the world's third largest rice exporter. As shown in figure 7.1, paddy production since 1989 has been on average about 25 percent higher than in the previous period, albeit with some variations from year to year due to the vagaries of weather. It is, however, unlikely that Viet Nam can expect further increases in paddy yield without substantial investments in irrigation and chemical fertilizers.

The stabilization program that Viet Nam adopted in 1989 was pure IMF orthodoxy, albeit without the IMF behind it. As it turned out, orthodox stabilization worked nowhere more successfully than in the unorthodox economy of Viet Nam. The two key components of the 1989 program were (1) raising interest rates and (2) devaluing and unifying the exchange rate. These measures, together with the legalization of gold trading, induced a strong portfolio adjustment by households in favor of dong assets and away from dollars and gold, which at the time were circulating widely in Viet Nam (Dollar 1993, 212). The effect of these measures was to bring inflation to a virtual halt in mid-1989.

The growth of central bank credit was also reduced, but as table 7.5 shows, it remained high at 233 percent for the year (1989). However, since credit growth in 1989 accommodated a shift in demand for real money balances, it allowed a significantly lower level of inflation (74 percent for the year). The portfolio shift was, of course, a once-and-for-all adjustment, and by 1990 a closer relationship between credit growth and inflation was observed. In 1991, there was serious backsliding on credit growth and inflation, but since then the inflation rate has been steadily reduced, an achievement that is owed mainly to fiscal restraint, which is the foundation of a sound monetary policy.

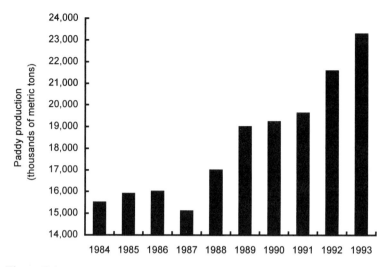

Figure 7.1
Rice paddy production in 1984–93. Source: World Bank (1994b, 130).

Table 7.5
Monetary indicators from 1988 to 1994 (percentages)

	1988	1989	1990	1991	1992	1993	1994
Growth of liquidity (M2)	443.3	237.8	32.4	78.8	3.7	8.9	27.8
Share in total liquidity							
Currency	40.0	27.4	32.9	31.6	39.0	44.0	45.2
Dong deposits	50.7	48.1	34.7	27.2	41.5	33.0	34.9
Foreign currency deposits	9.3	24.7	32.4	41.1	30.0	23.0	19.8
Share in domestic credit							
Government	25.4	38.7	40.5	28.0	11.1	14.5	12.6
Non-financial SOEs	64.5	53.7	53.3	64.6	72.6	57.1	54.9
Other	10.1	7.6	6.2	7.4	16.3	38.4	32.6
Inflation rate	308.2	74.3	36.4	82.7	37.7	8.3	9.3

Source: World Bank (1994b, 1995b).

Table 7.6
Fiscal policy indicators from 1988 to 1994 (percentages of GDP)

	1988	1989	1990	1991	1992	1993	1994
Revenue	11.3	13.8	14.7	13.5	19.0	22.3	24.7
Current expenditure	14.0	15.4	14.7	11.4	14.0	18.8	18.3
Government saving	-2.7	-1.6	0.0	-2.1	5.0	-3.5	-7.4
Capital expenditure	4.4	5.8	5.1	2.8	5.8	7.0	6.9
Primary balance	-7.1	-7.2	-5.1	-1.7	-0.8	-3.5	-0.3
Interest payments	0.1	0.3	0.7	0.8	0.9	1.3	1.3
Overall deficit	-7.2	-7.5	-5.8	-1.5	-1.7	-4.8	-1.8
Domestic borrowing	4.8	6.0	2.8	0.5	-0.7	3.4	0.4
Foreign borrowing	2.4	1.5	3.0	1.0	2.4	1.4	1.4

Source: World Bank (1994b, 1995b).

Since public sector deficits were the cause of the money growth that fueled inflation, the only way to stabilize the economy was to reduce the government deficit. This became all the more imperative since the only non-inflationary source of deficit finance, Soviet aid, was dwindling fast. Raising tax revenue was not an option for Viet Nam. Because of Viet Nam's weak tax base, most central government revenues came from taxing state enterprises, and their financial position was only getting worse as a result of being weaned from central bank credits and because of rising input costs resulting from the price liberalization. Thus, reducing the deficit meant reducing government spending, which the government did by a full six percentage points of GDP between 1989 and 1991 (table 7.6). In order to cut spending by that magnitude, subsidies to state enterprises were largely eliminated, the investment program was severely cut, wage increases for civil servants were restrained below the inflation rate, and about one-half million soldiers were demobilized (Dollar and Litvack 1994, 8). Since 1992, both revenues and expenditures have risen. The rise in revenues has been largely due to growth in oil revenues. In addition, since 1993 there has been a substantial increase in the inflow of foreign savings from both official (multilateral and bilateral) lenders and from private foreign investors, which allowed the government to finance a larger part of its deficit without going to the central bank.

Table 7.7
International trade from 1988 to 1994 (percentages of GDP)

	1988	1989	1990	1991	1992	1993	1994
Rate of change (%)							
Exports (in US$)	20.1	80.0	31.2	17.9	21.2	15.1	26.3
Imports (in US$)	19.2	18.3	6.1	18.9	20.4	38.5	28.3
Share in exports (%)							
Rice	0.0	23.9	18.0	11.0	12.5	12.0	11.9
Oil	10.7	15.1	22.5	28.5	30.5	28.0	24.0
Other primary goods	86.9	59.5	57.8	49.5	44.1	46.0	42.7
Manufactures	2.4	1.5	1.7	11.0	12.9	14.0	21.0

Source: World Bank (1994b, 128).

An important element in Viet Nam's successful stabilization program was the growth of exports. Viet Nam was dependent on imports of several important materials, including refined petroleum, steel, fertilizer, and cotton, most of which were obtained from the Soviet Union on credit. With the Soviet Union collapsing, Viet Nam faced the prospect of a severe compression of imports unless it could significantly increase the volume of exports to convertible currency countries. Through a combination of good policies and good luck this was achieved, as table 7.7 indicates, with export volume expanding at an annual rate of about 25 percent from 1989 to 1993. The good policies began in 1987 and 1988 with the lifting of many controls on trade, but of critical importance was the unification of the official and parallel exchange rates at the market clearing rate, which constituted a real devaluation of the official rate on the order of about 75 percent. This measure, together with the elimination of dual pricing in agriculture, immediately raised rice exports to an *unprecedented* level in 1989.[1] In 1990 and 1992, oil became the most rapidly growing export, a development that clearly had more to do with good luck than good policies. Since 1992, rice and oil have continued to be major exports,

---

1. Dollar (1993, 224) notes that part of the increase in rice exports occurred as households sold off hoarded rice they had accumulated during the period of hyperinflation.

though the commodity composition of the exports has become increasingly diversified.

It is often suggested that the experience of Viet Nam, like that of China, demonstrates the superiority of the gradual approach to transition to a market economy over the "big bang" approach followed in Eastern Europe and Russia. However, as the foregoing discussion should make clear, the pace of reform in Viet Nam from 1989 to 1991 was anything but gradual, and the stabilization program adopted in 1989 was certainly as ambitious as anything described as "shock therapy" in other countries. The mistake is to confuse the outcome of reforms with the reforms themselves. There can be no question that (1) privatizing the dominant sector of the economy (agriculture), (2) decontrolling prices, and (3) opening up the economy, all in a matter of a few years, constituted a radical reform program. The outcome was, nevertheless, very different from that in Eastern Europe and Russia, where "big bang" describes the "big collapse" in output that followed major reforms.

Viet Nam escaped a "big collapse" not as a result of differences in the relative pace of reform, but because there were fundamental differences in the structure of the economies of Viet Nam and those in Eastern Europe. Agriculture, the dominant sector in the Vietnamese economy, was simply in a better position to respond to the incentives provided by the reforms than was industry, the dominant sector in Russia and Eastern Europe. In fact, the reform and stabilization measures adopted in Viet Nam also had a severe effect on its industrial sector. Between 1988 and 1992, about 800,000 workers (one-third of the state enterprise labor force) left the sector, and the number of firms declined from 12,000 to 7,000 (Dollar and Litvack 1994, 8). Thus, if the industrial sector in Viet Nam had occupied a position comparable to its position in Eastern Europe, there would in all likelihood have been a "big collapse" about as great as the one in Eastern Europe. It is also worth noting that workers who left the state enterprise sector, along with the 500,000 who were demobilized from the military, were absorbed by their families rather than becoming a financial burden to the state, as they were in Eastern Europe.

Coasting on Success: 1992 to 1994

The main motivation for economic reform in Viet Nam, in both the 1970s and 1980s, was the threat of an imminent economic crisis, rather than any fundamental preference on the part of policy makers for a market economy, much less for capitalism. It was to be expected, therefore, that as economic conditions improved, the pressure for reform would diminish and with it the momentum of reform would decline, as indeed it has. Nevertheless, a number of additional reform measures have been taken in recent years and still more are either in the process of being implemented or are under consideration. It is useful to review the most important of these reforms, not only to complete the accounting of what has been accomplished, but also to gain an understanding of the limits beyond which the government appears to be unwilling to go in establishing a market economy.

Financial Sector Reform
One area in which important measures have been taken, but in which there is much more to be done, is the financial sector. Viet Nam had a single state bank that functioned as a de facto commercial bank and as a central bank until 1988, when the commercial banking functions of the State Bank of Viet Nam were handed over to four subsidiary state commercial banks, each specialized according to the area of its lending activities (agriculture, industry and commerce, construction, and foreign trade). Since then, the number of banking institutions in Viet Nam has risen to 60, but the four state-owned commercial banks still account for the bulk of deposits and for about 90 percent of the stock of total outstanding bank loans, 75 percent of which have gone to state-owned non-financial enterprises (Doanh 1994).

It is apparent that the banking system, which constitutes almost the entire financial system in Viet Nam, is biased against the non-state sector, since the latter's share in the economy (approximately two-thirds) is more than double its share of bank credits. Of course, the solution to this problem is to open up the financial system to competition, but the government so far has been unwilling to do that. In spite of the growing number of domestic and foreign banking institutions, there is little competition in the financial sector. Nor is there likely to be any increase in competition, not only because of government restrictions, but also because the current combination of reserve requirements, turnover taxes, and profit taxes makes financial intermediation unprofitable in Viet Nam (World Bank 1994b, 55). Not surprisingly, therefore, as table 7.8 indicates, the level of financial development in Viet Nam, as measured by the ratio of the money supply (M2) to GDP, is far below that of other countries in the region, even the poorer ones such as Indonesia and China.

State Enterprise Reform
A priority in recent years has been state enterprise reform. Many of Viet Nam's past economic crises stemmed from the "soft budget constraint" of state enterprises. To a large extent, the budget constraint of

Table 7.8
Financial deepening in Viet Nam and selected Asian countries (percentages)

	M2 as percentage of GDP
Thailand (1992)	75.3
Indonesia (1992)	45.8
China (1993)	95.8
Viet Nam	24.0

Sources: International Monetary Fund, *International Financial Statistics* (March 1995) and World Bank (1994b, 112, 124).

state enterprises has been hardened up, as state enterprises have been weaned from direct operating subsidies, denied automatic access to central bank credits, and forced to buy inputs and sell output at market prices. The result has been a significant improvement in the profitability and performance of state-owned enterprises, but not without painful adjustments, including the liquidation of about 2,000 enterprises and the merger of 3,000 others, lowering the overall number of state-owned enterprises from about 12,000 in 1990 to about 7,000 in 1993. This restructuring reduced employment in state enterprises by about one-third. Nevertheless, state-owned enterprises still account for the bulk of industrial production, amounting to about 7 percent of GDP, most of which is accounted for by about 300 medium- to large-scale enterprises. (World Bank 1994b, 30, 40.)

Although state-owned enterprises have gained considerable autonomy in recent years, the framework of bureaucratic controls that existed under the command economy system has remained largely intact. However, with the passage of the new state enterprise law, ownership rights over centrally controlled state enterprises (the 2,000 largest state-owned enterprises) have been transferred from the line ministries, which previously exercised ownership rights, to a bureau within the Ministry of Finance. This change in the hierarchy of the bureaucratic structure is potentially very important, in that it may be expected to mitigate the bias against non-state enterprises which has arisen from the line ministries' conflict of interest as both enterprise owners and industry regulators.

While the new state enterprise law should contribute to the ongoing process of decentralization in the state industrial sector, other measures taken recently work in the opposite direction. A case in point is the March 1994 decision to encourage the establishment of state-enterprise groups, or conglomerates. Apparently the view in the top policy circles in Viet Nam is that size and concentration are important for achieving efficiency and international competitiveness in industry. If this proposition were valid, the market would, of course, guarantee its outcome. The government of Viet Nam, however, is not disposed to leave industrial structure to the market, preferring instead to achieve its desired outcome by administrative fiat. Nor, for that matter, has the government revealed a sincere interest in privatization. A pilot project (launched in June 1992) to transform a number of medium-sized state enterprises into share-holding companies through acquisition of shares by enterprise employees is, with only three firms equitized so far, generally regarded as a failure, in large measure because of lack of government commitment to the project.

Legal Reform

Perhaps the first and foremost public good that government must supply in a market economy is a legal framework that lays out the rules of a market economy and a mechanism for enforcing them. Since 1986, Viet Nam has made significant progress in developing such a legal framework. Laws have been passed on civil and economic contracts, on private property rights, on domestic sole proprietorships and shareholding companies, on state enterprise, on foreign investment, on land use rights, and on bankruptcy. In 1994, a labor code was enacted which sets out the contractual rights of employers and employees regarding social insurance and rights to strike. A comprehensive civil code enacted in 1995 may require many existing laws to be revised to achieve consistency with the code.

In fulfilling the fundamental duty of government to establish the rules of a market economy, the authorities in Viet Nam have, perhaps, done too much of a good thing. A major problem of the legal framework in Viet Nam is the proliferation of highly differentiated laws applying separately to the many different legal forms of economic organization (World Bank 1994b, 47). In such circumstances, it is virtually impossible to honor the principle of equal treatment under the law, and avoid discriminating in favor of one class of business and against another. The proliferation of laws and numerous ordinances and decrees that are required to implement the laws constitutes a formidable entry barrier to private business, which in an economy trying to establish a market economy is counterproductive.

Trade Reform

Of all the "stylized facts" about economic development, none is as robust as the link between openness to trade and economic growth. As noted above, the importance of this link was recognized at the outset of *doi moi.*

Table 7.9
The structure of tariffs as of August 15, 1994

	Range of tariff rates (ad valorem percentage)
Fruits and melons	30–35
Meat and fisheries products	35–45
Beverages	80–150
Clothing	50–100
Fabrics	35–45
Hides and skins	5
Electrical batteries	20–30
Metal ores and concentrates	1–5

Source: World Bank (1994b, 63).

The early liberalization measures, combined with the devaluation and unification of the exchange rate, led to a significant increase in the level of trade (relative to GDP) and diversification of markets in favor of hard currency countries. These reforms have been further reinforced more recently by measures to promote exports, including the establishment of a duty drawback scheme and the approval of five export processing zones. Whereas in the past, in order to be granted permission to export, firms had to meet certain minimum size requirements, currently any enterprise with prospects of export orders is given the certificate that is required to engage in trade.

Importing is, of course, more closely regulated, with certificates, permits, and licenses being required on terms that vary from one product category to another. Aside from these administrative obstacles, the main barrier to imports in Viet Nam is tariffs, which are adjusted on a quarterly basis to meet what the government considers the "country's needs," of which an important if not paramount determinant is the protection of domestic producers of competing goods. Not surprisingly, this policy has resulted in an increasingly complex tariff schedule, which in 1993 contained 20 different duty rates ranging from zero to 200 percent, implying a high degree of variation in effective rates of protection across industries and hence the potential for very costly misallocation of resources. (See table 7.9.) As a recent World Bank (1994b, 66) report concludes, "The present system of import regulations reflects a philosophy of central control of the economy."

Table 7.10
Approved foreign direct investment in Viet Nam and selected other Southeast Asian counties (US$ million)

	1988	1989	1990	1991	1992	1993
Indonesia	4,412	4,714	8,751	8,778	10,323	8,144
Malaysia	1,863	3,193	6,517	6,204	6,977	2,444
Philippines	452	804	961	778	284	532
Thailand	6,250	7,995	14,127	4,988	10,029	4,293
Viet Nam	366	539	596	1,288	1,928	2,728
Total	12,936	17,245	30,952	22,036	29,552	18,141

Sources: *Viet Nam Investment Review* (1994) and Nomura Research Institute, *Nomura Asia Focus* (December 1994).

Foreign Investment Policy
As in many other areas, the trend of policy toward foreign investment has been toward increasing liberalization. Indeed, in some ways Viet Nam's foreign investment code is more liberal than that of other countries in the region. Of course a trend toward liberalization was inevitable given that Viet Nam started, in 1988, from a policy of total exclusion of foreign investment. Currently, Viet Nam allows foreigners to establish wholly owned enterprises or to go into joint ventures with Vietnamese partners, either in the private or state-enterprise sector. Since 1992, foreign investments in Viet Nam have been guaranteed against nationalization and have been offered generous tax treatment.

The change in attitude toward foreign investment and the overall success of economic reforms in Viet Nam have attracted a great deal of attention from potential foreign investors and the journalists who write about foreign investment. The attention that foreign investment in Viet Nam has received, however, far exceeds the money that has been invested. As table 7.10 indicates, the rate of growth of foreign investment (approvals) in Viet Nam has been extremely high (about 50 percent per year), but the amounts invested remain low compared to the amounts invested in other countries in the region. Indeed, the figures for foreign investment in table 7.10 probably exaggerate the level of investment by a significant factor, because these numbers include debt as well as equity, include the local contribution to joint ventures as well as the foreign contribution, and indicate the amounts approved for investment rather than the amounts actually invested, which according to the World Bank may differ by as much as four to one.

The relatively low level of foreign investment, given that Viet Nam has the second largest population and the lowest wage level in Southeast Asia, clearly indicates that there are some formidable obstacles to foreign investment in Viet Nam. The poor state of the physical infrastructure in Viet Nam is an obstacle, as is the cost of acquiring land use rights and the uncertainty about retaining those rights. However, at the top of most investors' lists of obstacles are the complex bureaucratic requirements and procedures for getting a project approved and implemented, which often take several years to complete (Bandaralage and Nguyen 1994). Typically this process requires the involvement of at least eight central government agencies and numerous local government entities. These bureaucracies consider the following issues, among others: (1) whether the foreign firm is offering the "appropriate" technology, by which is meant "state-of-the-art" technology; (2) whether there is a "need" for the investment, as determined by existing domestic supply and demand in the industry; and (3) whether the investment would threaten domestic firms in the industry. Thus, the philosophy of central control of the economy also permeates Viet Nam's foreign investment policy, as it does the many other areas of policy reform.

7.4   Interpreting the Transition Experience

Achieving Long-Term Growth

What unfolded under *doi moi* undoubtedly exceeded anything imagined by those who coined the slogan. When the Sixth Party Congress met in 1986, the economy was in a shambles, people were fleeing the country, and Viet Nam's principal foreign ally and benefactor was collapsing. In 1994, when the midterm party conference met, Viet Nam's leaders could take justifiable pride in five years of GDP growth at an average annual rate of 8 percent and an inflation rate in single digits. Even if many of those who fled the country were not returning, a good deal of their money was. In addition, Viet Nam was again receiving funds from multilateral development agencies, bilateral donors, and foreign investors from all over the world, including its former enemy, the United States.

In spite of this progress, Viet Nam remains a poor country. World Bank estimates put per capita GDP at about $250. In purchasing power parity terms, it might be as high as $750, which still leaves it one of the world's poorest countries. A recent World Bank household survey found that slightly more than half of Viet Nam's 14 million households is below the poverty line (Dollar and Litvack 1994). Moreover, Viet Nam will remain poor for a long time to come, even if it maintains its high GDP growth rate. At its current rate of per capita income growth, Viet

Nam will require 25 years to reach the level of per capita income in Thailand today ($2,500), and about 50 years to match Taiwan's present per capita income of about $12,000.

Obviously, Viet Nam has to grow fast *steadily* over a long period in order to reach the present income levels of its richer neighbors. Many developing countries have achieved spurts of growth for periods as long as five to ten years, but not many have experienced continuous per capita income growth at a rate of 7 percent or higher for several decades. The few that have achieved this growth rate are Viet Nam's neighbors. Their experience provides a proven path for Viet Nam to follow, provided that it is willing and able to take the measures required to implement the same development strategy. If Viet Nam is willing and able to do so, there is good reason to expect that it also will succeed. The export-oriented industrialization strategy that lies behind the success of the East Asian Tigers (including Korea, Taiwan, Thailand, Malaysia, and parts of China) is made to order for Viet Nam, a country rich in labor resources and poor in just about everything else (Riedel 1993). Viet Nam should therefore industrialize in line with its comparative advantage in relatively labor-intensive manufactures, which necessarily implies a strong export orientation.

What measures are required to make the export-oriented industrialization strategy work? The answer is found in the experience of those countries which have succeeded under the strategy, although admittedly not everyone agrees on the relative importance of the ingredients of the strategy.[2] What is common to most of the successful experiences of export-oriented growth, however, was (1) macroeconomic stability, (2) relatively high rates of saving and investment, and (3) if not free trade (as in Hong Kong and Singapore), then at least free access for exporters to imported capital goods and intermediate inputs (as in Taiwan and the other Tigers).

As the foregoing review makes clear, Viet Nam has made substantial, albeit incomplete, progress in each of these areas. Macroeconomic stabilization may be the government's greatest success, although in this realm success is fleeting and stability is only as secure as the latest government budget. Keeping the budget deficit at a manageable level is not easy in a country with a strong socialist orientation and a seriously deficient economic infrastructure, but the government of Viet Nam appears determined to try. After increasing government spending by ten percentage points of GDP between 1991 and 1993, allowing the deficit to GDP ratio to increase threefold from 1.5 to 4.7 percent, tax and expenditure measures were taken in 1994 to lower the deficit to 2.7 percent of GDP, keeping inflation in single digits (World Bank 1994b, 60).

---

2. Compare, for example, Riedel (1988) and Wade (1990).

Table 7.11
Saving and investment rates from 1990 to 1994 (percentages of GDP)

	1990	1991	1992	1993	1994
Gross domestic investment	11.7	15.1	17.0	19.4	19.9
Gross national savings	7.4	13.1	16.3	11.2	15.0
Public savings	0.0	2.1	5.0	3.5	6.6
Private savings	7.4	11.0	11.3	7.7	8.4
Foreign savings[a]	4.2	1.9	0.7	8.3	4.9

Source: World Bank (1994b, 16).
a. Current account deficit.

Viet Nam has also made substantial progress in raising the rates of domestic saving and investment (table 7.11). The disappearance of foreign savings (along with the Soviet Union) between 1990 and 1992, was more than made up for by increases in domestic savings in the public and private sectors. The return of foreign savings to Viet Nam in 1993, from different sources and in even greater proportions than before, was accompanied by a decline in the rate of public and private savings. It is, however, difficult to determine the direction of cause and effect in the apparent negative relation between domestic and foreign savings.

The third element of a successful export-oriented industrialization is access by exporters to imported capital goods and intermediate inputs. The introduction of a duty drawback scheme for exporters and the approval of five export processing zones are important steps in this direction. On the other hand, the complex bureaucratic procedures for importing, which imbue officials with enormous discretionary power to decide when trade is in the national interest, clearly work in the opposite direction. A duty drawback scheme and export processing zones are generally not sufficient to offset these kinds of bureaucratic obstacles. Indeed, these measures have worked in other countries only when they were part of a broader trade liberalization program, not when they were used to substitute for one.

The Missing Ingredient

In identifying stability, openness, and an ample availability of investible funds as the key ingredients of a successful industrialization strategy, we implicitly assume that there are actors in the economy who can, and

Table 7.12
Ownership structure in Vietnamese industry

	1992		1990	
	Number of firms	Employees (thousands)	Number of firms	Employees (thousands)
State enterprises	2,268	667.5	2,599	743.8
State cooperatives	5,723	207.2	8,829	501.1
Private corporations	1,114	47.2	959	19.5
Household firms	530,891	1,129.2	446,771	1,029.5

Source: *So Lieu Cong Nghiep Viet Nam (1989–1993)*, Nha Xuat Ban Thong Ke, Ha Noi (1994).

will, respond to those favorable conditions to generate growth. In the other Asian Tigers, the actors who responded most enthusiastically to the favorable conditions created by policy reform, and generated most of the resulting growth, were private entrepreneurs (or, as in China, their equivalent, the managers of Town and Village Enterprises). Are there sufficient private entrepreneurs in Viet Nam, and are they in a position to take advantage of the reforms?

One cannot but be impressed by the entrepreneurial spirit in Viet Nam. On the streets of Ho Chi Minh City one can "smell economics," and if it is different in Hanoi, it is only by a matter of degree. One gets the impression that everyone has at least one foot in the private sector, even those nominally employed in the public sector. Unfortunately, the official statistics needed to confirm or refute this impression are scant. The most recent statistics for the industrial sector, for example, are for 1992. While these data are no doubt outdated, given the changes that are taking place in the country, they do give some indication of the changing structure of ownership in the industrial sector.

The decline in the number of state-owned enterprises and state cooperatives is clearly revealed in the data presented in table 7.12. The growth of private sector activity, on the other hand, was until 1992 almost entirely among private household firms, which are extremely small, averaging two employees. The private enterprise (or corporate) sector, in which the average firm size is about 40 employees, showed very little growth and is extremely small, accounting for only 2 percent of industrial employment and 4 percent of industrial output.

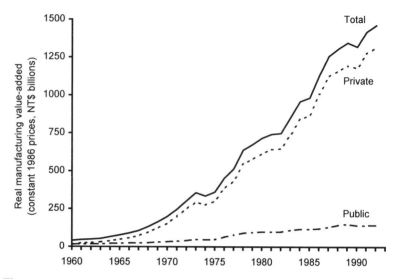

Figure 7.2
Real manufacturing value-added by Taiwanese private and public enterprises
(constant 1985 prices, NT$ billions). Source: *Taiwan Statistical Data Book* (1993).

Is the private corporate sector a missing ingredient of the export-
oriented industrialization strategy? Again, we can look to the experience
of the countries that have succeeded with the strategy for an answer.
Taiwan is perhaps the most appropriate comparator, since it shared many
of the same characteristics with Viet Nam when it launched the strategy
35 years ago—a high population density, a natural resource scarcity, and
a predominantly rural economy.[3] Of course, Taiwan was not initially a
socialist, command economy. It did, however, have a very large state-
owned enterprise sector in manufacturing, accounting for about half of
manufacturing value-added in 1960 (see figure 7.2). Moreover, the state-
owned manufacturing firms continued to expand even after the export-
oriented industrialization strategy was adopted in 1960, with output
growing at about 7 percent per annum from 1960 to 1993. Privatization
was attempted early on, but it never succeeded (Schieve 1995).

In relative terms, however, the state-owned firms declined dramatically. Their share of manufacturing value-added fell from 56 percent in
1952 to only 10 percent in 1993 (figure 7.2). The growth of manufacturing
in Taiwan was, therefore, generated predominantly in the private sector.

---

3. For a comparison of the two economies together with two other "Tigers,"
China and Thailand, see Riedel (1993).

Table 7.13
Characteristics of manufacturing enterprises in Taiwan by form of ownership in 1986

	Private corporations	Family firms	State enterprises
Number of firms	57,477	61,224	221
Employment (thousands)	2,299	337	93
Fixed capital (millions NT$)	1,013	101	294
Value-added (millions NT$)	2,835	170	325
Share in value-added (%)	85.2	5.1	9.7
Employment per firm (thousands)	40.0	5.5	420.0
Capital per employee (thousands NT$)	440.0	300.0	3,161.2
Value-added per employee (thousands NT$)	1,233.0	504.4	3,161.3
Output–capital ratio	2.8	1.6	1.1

Source: *The Report on the 1986 Industrial and Commercial Census*, Taiwan-Fukien Area, Republic of China (1988, 178).

Indeed, the private sector accounted for 91 percent of the incremental increase in real value-added in manufacturing between 1960 and 1993.

Like Viet Nam, the private manufacturing sector in Taiwan consists of two broad classes of firms, viz., family firms and corporations. Taiwan's family firms, averaging about five employees, are the most numerous form of business enterprise in manufacturing, but their contribution to manufacturing value-added is minuscule (only 5 percent); see table 7.13. By far the most important source of manufacturing value-added in Taiwan is private corporate enterprises, which, like their counterparts in Viet Nam, have on average about 40 employees. The output–capital ratio, which is a rough measure of the return to capital, is about three times higher in the private corporate sector than in the relatively capital-intensive state-owned enterprises, and almost two times higher than in the relatively labor-intensive family firms. It is therefore not surprising that the small to medium-sized private corporations became the dominant form of industrial organization in Taiwan.

If Viet Nam is to succeed with the export-oriented industrialization strategy, it too will have to develop a dynamic, small to medium-sized private enterprise sector in manufacturing. The government's role in the development of private enterprise is mainly to get out of the way and let it happen. So far, the government of Viet Nam has not been willing to do that. Its rules and regulations on trade, investment, and finance constitute formidable obstacles to private enterprise development. At the heart of the matter is a philosophy that is antithetical to the development of a dynamic private industrial sector. The government has accepted the necessity of a market economy, but seems to prefer one it can control and command. Unfortunately, world economic history is replete with examples of failed market economies, and in most cases the reason for their failure can be traced to governments' attempts to restrict market freedom.

7.5 Conclusions

What are the lessons of Viet Nam's transition experience? Clearly, the "pitfalls of partial reform" constitute an important lesson also found in the experiences of most of the other transition economies (Murphy, Shliefer, and Vishny 1992). Contrary to popular opinion, Viet Nam does not provide evidence of the superiority of a gradual approach. On the contrary, Viet Nam's attempts to introduce market reforms step-by-step failed. Success only came after it launched its ambitious structural adjustment and stabilization program in 1989. The reason for the confusion on this point, we suggest, is that observers of the economic reform process often confuse the outcome of the reforms with the reforms themselves. The reason Viet Nam did not suffer a "big collapse" was not because its economic reforms were more timid than those in Eastern Europe or Russia, but because of fundamental structural differences in their respective economies (Riedel 1993).

Another popular perception about Viet Nam's experience that we cast in some doubt is its degree of success. The point is not to diminish the tremendous gains that have been made. As has been noted, "Vietnam's development over the past decade represents one of the more dramatic turn-arounds in economic history" (Dollar and Litvack 1994, 1). It is, nevertheless, only a turn-around; Viet Nam is now facing in the right direction, but it still has a long way to go, and it will take a long time to get there. To complete the journey Viet Nam needs a sound strategy for long-term growth. It is suggested here that the experience of Viet Nam's successful neighbors offers such a strategy, one that is tailor-made for Viet Nam (Riedel 1995). However, while the country has taken many of the measures required to implement the strategy, a missing ingredient remains: the acceptance by the government of an unfettered private enterprise economy. Rather than creating the conditions in which private enterprise can thrive, the government's attention is focused on the problems of the state-owned industrial enterprises. Encouraging state-owned firms to become more efficient or to privatize themselves is a worthy cause, but only if it does not divert attention from the even more important objective of fostering development of private enterprise in the industrial sector. For it is the performance of these firms that will largely determine what kind of market economy Viet Nam will have—a mediocre, cumbersome one, like so many market economies in the third world, or a dynamic, prosperous one, like those that surround Viet Nam in Southeast Asia.

III

Components of Reform Programs

8

East Asian Lessons from Economic Reforms

Vinod Thomas and Yan Wang

The hastier you are, the later you will reach your goal.

Lunyu (*The Analects of Confucius*)

You cannot jump over an abyss in two steps.

A Russian proverb

8.1 Summary

The East Asian economies have had enormous success in their economic reforms. The market economies of Indonesia, Korea, Malaysia, and Thailand grew at more than 5 percent a year during the 1980s, when they stepped up economic liberalization. China has been expanding at 9 percent a year since the start of reforms in 1978, and Viet Nam and Laos at about 7 percent since 1989. Meanwhile, other low- and middle-income countries that were in the midst of reforms fared less well, growing at less than 3 percent a year. The countries of the former Soviet Union and Eastern Europe, which have been reforming since the early 1990s, have suffered large losses in output initially.

Why are there differences? Why has East Asia managed to get greater payoffs from its reforms? Some people credit the gradual and evolutionary nature of changes in East Asia, especially in socialist transitions, in contrast to the shock therapy adopted elsewhere. East Asia's more favorable initial conditions also take some of the credit for making reforms more productive. Certainly, more favorable initial conditions make a gradual approach more feasible.

The real answer is likely to be more complex, however. Consider first the issue of speed. Rapid and comprehensive reforms are desirable because they bring larger benefits sooner. But other considerations, such

We are grateful to Stephen Parker, Wing Thye Woo, and others for comments and suggestions. Remaining errors and omissions are solely our responsibility.

as social costs, sequencing, learning by doing, institution-building, administrative capacity, and reversing paths under uncertainty, argue for a gradual approach. This paper concludes that the East Asian experience, though full of incremental changes, can hardly be classified as gradualist across the board. In areas where swift actions were needed, swift actions were taken. It is also useful to note the rapid pace of decision making and taking ownership in reform programs, even when implementation had to be phased. Finally, when the need for reform was a binding constraint on actions elsewhere (for example, when macroeconomic instability required immediate action), changes were swift. When necessary changes were delayed, the results were costly.

The steady pace of implementation and institution-building also had its rewards. The East Asian experience suggests that government has a major role in institution-building; laissez-faire is not optimal. Having market-oriented institutions in place while old institutions are torn down is crucial for rapid reforms to take hold. Here, China's experimentation with market institutions might shed light. When institutional changes lagged, the East Asian economies reaped poor results.

On the issue of initial conditions, we find that East Asian economies in general had less macroeconomic instability and fewer market distortions than economies in Eastern Europe, Central Asia, or the former Soviet Union. In most cases, however, this was not the result of good luck, but rather the consequence of prompt attention to policy problems earlier on. While favorable initial conditions help, it was the continued policy reforms that had the greater impact on outcomes.

8.2 Performance of East Asian Reformers

No economic reform in recent history has been as momentous as the socialist transition that is sweeping the world. All across the developing world over the past decade and a half, countries have been carrying out policy reforms. East Asia has experienced the financial liberalization and macroeconomic stabilization of Indonesia, the trade reform in Korea in the 1980s, the trade reform and deregulation of Thailand in the 1980s and early 1990s, and the financial sector liberalization in Taiwan (China) after 1987. These countries were joined by socialist China, which started its transition from central planning to a market-based economy in 1979. Viet Nam and Lao PDR started their market reforms in the late 1980s.

Most reforming East Asian economies, non-socialist and socialist alike, have achieved spectacular economic growth and poverty reduction (table 8.1). China and Korea both registered the highest growth rates in GNP per capita during 1980–93 (8.2 percent) (World Bank 1995d).

Table 8.1
Performance of East Asian reforming countries, 1980–1994

Countries	Reform periods	Growth of GNP per capita	GDP growth	Growth of exports [imports]
Non-socialist reformers				
Korea	1981–	8.5	8.9	10.8 [11.5]
Indonesia	1982–90	4.0	5.9	4.6 [1.9]
Malaysia	1983–90	3.2	6.4	11.7 [10.5]
Thailand	1984, 1990	6.0	8.3	14.7 [13.4]
Philippines	1986–89, 1991	–1.0	1.5 (5.2 in 1986–89)	4.9 [6.0]
Socialist reformers				
China	1979–	7.6	9.5	10.4 [7.7]
Cambodia	1991–	—	5.0^a	$35.0 [25.9]^a$
Lao PDR	1986–	4.7^b	7.6^b	$20.0 [19.5]^b$
Mongolia	1990–	—	-4.0^c	$5.7 [-8.0]^c$
Viet Nam	1989–	4.8^d	7.4^d	$28.0 [24.0]^d$
For 1980–93:				
East Asia		6.4	7.8	10.8 [9.2]
South Asia		3.0	5.2	7.3 [3.7]
Sub-Saharan Africa		–0.8	1.6	2.5 [–2.2]
Europe and Central Asia		–0.3	0.4	—
Middle East and North Africa		–2.4	2.2	–1.0 [–3.9]
Latin America and Caribbean		–0.1	1.9	3.4 [0.3]

Sources: World Bank (1995d) for 1980–94 unless otherwise noted.
a. Data is for 1989–94 based on World Bank staff estimates, 1995.
b. Data is for 1988–94. World Bank staff estimates, 1995.
c. Data is for 1991–94. World Bank staff estimates,1995.
d. Data is for 1989–94. World Bank staff estimates, 1995.

Table 8.2
Performance of Eastern European and Central Asian reformers

Countries	Reform periods	1980–1993	1991	1992	1993	1994	Growth of export [import] 1993
		GDP growth					
Albania	1992–	−1.3[a]	−27.7	−9.7	11.0	7.4	−2.1
							[−18.9]
Bulgaria	1991–	0.9	−11.7	−6.0	−4.7	−0.8	4.7
							[22.5]
Czech Republic[b]	1991–	−1.3	−14.2	−6.6	−0.3	3.0	—
Hungary	1990–	−0.5	−11.9	−4.5	−2.3	2.6	−11.6
							[13.8]
Poland	1989–	0.4	−7.6	1.0	3.8	5.5	−3.0
							[3.7]
Romania	1990–	−1.9	−12.9	−13.8	1.2	2.4	—
Russia	1992–	−0.5	−12.8	−19.0	−12.0	−15.0	—
Slovak Republic[b]	1991–	−1.3	−14.5	−7.0	−4.1	5.3	−9.3
							[−6.5]
Ukraine	1992–	0.0	−13.4	−17.0	−14.0	−23.0	−16.0
							[−23.4]

Source: World Bank (1995d) and staff estimates, 1995.
Note: 1994 numbers are based on World Bank staff estimates, 1995.
a. This number is for 1980–92.
b. Slovak became independent in January 1993. Data here include that for the Czech and Slovak Federal Republics.

Viet Nam's performance has been remarkable, with an annual growth rate of 7.1 percent during 1988–93, declines in inflation from over 400 percent in 1988 to 14.6 percent in 1993; and increases in exports at around 30 percent a year. Agricultural reform and price liberalization have transformed Viet Nam from a major rice importer to the third largest rice exporter in 1989.

In contrast, almost all reforming countries in Eastern Europe and Central Asia initially suffered severe economic and financial crises with large losses in output, mounting inflation, and unemployment (table 8.2). Several Eastern European countries (Albania, the Czech Republic,

Romania, and Poland) have shown encouraging signs of macro-economic stabilization in 1993, followed by strong economic recovery in 1994. But Russia and Ukraine, and most countries of the former Soviet Union, are still in recession.

The contrast is striking between East Asia, and Eastern Europe and the former Soviet Union (EEFSU). What accounts for this remarkable difference in the outcome of reforms—in East Asia being able to get higher payoffs from reform measures? This paper explores this question by focusing on two factors: (1) the speed at which reforms are undertaken and (2) the macroeconomic, political, and social conditions before reform that affect its success. The paper identifies the most important factors and policies that determine the outcomes of reform.

8.3 Two Clarifications on the Pace of Reforms

The issues of pace and initial conditions are rather complex. Rapid and comprehensive reforms are desirable because they bring larger benefits sooner; however, some circumstances argue for a gradual approach. Although East Asian countries experienced many incremental changes, their general approaches to reform can hardly be classified as gradualist across the board. When swift actions were needed, swift actions were taken. In this regard, it is instructive to view the rapid pace of Chinese reform in historical perspective. It is also useful to note the following experience in East Asia. First, the pace of decision making was rapid, even when implementation had to be phased. Second, when the need for reform constrained actions elsewhere, changes were usually made quickly. When they have not been rapid, the results have been costly.

Speed in Historical Perspective

From 1921 to 1945, the U.S. average nominal tariff varied from 30 to 59 percent.[1] After 40 years and seven rounds of GATT negotiations, the average tariff of industrial countries was lowered from 40 percent to about 5 percent at the Tokyo Round. Tariffs escalated again following the Tokyo Round (1974–79), reaching 30 percent for some processed commodities, an effective rate of protection of more than 100 percent (Yeats 1987, 119; Finger and Olechowski 1987). After almost 50 years, trade liberalization of agriculture in industrial countries is still unfinished even with the Uruguay Round Agreement.

---

1. U.S. Department of Commerce, *Historical Statistics of the United States: Colonial Time to 1970*, Series U 207–12, p. 888. We use the ratio of duties to total dutiable imports as the average nominal tariff.

Table 8.3
Speed in reform decision versus implementation

Reform implementation	Reform decisions	
	Fast	Slow
Fast	In areas with proven results: • exchange rate reform • some trade reforms (quantitative restrictions first) • government expenditure cuts • monetary control • price liberalization	In areas with uncertain results or politically difficult decisions: • rationalization of certain expenditures • land reform • liberalization of prices of certain necessities
Slow	Proven results but implementation takes time: • an independent central bank • commercial banking • securities markets • open capital account • a social safety net • legal infrastructure	Uncertain results and difficult to implement: • intergovernmental relations: tax and expenditure assignments • privatization of large state-owned enterprises

Compared to the lengthy process in industrial countries, the pace of trade reforms has been fast in some developing countries and formerly socialist countries, which have liberalized much of their trade in just 5 to 15 years. This catching-up in market development is an advantage that latecomers can seize upon only through a rapid opening up of their economies. China has accomplished in 15 years the institution-building and economic development that took several decades in industrial countries.

The economic integration of the world has provided the external conditions for accelerating the development of market institutions in reforming countries. But efficient reformers learn faster than others, so how quickly a country learns and catches up in developing market institutions depends not only on its initial endowments and conditions, but also on its way of learning.

The Decision to Reform and Its Implementation

Where theory and experience have demonstrated the benefits, the decision to reform can be announced quickly and clearly at the outset, even if implementation takes years. In areas where results are uncertain, or politically difficult to accept, even the decisions to reform need to be made cautiously. This uncertainty often characterizes socialist economies in transition, because much more is known about initial conditions and goals than about how to get there (table 8.3).

Initial Conditions Affecting Speed

Macroeconomic Conditions
Countries with relatively stable political and macroeconomic conditions usually feel no particular urgency to reform, so they can afford to conduct reforms in an evolutionary fashion, rather than risk political and economic chaos. China and most East Asian countries belong to this group. China had far more severe structural distortion than did other East Asian economies, from the domination of state ownership and heavy industry to distorted prices and a closed economy. (See table 8.4.)

Countries experiencing massive macroeconomic imbalances cannot afford to reform slowly—they need a strong dose of medicine quickly. The political opportunity to reform may not last long. For these countries, the "big bang" approach may be more appropriate. Countries in this group include Viet Nam in 1988, and most countries in Eastern Europe and the former Soviet Union, which had more structural distortions and a much higher degree of industrial concentration than China had before reforms. Many Latin American countries are also in this group.

Degree of Specialization and Labor Market Conditions
Developing countries with a large and mostly self-sufficient agricultural sector, a low degree of specialization, and abundant surplus labor, can afford to delay privatization of large state enterprises, allowing the non-state sector to outgrow the state sector and improving productivity in both sectors. (See table 8.5.) China and Viet Nam are cases in point. The productivity increase is triggered first in rural areas. Then increased competition in domestic markets, rather than the privatization of large state enterprises at the outset, forces state-owned enterprises (SOEs) to become more efficient in order to survive.

Most countries in EEFSU have little surplus labor and a high degree of specialization among workers. For them, the restructuring of the state and sector unavoidably involves more severe displacement of highly specialized workers and the disruption of production.

Table 8.4
Initial conditions: An illustration of different countries at different times

Structural problems	Macroeconomic instability	
	Mild • mild inflation • small fiscal deficits • small current account deficits	Severe • high inflation • large fiscal deficits • large current account deficits
Mild • some price distortions • some exchange rate distortions • some financial distortions	Indonesia (early 1980s) Korea (early 1980s) Malaysia (early 1980s) Thailand (early 1980s)	
Severe • public ownership dominates • massive distortions • a relatively closed economy • heavily monopolistic industrial structure in some countries	China (1980s) Lao PDR (late 1980s) India (1980s)	Brazil (1980s) Mexico (early 1980s) Ghana (1970s) EEFSU (1980s to early 1990s) Viet Nam (1988)

Note: This table is for illustration only; it is far from comprehensive.

8.4 East Asia's Success: Initial Social Conditions or Public Policies?

The Debate

What explains the remarkable success of East Asian reformers? Several different views are heard. The market-friendly view stresses the role of government policies in four areas: investing in people, providing a competitive environment for private enterprises, keeping the economy open to international trade, and maintaining a stable macroeconomy. Recognizing that the "early birds" and "latecomers" in East Asia chose different types of policies, *The East Asian Miracle* (World Bank 1993a) divides public policies into fundamentals and selective interventions. In general, fundamental policies are found to be crucial to East Asia's success. They encompass macroeconomic stability, investment in human capital, stable and secure financial systems, limited price distortions, and openness to foreign technology. "Export-push strategies have been by far the most successful combination of fundamentals and

Table 8.5
Initial conditions: Specialization and labor markets

Labor market condition	Degree of specialization and division of labor	
	Low • large agricultural sector • small manufacturing sector • self-sufficiency in many areas • low interdependency across regions and sectors	High • small agricultural sector • big manufacturing sector • regional specialization • high degree of interdependency
Loose • surplus labor • labor mobility limited • low wage and salaries • labor unions are weak	China Lao PDR Mongolia Viet Nam	
Tight • few surplus labor • labor mobility allowed • relatively higher wages and salaries • labor unions are strong		Eastern European countries and middle-income countries in the former Soviet Union

policy interventions." (World Bank 1993a, 24.) The other two selective interventions examined, industrial promotion and directed credit, did not work or involved high uncertainty.

Among those who take a different view, some focus on initial conditions and some emphasize industrial policies (for example, Amsden 1994, Lall 1994, Fishlow and Gwin 1994, Haggard 1994, and Wade 1994). In an interesting paper, Dani Rodrik (1994b) argues that initial social conditions, especially education and income equality, are crucial factors in East Asia's success.[2] Using coefficients from an

---

2. In this section, we focus on initial social conditions often used in growth models, such as initial income level, initial primary and secondary school enrollment, initial infant mortality rate, and initial equality indicators. These are different from initial structural conditions, such as the level of specialization and labor market conditions.

empirical analysis of data from 41 countries, Rodrik shows that initial social conditions can explain 74 to 107 percent of the growth in selected East Asian countries.

Initial Social Conditions are neither Sufficient nor Self-Generating

Except for certain naturally endowed conditions, most initial conditions do not just happen; often they are the results of earlier government policies or the consequences of the development process. For example, the good standing of Korea and Taiwan (China) on income equality in 1960 was the result of successful land reforms in the 1950s. The better health status and educational attainment are also outcomes of government policies for improving public and private education and health services. The remarkable macroeconomic stability in East Asia reflects prompt government attention to macroeconomic problems as soon as they appear. The response of the Malaysian government to the banking crisis in 1985–86 is a good example of such prompt attention (see "Experience of East Asian Reformers" below).

Initial social conditions alone cannot ensure good performance in development. Many of the former socialist economies of Eastern Europe and the former Soviet Union had good initial social conditions before reforms: low infant mortality, high life expectancy, high primary and secondary enrollment, and low income inequality. However, these economies were mostly closed to the non-socialist world outside, and their prices, interest rates, and incentives were severely distorted. Thus their economies stagnated. This experience shows, intuitively, that initial conditions in education and income equality are important, but alone they will not propel a country down the road to rapid growth.

To investigate the relationship between initial social conditions, public policies, and growth performance, we employed an endogenous growth model with data from 87 countries, including transitional economies, for 1970–88. The data set included variables on performance (growth rate of GDP per capita); initial social conditions (GDP per capita in 1970, primary and secondary enrollment, infant mortality, and total fertility rate); and macroeconomic stability and public policies (trade, investment, government consumption, and inflation rates). Among them, openness to trade is proxied by an instrumental variable, deviations in trade shares (DEVTRDS). Appendix 8 presents the framework, data, and methodology.

First, we ran regressions similar to those of Rodrik (1994b), incorporating initial social conditions alone or with regional dummy variables. Second, we ran our main regressions, which included initial social conditions, policy variables, and regional dummies.

Table 8.6
Comparative regressions on initial conditions

Variables	1		2		3	
Dependent variables	ZGDPCAP	t	ZGDPCAP	t	ZGDPCAP	t
Constant	4.4607	2.09				
GDPCAP70	−0.0002	−2.17			−0.0002	−2.23
PENROL70	0.0020	0.17			0.0049	0.48
SENROL70	0.0027	0.15			−0.0207	−1.21
IMR70	−0.0162	−1.98			−0.0111	−1.55
TFR70	−0.2734	−0.89			−0.5262	−2.01
POPGRO	−0.0124	−0.03			0.2278	0.56
AFRICA			−0.1014	−0.32	4.1464	2.21
EASIA			4.0911	8.30	7.3593	3.95
SASIA			1.7897	2.42	6.0227	2.95
EECA			1.6509	2.23	4.2575	2.18
LAC			0.7757	2.29	4.4361	2.24
MENA			3.0081	6.10	7.0010	3.38
HIGHINC			2.2949	6.94	6.6607	2.84
Adj. R^2	0.2330		0.6524		0.7001	
F value	5.354		24.330		16.620	
n	87		87		87	

ZGDPCAP: Annual growth rate of GDP per capita, 1970–88.
GDPCAP70: GDP per capita in USD in 1970.
PENROL70: Primary enrollment rate in 1970.
SENROL70: Secondary enrollment rate in 1970.
IMR70: Infant mortality rate in 1970.
TFR70: Total fertility rate in 1970.
POPGRO: Population growth rate in 1970–88.
HIGHINC: A dummy variable for high-income countries.
AFRICA, EASIA, SASIA, LAC, MENA, and EECA are regional dummies.

For the first regression, regression 1 in table 8.6, we used the following as indicators of initial social conditions: GDP per capita, primary and secondary enrollment, infant mortality, total fertility in 1970, and the average population growth rate in 1970–88. The regression incorporated no policy indicator (population growth was assumed not to be significantly affected by family planning policy before 1988). Only GDP per capita and infant mortality in 1970 were found to be significantly and negatively associated with growth, with the adjusted R^2 only 0.23.

For regression 2 we used regional dummies as independent variables, reasoning that a country's geographic location is purely exogenous and can be considered an initial condition. The regional dummy variable also reflects to some extent the impact of geographic proximity. If proximity effects are present, the growth rates of neighboring countries should be closely related. The results show that all regional dummies are significantly related to growth, except for Africa. Both the adjusted R^2 (0.65) and the F value (24.33) are higher than those for regression 1.

For regression 3, we included both initial social conditions and regional dummies. Only two out of six indicators of initial conditions are significant: total fertility in 1970 and GDP per capita are negative and significant. The effects of enrollment rates and population growth are ambiguous. In addition, all regional dummy variables are significant, with the biggest coefficients and t-statistics for East Asia.

Policies Determine Outcomes

For our main analysis, we included indicators of government policies and stability, all six indicators of initial social conditions, as well as regional dummy variables (see table 8.7).

Regression 1 included initial social conditions and policy variables, but not regional dummies. None of the initial conditions are significant. The policy indicators, trade (DEVTRDS) and investment (SGDINV), are positively and significantly associated with growth. Government consumption (SGCON) and inflation (CPICHG), an indicator of stability, are insignificant.

Our full model, regression 3, includes all three groups of variables, and the results make intuitive sense. Among initial conditions, GDP and total fertility in 1970 are negatively and significantly associated with growth. All three policy indicators, trade (DEVTRDS), investment (SGDINV), and government consumption (SGCON) are significantly related to growth with the expected signs. Regional dummies are very significant, especially for East Asia. The adjusted R^2 is 0.74. A few other specifications are attempted for sensitivity test. In regression 2, when enrollment and population growth rates are excluded, the results are consistent with those of the full model. The estimated coefficients and level of significance do not change much, indicating the robustness of the results.

Table 8.7
Main regressions with both initial conditions and policy variables

Variables	1		2		3 (full model)	
Dependent variable	ZGDPCAP	t	ZGDPCAP	t	ZGDPCAP	t
Constant	2.7438	1.26				
GDPCAP70	−0.00001	−1.62	−0.0002	−2.05	−0.0002	−2.11
PENROL70	0.0009	0.07			−0.0018	−0.18
SENROL70	0.0133	0.77			−0.0095	−0.57
IMR70	−0.0100	−1.26	−0.0082	−1.44	−0.0100	−1.37
TFR70	−0.2082	−0.72	−0.3779	−2.43	−0.5176	−2.09
POPGRO	−0.0540	−0.12			0.2108	0.54
DEVTRDS	0.5218	1.79	0.4310	1.82	0.4399	1.82
SGDINV	0.0655	2.55	0.0538	5.54	0.0509	2.30
SGCON	−0.0573	−1.57	−0.0805	−2.55	−0.0808	−2.42
CPICHG	−0.0030	−1.32	−0.0018	−0.96	−0.0016	−0.80
AFRICA			3.5851	3.06	4.4160	2.25
EASIA			6.0613	5.73	6.9896	3.63
SASIA			5.0858	4.37	6.0958	2.98
EECA			2.4253	2.26	3.5149	1.73
LAC			3.8296	3.74	4.7853	2.40
MENA			6.1621	5.11	7.2341	3.31
HIGHINC			5.2650	4.39	6.6301	2.78
Adj. R^2	0.3253		0.7449		0.7365	
F value	5.147		19.141		15.304	
n	87		87		87	

ZGDPCAP: Annual growth rate of GDP per capita, 1970–88.
GDPCAP70: GDP per capita in USD in 1970.
PENROL70: Primary enrollment rate in 1970.
SENROL70: Secondary enrollment rate in 1970.
IMR70: Infant mortality rate in 1970.
TFR70: Total fertility rate in 1970.
POPGRO: Population growth rate in 1970–88.
DEVTRDS: Deviations of the actual trade share in GDP from the predicted.
SGDINV: Share of gross domestic investment in GDP.
SGCON: Share of government consumption.
CPICHG: Inflation (changes in consumer price index).
HIGHINC: A dummy variable for high-income countries.
AFRICA, EASIA, SASIA, LAC, MENA, and EECA are regional dummies.

F-tests are conducted to compare the full model (equation 3 in table 8.7) and the restricted models, the other five equations in tables 8.6 and 8.7. Our null hypothesis is that the full model which includes policy variables is not significantly different from the restricted models. The results reject the null hypothesis in all cases except one—equation 3 is not significantly different from equation 2 in table 8.7. In sum, our results suggest the following.

• A growth model is mis-specified if it includes initial social conditions alone, ignoring regional dummies and other factors potentially important to growth.

• Model specification is improved as policy variables such as trade, investment, and government consumption, as well as indicators of stability, are incorporated in a growth equation, together with initial conditions and regional dummies. Investment and openness to trade are positive and significant, and government consumption is negative and significant. *F*-tests also show that our full models which incorporate policy variables are superior to models without them.

In other words, initial conditions in education and income equality are necessary but not sufficient conditions for a country to take off on the income growth path. The right policy mix, especially of policies conducive to international trade and private investment, matters significantly for the outcomes of development and reform.

Experience of East Asian Reformers

East Asian reformers, socialist or non-socialist, have experienced remarkable successes in structural reforms. Although the approaches adopted vary substantially, some commonalities in initial conditions, pace of reform, and content of reforms stand out. The commonalities in initial *structural* conditions before reforms are generally obvious.

• Most East Asian reformers had only mild macroeconomic stability problems, except for Viet Nam (1988) and Mongolia (1990–92). Structural distortions are more severe in socialist reformers than in non-socialist reformers (table 8.4).

• Most East Asian reformers had low levels of specialization and large shares of agriculture and surplus labor, especially when compared with Eastern Europe and the former Soviet Union (table 8.5). For the East Asian socialist countries, however, the high level of investment in human capital and the more equal income distribution compares well with Eastern Europe and the former Soviet Union.

Commonalities in the content of reforms are also apparent. There is, however, less similarity in the pace of reform.

• Land reforms, agricultural price liberalization, and other rural reforms are generally conducted first among structural reforms. Korea and Taiwan (China) in the early 1950s and China and Viet Nam in the 1980s are cases in point.

• Openness to international trade and investment is at the center of reforms, although early birds and latecomers have different approaches. Expansion of labor-intensive exports was the key to takeoff on the growth path. Integration into the global market allowed technological catch-up and industrial upgrading to take place.

• Most East Asian countries have strong governments and have maintained relative political stability (World Bank 1993a, 1993b). Most of these countries also worked to build strong market institutions, some earlier (Korea from 1963 on) and some later (Thailand and China in the 1980s).

Stabilization

Where macroeconomic imbalances are severe, swift and decisive actions are more effective than incremental reforms (Bolivia, Israel, Mexico, Malaysia, and Viet Nam). Viet Nam's hyperinflation in 1988 was brought under control by raising interest rates (to 12 percent a month) and curbing credit financing of the budget deficit. During Malaysia's banking crisis in 1985–86, the central bank acted decisively to recapitalize banks and take over institutions that were unable to recapitalize. Thus contagion effects were prevented. Government deficits can be reduced relatively rapidly, as many developing countries have demonstrated. Viet Nam cut its fiscal deficit from 11.4 percent of GDP in 1989 to 3.8 percent in 1992 by streamlining the public sector significantly: budget subsidies to state enterprises were eliminated, and over 1 million workers and soldiers were cut from public sector payrolls (Dollar 1994). Not all fiscal reforms can be accomplished as quickly. Tax reform takes more time, and institutional reform in intergovernmental relations is an unfinished task in most countries.

Exchange Rate Reform and Policies

Exchange rate reform seems less sensitive to pace. Both rapid and gradual reform are effective. Viet Nam reformed rapidly, while China and other East Asian countries chose a more gradual pace. All achieved their targets. Mexico's exchange rate reform followed a pre-announced, step-by-step program in the late 1980s.

Aggressive exchange rate policies were common in East Asia, with devaluations under a fixed-rate regime followed by strict maintenance of a depreciated and stable exchange rate thereafter. Two-tier exchange rates were not uncommon during the interim. Korea had the lowest variability in real exchange rates among developing countries. Thailand's currency, tied to a basket of currencies, depreciated by 30 percent in real terms during the second trade reform in 1983–91. China's real exchange rate has depreciated substantially against other currencies since 1978. After a prolonged period of two-tier exchange rates and the development of a "swap" market, China's exchange rates were unified smoothly at the swap market rate in January 1994. Malaysia maintained a stable real exchange rate during 1960–83 through a policy of macroeconomic stability and minimum trade intervention. Viet Nam's exchange rates were unified and devalued sharply at the black market rate in 1989.

Openness to Foreign Trade

Trade policy has been an important component of East Asian development strategy, with considerable variations among early performers and latecomers. Most economies (except Hong Kong and Malaysia) had a period of import protection and substitution, followed by trade reforms. Singapore (1959–64), Taiwan (1953–58), Thailand (1960–79), and Indonesia (1973–80) had import-substitution policies. Korea (1960–79) had high levels of import protection despite its export emphasis.

When they introduced trade reforms, East Asian countries promoted exports first and liberalized imports later. Decisions on trade reforms were made quickly and announced clearly at the outset to give the right signals to producers and investors, but implementation was usually phased in slowly. Korea had a long period of export promotion and import protection during the 1970s, followed by trade liberalization in the 1980s. Devaluations, aggressive exchange rate management, and export policies ensured that import protection did not tip the terms of trade against exports. Similarly, Thailand conducted its second trade reform in the early 1980s and lowered tariffs on manufactured imports after 1990. When China started to reform, one of its first moves was to open up foreign trade in the late 1970s. Exports were promoted first, and foreign direct investment and imports were liberalized later. In Viet Nam, exports grew explosively at 30 percent a year after the liberalization of foreign trade and investment.

Openness to Foreign Investment

Openness to foreign investment is another key factor in East Asia's technological catching-up and growth in productivity. Some economies opened to foreign investment earlier (Indonesia, Singapore, and Malaysia), others later (Korea, Thailand, China, Viet Nam, and Lao PDR). The emerging capital markets in East Asia have become increasingly more attractive to foreign investors since the late 1980s. Private capital inflows to East Asia in 1994 totaled US$77.3 billion, in which 33 percent is port-folio investment ($25.8 billion) and 55 percent is foreign direct invest-ment ($43.0 billion). China has become the most attractive destination for foreign direct investment among developing countries, netting $23 billion in 1993 and nearly $30 billion in 1994.[3]

Agricultural Reforms
East Asian economies have given close attention to agricultural reforms, including land reforms and agricultural price liberalization. Several East Asian economies introduced land reform early on: Korea in 1950 and Taiwan (China) in 1949–52. Farmers in Indonesia have more equitable land tenure arrangements than farmers in other East Asian countries, for their rewards are tied directly to their efforts. This creates the pre-conditions for more broad-based growth of agricultural production.

China began its agricultural reforms by providing both ownership and price incentives. Land was returned to individuals on a long-term lease basis, and relative agricultural prices were increased 25 percent in real terms (with further increases later). The output response was rapid (average annual growth of 6 percent in 1979–89), and large cash savings created a surplus for investment. The agricultural reforms also released a pool of labor for new sources of employment, thus promoting the rapid development of township and village enterprises (TVEs) (Harrold 1992).

In Viet Nam, collective farms were dismantled, and family farming returned on the basis of long-term leases in 1989. Price controls were lifted in the agricultural sector, and price reform in industry and services was nearly as comprehensive. Agricultural output responded immediately. In the year that reforms were decisively undertaken, Viet Nam switched from a rice importer to a rice exporter. The increase in rural incomes had a spillover effect on the construction and service industries, which became the leading sectors during 1990 (Dollar 1994).

Financial Reforms and Development
Development of the financial sector and capital market in East Asia has been crucial for channeling funds from savers to productive oppor-tunities. There is a strong case for sequencing the liberalization of the financial sector. Deregulation of interest rates generally comes first,

---

3. There is, however, a certain amount of "roundtriping" of capital flows to China, i.e., illicit capital outflows being repatriated and disguised as foreign direct investment (FDI). A rough estimate puts it at around 25 percent of the annual FDI flows. See Shilling and Wang 1995, *Managing Capital Flows in East Asia.*

accompanied or followed by development of commercial banking and non-bank institutions. Development of a securities market takes longer, because it requires institution-building and the establishment of a legal infrastructure. Malaysia now has the world's ninth largest equity market in terms of market capitalization, and Korea and Thailand rank among the top twenty. Most East Asian countries maintained positive real interest rates. Active institution-building contributed to significant financial deepening and the development of equity and bond markets. Thailand developed a well-functioning commercial banking industry first, in the 1960s and 1970s, and then deregulated interest rates in the 1990s. Indonesia liberalized the financial sector early on; Korea and Taiwan (China) did the same much later in their development process, in the late 1980s and early 1990s.

Privatization

Most East Asian reformers have been cautious about privatizing large state-owned enterprises. But small-scale private sector development has been pursued aggressively. In China the non-state sector, especially the township and village enterprises, grew rapidly and now accounts for over half of industrial output.

China's approach to large state enterprises is similar to that of Korea: corporatization first, privatization later. Korea converted some government agencies to corporations (Tobacco Corporation and Telecom Corporation) and then sold shares through public offerings. In China, more than 25,000 companies have issued stocks to employees and other private shareholders. As of December 1995, 323 of these companies were allowed to list their shares on the country's two stock exchanges, and about 20 companies were allowed to list their stocks on overseas exchanges. Most equity joint ventures are also partially owned by foreign investors. Recently, most small and medium-sized state enterprises have been allowed to merge or to be acquired by other enterprises, private or public. Several hundred SOEs were allowed to go bankrupt in the last few years. Meanwhile, the non-state sector is growing at a spectacular speed, accounting for over 60 percent of the industrial output.

The Philippines sold 81 government-owned and controlled corporations by 1993, generating P28 billion in revenues. Malaysia privatized 106 public enterprises between 1985 and 1990. Indonesia had privatized ten state enterprises as of early 1993. Thailand had reduced the number of state enterprises from 100 to 63 by 1993; it sold 25 percent of Telecom Asia (50 percent of it to foreign investors) and 15 percent of the Bank of Asia in 1993. Privatization in the Lao PDR takes the form of leasing and joint ventures. Mongolia has privatized large state enterprises through vouchers distributed to the population.

Mass privatization gives firms a corporate structure, but it does not provide firms with the right incentives and corporate governance overnight (Fan and Schaffer 1994).[4] Firms become more efficient if, first, state subsidies are stopped and sound corporate governance structure is established; and second, a competitive external environment is established in the product market. Poland and Viet Nam cut state subsidies to public enterprises. China has been introducing competition in the product market. Both can be conducted through a pre-announced step-by-step fashion.

Lessons from the experience of East Asian reformers include a strong commitment to reform programs, careful maintenance of macro-economic stability, and openness to international trade and investment. Such openness allows a country to develop its industries according to its comparative advantage and to upgrade as factor endowment changes. Integration into the global market also allows countries to catch up technologically and to upgrade their labor force and industries (table 8.8).

8.5 Conclusions

Successful East Asian reformers made structural changes incrementally, but their experience is an endorsement not so much of gradualism as of timely action to avoid the need for shock therapy.

The economic arguments for early announcement of reforms in all areas and for rapid implementation in many remain strong. Socio-political realities, however, usually dictate an actual speed that is quite a bit slower than the optimal speed. After all, social and political stability have proved to be as vital an ingredient for success as economic stability (World Bank 1993a, 1993b). As long as macroeconomic instability is not a critical handicap requiring immediate action, a country, depending on structural characteristics, may be able to afford to pace the transition to accommodate broader acceptability. Moreover, the more specialized is a country's labor force, the more severe a disruption of production and displacement of workers the country can expect. Countries of Eastern Europe and the former Soviet Union are thus likely to experience a longer recession than low-income reforming countries.

---

4. A study, sponsored by the British government, of 27 privatized or privatizing firms in Russia in early 1993 concluded that enterprise behavior had not changed much as the result of privatization; firms continued to adjust in a fairly conservative, non-entrepreneurial fashion (KPMG Management Consulting 1993). A larger survey of 92 privatized Russian firms in October 1993 conducted by the World Bank and the EBRD concluded that insiders, namely managers, were in practice clearly in control of their enterprises (World Bank and EBRD 1993).

Table 8.8
Speed and types of reforms: East Asian reformers relative to others

Types of reforms	Rapid reform		Gradual reform	
	Countries	Results	Countries	Results
1. Macroeconomic stabilization	Bolivia, Mexico, and Israel	Successful	Brazil	Failed
	Poland (1989–90), Yugoslavia (1989–90)	Positive and big social cost	Hungary	Mixed
	Czechoslovakia, Bulgaria, and Romania (1991)	Positive and unfinished		
2. Exchange system				
Devaluation	Many countries	Positive with costs	China and other East Asians	Successful
Open capital account	U.K.	Successful	Israel	Successful
	Argentina, Chile, and Uruguay (1970s)	Failed	Mexico (1980s)	Successful
3. Trade liberalization				
Remove quantitative restrictions	Chile (1977–79)	Successful	EEC (1950–60)	Successful
	Mexico (1985–88)	Successful	Israel (1960s)	Successful
Reduce tariffs	Viet Nam	Successful	Korea (1980s)	Successful with costs
	EEFSU	Positive	China (1980s)	Successful, unfinished
4. Agricultural reform	Korea and Taiwan (1950s)	Successful		
Land reform	China (pseudo land reforms 1978–83)	Successful	Philippines	Unsuccessful

Table 8.8 (continued)

Types of reforms	Rapid reform		Gradual reform	
	Countries	Results	Countries	Results
Agricultural prices	Chile (1973)	Large short-term costs, large long-term gains	Columbia	Mixed
			China (1978–)	Positive, unfinished
	Viet Nam	Successful		
5. Price reforms				
Free most prices	Viet Nam	Successful		
Price of necessities	EEFSU	Positive, with big social costs	China (1979–)	Positive with costs
6. Financial reforms				
Interest rates and credit	Indonesia (1970-80s), Philippines	Mixed	Japan, Taiwan, Korea, and Singapore	Successful
De-monopolized banking	EEFSU	Unfinished		
Capital markets			China (1984–)	Positive, unfinished
7. Ownership reforms				
Small private enterprise	China (TVEs), Viet Nam, and EEFSU	Successful		
Privatization of large SOEs	Czech Republic	Some success	China (1984–) (partial)	Mixed, some positive results
	Russia and Poland	Some positive results		
8. Institution-building				
Legal infrastructure	Many countries	Positive, unfinished	Many countries	Positive, continuous
Social safety net	Viet Nam, EEFSU			
Fiscal decentralization	China (started early, still continuing)	Positive, unfinished	China (1983–)	Positive, unfinished

Initial conditions affect the need for speed, but they do not determine outcomes. Nor are they sufficient to ensure good growth performance. Policies that are conducive to investment and openness are more significantly related to growth. Direct foreign investment and openness to trade promise much greater gains than trade protection could ever provide.

The East Asian experience also suggests, however, that government has a major, positive role in reforms—laissez-faire is not optimal. The government's role is crucial in making markets work, dealing with externalities, and facilitating public investments. Reforms fail not because market liberalization proceeds too quickly, but because supportive, institutional reforms proceed too slowly.

Rapid market reform depends on having in place market-oriented institutions (a central bank and commercial banks, for example) and market-specific human capital (experts trained to run a central bank). The inadequacy of such institutions in countries in Eastern Europe and the former Soviet Union has hindered the effectiveness of liberalization. Those countries need to build a market-ready foundation of institutions and skilled people to allow rapid reforms to take hold and have an impact. China's approach works at the margin, building market institutions incrementally, as the role of old planning institutions is cut back. This strategy has worked in China, and may have some implications for other low-income transitional economies. It may or may not be replicable, however, in countries with different characteristics, just as Japan's experience with industrial policies.

Appendix 8 Framework, Data, and Methodology

The model used in this analysis is based on Barro (1989, 1990), where government policies on public services, taxation, and investment of human capital affect an economy's long-term growth in per capita income. The representative household in this economy seeks to maximize a utility function with a constant elasticity with respect to consumption. The production function is of the Cobb-Douglas form, with k, capital per person, and g, public services provided by government, as two major inputs. The resulting function for income growth includes some variable reflecting initial income level (GDP in 1960), some indicators of government expenditures, investment, schooling, population growth, regional dummies, and other variables. We modify this standard model by adding one indicator of openness to trade and investment. Here we split k into k_1, domestically produced capital goods, and k_2, which is goods imported from abroad. Openness then can affect growth through its effect on the level of k_2 and on the productivity (or rate of returns) of both k_1 and k_2 (see Easterly et al. 1992, 21). The resulting equation for growth rates can be specified as:

$$G_i = \alpha_0 + \Sigma \beta_j I_j + \Sigma \delta_j P_j + \Sigma \gamma R,$$

where G_i is the average growth rate of GDP per capita in country i, I is a set of initial conditions, P is a set of public policy indicators, and R is a set of dummy variables for regions where the country is located.

The data set is compiled based on the World Bank central database, from 87 countries for the period of 1970 to 1988, including 63 low- and middle-income countries (LMICs), 20 high-income countries, as well as four Eastern European countries. The cutoff point of 1988 is chosen because this is the year before the breaking-up of the former Soviet Union, and before the economic crises in the Eastern European countries began. The purpose is to avoid the problem of comparing countries in deep crises and those not in crisis. The regressions use the data set as a cross section, not as a panel, since our focus is on factors influencing *long-term* growth rates which can be reflected by the average growth rate in the 19-year period of 1970–88.

The data set includes the following variables: growth rate of GDP per capita; indicators of initial conditions, such as GDP per capita in 1970, education and health in 1970; and indicators of stability and public policies, such as shares of trade, investment, government consumption, and inflation rates. In addition, a set of regional dummy variables are defined and used in regressions to control for the impact of geographical proximity. See appendix table 8A.1.

The first two groups of variables are straightforward. The dependent variable in the regressions is the average annual real growth rate of GDP per capita (in constant 1987 dollars) in 1970–88. Indicators of initial conditions include GDP per capita in 1970, primary and secondary enrollment rates in 1970, infant mortality rate and total fertility rate in 1970, as well as average population growth rate during 1970–88. These initial conditions, except for the last, are time-invariant, and so are the regional dummies.

The third group consists of stability and government policy indicators. Gross domestic investment and government consumption are straight from the national income account, and shares are calculated as percentages of GDP in local currencies. Inflation rates are calculated based on the CPI data from the IMF international finance statistics.

Openness to trade is indicated by an instrumental variable, deviations in trade shares (DEVTRDS). As is well known, trade shares in GDP are affected by the size of a country's domestic market. Thus, it cannot be used directly to reflect "openness in trade." In this paper, we use an instrumental variable procedure to estimate a function for trade shares, and then use the calculated percentage deviations in trade shares as an indicator of openness. The function for trade shares is specified as follows:

$$T = f(p, a, l),$$

where T is the share of total trade (exports plus imports) in GDP, p is the population, a is the surface area and l represents the arable land of the countries. The rationale behind this specification is that surface area and population reflect the size of domestic market and demand. The larger the area and population, the larger the domestic market and, presumably, the less important the international trade. Arable land is incorporated because it can be considered a proxy for the agricultural sector, which also reflects the countries' dependency on international trade for food.

Deviations in trade shares, DEVTRDS, is then calculated as the ratio of the residual between actual and predicted trade share in actual trade share. Specifically,

$$DEVTRDS = \frac{(T - \hat{T})}{T},$$

where T is trade share and $\hat{T}$ is the trade share predicted based on the above estimated equation. DEVTRDS is then included in the main regressions representing the degree of openness to trade. Table 8A.1 lists the results of DEVTRDS for selected countries and regions.

The calculated deviations in trade shares make intuitive sense. DEVTRDS is the highest in East Asia among all regions, indicating East Asia is the region most open to trade. Across countries, DEVTRDS is the highest in the U.S. and lowest in Japan. This result implies, after controlling for the size of domestic market, that the U.S. is a country most "open" to trade in the world considering its low tariff and non-tariff barriers. Japan could have higher trade share, considering its small domestic market. China is the most open country among East Asian countries, controlling for population and land area. China's average trade share, at 23.96 percent during 1970–88, is the second highest among larger countries including Canada (43.62), Brazil (15.15), India (13.68), former USSR (estimated at 14.4, excluded in regressions) and the U.S. (15.84).

Regression results are presented in tables 8.6 and 8.7.

Table 8A.1
GDP growth and deviations in trade shares, 1970–88

Countries and regions	n	Growth in GDP per capita (%)	Trade shares in GDP (%)	Deviations in trade shares
Africa	22	–0.10	73.24	–0.07
East Asia	9	4.09	98.95	0.23
China	1	5.62	23.96	1.05
Indonesia	1	3.91	50.91	–0.90
Korea	1	6.87	57.92	–0.14
Malaysia	1	3.83	97.42	0.33
Thailand	1	4.14	49.57	–0.25
South Asia	4	1.79	33.30	–0.72
India	1	1.86	13.68	–0.20
Eastern Europe and Central Asia	4	1.65	47.91	–0.043
Albania	1	–0.40	38.62	–0.74
Hungary	1	3.23	69.15	0.05
Poland	1	0.40	39.37	–0.60
Romania	1	3.36	44.51	–0.45
Latin America	19	0.78	46.21	–0.55
Middle East and North Africa	9	3.00	66.75	–0.22
High income	20	2.29	49.94	–0.26
Canada	1	2.74	43.62	0.47
Japan	1	3.20	17.05	–2.71
U.S.A.	1	1.63	15.85	1.29

Note: This table is provided for the purpose of checking on DEVTRDS (deviations of the actual trade share in GDP from the predicted). Data for Eastern European countries are mainly from 1980–88.

9

An Overview of Stabilization Issues Facing Economies in Transition

Jeffrey D. Sachs

9.1 The Mechanics of Inflation

Most economies in transition face difficulties of maintaining price stability. High inflation has affected transition economies in Eastern Europe and the former Soviet Union, as well as in East Asia, including China and Viet Nam. This section outlines the main issues involving macroeconomic stabilization.

High inflation is almost always the result of two factors: *fiscal imbalances* and *low confidence* in macroeconomic management. These factors result in (1) rapid growth of the money supply, combined with (2) a flight from the currency. Usually, it is the combination of these forces which produces high inflation.

To separate the roles of fiscal imbalances and confidence, it is useful to start with the basic monetary identity: $M*V = P*Q$. Here, M is the money supply, V is velocity, P is the average price level, and Q is the level of real GDP. Nominal GDP is equal to $P*Q$. Then, by simple mathematical manipulation, we can see that

$$\dot{M}/M + \dot{V}/V = \dot{P}/P + \dot{Q}/Q \qquad (9.1)$$

where for any variable, $\dot{X} = dX/dt$, the rate of change of X. Let $\mu = \dot{M}/PQ$. That is, μ is the growth of the money supply measured as a percentage of GDP. Then we can rewrite (9.1) as

$$\dot{P}/P = \mu*V + \dot{V}/V - \dot{Q}/Q. \qquad (9.2)$$

Equation (9.2) shows that inflation will be high in the following conditions:

(a) a rapid increase in the money supply measured as a percent of GDP, μ;

(b) a high velocity, V, which interacts with high money growth in the term $\mu*V$; and

(c) a rapidly rising velocity, $\dot{V}/V$.

Note also that a low rate of real GDP growth, $\dot{Q}/Q$, will be associated with higher inflation. However, in cases of very high inflation, it is monetary factors (μ, $\dot{V}/V$, and V) which are the most important in determining the course of stabilization. Changes in output, $\dot{Q}/Q$, are important mainly as they affect the fiscal deficit, rather than as they affect the demand for money.

In practice, therefore, the main sources of high inflation in transition economies have been a rapid increase in the money supply, μ, and a flight from the currency, resulting in high and rising values of V.

Fiscal imbalances are the *main* sources of rapid money growth. Typically, the government borrows from the central bank to fund its activities, resulting in a rapid increase in the money supply. Of course, not all fiscal activities show up in the budget, since many government activities are hidden as "quasi-fiscal operations" that are off the balance sheets of budgetary units. Therefore, we refer to "fiscal deficits" as the broad category of government actions which must be financed, and "budget deficits" as the subset of those activities which appear in a formal budget. Two key examples of quasi-fiscal deficits are (1) extra-budgetary funds for social or regional spending, and (2) loans by the central bank and other state banks to state-owned enterprises. Thus, the money supply may grow excessively as a result of three main factors: budget deficits, extra-budgetary expenditures, and loans from the state banking system.

Loss of confidence in the money, resulting in rising V, can come from many factors. Low interest rates on deposits in the banking system may induce currency substitution and capital flight, resulting in a rising level of V. High inflation will similarly induce a flight from money, especially from holdings of currency. Expectations of future budget deficits will also induce a flight from the currency, in expectation of future inflation or future increases in taxation. Fears of currency confiscation, as have occurred in Russia during 1991 and 1993, may also induce a flight from the currency.

Note that in extreme circumstances, a loss of confidence can be self-fulfilling. Money holders believe that inflation will be high, so they try to convert their money holdings into foreign currency. As a result, V rises rapidly. In turn, the rise in V produces the high inflation that was feared by the money holders. In this sense, the loss of confidence in the currency has become a self-fulfilling prophecy.

9.2 Fiscal Consolidation

The most important step in macroeconomic stabilization is fiscal consolidation, that is, the elimination of the underlying fiscal and quasi-fiscal deficits that are the cause of the high inflation. Deficit reduction almost always requires actions on both expenditures and taxes. This is especially the case in transition economies. To see exactly what is required, it is useful to understand the fiscal structures of the transition economies in comparison with market economies.

In table 9.1 we examine the structure of general government revenues and expenditures in Poland in 1987, two years before the start of Poland's transition to the market economy, and 1993. Poland (and other transition economies in Central and Eastern Europe) began its reforms with several unusual budgetary characteristics.

On the revenue side, a large proportion of taxation came from profit taxes on state enterprises. Indirect taxes, moreover, were in the form of turnover taxes on state enterprises rather than the more efficient and modern system of value-added taxation. There was no individual income taxation. The traditional sources of revenue in the transition economies, viz., taxes on state enterprises, tend to decline sharply when market reforms begin, largely because market liberalization offers new ways for the state enterprises to avoid tax collections, and because an increasing proportion of GDP originates in the private sector. The simplest method of tax avoidance is for the state enterprises to pay high wages and benefits to the workers, so that the profits of the state enterprises decline.

The key steps in tax reform, and fiscal consolidation, typically involve the move from a tax system based on the state enterprise (profits taxes and turnover taxes) to a system based on value-added taxes (VAT) and individual income taxes. Note that in Poland, corporate (mostly state enterprise) taxation declined from 12.5 percent of GDP in 1987 to merely 4.2 percent of GDP in 1993. Individual income taxes, by contrast, rose from nothing to 9.0 percent of GDP. Overall, there was a modest decline in revenues of the general government, from 52.4 percent of GDP in 1987 to 47.6 percent of GDP in 1993.

On the expenditure side, the main difference between the transition and market economies is the high level of subsidies to the state enterprises before the start of reforms. In 1987, Poland's government (at all levels) expended a remarkable 11.8 percent of GDP in enterprise subsidies. Poland's reliance on subsidies was even larger than indicated, however, because of the use of off-budget subsidization, especially in the form of soft credits to state enterprises from the banking system. Another key characteristic of the pre-reform economies is the large government expenditure on investment. Capital expenditure in Poland was 7.9 percent of GDP in 1987.

Fiscal consolidation typically involves sharp cuts in subsidies, and a sharp cut in public investment spending, with much of the investment spending transferred from the budget to the enterprises themselves. We see in table 9.1 that by 1993, subsidies to the state enterprises had been cut dramatically, down to just 1.9 percent of GDP. Similarly, capital expenditure declined to just 3.3 percent of GDP.

It is notable, however, that Poland's spending on government goods and services (mainly health care, education, and public administration) and on social transfers, increased markedly over the same period, thus offsetting the fiscal gains that came from the cuts in subsidies and capital expenditures. Overall, total government expenditures remained nearly unchanged as a percentage of GDP, declining marginally from 50.4 percent of GDP in 1987 to 49.9 percent of GDP in 1993. I will return to the crucial issue of social spending in section 9.6, when I consider long-term issues in fiscal policy.

Poland's main gains in stabilization came from the end of quasi-fiscal deficits, mainly cheap credits from the state banks, rather than from a large and persistent reduction in the budget deficit itself.[1] Poland, like many of its neighbors, succeeded in accomplishing a major structural shift to a market-based fiscal system, including six main steps: the introduction of individual income taxes, the introduction of the VAT, the decline in reliance on state enterprise profit taxation, the end of the turnover tax, the cut in subsidies to state enterprises, and the cut in public investment spending. But, also like many of its neighbors, Poland did not succeed in reducing the overall share of government expenditures in GDP, since higher social transfers and spending on education and health compensated for the cuts in subsidies and capital spending. Therefore, Poland has not yet definitively ended its budgetary pressures.

9.3 Other Financial Steps Towards Stabilization

In addition to tax reform and expenditure cuts, it is important for the government to develop new methods for non-monetary financing of budget deficits in the short term. For example, a government Treasury bill market can add important flexibility to fiscal policy and to anti-inflation policy in economies in transition, by allowing governments to borrow from the domestic public, rather than from the central bank. Most economies in transition have taken steps to spur the development of Treasury bill markets.

---

1. In addition, the budget deficit widened enormously during the political turmoil of 1988 and 1989, so that part of the large fiscal adjustment in 1990 involved reversing the serious fiscal deterioration of the previous two years.

Table 9.1
Government revenues and expenditures in Poland (percent of GDP): pre-reform (1987) and post-reform (1993)

	1987	1993
Revenues:	52.4	47.6
Corporate taxes	12.5	4.2
Individual taxes	0.0	9.0
Indirect taxes	15.4	11.4
Other revenues	24.5	23.0
Expenditures:	50.4	49.9
Capital	7.9	3.3
Current goods and services, interest	10.2	15.6
Enterprise subsidies	11.8	1.9
Pensions, other benefits, and other transfers to households	12.2	21.0
Other	8.3	8.1
Deficit	−0.8	−2.6

Source: Antczak et al. (1995).

Foreign borrowing can also play an important role in reducing the dependence on monetary financing of the deficit. If the government can borrow from the international financial markets (e.g., the international bond market or the IMF), it does not have to borrow from the central bank. Hence, the same size budget deficit can be financed without increasing the money supply.

In accounting terms, the fiscal deficit as a percentage of GDP (d) can be financed by monetization of the central bank (μ), or by foreign borrowing (f), or by domestic bond financing (b). Therefore, $d = \mu + f + b$. For a given deficit, a higher level of f or b will result in a lower level of μ.

Privatization can play an additional role in fiscal consolidation in several ways. To a modest extent (which is often exaggerated in government plans), the government may be able to raise revenue from the sale of state-owned assets. More importantly, the transfer of state enterprises to private owners usually allows the government to escape from the political obligation to provide subsidies to loss-making firms. In this indirect way, privatization may thereby reduce the outflow of funds associated with the "soft budget constraint" of the state enterprise sector. More subtle methods of privatization, such as the transfer of state assets to (private) pension funds, to help cover the costs of social security obligations, may also allow the government to use the privatization of state assets to reduce budgetary costs.

9.4 Structural Aspects of Moderate Inflation

When inflation is very high, monetary factors dominate the inflationary process. Thus, ending budget deficits and rapid credit expansion are usually sufficient to end high rates of inflation. After inflation has come down to relatively low rates (e.g., below 30 percent per year), various structural factors can raise the costs of further disinflation. To put the issue more precisely, fiscal and monetary discipline will still be necessary to eliminate the remaining inflation. Nonetheless, the *costs* of disinflation (in terms of lost output or temporarily higher unemployment), can be affected by various structural factors in the economy.

Structural impediments to stabilization include (1) widespread indexation of wages and prices, (2) lack of competition among enterprises, and (3) an extensive labor force in state-owned enterprises. Indexation of wages and prices can contribute to an ongoing wage–price spiral even after restrictive monetary and fiscal policies have been put in place. The lack of competition among enterprises (particularly in the service sector or in manufacturing sectors that are sheltered from international competition) can also result in persistent inflation even after macroeconomic policies have become restrictive. Eventually, the monopolistic enterprises will stabilize their prices, but often at levels far above costs, and with a substantial loss in output and efficiency.

A high proportion of the labor force in state-owned enterprises can also lead to persistent wage increases despite restrictive macroeconomic measures, because wage negotiations in state enterprises are often dominated by political rather than economic considerations, and because state enterprise managers are often willing to grant wage increases even when the state enterprise is facing restrictive credit conditions, using enterprise "profits" to pay higher wages. (This reflects the obvious fact that the "profits" do not belong to real owners.) Other kinds of restrictive labor market practices can also lead to short-term persistence of wage inflation, and eventually to high unemployment. Restrictions on firing workers can strengthen the bargaining power of workers to press for wage increases even when unemployment is rising.

For these reasons, disinflation programs often include de-indexation of wages, liberalization of international and domestic trade (to increase competition), partial deregulation of domestic labor markets, and privatization, to promote market-based disciplines on enterprise behavior.

Many countries have experimented with wage–price controls or other forms of "income policies" as accompaniments to stabilization. It is very clear from experience that price controls lead to shortages and distortions that make them highly undesirable. They also tend to increase political conflict, as consumers and suppliers argue vigorously about the "appropriate" levels for particular controls. This political conflict can weaken or defeat a government attempting to carry out a stabilization program. There may be a slightly stronger case for temporary wage controls, at least with respect to workers in state-owned enterprises. As with price controls, however, the introduction of wage controls imposes distortions and invites extreme political conflict within the economy. If any wage controls are used, they should be very short-term and restricted to state enterprises.

9.5 Monetary Policy to Support Stabilization

In most situations with high inflation, there is little independence of monetary policy. The central bank is forced to lend money to the government to cover large budget deficits, so that the money is a "hostage" of the fiscal deficit. In this sense, the most important step towards monetary stabilization is, in most cases, not really monetary policy, but fiscal policy. Nevertheless, there are many monetary choices that accompany a successful stabilization program.

The most practical choice is the kind of exchange rate regime. Should the exchange rate be freely floating, or should the central bank announce an official rate of foreign exchange, and then intervene in the foreign exchange market in order to stabilize the exchange rate at the promised level? There is considerable debate about these economic choices. In my opinion, the lessons of history suggest the following three ideas.

1. For large or medium-sized countries that have already achieved low inflation, a floating exchange rate system is the most flexible and realistic system.

2. For very small countries, which are very open to trade, a fixed exchange rate system, linked to the major trading partner, is the most realistic.

3. For countries trying to end a high inflation, a *temporary* period of a pegged exchange rate is a useful accompaniment to fiscal consolidation.

There are many reasons to prefer a floating exchange rate system for most countries that are already operating at low rates of inflation. Most importantly, the floating rate system can help the economy to adapt to international shocks. When a country suffers a decline in the terms of trade (e.g., a fall in oil prices for an oil-exporting country, or a rise in interest rates for a debtor economy), it is almost always necessary to reduce domestic expenditures and to expand exports. In order to carry out such an adjustment, the price of tradeable goods (both exportable goods and import-competing goods) must increase relative to non-tradeable goods. A depreciation of a floating exchange rate is usually an effective mechanism to achieve the necessary adjustment. The alternative approaches are (1) a devaluation of a previously pegged exchange rate; or (2) a fall in domestic prices, brought about by a domestic recession. A devaluation of a pegged rate is usually more traumatic politically than a depreciation of a floating rate. A fall in domestic prices is usually very painful in terms of unemployment and lost output.

Another crucial reason to prefer a floating exchange rate in the long term is that a pegged exchange rate might become uncompetitive over several years as a result of excessive nominal wage increases in the domestic economy. Many countries which attempted to maintain a pegged rate in the long run have found themselves losing long-term competitiveness, even when the economy has not been hit by a large external shock. Clearly this occurred in West Africa to countries pegged to the French franc. It has happened to many countries in Central and South America that tried to maintain a long-term pegged rate to the U.S. dollar.

Despite the general presumption in favor of flexible exchange rates, there are still important cases when a pegged exchange rate is useful. When a country is attempting to end a period of very rapid inflation, pegging the exchange rate can be an important part of early stabilization. There are several reasons why a pegged exchange rate is useful at the start of stabilization. One important reason is symbolic: the commitment to a pegged exchange rate is a very visible signal of the government, that may increase confidence and stop a flight from the currency. Thus, if velocity has been rising rapidly, a commitment to peg the exchange rate, backed by a supply of international reserves (perhaps supplied by the IMF or other governments), can restore confidence in the domestic currency.

There is a second, and more subtle reason, but one that is very important and poorly understood. At the end of a period of high inflation, real money balances (M/P) tend to be very low, since households and businesses have reduced their money holdings as much as possible to avoid the inflationary losses on money. Instead of using domestic money in the high inflation, economic agents use foreign money or inventories of commodities as stores of value (and foreign money as a means of payment, usually for expensive items such as houses, cars, real estate, and capital equipment). Therefore, once stabilization is achieved, M/P will rise, as households and firms convert their foreign currency and physical assets back into money.

Under a pegged exchange rate, the conversion of these assets back into domestic money is fairly automatic. As the demand for domestic money increases at the start of stabilization, households attempt to sell dollars and to buy domestic money. This causes the exchange rate to begin to appreciate in nominal terms. The central bank, which is committed to a pegged exchange rate, is forced to intervene in the foreign exchange market to stop the appreciation, by buying dollars and selling domestic currency. As a result, M/P tends to rise. The supply of money automatically adjusts to the demand for money.

Under a floating exchange rate, however, the automatic adjustment cannot take place. Instead, the exchange rate appreciates but the central bank does not intervene. Therefore, the money supply M does not increase. The result can be an overvalued currency and very high real interest rates, since the supply of money M/P remains very low even after inflation ends. Since domestic wages and non-tradeable prices will tend to fall very little even when the exchange rate appreciates significantly, the result will be low real money balances, high real interest rates, and an overvalued currency.

For these reasons, stabilization with a pegged exchange rate has tended to be less costly than stabilization with a floating exchange rate. Most successful stabilizations in the past decade have relied on a pegged exchange rate for at least a short period after the start of stabilization. This includes Bolivia (1985), Israel (1985), Mexico (1987), Poland (1990), Argentina (1991), and Estonia (1992). Several countries have stabilized with a floating exchange rate, such as Peru (1990) and Latvia (1992), but it seems that the output costs of disinflation have been much higher. (Even in these cases, however, there was a subsequent economic recovery.)

Without question, there is a need for long-term institutional change in monetary management to support stabilization. In order to prevent a reversion to money-financed budget deficits, it is important to give the central bank enough independence to be able to refuse demands for credits that may come from the Treasury or the president. There is evidence that countries with independent central banks, particularly banks in which the governor of the central bank cannot be fired by the government or the Parliament, are better able to resist the political pressures for money expansion than are countries with central banks that are under the political control of the government. The law governing the central bank should also be explicit in underscoring that the preeminent goal of the central bank is price stability.

One recent idea that has become popular in some circles is to eliminate the central bank altogether, and to create a currency board, in which the only responsibility of the monetary authorities is to maintain a permanently fixed exchange rate to an international currency. Under a currency board, the monetary authority buys and sells domestic money in exchange for foreign money at a predetermined, fixed rate. The currency board is prohibited by law from making any loans to the government or the banking sector. Currency boards were the main instrument of monetary control in the British Empire. Colonial administrations linked the local currency one-to-one with British sterling. Since 1970, four countries have adopted systems like currency boards: Argentina, Estonia, Hong Kong, and Lithuania. The French African Franc Zone operated like a currency board arrangement until the devaluation last year. Panama also operates according to currency board rules.

The currency board approach has serious flaws, except for a few very small, very open economies (e.g., Hong Kong). First, there is a tendency for the real exchange rate to become over-valued in the long run, with serious consequences for economic growth (as in French Africa). Second, the country's banking system becomes vulnerable to panics as a result of a currency board system, since the central bank can no longer play the role of "lender of last resort," which is often vital for banking stability. Thus, Argentina suffered a serious banking crisis early in 1995, which required an international financial bailout. Third, there seem to be better, and more flexible, ways to establish monetary stability than a strict currency board. As I have already argued, central bank independence, combined with responsible budgetary policies, can do the job of providing long-term price stabilization.

9.6 Long-term Issues of Fiscal Restructuring

Short-run fiscal stabilization may be enough to end a high inflation, but long-term fiscal reform is needed to keep the inflation rate low. Most of the advanced industrial economies are under chronic, long-term fiscal stress in the past decade because of political and economic pressures tending towards higher budget deficits and higher government spending. These pressures can possibly be avoided in the developing countries if they plan ahead by making long-term structural reforms.

The main source of budgetary pressures in the advanced economies is social spending by the government, usually in the form of government transfers for pensions, health care, child support, unemployment compensation, and welfare payments for low-income groups.

Table 9.2
Social spending in selected countries, averages for 1985–90 (percent of GDP)

	GDP per capita	Social	Education	Health	Total
Developing countries:					
South Asia	1,260	0.7	3.4	1.4	5.5
East Asia	3,210	3.4	2.8	2.2	8.4
Latin America	5,360	3.4	4.2	2.4	10.0
Eastern Europe	5,210	14.9	4.8	5.2	24.9
Developed countries:					
OECD	19,000	16.3	4.9	5.9	27.1

Source: United Nations, *World Development Handbook* (1994).
Note: GDP per capita is measured in purchasing power parity terms, in 1991 US$. OECD is the group of countries of the Organization of Economic Cooperation and Development. All variables are averages for 1985–90.

Of these expenditures, pension payments are by far the largest, followed by government spending on health care. Some indication of public expenditures for social purposes is shown in table 9.2, using cross-country data for 1985–90 from the United Nations. As shown in the table, the governments of the advanced industrial countries spent around 27 percent of GDP on social expenditures, with about half of that in pension payments. Eastern Europe, though much poorer than Western Europe, also spent a huge amount on social functions, reaching 24 percent of GDP during 1985–90. As table 9.3 demonstrates clearly, this social spending continued to increase during the reforms of the 1990s, so that Eastern Europe now spends approximately the same as Western Europe, despite a per capita GDP of about one-fourth the level of the richer countries in Western Europe.

This level of social spending is contributing to severe long-term budget and political crises in the advanced economies and in Eastern Europe. In order to cover such large social transfers, these countries must impose very high tax rates. In turn, these high tax rates lead to serious distortions of incentives, to capital flight, and to considerable tax evasion and illegal economic activities in the tax-free black market. Therefore, there are strong pressures to cut back on the generosity of the social transfers, yet there are also huge political obstacles to cutting back on these expenditures.

Table 9.3
Changing patterns of social expenditures and subsidies (percent of GDP): pre-reform (1989) and post-reform (1993)

	Social expenditures		Subsidies	
	1989	1993	1989	1993
Bulgaria	10.4	12.9	15.5	3.9
Czech Republic	13.2	14.6	16.6	n.a.
Estonia[a]	10.4	8.8	2.5	1.3
Hungary	15.8	22.5	10.7	3.1
Poland	10.0	21.0	12.9	3.3
Slovakia	13.2	17.0	16.6	4.8
Slovenia	25.9	30.5	3.4	4.1

Sources: European Bank for Reconstruction and Development, *Transition Report* (1994, table 6.6, 87), except for Poland (1989, 1994) and Slovenia (1994), which are based on national data.
Note: the 1989 data for the Czech Republic and Slovakia are the 1989 figures for Czechoslovakia.
a. Data are for 1991 rather than 1989.

The best strategy for countries in Latin America and East Asia that have not yet developed comparable levels of social spending is to look for new mechanisms to achieve social goals such as old-age support, but without burdening the state so severely. There are many promising approaches that are now being tried. Most notably, Chile has introduced a *private*, but regulated, pension system that accomplishes many of the goals of old-age support, but is based on household savings rather than government taxes and transfers. Many other countries in Latin America (e.g., Argentina, Bolivia, Colombia, and Peru) are currently copying the Chilean approach, and I believe that it has important lessons for Eastern Europe and East Asia.

Another important issue for long-term fiscal reform is "fiscal federalism," the division of tax and spending responsibility between central and local governments. One of the legacies of World War II and postwar development strategies was the highly centralized state. Until recently, most countries concentrated the core of fiscal powers at the national level, and local governments had little fiscal authority. Often the local governments were simply administrative offices appointed by the central government. In recent years, there has been a powerful trend towards increased power of local governments. It has been recognized that local governments can increase political legitimacy, representation, and public participation, and can make more effective decisions in many cases regarding local infrastructure and social expenditures. Thus, in Brazil, Canada, China, India, Russia, and the United States, there is a sharp discernible trend towards more power for local governments.

It is therefore crucial that tax and spending systems adjust harmoniously to these trends in political organization. Local governments need adequate sources of funding, and more authority to design expenditure programs. It is important to encourage local governments to compete with each other by improving local business conditions. At the same time, this competition should not be destructive of the national market (e.g., local governments should not be able to impose limits on trade with other regions), and should not force local governments to cut taxes below the levels needed to fund local public goods. Fiscal federalism involves many unsolved, yet extremely important, problems of political and economic organization.

In addition to substantive reforms of budgetary policies, there may be a need for reforms of the budgetary process. Countries differ significantly in their *procedures* for approving the annual budget. For example, fiscal pressures tend to be greater in countries in which the Parliament has widespread powers to adopt expenditure programs beyond those requested by the government. Conversely, fiscal pressures are reduced when parliamentary procedures limit the power of special interests to push for spending programs outside of the boundaries set by the government.

In addition to budgetary control, two other issues should be mentioned as priorities for long-term macroeconomic management. The first is the development of a healthy banking sector. This involves privatization of state banks, recapitalization of loss-making banks, opening the banking sector to international competition, and proper regulatory supervision of the banking system to avoid future banking crises. The second issue is the development of a workable system for enterprise bankruptcies. In both cases, the fiscal costs of inadequate policies could be very high. Government bailouts of bad banks and bad enterprises add substantially to fiscal burdens. Much is already known about these topics, but unfortunately the subjects are complex, and go beyond the scope of this paper.

10 Trade Policies in Transition Economies: A Comparison of European and Asian Experiences

Georges de Menil

10.1 Introduction

Large increases in international trade have been a major feature of successful transitions to date from central planning to a market economy. Reformers have viewed trade as both a means and an end—a means for appropriating capitalist efficiency and introducing competition into domestic markets, and an end in itself, in that it provides access to the material goods associated with the standard of living of developed countries. This chapter is an attempt at a comparative analysis of the principal causal factors influencing trade performance in Poland, Czecho-slovakia, Hungary, Viet Nam, China, and the Russian Federation.

The most widely accepted explanation of the trade performance of transition economies is an extension of the standard post-Keynesian analysis which holds that the key to success is a sharp real devaluation, accompanied by restrictive macroeconomic policies to reduce domestic absorption. When the devaluation is decisive, and tight macroeconomic policies are forcefully implemented, the trade balance improves and trade expands. When either one is indecisive or insufficient, the adjustment fails.[1]

Jacques Delpla provided invaluable assistance with data collection. I am grateful for advice and help with data sources from Luca Barboni, Olivier Bouin, Timothy Helleniak, Bart Kaminsky, Marcelo Selowsky, and Wing Thye Woo, and for comments and criticisms from Jacques Delpla, Marek Dabrowski, Zdanek Drabek, Laslo Halpern, Stephen Parker, Richard Portes, Dani Rodrik, and Wing Thye Woo. The opinions and errors are my own.

1. These are the bare bones of what Bruno (1993) calls the "real fundamentals" of "orthodox stabilization" (see table 8.1, 269). Rodrik (1994a) suggests that these two classical macroeconomic measures are "the only serious contenders" as explanations of the boom in Visegrad exports to the West. Portes (1994, 6), also commenting on the Central and Eastern European countries (CEECs), states that their "trade performance (in terms of net exports) ... is perhaps not astonishing in view of the deep fall in output and ... the continuing substantial under-valuation of their exchange rates relative to PPP." (See also Faini and Portes

In this chapter I allow for a different emphasis. In each case, I consider the possibility that the intensity and comprehensiveness of the trade liberalization measures may have had an independent and long-lasting effect, in and of themselves. I do not deny that, where they were observed, devaluation and the compression of domestic demand increased net exports. However, I focus attention on the positive effects on supply of the dismantling of the trade restrictions associated with central planning.

Poland, Czechoslovakia, Hungary, and Viet Nam, which implemented comprehensive reform programs featuring the rapid liberalization of domestic markets and trade, are analyzed as a group in section 10.2. The two major powers in the former communist world, China and the Russian Federation, call for special treatment. China's trade policies and trade performance are analyzed in section 10.3, and Russia's in section 10.4. Section 10.5 attempts to knit together the common threads of these six experiences.

10.2 Four Cases of Rapid and Comprehensive Liberalization

When the Berlin Wall came down, the conventional wisdom in Europe was that rapid trade liberalization could not succeed. Enterprises in communist countries were said to produce goods of such poor quality, and so inefficiently, that they could not possibly compete with their Western counterparts. The reconstruction of Western Europe after World War II was held up as an example; it was more than ten years after the War before the Western European nations attained current account convertibility. It was argued that the European Payments Union (1950–1957) was the kind of institutional arrangement Central Europe should set up to preserve regional trading patterns while awaiting convertibility.

Defying admonitions to proceed slowly, the political leaders of Poland, Czechoslovakia, and Hungary implemented the most rapid and comprehensive trade liberalization measures to have been attempted anywhere in the world in recent history. In Viet Nam trade reform was slower, and it did not go as far. But even there, the speed of implementation compared favorably with that in Chile (1974–1979).

Trade Policies of the Rapid Reformers: The Main Features

Poland. Opening the country to world markets was central to the logic of the Polish reform strategy. International markets were seen as

---

1995, 4.) Focusing on the "differences in the time pattern of [export] growth between the three Visegrad countries," Drabek and Smith (1995) assert, "It is tempting to relate these differences to the differences in the evolution of real exchange rates."

providing a solution to the critical problem of phasing. As long as all industry remained in gigantic state-owned enterprises (SOEs), freeing prices was unlikely to generate efficient signals and incentives. But breaking up and privatizing industry would take time, and did not seem possible in the absence of meaningful relative prices with which to value the parts. With trade liberalization, Poland could import, with one stroke of the pen, both world relative prices and international competition. Furthermore, by locking its economy into the world trading system, its leaders hoped to bolster the irreversibility of the regime change.

Before 1989, trade was largely set by the central plan. Foreign exchange was recovered and rationed at an official rate below the parallel market rate. World prices were deprived of value as signals through their systematic equalization with domestic prices by means of a complex and detailed system of taxes and subsidies.

On January 1, 1990, Poland abolished most price controls, dismantled the remnants of centralized allocation of products, terminated the state monopoly of foreign trade, and eliminated almost all remaining equalizing taxes and subsidies. A central feature of the strategy was the conscious rejection of sectoral policy objectives.

There remained an obligation to repatriate foreign currency export earnings, but they were exchanged into zlotys at the same rate (minus a normal commission) at which importers bought the foreign exchange. Although transfers in and out of the country required authorization, domestic financial institutions could offer demand deposits, time deposits, and securities in foreign currencies.

As to trade policy, the only significant instruments retained were import duties. The schedule of import duties, which had been established a year before, was low and relatively uniform. The average potential rate was 18.3 percent, but the average effective rate was 10 percent.[2] To promote competition, the government abolished many of these duties: by August 1990 it had removed all duties on 60 percent of Poland's imports, and the average potential tariff rate had fallen to 5.5 percent. In the estimation of the GATT secretariat, by the end of 1990 Poland's commercial policy was "one of the most liberal of Europe."[3]

After August 1991, Poland's commercial policy experienced some backsliding. Most of the import duties which had been reduced the previous year were restored to their original values, and some were raised. These increases were motivated by a desire to establish a higher baseline for planned further reductions negotiated with GATT and the

2. OECD (1992, 149 and table 1, 151).
3. GATT (1993, 9).

European Union (EU). They were also responses to increasing political pressure for some form of protection.

In September 1993, legislative elections gave a majority to a coalition led by the SDRP (Social Democracy of the Polish Republic, the former Communist Party) and the PSL (allied Polish Peasant Party). The new government has continued the basic strategy of its predecessors, but has announced its intention to implement an industrial policy and intervene in sectoral decisions.

The Other Visegrad Reformers

Czechoslovakia.   Price and trade liberalization were roughly as extensive, as deep, and as rapid in Czechoslovakia as in Poland. The tariffs and occasional quotas which replaced the former system of state management and allocation were initially slightly more restrictive than Poland's. The average potential import tariff rate was only 5.9 percent,[4] but imports of consumption goods were subject to a temporary 20 percent surcharge. Quotas were put into effect, not only on a few sensitive exports and exports subject to international voluntary restraint agreements, but also on some imports (agricultural products). But by the end of 1992, Czechoslovakia's restrictions had come down,[5] and since Poland's had been raised, the two countries were in about the same position. Since the break-up of Czechoslovakia, the Czech Republic has maintained low tariffs.

Hungary.   By 1991 Hungary had a long history of gradual reforms. The New Economic Mechanism introduced in 1968 replaced direct quantity allocations with an indirect mechanism which relied on a complex system of price regulations, price controls, subsidies, and taxes. Some forms of private economic association had been introduced in 1981 on the occasion of entry into the IMF. Between 1987 and 1991, the state trading monopoly was relaxed, and access to the foreign exchange market (unified since 1981, but still rationed) was increased. The percentage of retail prices which were free had moved from 41 percent in 1987 to 77 percent in 1990.[6] Nonetheless, in 1990 the state still had control of a substantial part of trade; imports of consumption goods were subject to a global quota, and licenses were still required in 1990 for 30 percent of imports.

In January 1991 the government announced a new four-year program of further liberalization, and accompanied the announcement with a modest devaluation of the forint. All but 10 percent of retail prices were

---

4. See OECD-CCET (1994a, table 1.1, 34).
5. The import surcharge was lowered to 10 percent in January 1992.
6. See Riecke and Antal (1993, table 4.2, 111).

freed, and the state trading monopoly was abolished.[7] In addition, the quota on consumption goods imports was raised to such a degree that it became inoperative, import licenses were rendered automatic, and export licenses were largely eliminated. In 1992 a free, inter-bank market for foreign exchange was introduced. By the end of 1992, Hungary bene-fited from the three internal convertibility provisions which had been introduced by all of Central Europe's rapid reformers: free access of enter-prises to foreign exchange for imports, the right for foreigners to repa-triate investment income and capital gains, and liquidate their investment, and the right for domestic residents to hold foreign currency accounts.[8]

However, by the end of 1993, deterioration of the trade balance and pol-itical pressure were producing what Winters (1995a) calls "liberalization fatigue." In December 1993, the government presented a program to reduce the foreign deficit through promoting exports and curtailing imports.

Viet Nam

It is somewhat paradoxical to present Viet Nam's reform experience alongside those of Visegrad countries. Unlike them, Viet Nam is an underdeveloped country, engaged predominantly in traditional agricul-ture.[9] Nevertheless, Viet Nam's initial conditions and policies resemble in some ways those of the rapid reformers in Central Europe.

Viet Nam was initially, like the Visegrad countries, a fully integrated member of the centralized trading system of the Soviet Union, the Council on Mutual Economic Assistance (CMEA). In 1986, 38 percent of Viet Nam's exports were shipped to CMEA partners. Comparable figures for Poland, Czechoslovakia, and Hungary in 1989 were 37 percent, 48 percent, and 36 percent. (See also Appendix 10, tables 10A.1, 10A.2, 10A.4, and 10A.5).[10]

Like Poland, Viet Nam wrestled with hyperinflation in the months which preceded its "jump to the market" in 1989. The leadership experi-mented with piecemeal market-oriented reforms between 1980 and

---

7. The state retained management of trade in three commodities: pork, scrap iron, and waste paper. See OECD-CCET (1994a, table 1.1, 34).

8. See OECD-CCET (1994b, table 1, 52).

9. In 1988, agriculture accounted for 72 percent of total employment in Viet Nam, but only 29 percent of employment in Poland, 14 percent in Hungary, and 11 percent in Czechoslovakia. In 1993, GDP per capita was $3,510 in Hungary, $3,074 in Czechoslovakia, $2,233 in Poland, and only $180 in Viet Nam. See World Bank (1994b, table 1.3); Berg and Sachs (1992, table 4); Hare and Revesz (1992, table 9b); and Begg (1991, table 3).

10. All the trade data reported in this paper must be reviewed with cir-cumspection. Pre-reform and post-reform domestic currency flows are not comparable because of the extensive change in relative prices brought about by reform. Simple translation into dollars with average exchange rates masks the major distortions which can be associated with these changes in relative prices.

1985, but the result was an inflation rate approaching 30 percent per month for several months in 1986. Another bout of near-hyperinflation and a balance-of-payments crisis in 1988 led to the adoption of a radical strategy of reform and stabilization.

Between January and June 1989, price controls, state procurement, and rationing were eliminated for most goods. The number of foreign trade companies (whose conditions of establishment were liberalized) doubled to close to 160. Most importantly, in March 1989 the official exchange rate was dramatically devalued (the dong/dollar rate for transactions within the plan went from 900 to 4,500), and the official and parallel exchange markets were unified. The devaluation was accompanied by a sharp increase in real interest rates, which became positive, and by measures to reduce the government deficit, which had grown to 7.2 percent of GDP.

The liberalization of exports continued, and by April 1994 the World Bank (1994b, 60) was able to report that "any enterprise with prospects for receiving an export order is granted the authority to export the products it produces, and to import inputs that are needed for export production. ... No products are subject to export quota, and except on raw materials, export taxes have been eliminated or reduced to minimal levels." The liberalization of imports did not proceed as far. In the same report, the World Bank (1994b, 62) states that permits and quotas were still in place for 15 products, and the tariff code was complex, characterized by escalating and variable rates ranging from 0 to 200 percent. The average, unweighted rate was 11.9 percent in January 1993. The persistence of this distortionary schedule of import duties is one of the important remaining differences between Viet Nam's policy experience and the otherwise similar experiences of the Visegrad countries.

Trade Performances of the Rapid Reformers

How did the trade flows of Poland, Czechoslovakia, Hungary, and Viet Nam evolve in the years that followed their reforms? The story is one of dramatic restructuring; see tables 10A.1–10A.7 in Appendix 10.

Two important caveats about the data are in order. The first is that most of the numbers are derived from official, national data sources. These sources are well known to under-report trade flows in the first years of transition because of the disorganization of the state, the lack of training of the civil service, and the proliferation of informal transactions. Clear evidence of this under-reporting can be found by comparing national source data with measures of the same flows obtained by summing the "mirror statistics" of each country's trade partners.[11]

11. For instance, Poland's official data on its exports to the EU can be compared with the sum of all imports from Poland recorded by EU members.

Wherever possible, I will base my evaluations on series of "mirror statistics," found in tables 10A.1, 10A.2, 10A.4, and 10A.8. These statistics are more difficult to compile, and not as comprehensive as the official data published by the World Bank and the IMF.

The unification of Germany is the second consideration which complicates the interpretation of the data. Before October 1990, its Eastern Laender were a separate country and an important member of the CMEA. Since Poland, Czechoslovakia, and Hungary each had major trade flows with the former GDR, unification mechanically reduced their reported CMEA trade and increased their reported trade with the EU. To obtain an accurate measure of the true economic shift, one has to adjust for that effect.[12]

Trade Performances: Exports
Turning to tables 10A.1–10A.5 in the appendix, the first thing one observes is that in all four countries, exports to former CMEA partners dropped dramatically from the late 1980s onwards. The trend is gradual in Hungary, marked in Poland and Czechoslovakia, and sudden in Viet Nam. The unification of Germany artificially magnifies the phenomenon in the official data, but it is already visible in Hungary in 1987 and in Poland in 1989. For Viet Nam, which is not an immediate neighbor, the German distortion is presumably less significant. Viet Nam's official exports to former CMEA partners dropped to almost zero in 1991 and to zero in 1992.

The second thing one observes is that exports to non-CMEA countries rose just as dramatically. The net result was that in all four countries, total exports rose for the first two years following radical reform.[13] (In Viet Nam, total exports experienced a steep increase, and continued growing through the end of the period.)

Tables 10A.1, 10A.2, and 10A.4 report "mirror" data on Visegrad trade with the EEC. (Comprehensive mirror data are not available for Viet Nam.) In these tables, mirror data is first presented for the total EEC, including Germany, to make it possible to compare this data directly with official data for the same flows. One observes that in the first years of transition (1989 and 1990), the mirror series record substantially larger flows than the official series, but that the two then come into

---

12. The division of Czechoslovakia into the Czech and Slovak Republics on January 1, 1993 is another border change which complicates statistical measurement. What were formally internal flows between the two parts of the Federation became official exports and imports, thereby making the combined trade of the two independent republics mechanically larger than the consolidated trade of the former Federation.
13. The effect of German unification is neutral on this measure of the growth of total exports: it influences the composition, but not the total.

balance, and the larger of the two is sometimes the one, sometimes the other.

The mirror data in the next line of the tables measures trade flows with the EEC, excluding Germany. It is from these numbers that we can infer the most undistorted picture of the progression of Visegrad exports to market economies. Table 10.1 summarizes the average annual compound rates of growth of these flows from the last year prior to major trade liberalization through 1993. As measured by these statistics, the growth of exports to market economies ranged from 6 to 10 percent per year, depending on the country. Viet Nam's record is even more dramatic. Between 1988 and 1993, exports to market economies compounded at 36 percent per year, according to official national statistics.

Trade Performance: Imports

The evolution of imports was similar overall to the evolution of exports. In every case, imports from the former CMEA declined rapidly, while imports from market countries grew. The latter did not make up for the former in every country and every year. In Poland and Czechoslovakia, CMEA imports fell by more than market imports rose during the first year of reform, and thus total imports fell. The combination of increasing total exports and declining total imports resulted, for Poland and Czechoslovakia, in an improvement of the official trade balance in the first year of reform. In both countries, however, the positive change in the official trade balance was reversed the next year.

Tables 10A.5–10A.8 show that even though total imports to Viet Nam from convertible currency areas grew throughout the reform period, the official trade balance improved continuously for the first four years of reform, because increases in exports exceeded increases in imports. Table 10.1 shows the spectacularly high average growth rates of exports to and imports from convertible currency areas from 1988 through 1993.

Table 10.1 also confirms that the dominant characteristic of the four rapidly reforming countries during 1988–93 was the rapid growth of trade with market economies.

Trade Performance: Product Mix

In each of these four countries, the shift from the state trading patterns of the CMEA to free markets entailed shifts in product mix. In the Visegrad countries, electrical machinery had accounted for the lion's share of all exports to the CMEA; exports to the market economies were divided more evenly—the four principal product groups being minerals and metals, agricultural products and food, light manufactures, and electrical machinery. Table 10.2 shows the commodity composition of

Table 10.1
Trade expansion in transition economies (average annual compound growth rate, in US$)

Poland (1989–1993)	
Exports to EEC (ex. Germany)	9.9%
Imports from EEC (ex. Germany)	25.3%
Czechoslovakia (1990–1993)	
Exports to EEC (ex. Germany)	8.0%
Imports from EEC (ex. Germany)	25.5%
Hungary (1989–1992)	
Exports to EEC (ex. Germany)	6.1%
Imports from EEC (ex. Germany)	16.3%
Viet Nam (1988–1993)	
Exports to convertible currency areas	36%
Imports from convertible currency areas	35%
China (1978–1993)	
Exports	15%
Imports	15%
China (1978–1981)	
Exports	27%
Imports	23%
Russia (1991–1993)	
Market economy exports	–6%
Market economy imports	–23%

Sources: Appendix tables. Figures for Poland, Czechoslovakia, and Hungary are based on "mirror" statistics. Figures for the other countries are based on official national data as adjusted by the World Bank or the IMF.

Polish trade in 1989 and 1991. This product characterization remained stable as CMEA exports collapsed and the share of exports going to the West increased. The shift from one region to the other therefore implied a change in the aggregate product mix.

In Viet Nam, the expansion of exports to convertible currency areas was also accompanied by a shift in the product mix (see table 10A.5). The country's two principal export staples, rice and petroleum, rapidly grew from insignificant amounts to 30–40 percent of total convertible currency exports. Labor-intensive handicrafts and light industrial products also grew to 14 percent of the convertible currency total.[14]

___

14. There is insufficient information to analyze the structure of Viet Nam's imports, or of trade in any direction with the non-convertible currency area.

Table 10.2
Commodity composition of Polish trade with CMEA, former CMEA, and the
rest of the world, in 1989 and 1991

	1989	1991[a]
Market exports, total (trillion zlotys)	12.87	131.2
Market export composition (% of total)		
Fuels	11.5	10.6
Minerals and metals	16.1	21.8
Food and agriculture	19.0	17.2
Electrical engineering	25.3	19.3
Chemicals	11.3	10.3
Manufactures[b]	15.8	20.8
CMEA exports, total (trillion zlotys)	6.61	26.52
CMEA export composition (% of total)		
Fuels	5.9	11.0
Minerals and metals	3.3	7.2
Food and agriculture	3.5	13.4
Electrical engineering	63.8	37.6
Chemicals	9.1	18.1
Manufactures	14.4	12.6
Market imports, total (trillion zlotys)	10.67	135.39
Market import composition (% of total)		
Fuels	5.4	10.3
Minerals and metals	10.4	5.8
Food and agriculture	19.5	15.4
Electrical engineering	32.6	41.1
Chemicals	18.8	13.9
Manufactures	13.2	13.5
CMEA imports, total (trillion zlotys)	4.75	31.35
CMEA imports, total (% of total)		
Fuels	28.0	55.1
Minerals and metals	9.4	6.8
Food and agriculture	2.7	5.9
Electrical engineering	44.4	21.2
Chemicals	7.2	6.9
Manufactures	8.2	4.2

Source: Polish Central Statistical Office.
a. "CMEA" in 1991 means former CMEA countries.
b. Includes wood and paper products, textiles, wearing apparel and leather
goods, construction, forestry, and other industries.

Explanations for the Trade Performances of the Rapid Reformers

What explains the dramatic record of trade expansion of the Visegrad countries and Viet Nam? I contend that liberalization per se was a large part of the story. I argue that the dismantling of central planning and the introduction of decentralized incentives (even prior to the widespread introduction of private property) uncovered large, previously hidden opportunities for commercial gain, and unleashed previously suppressed entrepreneurial energies. Exports and imports grew, in considerable part, because individuals and enterprises (including public enterprises) found themselves suddenly free to take advantage of profitable opportunities to trade.

But there are alternative explanations. In the section below, I examine the following arguments:

1. The collapse of the CMEA forced restructuring on its former members.

2. Previous barriers in the market economies to exports from these economies were reduced or eliminated.

3. The macroeconomic policies of the reforming countries, by pushing net exports, were primarily responsible for the trade expansion.

The Collapse of the CMEA
The CMEA was a closed system of state barter, in which the dominant flows from Central Europe were exchanges of manufactures for Soviet energy and raw materials. Viet Nam exchanged primary products for Soviet petroleum and Soviet manufactures. The participating governments had no alternative options, and their enterprises had no say in the bargaining. Bilateral balances were supposed to be equilibrated. The system was totally contrary in its conception and nature to the working of a free market. In addition, as the CMEA was perceived in the CEECs as an instrument of Soviet domination, the Visegrad reformers were particularly determined to break up the CMEA.

As it turned out, the system was incapable of surviving anyway. As trade became decentralized in the USSR and Eastern Europe, governments lost procurement powers, and thus were unable to fulfill CMEA obligations. Furthermore, the financial difficulties of the Soviet government forced it to stop subsidizing trade. The upshot was that the CMEA was abolished at the beginning of 1991. Its demise had the effect of imposing a dramatic liquidity constraint on transactions.

The important question for our purposes is: Was the increase in the share of these countries' non-CMEA exports between 1989 and 1993 simply an arithmetic consequence of the collapse of their exports to the

CMEA? The answer is negative. In each of the four countries, exports to non-CMEA markets displayed strong independent growth rates during the period. Were the same goods which were not being sold to the CMEA pushed onto Western markets? Our data suggest that CMEA exports and much of the corresponding production simply disappeared, and that other products were produced for the West.[15]

The Reduction of Barriers to Imports into the Market Economies
Another possible explanation of the trade expansions of Poland, Czechoslovakia, Hungary, and Viet Nam might be that governments in market economies dramatically reduced previous barriers to imports from these countries.

It is easy to dismiss this explanation in the case of Viet Nam. Though foreign trade relations with Western European and Asian countries had been reestablished quickly in 1976 after the end of the Viet Nam War, they were cut off again in 1979 when Viet Nam became militarily involved in Cambodia. In the opinion of the World Bank,

Viet Nam's poor export performance in the first half of the 1980s was the result both of the embargoes and of its own internal policies which created weak incentives to export. It is difficult to sort out the relative importance of the two factors, but it is the case that trade and exchange reforms in 1989 led to a surge in trade with the convertible area, despite continuing embargoes. In many cases, Vietnamese goods found their way to western markets through indirect routes, such as Hong Kong or Singapore.   (World Bank 1990b, 61)

Thus, in the case of Viet Nam, trade expanded in spite of the maintenance of embargoes, not because they had been reduced.

The issue is more complex in the case of the Visegrad countries. Prior to the 1990 and 1991 reforms, Central European access to Western markets had indeed been restricted by a number of obstacles. Numerous trading powers, including the EEC, applied discriminatory quotas intended to counter the distortionary nature of state trading. Several OECD countries (including the United States) did not confer most-favored-nation (MFN) status to many communist countries. None appointed Generalized System of Preferences (GSP) rates to these countries.

In the wake of the reforms, most OECD countries removed their discriminatory state-trading quotas for those Central European countries, and granted them MFN and GSP status. The elimination of the discriminatory quotas was clearly an important necessary condition for trade to develop. However, MFN and GSP do not appear to have

---

15. Rodrik (1994a) presents some further rough disaggregated data in support of the view that the goods which had been delivered to the CMEA were not the same as those which were subsequently sold to the West.

provided substantial immediate benefits.[16] Significant barriers continued to restrict entry of the products in which the export potential of the CEECs was greatest.

There was no significant market in the West, for technological and quality reasons, for the machinery which had figured so prominently in Central European exports to the CMEA. Where Central Europe had and has current export potential is in primary products (iron, steel, and chemicals), textiles, and agricultural and food products. These are precisely the "sensitive" areas where MFN and GSP tariffs remain relatively high, and where major, additional non-tariff barriers restrict access. Various quotas and voluntary export restraint schemes limit iron and steel; the Multi-Fiber Agreement (MFA) sets quotas for textiles; and the farm support programs of all the OECD countries, most notably the European Union's Common Agricultural Policy (CAP), restrict imports of agricultural and food products. The natural tendency in all Voluntary Export Restraints (VERs) (e.g., the MFA) for quotas to be based on the past history of exports has kept the allotments of the new Central European democracies low.

Similar reservations apply to the important Europe Agreements which the European Union negotiated with Poland, Hungary, and Czechoslovakia at the end of 1991.[17] These comprehensive agreements, which aim at bringing a broad range of economic regulations in the reforming countries into harmony with those of the EU, constitute an important political commitment to the Central European countries, and are a central part of a process which may eventually lead to EU membership. They include a schedule and calendar for tariff and quota reductions—some rapid, others spread out over 10 years beginning March 1992.

The Europe Agreements have been the subject of intense professional debate. Supporters claim that they offer the Central European participants important short- and long-term trade advantages, and critics argue that the immediate benefits are very limited.[18] The central issue in

16. For a different interpretation, see Inotai (1994) and Faini and Portes (1995).
17. The Polish and Hungarian agreements were signed in December 1991. Final agreements with the Czech and Slovak Republics were delayed by the breakup of the Federation, and were not signed until October 1993. Ratification by all the member states of the EU has followed some time after agreement. However, the trade provisions of the original three agreements, including that with Czechoslovakia, went into effect in March 1992. Ratification was not required for the trade provisions because the European Commission has full authority on trade. (In the case of Czechoslovakia, the trade provisions were implemented under an interim agreement.) See OECD-CCET (1994a, table 4, 3) and OECD (1992, 144, 145, and Annex 1).
18. See Hamilton and Winters (1992), OECD-CCET (1994a, 71), OECD (1992, 142–5), and GATT (1993, 14–17).

the short term is "sensitive products." In the case of Poland, these are estimated to have accounted for 50 percent of the country's exports to the European Community in 1990.[19] The Europe Agreement signed with Poland did provide for immediate partial reduction of Europe's quotas for Polish imports of iron and steel. (Poland made comparable concessions.) But increases in textile quotas were necessarily made conditional on international revision and renegotiation of the MFA, and provisions relative to imports of agricultural and food products remained very complex and limited.

In summary, one can reasonably conclude that the Europe Agreements did not result in massive increases in imports during 1989–1993. A similar conclusion can be reached with regard to the trade agreements these countries signed with EFTA, after completion of their negotiations with the EC.

The relaxation of trade restrictions in the OECD has certainly favored the expansion of exports from Poland, Czechoslovakia, and Hungary. The elimination of previous discriminatory state-trading quotas were probably a necessary condition. But it is clear from the partial nature of the relaxation, particularly for sensitive products, that it is not sufficient to explain the export boom observed between 1989 and 1993. To identify the causes of this phenomenon, one must look to the policies of the Central European countries themselves.

The Trade Effect of Macroeconomic Policies
The main alternative explanation for the successful trade performances of the Visegrad countries and Viet Nam is that their macroeconomic policies favored trade expansion. Most of the rapid reformers accompanied their liberalizations with macroeconomic stabilization programs modeled on IMF orthodoxy.

Poland, having devalued the zloty thirteen-fold with respect to the dollar in a succession of steps during the inflation of 1989, devalued it again by 46 percent in January 1990. Czechoslovakia devalued the crown 107 percent with respect to the dollar in 1990, prior to the introduction of its reforms. In Viet Nam, the official exchange rate between the dong and the dollar was devalued fivefold in March 1989, bringing it to the black market rate. Tables 10.3 and 10.4 summarize the corresponding evolution of the real exchange rate in these countries.

---

19. OECD (1992, 197).

Table 10.3
Nominal and real exchange rates for six transition economies

	1978	1980	1984	1985	1986	1987	1988	1989	1990	1991	1992	1993
Poland: nominal[a]	—	—	—	148	198	316	503	6,500	9,500	10,957	15,767	21,344
Poland: real[b] (1985=100)	—	—	—	100	86	65	63	16	73	103	100	98
CFSR[c]: nominal	—	—	—	16	14	13	14	14	28	28	29	30
CFSR: real (1985=100)	—	—	—	100	109	117	103	99	53	80	83	95
Hungary: nominal	—	—	—	50	46	47	50	59	63	75	81	100
Hungary: real (1985=100)	—	—	—	—	—	100	104	99	113	123	135	138
Viet Nam: nominal	—	—	—	—	22.5	281.3	1,125	5,375	8,125	11,500	10,565	10,825
Viet Nam: real (1986=100)	—	—	—	—	100	25	30	8	8	10	12	12
China: nominal	1.577	1.530	2.796	3.201	3.722	3.722	3.722	4.722	5.222	5.417	5.799	5.806
China: real (1978 = 100)	100	87	43	—	35	44	44	35	31	30	29	34
Russia: nominal	—	—	—	—	—	—	—	—	—	1.67	415.5	1,249
Russia: real (1991 = 100)	—	—	—	—	—	—	—	—	—	100	10	32

Sources: Poland, Hungary, Czechoslovakia, Czech Republic, and U.S.: IMF, *International Financial Statistics*. Viet Nam: Exchange rate from IMF, *International Financial Statistics*, CD-ROM. The nominal rate in this case is a market rate. CPI from the World Bank, private communication. China: Lardy (1992, 148); Bell, Khor, and Kochhar (1993, 7); and World Bank, private communication. Russia: IMF, *International Financial Statistics, Supplement on Countries of the Former Soviet Union*, and *Russian Economic Trends*.

a. Nominal exchange rate is the national currency per U.S. dollar, end of year.
b. Real exchange rate is domestic prices/foreign prices, i.e., domestic price index × domestic currency price of a dollar), end of year, using consumer price indices and the official exchange rate.
c. Czech Republic in 1993.

Table 10.4
Average annual real exchange rate appreciation or depreciation (relative to US$) in transition economies

Poland (1989–93)	+45%
Czechoslovakia (1990–93)[a]	+9%
Hungary (1989–92)	+10%
Viet Nam (1988–93)	−18%
China (1978–93)	−7%
Russia (1991–93)	−58%

Sources: See table 10.3.
Note: For all countries, the figure is based on year-end values of dollars per unit of the national currency (at the official rate), deflated by the ratio of the U.S. consumer price index to the national consumer price index. The annual rate of real appreciation is the growth rate from year-end to year-end of this number. (It is calculated as the yearly change in the logarithm of this number.) It is affected by fluctuations of the U.S. dollar as well as fluctuations of the currencies of the transition economies.
a. Based on the real exchange rate of the Czech Republic in 1993.

Poland, Czechoslovakia, and Viet Nam accompanied their devaluations with restrictive macroeconomic policies. As table 10.5 shows, Poland's budget switched from deficit to surplus between 1989 and 1990; Czechoslovakia ran a small budget surplus the year it devalued (1990); and Viet Nam began a slow process of deficit reduction in 1989 which was to last three years.

Monetary policy was also initially tight in these three countries. Table 10.6 provides a summary of the evolution of real interest rates. Largely negative throughout the period, they turned positive in Poland in 1990. 1991 was also a period of relative tightness in Hungary and Czechoslovakia. Comparable data are not available for Viet Nam; however, real interest rates went from being highly negative to highly positive in 1989, and then fluctuated, but they were more often positive than negative during the remainder of the period.[20]

Restrictive macroeconomic policies free additional capacity for the increased net exports stimulated by real devaluation. Not surprisingly, the trade balance improved in the first year of reform in Poland, Czechoslovakia, and Viet Nam. The phenomenon is most marked in Poland, where a small trade surplus of $47 million in 1989 increased to $3.6 billion in 1990. But it is also visible in Czechoslovakia, where a trade

---

20. See World Bank (1992c, 2, 8) and World Bank (1994b, 12) for data on real rates of interest for household deposits.

Table 10.5
Overall government budget balances (% GDP)

	1988	1989	1990	1991	1992	1993
Poland	—	−7.4	3.1	−6.5	−6.7	2.9
Czechoslovakia[a]	—	−2.4	0.1	−2	−3.3	1.4
Hungary	—	−1.3	0.5	−2.5	−5.5	−5.9
Viet Nam	−7.2	−7.5	−5.8	−1.5	−1.7	−4.8
Russian Federation	—	n.a.	n.a.	n.a.	−18	−11

	1978	1979	1980	1981	1982	1983
China	0.3	−5.1	−3.3	−1.3	−1.4	−1.7

	1984	1985	1986	1987	1988	1989
China (continued)	−1.5	−0.5	−2.0	−2.2	−2.4	−2.3

	1990	1991	1992	1993		
China (continued)	−2.1	−2.5	−2.5	−2.1		

Sources: Statistical tables, EBRD, *The Economics of Transition* (1994), vol. 2, no. 2 (December); Tseng et al. (1994, 2); Bell, Khor, and Kochhar (1993, 7); World Bank (1994b); and Delpla and Wyplosz (1994).
a. The Czech Republic in 1993.

deficit of $1.4 billion in 1990 was reduced to $121 million in 1991. It is very clear in Viet Nam, where a trade deficit of $679 million was cut roughly in half to $350 million in 1989, and kept nearly at zero for the three following years. (See tables 10A.1, 10A.2, and 10A.7 in Appendix 10.)

The export push argument does not apply in the Hungarian case. Macroeconomic policy did not follow IMF principles in 1991. In real terms, the forint appreciated rather than depreciated, the budget balance deteriorated, and the real refinancing rate remained negative (although slightly less than before). (See tables 10.3–10.6.) Nonetheless, both exports to and imports from the EEC grew, as the mirror statistics in table 10A.4 show.

But the export push argument does not completely explain the expansion of trade between 1989 and 1993 in Poland and Czechoslovakia either. For one thing, the two countries' macro policies reversed in this period. The decision in both countries to use the exchange rate as a nominal anchor, combined with the persistence of high inflation in Poland and the inevitability of some price increases in Czechoslovakia, caused the real

Table 10.6
Real interest rates (percent annual rate)

	1989	1990	1991	1992	1993
Poland	−196	+67.3	+20.9	+5.3	+4.6
Czechoslovakia[a]	n.a.	−11.7	−2.5	−2.0	−7.6
Hungary	−5.8	−15.5	+8.3	+5.6	−0.3
Russian Federation	n.a.	n.a.	n.a.	−192	−148

Sources: *International Financial Statistics*, various issues, and *International Financial Statistics, Supplement on Countries of the Former Soviet Union*, supplement 16; and statistical tables, EBRD, *The Economics of Transition* (1994), vol. 2, no. 4.
Note: The real interest rate is the refinancing rate at the end of the first quarter of each year minus the December to December CPI increase for the same year. For Poland in 1990, Czechoslovakia in 1991, Hungary in 1991, and Russia in 1992, the rate of inflation which is subtracted form the nominal refinancing rate is the April to December CPI percentage increase (annualized) for the same year. This is done to remove from the calculation of inflation the surge of prices which accompanies the first three months of liberalization. (When monthly CPI indices are not available, quarterly indices are used instead, and rates of change are fourth quarter to fourth quarter, or first quarter to fourth quarter annualized.)
a. The Czech Republic in 1993.

exchange rate to appreciate substantially after the initial introduction of the program in both countries. As table 10.3 shows, the appreciation was already substantial in the first year of reform, and by 1993 Czechoslovakia had almost returned to the real exchange rate of 1989, and was well above the real exchange rate of 1990.

Demand policies also changed, as the fiscal balance shifted dramatically from surplus to deficit in Poland between the first and second years of reform, and Czechoslovakia's modest deficit increased (table 10.5). Real refinance rates also declined in the three Visegrad countries (table 10.6). In a manner that is consistent with these reversals, the characteristic first-year trade balance improvements of Poland and Czechoslovakia became trade balance deteriorations in the second and subsequent years. Over the full period, 1989–1993, there does not appear to be a positive export bias on average to Poland and Czechoslovakia's macroeconomic policies. Macroeconomic policy considerations alone, therefore, cannot explain the growth of exports over that period in these countries.[21]

21. Richard Portes pointed out in private correspondence that whatever the stance of macroeconomic policies was in Poland in 1991 and Czechoslovakia in 1992, output fell in both countries in those years. Negative demand shocks coming from elsewhere than the budget or interest rates could have freed up resources for export growth.

Of the four rapid reformers, Viet Nam (which received no IMF aid) fits the IMF scenario best. Most of the initial real devaluation was preserved by what was, in effect, a crawling peg. The fiscal balance became progressively tighter rather than looser, and real interest rates, though variable, remained mostly positive. (See tables 10.3–10.5.) Not surprisingly, the improvement in the trade balance of the first two years was maintained through 1992. However, although the real exchange rate and macroeconomic demand management seem to explain the movement of net exports reasonably well, they leave the phenomenal growth of imports during this period unexplained.

Synthesis and Evaluation
In all four countries being considered in this section, the real story is not what happens to the trade balance, but rather the expansion of gross trade flows. Both imports and exports increase in every case during 1989–93 (see table 10.1). No macroeconomic export bias could have explained the major shift in the degree of openness of these four economies in the years which followed their implementation of rapid trade liberalization. One is therefore left with the conclusion that liberalization *per se* was an important cause of the impressive trade performances of Poland, Czechoslovakia, Hungary, and Viet Nam. I do not deny that real devaluation and the compression of domestic demand prompted, where they were observed, increases in net exports.

It is striking that, at the time of the major loss of their CMEA market, the Visegrad countries and Viet Nam expanded their trade with market economies in spite of resistance to their imports. Moreover, this transformation was brought about before significant privatization had occurred (Hungary is an exception). In Poland, Czechoslovakia, and Viet Nam, the changes were wrought in large part by firms that were still state-owned. When privatization is slow to materialize, decentralization and radical trade liberalization can nonetheless so alter the external environment as to bring about a marked change in the performance even of SOEs.

10.3 China

The first thirty tumultuous years of communism in China were passed in near-total autarky. Exports were tolerated to the extent that they were necessary to obtain foreign exchange for importing otherwise irreplaceable materials.

In December 1978 Deng Xiaoping introduced the strategy of "Reforms and Opening Up" during the Eleventh Central Committee of the Chinese Communist Party. Trade was a central part of reforms: during the 15 years after 1978, exports and imports rose fourfold, growing at an average of 15 percent per year in dollar terms. Tables 10.1, 10A.8, and 10A.9 rely almost exclusively on official national statistics. A short series of "mirror" estimates of China's exports, obtained from trading partners, appear in italics in table 10A.8. These data suggest that the degree of under-reporting has increased as liberalization has progressed and openness has increased. If the "mirror statistics" are correct, the effective average annual rates of growth of exports and imports in dollars are greater than the numbers reported in table 10.1.

China: Explanations for its Trade Performance

As China was not a member of the CMEA, there was no analog in the Chinese case to the pressure that the collapse of the CMEA put on the Visegrad countries and Viet Nam to find new outlets for their products.

China's own macroeconomic policies were not a determining factor either. Far from implementing anything like an IMF stabilization program, the central government acted paradoxically at times, and had difficulty exercising effective control over internal and external balances at other times. During the first two years of reform (1979 and 1980), the overall government budget balance deteriorated sharply, and the government actually appreciated the nominal value of the yuan.[22]

The 15-year period of trade reform was marked by two significant episodes of overheating, in 1985–86 and 1988–89. In the first episode, the annual inflation rate rose to 8.8 percent and the trade balance fell to –14.8 percent of GDP. In the second, the annual inflation rate rose to 18.6 percent and the trade balance fell to –7.7 percent of GDP.

In an explicit effort to promote exports, the Chinese authorities increased the frequency and the magnitude of yuan devaluations from 1984 on, and, as a result, succeeded in lowering the currency's real effective exchange rate 30 percent between 1984 and 1991. (See table 10.3.) This clearly helped exports, but it cannot be considered one of the causes of the dramatic expansion of imports.

The Nature of the Trade Regime in China

This catalogue of unsatisfactory explanations forces us to turn again to liberalization as the possible principal cause of China's dramatic trade expansion between 1978 and 1993. However, a careful examination of trade reforms at the national level during this period leaves us with a

---

22. From an annual average of 1.68 yuan/dollar to 1.50 yuan/dollar (Lardy 1992, Appendix A, 148).

puzzle. Although the regime was liberalized progressively after 1978, it remained, on paper, highly restrictive and rigid by external standards as late as 1988. How could exports and imports have grown the way they did in the restrictive regime that was still officially in place throughout most of the period? Before turning to a possible explanation, I will review the character and pace of the principal trade reforms at the national level.

The regime was progressively liberalized in the following three main respects: (1) the quantitative controls of the planning authorities were relaxed, (2) the central government's monopoly of foreign trade was broken, and (3) foreign exchange control was loosened.[23]

1. The management of exports and imports was released from some of the centralized strictures of the plan as early as 1979. The percentage of exports covered by command planning, which had been 100% in 1978, declined progressively to 45 percent by 1988. The coverage of mandatory plans for imports declined in a similar progressive fashion. By 1984, 40 percent of China's imports were subject to a central system of "unified management." (Fukusaku and Wall 1994, 27.) Exports and imports not controlled by the plan did not, however, thereby become market-determined, as I shall point out later.

2. The number of national foreign trading companies (FTCs) was about a dozen in 1979. By the mid-1980s, 800 import and export corporations had been approved by the Ministry of Foreign Economic Relations and Trade. In 1990 there were over 5,000 foreign trading companies. (Lardy 1992, 39.) Some of the FTCs were the creatures of national production ministries, some were created by provincial governments, and some were set up by large state enterprises.

3. A third decisive development at the national level involved the partial relaxation of exchange controls. Before reforms, all foreign exchange earnings had to be sold to the Bank of China at the official exchange rate. Beginning in 1979, export-producing enterprises and their immediate local authorities were allowed to retain a share of their foreign export earnings. The value of these retention rights was increased by the introduction, in October 1980, of a procedure for selling surplus foreign exchange at a more favorable, though not yet free, market rate. (Retention rates initially varied between 15 and 40 percent; see Lardy 1992, 52–3.)

---

23. This three-point synthesis constitutes a radically simplified summary of complex processes described in greater detail in Lardy (1992); Bell, Khor, and Kochhar (1993); Tseng, Khor, Kochhar, Mihaljek, and Burton (1994); and Fukasaku, Wall, and Wu (1994).

The first formally recognized arrangement which could be considered a market for foreign exchange was the "foreign exchange transaction center," opened in 1985 in the Shenzhen Special Economic Zone, in which enterprises with surplus retention rights could trade directly with enterprises in need of foreign exchange. Such centers, soon to be known as "swap" centers, multiplied rapidly. Originally limited to enterprises with foreign investors, the centers were opened to and quickly became dominated by domestic enterprises. By 1988, the year in which retention rates were widely liberalized,[24] there were 39 swap centers across China. On these exchanges, which remained partially controlled until the end of the decade, the dollar fluctuated, but was systematically above its official rate.[25] The process of progressive decontrol culminated January 1, 1994 in the unification of the official and swap markets at the swap market rate of 8.7 yuan/dollar. (The official rate was devalued from 6.2 to 8.7 yuan/dollar.)

It bears emphasizing that, with the exception of the unification of the exchange markets at the beginning of 1994, China has stopped far short of trade liberalization. In the late 1980s, the 60 percent of China's exports that were not directly regulated by the plan were, nonetheless, subject to restrictive and discretionary licensing requirements. On the import side, 45 percent were controlled by the plan, and 45 percent by licensing.[26] Licensed imports were also subject to a high and escalating tariff schedule.

If, then, China's official trade regime remained as restrictive as it was in the late 1980s, what explains the dramatic expansion of trade?

China: The Role of the Municipalities and the Provinces

The most plausible answer is that broad exemptions from central regulation and control, liberally granted by local authorities, were the main secret of China's trade success.[27] What appeared to be, at the central official level, a highly restrictive trade regime at the end of the 1980s, had in fact become, in the coastal provinces where most of the trade took place, an environment with few controls, minimal taxes, and minimal tariffs.

One of the first components of the reform strategy introduced in 1978 was the creation of Special Economic Zones (SEZs), in which state-owned enterprises and newly admitted foreign enterprises were free of

---

24. Retention rates had been raised to 70 percent for light industry, arts and crafts, and garments in September 1987 (Lardy 1992, 56).
25. The average premium in 1988 was 33 percent (Lardy 1992, 58, 61).
26. See Fukasaku, Wall, and Wu (1994, 27, 30, 31).
27. For similar views see Panagariya (1993) and Fukasaku, Wall, and Wu (1994).

central regulations and controls. Within two years, four SEZs had been established in the coastal provinces of Guangdong and Fujian. They were Shenzhen (near Hong Kong), Zhuhai (near Macao), Shantou, and Xiamen (across from Taiwan). These SEZs were to play a central, catalytic role in the opening up of the country.

Unlike their predecessors, the Export Processing Zones of East and Southeast Asia, the SEZs were not simply preferential tariff and tax areas managed directly by the central government. They were, on the contrary, autonomous regions with their own governmental bodies, and were explicitly encouraged to experiment with free-market reforms which would have been politically unacceptable if introduced at the national level. These reforms included the acceptance and encouragement of foreign direct investment, freedom from plan directives, broad freedom to retain and use foreign exchange, and the elimination of all import and export duties and licenses.

With obstacles and restrictions thus lifted, trade flourished in the SEZs. The further extension of rights of autonomy to fourteen coastal cities and other Open Economic Zones (OEZs) in the mid-1980s expanded the privileged area of exclusion from central controls, and stimulated further growth of trade. Within the provinces that harbored the OEZs, there was a contagion effect: municipalities without special status vied with those that did, and adopted some of their innovations. As a consequence, the open provinces contributed an increasing share of total exports. In 1984, Guangdong and Fujian Provinces exported 12 percent of total national exports. By 1990, they exported 21 percent of a rapidly growing total. By 1992, their share had risen to 27 percent.[28]

There was a close relationship between these OEZs and China's most dynamic forms of non-state entrepreneurship, the Foreign Funded Enterprises (FFEs) and the Township and Village Enterprises (TVEs). The FFEs first appeared and subsequently proliferated in the OEZs, where they benefited from special tax, exchange control, and other provisions. These were often managed and/or funded by expatriates, who brought with their investments their commercial know-how to promote exports. Their contribution to China's total exports grew from 1 percent in 1984, to 10 percent in 1990, and 20 percent in 1992. The TVEs likewise gravitated to the coastal OEZs in search of entrepreneurial flexibility, even when the towns which they served were located far inland. By 1992, they are estimated to have contributed more than 25 percent of the country's total exports. (See Bell, Khor, and Kochhar, 1993, 45.)

---

28. Data on exports by provinces are from Hsueh Tien-tun, Li Quian, and Liu Shucheng (1992), series v11b1, and *Almanac of China's Foreign Economic Relations and Trade* (1993, 1994). Data on total national exports are from Bell, Khor, and Kochhar (1993, 7).

A final indicator of the central importance of local exemptions in the Chinese trade regime is the disparity between the average effective rate and the potential statutory rate of import duties. In 1992, the unweighted average rate of import duty was 42.8 percent; tariff revenue as a percentage of actual imports was 5.6 percent. The difference was primarily due to exemptions, most of which were granted by local authorities.[29]

China: Foreign Direct Investment and Comparative Advantage

Foreign direct investment (FDI) has played an additional, unique role in China's trade expansion. Attracting foreign direct investment was an early priority of the "Reforms and Opening Up" strategy of 1978. Protection for the full range of investments from joint ventures to fully owned subsidiaries was guaranteed by law in 1979 and subsequently written into the constitution in 1982.

Powerful tax and other regulatory incentives written into a new law in 1986 triggered an investment boom which lasted through 1993. By the end of 1994, accumulated realized investment was approaching $100 billion. In that same year, the flow of new planned commitments to China was over $100 billion (see Cheng 1995, table 1). None of the other transition economies reviewed in this survey benefited from a similar level of foreign investment. Prior to 1993, the only other country to have received significant inflows of FDI was Hungary.

Even more than trade expansion, FDI was concentrated almost exclusively in the coastal provinces. The lion's share of such investment originated with expatriates from Hong Kong, Taiwan, and elsewhere.[30]

The correlation between foreign direct investment and export growth reflects causal relationships going in both directions: the promise of export sales attracts direct investment, and direct investment facilitates the production and commercializing of exports. The managerial and commercial knowledge that investors, particularly expatriate investors,

---

29. Fukasaku, Wall, and Wu (1994, 149) provide further details: "Tariff exemptions are granted for imports used to produce exports, for import requirements of capital goods by enterprises considered to be raising the level of technology in China, for raw materials, and intermediate and capital goods imported into the Special Economic Zones, Economic and Technological Development Zones, and for those imported by Sino-foreign joint ventures and co-operative enterprises. Tariffs are also reduced by 50 per cent for consumers in the Special Economic Zones." Four of the six categories mentioned (including imports for exports) are by their nature concentrated in Open Economic Zones.
30. As of 1993, 90 percent of realized FDI since 1979 was directed to the coastal regions, and 71.6 percent of accumulated realized FDI by 1993 came from Hong Kong, Macao, or Taiwan (Cheng 1995).

brought with them was an important factor that accelerated the speed with which China was able to exploit its comparative advantage.

China's natural long-term comparative advantage in labor-intensive manufactures provided an additional important stimulus for trade. Abundant low-cost labor, initially employed in inefficient, traditional agriculture, was ready to migrate to produce labor-intensive manufactures for export. The comparatively low levels of GDP per capita in China (an indirect indicator of underlying differences in real wages) suggest that China's incentives to exchange with the OECD are far more powerful than those of temporarily depressed Central Europe.

This structural argument also applies to Viet Nam. In both countries the unique potential profitability of trade interacted positively with other forces conducive to trade, whether from the side of supply or demand.

In summary, the story of China's trade expansion is again one in which trade liberalization played a critical role. Real devaluation, natural comparative advantage, and the entrepreneurial energies of a receptive expatriate community also contributed to China's trade performance. But it is doubtful that trade would have grown in the way that it did, if restrictive national regulations had not been substantially mitigated by local authorities taking advantage of the possibilities offered by extensive decentralization.

10.4   The Russian Federation

The Russian Federation: The Trade Record

The trade experience of the Russian Federation during 1992–93 is interesting, first, because it provides a contrasting and striking example of poor trade performance, and second, because trade flows failed to expand in that country despite *both* real devaluation *and* significant trade liberalization. Indeed, far from growing, Russia's trade collapsed. Tables 10A.10–10A.12 tell the story. Russia suffered not one, but two major trade shocks. The first was the collapse of the CMEA in 1991. The dollar value of Russia's exports to its former CMEA partners dropped that year to 43 percent of what it had been in 1990. The dollar value of its imports from the former CMEA dropped to 34 percent of the previous year's level.[31] The second was the collapse of the Soviet Union,

---

31. See table 10A.10, which reports official data on trade flows at transaction prices, converted to dollars at official exchange rates. It is well known that the resulting prices are far removed from world prices, both in the absolute and relatively. However, to the extent that the relative distortions remain stable between 1990 and 1991, the implied percentage drop is a biased but not meaningless measure of volume decline.

which was accompanied by a similarly dramatic decline of the volume of inter-republic trade. The pervasive price distortions make it very difficult to estimate trade flows between the republics on a basis that would make them comparable to normal international flows. Senik-Leygonie (1994) has calculated dollar estimates of Russian trade with the former republics and with the rest of the world by revaluing four-digit Standard Industrial Trade Classification (SITC) flows at world prices in 1990, 1992, and 1993. Table 10A.11 reproduces her table 21. She finds that in 1992, the dollar value of Russian exports to the former Soviet Union (FSU) was 40 percent of its 1990 level; the figure for imports was 56 percent. Russia's favorable terms of trade with both the former CMEA and the FSU was no compensation.

Both of these trade shocks could be expected to have multiplier effects on output, and thus to lead to further, induced reductions of imports and exports. In the Visegrad countries and Viet Nam, however, as section 10.2 has shown, the CMEA shock was accompanied by an *increase*, not a decrease, of non-CMEA trade. Between 1990 and 1992, Russia's exports to market economies fell by 12 percent in dollar terms, and its imports by 46 percent. Why did Russia's trade with market economies fail to increase, and fill at least some of the gap, as the market trade of the Visegrad countries and Viet Nam had done?

Russia: Explanations

One possible explanation is that standard IMF macroeconomic policies were not consistently followed. The ruble was sharply devalued at the outset. The controlled commercial rate was dropped from 1.67 rubles to the dollar to 55 rubles to the dollar, a devaluation of 330 percent. The degree of nominal devaluation rose to a factor of 100 when the exchange rate was unified at the inter-bank rate of 168 to the dollar in August 1992.

Continuing inflation eroded the corresponding reduction in the real rate, however. Prices were raised by a factor of 3.4 in January. They had increased by a factor of 12 by the time the exchange rates were unified in August. The real devaluation as of that point was still over eightfold. But prices rose much more rapidly than the ruble depreciation over the next year and a half. Consequently, the real ruble/dollar exchange rate appreciated 166 percent between August 1992 and the end of December 1993. By that point, although the ruble was nominally worth 1,247 per dollar, the real devaluation from the pre-reform official rate of 1.67 had been reduced to a factor of 3.2.[32]

---

32. These calculations use the inter-bank exchange rate and the CPI. The source is *Russian Economic Trends*.

Demand management was also not conducive to an export push. Fiscal and monetary policy were very loose by the summer of 1992, even though budget reductions had been announced in January. Delpla and Wyplosz (1994) present estimates for the consolidated deficit for 1992 which range from 18 to 40 percent, depending on the way in which central bank subsidies are treated. The real rate of interest on central bank refinancing was increasingly negative throughout the year. It was not until the summer of 1993 that both fiscal and monetary policy began to be tight. The Delpla and Wyplosz range for the consolidated budget deficit that year is from 11 to 14 percent. Real refinancing rates turned sharply positive in the fall.

It is likely that real appreciation of the ruble and the volatility of macroeconomic policy contributed to Russia's poor trade performance in 1992 and 1993. But by the end of 1993, the ruble was still benefiting from substantial real devaluation. That this real devaluation did not translate into export growth suggests that trade obstacles with an anti-export bias were also a part of the explanation.

Russian Trade Policies: Inadequate Liberalization

In January 1992 the Yeltsin-Gaidar government liberalized 90 percent of all retail prices and 80 percent of all producer prices, dismantled much of the apparatus of quantitative allocations under the central plan, and moved rapidly toward ruble convertibility for residents' current account transactions (this was realized with the unification of the exchange rates in August). But the government did not abolish the foreign trade monopolies of the past; it continued to administer 45 percent of the country's total imports and all exports of "strategically important raw materials," including oil and gas. From July 1992 these exports were carried out exclusively by enterprises specially licensed by the Ministry of Foreign Economic Relations. In January 1993 the system was tightened, and 25 percent of all exports outside the former Soviet Union were returned to the direct control of central foreign trade organizations.

In addition, through 1992 almost all official export and import trade with the new republics of the former Union was conducted on a state-to-state barter system. Even after "free trade" and MFN agreements had been negotiated with most of the new republics (February 1993), a substantial part of the exchanges were still carried out at the government level, on barter terms and subject to quotas.

Restrictions on non-centralized imports were initially relatively low. Quotas were the exception and were limited to security and health reasons. During the first six months of 1992, non-centralized imports were allowed in free of duty. In July, a tariff of 5 percent was imposed (with the rate for most luxury goods 10–25 percent). In September the average rate was tripled to 15 percent, and new duties of 20–50 percent were introduced for alcohol products. The latter were raised a month later to 100 percent. A new tariff schedule with MFN rates was introduced in April 1993, with some duties going down to 5–15 percent, and a few (for luxury goods) increasing to 25–150 percent.

The puzzling thing about Russian trade policy and Russian trade performance is that the export restrictions, which were still in place in the spring of 1996, were predominantly concentrated in the energy and raw materials sectors. Manufacturing exports, however, came to be substantially liberalized. By 1994 the degree of liberalization for exports of manufactured products was roughly comparable in Russia and Hungary (slightly less than the degree of liberalization in Poland).[33] Nonetheless, exports of manufactured products from Russia stagnated.

Not surprisingly, Russia's resistance to abandoning export controls over oil and gas led to the loss of potential hard currency revenues in those sectors. Between 1991 and 1993 the dollar value of exports of energy products outside the FSU remained flat.[34] By contrast, Viet Nam, a very small oil producer, liberalized energy exports in 1989, and saw the dollar value of its energy exports to convertible markets rise 29 percent per year over the next three years.[35]

What is surprising is that manufacturing exports to Europe, America, and the free markets of Asia did not grow. One possible explanation is that the segmentation of this large country, combined with the disrupted transportation and communication networks during this period, constituted, de facto, an obstacle to commerce that was more significant than the favorable legislation on the books at the national level.[36]

---

33. This evaluation is based on conversations with Marek Dabrowski, Laszlo Urban, and Boris Fedorov.

34. See Senik-Leygonie (1994, 20). The stability of dollar exports is the result of some volume increase (40 percent between 1991 and 1993 for petroleum, and 7 percent for gas) and offsetting declines in prices. See *Russian Economic Trends* (November 1994, table 5). The dollar value of these exports would have been higher if production and commercialization had not been restrained by quotas and other restrictions.

35. World Bank (1994b, 59). Part of this difference is a reflection of swings in the oil market. The Kuwait crisis and the Gulf War sparked a surge in demand and prices in 1990 and 1991. By 1992 and 1993, demand and prices were declining.

36. For a comparable view, see Vincentz (1994, 20), who argues that "hindrances of various kinds, including transportation and information costs, still impede the functioning of the market, making it harder for foreign companies to compete." Kaminski, Winters, and Wang (1996, 40–45) reach a somewhat different conclusion in their survey of trade policies and performances. They attribute Russia's failure to increase exports to the market economies to what they deem to be the incomplete nature of price liberalization and the failure of macroeconomic stabilization. The causal relationships between these factors remain unclear.

10.5   Conclusion

A common theme runs through this survey of the trade policies of Poland, Czechoslovakia, Hungary, Viet Nam, China, and Russia: the degree to which the trade constraints of the central planning regime were lifted (or not lifted) had a decisive effect on the subsequent pattern of trade expansion.

The strongest examples of rapid and comprehensive trade liberalization are Poland, Czechoslovakia, and Viet Nam. The pattern in Hungary is similar but not as dramatic. The result has been rapid growth of trade in all four countries. The record of trade expansion in China is also striking. It fits the picture (the restrictions of its post-reform trade regime notwithstanding), once one takes account of the pervasive nature of the exemptions from controls of all sorts granted by local authorities in the coastal provinces.

The first two years of the Russian Federation provide a puzzling contrast. Russia is distinguished by its persistent restrictions on energy and raw material exports, the volatility of macroeconomic conditions, and the chaotic nature of trade and communications within the country. In Russia, alone among the cases studied, trade with market economies failed to grow.

Real devaluation and restrictive demand policies (or their absence) do not provide a satisfactory sole explanation of the trade performances of any of these six countries. Exports remained high after real devaluation was reversed in Poland and Czechoslovakia. They expanded in China during the first phase of reform, even though the real value of the yuan was appreciating. Most importantly, devaluation and restrictive macroeconomic policies obviously cannot explain the great growth of imports that occurred.

This is not to say that real devaluation and macroeconomic restraint—and the current account improvement that should accompany them—are not important at the beginning of transition. Without the support of such prudent macroeconomic policies, trade liberalization might not be sustainable. But the experience of these six countries suggests that comprehensive trade liberalization is an essential ingredient of successful trade performance.

Appendix 10 Additional Trade Data

Table 10A.1
Poland: Foreign trade by destination (including alternate "mirror statistics" for trade with the EEC), in US$ million

	1985	1986	1987	1988	1989	1990	1991	1992	1993
Exports (US$ million)									
EEC	2,487	2,497	2,958	3,620	3,754	6,338	8,285	7,632	8,951
EEC (alternate estimates)	—	—	—	—	4,440	6,720	7,788	9,132	8,987
EEC (ex. Germany)	—	—	—	—	2,332	3,492	3,413	3,805	3,768
CMEA	5,626	5,651	5,171	5,919	5,014	3,327	2,506	2,026	1,869
Other	3,376	3,926	4,076	4,421	4,698	4,657	4,112	3,529	3,323
Total	11,489	12,074	12,205	13,960	13,466	14,322	14,903	13,187	14,143
Imports (US$ million)									
EEC	1,959	2,302	2,590	3,137	3,290	4,294	7,835	8,446	10,784
EEC (alternate estimates)	—	—	—	—	4,332	5,664	9,792	10,584	11,580
EEC (ex. Germany)	—	—	—	—	2,051	2,730	4,660	5,291	5,635
CMEA	5,986	5,964	5,105	5,240	3,572	2,270	2,962	2,589	2,531
Other	3,240	3,269	3,520	4,335	3,797	3,216	4,959	4,878	5,519
Total	11,185	11,535	11,215	12,712	10,659	9,780	15,756	15,913	18,834
Trade balance (US$ million)									
EEC	528	195	368	483	464	2,044	450	-814	-1,833
EEC (alternate estimates)	—	—	—	—	108	1,056	-2,004	-1,452	-2,513
EEC (ex. Germany)	—	—	—	—	481	762	-1,247	-1,486	-1,867
CMEA	-360	-313	66	679	1,442	1,057	-456	-563	-662
Other	136	657	556	86	901	1,441	-847	-1,349	-2,196
Total	304	539	990	1,248	2,807	4,542	-853	-2,726	-4,691

Sources: Data in normal type are national source data, adjusted by World Bank, from World Bank (1994a). Data in italics are "mirror statistics," from OECD, Economics and Statistics, *Monthly Statistics of Foreign Trade*, various issues.

Table 10A.2
Czechoslovakia: Foreign trade by destination (including alternate "mirror statistics" for trade with the EEC), in US$ million

	1989	1990	1991	1992	1993
Exports (US$ million)					
EEC	1,872	2,507	4,670	n.a.	n.a.
EEC (alternate estimates)	*2,868*	*3,432*	*5,064*	*7,140*	*7,013*
EEC (ex. Germany)	*1,540*	*1,750*	*1,993*	*2,467*	*2,224*
CMEA	3,525	3,387	4,314	n.a.	n.a.
Other	1,886	2,247	2,490	n.a.	n.a.
Total	7,283	8,141	11,474	n.a.	n.a.
Imports (US$ million)					
EEC	1,748	2,946	3,861	n.a.	n.a.
EEC (alternate estimates)	*2,628*	*3,324*	*4,740*	*8,112*	*8,471*
EEC (ex. Germany)	*1,165*	*1,396*	*1,738*	*2,808*	*3,000*
CMEA	3,193	3,553	4,419	n.a.	n.a.
Other	1,782	2,706	2,879	n.a.	n.a.
Total	6,723	9,205	11,160	n.a.	n.a.
Trade balance (US$ million)					
EEC	124	−439	809	n.a.	n.a.
EEC (alternate estimates)	*240*	*8*	*324*	*−972*	*−1,458*
EEC (ex. Germany)	*375*	*354*	*155*	*−341*	*−776*
CMEA	332	−166	−105	n.a.	n.a.
Other	104	−459	−389	n.a.	n.a.
Total	560	−1,064	314	n.a.	n.a.

Sources: Adjusted official data from the World Bank, directly supplied by the World Bank. "Mirror statistics" from OECD, Economics and Statistics, *Monthly Statistics of Foreign Trade*, various issues. "Mirror statistics" on trade flows for "Czechoslovakia" in 1993 are the sum of the corresponding flows for the Czech and Slovak Republics.

Table 10A.3
The Czech and Slovak Republics: Foreign trade by destination (US$ million)

	Czech Republic			Slovak Republic		
	1992	1993	1994	1992	1993	1994
Exports						
EEC	6,038	7,220	8,990	1,795	1,892	2,403
Former CMEA	8,524	7,687	6,942	5,167	4,598	5,072
Other	686	3,053	3,569	1,087	1,161	1,663
Total	15,248	17,960	19,501	8,049	7,651	9,138
Imports						
EEC	5,855	7,360	8,930	1,487	1,691	2,099
Former CMEA	8,433	7,219	6,866	6,388	5,181	4,766
Other	611	3,071	4,048	973	1,417	1,631
Total	14,899	17,650	19,844	8,848	8,289	8,496
Trade balance						
EEC	183	−140	60	308	201	304
Former CMEA	91	468	76	−1,221	−583	306
Other	75	−18	−479	114	−256	32
Total	349	310	−343	−799	−638	642

Sources: Adjusted official data from the World Bank, directly supplied by the World Bank.

Table 10A.4
Hungary: Foreign trade by destination (including alternate "mirror statistics" for trade with the EEC), in US$ million

	1985	1986	1987	1988	1989	1990	1991	1992	1993
Exports (US$ million)									
EEC	1,295	1,534	1,853	2,190	2,384	3,089	4,659	5,327	4,146
EEC (alternate estimates)	—	—	—	—	*2,904*	*3,852*	*4,620*	*5,208*	*4,613*
EEC (ex. Germany)	—	—	—	—	*1,472*	*1,823*	*2,037*	*2,238*	*1,878*
Former CMEA	3,960	4,361	4,230	3,883	3,426	2,707	1,981	2,081	1,999
Other	3,012	2,955	3,116	3,626	3,795	3,792	3,547	3,297	2,763
Total	8,267	8,850	9,199	9,699	9,605	9,588	10,187	10,705	8,908
Imports (US$ million)									
EEC	1,711	2,168	2,368	2,347	2,557	2,683	4,682	4,734	5,040
EEC (alternate estimates)	—	—	—	—	*3,312*	*3,684*	*4,332*	*5,256*	*5,738*
EEC (ex. Germany)	—	—	—	—	*1,368*	*1,595*	*1,784*	*2,249*	*2,622*
Former CMEA	3,467	4,115	3,937	3,439	2,917	2,408	2,538	2,612	3,468
Other	2,668	2,980	3,143	3,330	3,346	3,555	4,163	3,732	4,022
Total	7,846	9,263	9,448	9,116	8,820	8,646	11,383	11,078	12,530
Trade balance (US$ million)									
EEC	-416	-634	-515	-157	-173	406	-23	593	-894
EEC (alternate estimates)	—	—	—	—	*-408*	*168*	*288*	*-48*	*-1,125*
EEC (ex. Germany)	—	—	—	—	*104*	*228*	*253*	*-11*	*-744*
Former CMEA	493	246	293	444	509	299	-557	-531	-1,469
Other	344	-25	-27	296	449	237	-616	-435	-1,259
Total	421	-413	-249	583	785	942	-1,196	-373	-3,622

Sources: Figures in roman type are national source data, adjusted by the World Bank, directly supplied by the World Bank. Data in italics are "mirror statistics," from OECD, Economics and Statistics, *Monthly Statistics of Foreign Trade*, various issues.

Table 10A.5
Viet Nam: Exports (in US$ million)

	1986	1987	1988	1989	1990	1991	1992	1993
Total exports (US$ million)	494	610	733	1,320	1,732	2,042	2,475	2,850
Convertible area (US$ million)	307	430	465	977	1,257	2,024	2,475	2,850
Breakdown by product (%)								
Rice	0	0	0	32.34	21.64	11.12	12.12	11.93
Petroleum	0	6.98	16.99	20.47	31.03	28.71	30.55	28.04
Coal	9.45	2.33	2.80	2.15	3.02	2.37	1.90	2.46
Rubber	0.65	1.40	1.29	1.43	1.27	2.47	2.18	2.39
Tea	1.30	0.47	0.65	0.31	0.16	0.69	0.65	0.70
Coffee	0.65	5.58	5.38	3.17	1.99	3.66	3.47	3.65
Marine products	30.94	26.28	26.67	13.61	17.50	14.08	12.20	13.26
Agriculture/forestry	35.83	32.09	42.37	21.60	16.15	21.74	17.54	17.26
Handicrafts and light industrial	21.17	6.98	3.87	2.05	1.59	11.07	12.97	14.04
Non-convertible area (US$ million)	187	180	268	343	475	18	0	0
Breakdown by product (%)								
Coal	1.04	0.44	0.31	0.24	0	0	—	—
Rice	0	0	0	0.49	3.42	20.93	—	—
Rubber	5.83	4.89	4.04	3.64	0	0	—	—
Tea	2.71	3.11	0.62	2.31	0	0	—	—
Coffee	2.92	0.89	1.09	5.22	5.27	4.65	—	—
Marine products	2.50	0	0	0	0	0	—	—
Agriculture/forestry	21.88	35.56	31.83	31.55	25.02	0	—	—
Other	63.13	55.11	62.11	56.55	66.29	74.42	—	—

Source: World Bank (1994b), *Viet Nam Public Sector Management and Private Sector Incentives* (No. 13143-VN), September 26.

Table 10A.6
Viet Nam: Imports (US$ million)

	1986	1987	1988	1989	1990	1991	1992	1993
Total imports (US$ million)	1,121	1,184	1,412	1,670	1,772	2,105	2,535	3,505
Convertible area (US$ million)	453	465	603	985	1,431	1,859	2,535	3,505
Breakdown by product (%)								
Petroleum	0	0	0	0	24.88	26.09	24.26	20.43
Fertilizer	20.75	21.08	11.94	4.67	14.68	13.23	12.62	4.28
Steel	21.19	33.76	44.94	0	1.61	1.34	4.10	4.28
Machines/spare parts	0	0	0	0	0	0	3.94	15.66
Other	58.06	45.16	43.12	95.33	58.84	59.33	55.07	55.35
Non-convertible area (US$ million)	668	719	809	685	341	246	0	0
Breakdown by product (%)								
Petroleum products	28.91	30.76	28.63	27.33	21.29	0	—	—
Cotton textiles	1.47	1.33	1.65	1.22	1.70	0	—	—
Fertilizer	18.86	18.95	16.89	23.13	14.26	3.86	—	—
Raw cotton	3.11	3.59	3.35	4.56	6.73	0	—	—
Steel products	4.17	4.17	4.53	6.33	4.07	2.74	—	—
Sugar	0.47	0.70	0.36	0.61	0.59	0	—	—
Other	43.01	40.50	45.16	36.82	51.37	93.40	—	—

Source: World Bank (1994b), *Viet Nam Public Sector Management and Private Sector Incentives* (No. 13143-VN), September 26.

Table 10A.7
Viet Nam: Balance of payments (US$ million)

	1986	1987	1988	1989	1990	1991	1992	1993
Current account balance	-655	624	-751	-586	-259	-132	-8	-869
Exports, total	494	610	733	1,320	1,731	2,042	2,475	2,850
Imports, total	-1,121	-1,184	-1,412	-1,670	-1,772	-2,105	-2,535	-3,505
Trade balance	-627	-575	-679	-350	-41	-63	-60	-655
Services and transfers	-28	-49	-72	-237	-218	-69	51	-214
Interest	-94	-94	-153	-208	-238	-248	-282	327
Private remittances	30	10	4	9	50	36	—	—
Official transfers	27	17	13	—	88	55	64	194
Freight, insurance, other	10	18	63	-38	-118	88	—	330
Capital account balance	363	387	405	300	122	-60	271	-161
Disbursements	517	574	727	763	233	65	487	241
Scheduled amortizations	-265	-233	-363	-350	-279	-256	-435	-644
Short-term loans (net)	111	37	41	-213	48	-89	-41	-58
Direct foreign investment	—	—	—	100	120	220	260	300
Errors and omissions	-23	-51	26	67	-6	142	5	-76
Overall balance	-315	-297	-320	-220	-142	-50	268	-1,106

Source: World Bank (1994b), *Viet Nam Public Sector Management and Private Sector Incentives* (No. 13143-VN), September 26.

Table 10A.8
China: Exports and imports (US$ million)

	1980	1985	1986	1987	1988	1989	1990	1991	1992	1993
Exports, total	18,188	22,020	30,942	39,437	47,518	52,537	62,063	71,910	84,998	91,763
Mirror estimates	*n.a.*	*27,751*	*31,903*	*42,593*	*55,309*	*68,402*	*82,327*	*96,001*	*n.a.*	*n.a.*
Breakdown by product (% of total)										
Primary goods	50.24	50.56	36.43	33.55	30.32	28.70	25.55	22.55	23.07	21.48
Food	16.49	13.90	14.38	12.12	12.40	11.70	10.62	10.05	8.37	7.56
Non-food	9.49	9.70	9.40	9.26	8.96	8.02	5.70	4.85	4.04	4.44
Mineral fuels	23.49	26.08	11.90	11.52	8.31	8.22	8.42	6.70	6.61	5.31
Other	0.76	0.88	0.75	0.65	0.65	0.76	0.81	0.94	4.04	4.17
Manufactured goods	49.76	49.44	63.57	66.45	69.68	71.30	74.45	77.46	76.93	78.52
Chemicals and related products	6.19	4.97	5.60	5.67	6.10	6.09	6.01	5.31	4.85	4.79
Light industry	22.10	16.43	19.02	21.73	22.07	20.74	20.26	20.10	18.00	17.29
Machinery & transport equipment	4.65	2.82	3.54	4.41	5.83	7.37	9.00	9.94	16.17	17.26
Other	16.82	25.22	35.41	27.78	28.75	32.27	31.40	33.81	35.62	39.18
Imports, total (US$ million)	19,950	42,252	42,904	43,216	55,275	59,140	53,350	63,791	80,610	103,950
Breakdown by product (% of total)										
Food	16.10	4.45	4.67	7.07	7.58	8.91	8.39	5.83	5.12	3.06
Petroleum (mineral fuels)	1.02	0.41	1.17	1.25	1.42	2.79	2.38	3.31	1.36	0.81
Intermediate	53.33	45.38	40.91	38.80	42.32	39.59	34.35	36.35	34.11	32.68
Consumer goods	2.73	5.51	5.67	4.03	3.18	3.16	3.84	3.93	9.86	8.34
Manufactured	26.83	44.24	47.58	48.85	45.50	45.55	51.03	50.58	49.55	55.11

Sources: Official data from World Bank *China Report* [1994, table 3.1, 181 (source: China Statistical Yearbook 1993, 573, on customs basis)] and Customs Statistics IV/1993 for 1993. "Mirror statistics" data are from World Bank Country Study, *China–Foreign Trade Reform* (1994, table A1.1, 262).
Note: Data from 1980–91 are based on Standard Industrial Trade Classification (SITC); 1992–93 categories on Harmonized System (HS).

Table 10A.9
China: Destination of exports and sources of imports (US$ billion, percent)

	1980	1985	1990	1993
Exports	19.5	27.3	63.2	91.3
Total value (US$ billion)	100.0	100.0	100.0	100.0
Share (%)				
Newly industrialized countries	24.6	33.7	38.6	39.8
Other East Asian	4.0	2.7	2.9	2.4
Japan	20.7	22.3	14.2	13.6
North American OECD	5.7	9.4	9.1	17.6
Oceanian OECD	1.3	0.8	0.8	1.2
European OECD	12.2	8.4	9.5	11.3
Former USSR	1.2	3.8	3.2	3.0
Rest of the world	30.3	18.9	21.7	11.1
Imports				
Total value (US$ billion)	19.8	42.5	59.2	104.1
Share (%)	100.0	100.0	100.0	100.0
NIEs	26.5	27.4	49.4	41.5
Other East Asian	2.3	2.1	3.7	3.7
Japan	26.1	35.7	12.9	19.2
North American OECD	23.4	14.9	13.6	13.1
Oceanian OECD	6.2	3.0	2.5	2.4
European OECD	14.2	14.5	14.2	13.7
Former USSR	1.3	2.4	3.7	6.4
Rest of the world	22.6	15.6	23.6	11.5

Sources: Garnaut and Huan (1995, table 8, 32). From International Economic Data Bank, Australian National University data compiled from the IMF's "Direction of Trade Statistics." Asia Pacific Economics Group (1994) "Asia-Pacific Insights '94," Australian National University, Canberra.

Table 10A.10
Russia: Foreign trade, main trading partners outside the FSU (US$ million)

	1990	1991	1992	1993
Exports (US$ million)				
Former centrally planned economies	35,599	15,249	11,980	10,896
Eastern Europe, Viet Nam, Mongolia, and Cuba	30,723	11,660	7,983	7,452
China, North Korea, Laos, and Yugoslavia	4,885	3,589	3,997	3,444
Market economies	35,549	35,662	27,987	31,700
Developed market economies	25,584	28,764	23,843	25,817
Developing market economies	9,965	6,898	4,144	5,883
Baltic countries	0	0	682	473
Total	71,148	50,911	40,649	43,069
Imports (US$ million)				
Former centrally planned economies	41,482	13,997	7,929	7,561
Eastern Europe, Viet Nam, Mongolia, and Cuba	36,293	10,917	5,347	3,059
China, North Korea, Laos, and Yugoslavia	5,189	3,080	2,582	4,502
Market economies	40,269	30,476	27,052	19,290
Developed market economies	32,480	25,857	22,555	14,853
Developing market economies	7,789	4,619	4,497	4,437
Baltic countries	0	0	333	108
Total	81,751	44,473	35,314	26,959
Trade balance (US$ million)				
Former centrally planned economies	−5,883	1,252	4,051	3,335
Eastern Europe, Viet Nam, Mongolia, and Cuba	−5,570	744	2,636	4,393
China, North Korea, Laos, and Yugoslavia	−304	508	1,415	−1,058
Market economies	−4,720	5,186	935	12,410
Developed market economies	−6,896	2,907	1,288	10,964
Developing market economies	2,176	2,279	−353	1,446
Baltic countries	0	0	349	365
Total	−10,603	6,438	5,335	16,110

Source: Goskomstat, *Russian Economic Trends.*

Table 10A.11
Russia: Foreign trade, outside the FSU, geographic breakdown (US$ million)

	1990	1991	1992	1993
Exports: share of total				
Europe	52,551	37,194	29,913	29,239
Asia	12,728	10,453	8,145	10,553
Americas	3,592	2,149	1,406	2,833
Africa	2,225	1,097	491	436
Oceania	52	18	12	10
Total above	71,148	50,911	39,967	43,071
Imports: share of total				
Europe	57,735	27,868	21,969	14,319
Asia	12,075	7,723	7,409	9,500
Americas	10,144	7,491	4,858	2,660
Africa	1,190	834	686	369
Oceania	610	554	59	111
Total above	81,754	44,470	34,981	26,959
Balance of trade: share of total				
Europe	−5,184	9,326	7,944	14,920
Asia	653	2,730	736	1,053
Americas	−6,552	−5,345	−3,452	173
Africa	1,035	263	−195	67
Oceania	−558	−536	−47	−101
Total above	−10,606	6,438	4,986	16,112

Source: Goskomstat, *Russian Economic Trends*.
Note: The totals in this table differ slightly from those in Table 10A.10 because of
differences in sources for the different breakdowns.

Table 10A.12
Russia: Foreign trade evaluated at world prices, FSU and non-FSU (US$ billion)

	1990	1992	1993
Exports (US$ billion)			
Non-FSU	46	38	41
FSU	84	34	28
Total	130	72	69
Imports (US$ billion)			
Non-FSU	47	32	24
FSU	52	29	39
Total	99	61	63
Balance of trade (US$ billion)			
Non-FSU	−1	6	17
FSU	32	5	−11
Total	31	11	6

Source: Senik-Leygonie (1994, table 21, 62). Author's calculations based on CEA data for non-FSU and Goskomstat data for FSU.
Note: These estimates are built up from disaggregated data in constant rubles. They are converted to dollars, product by product, by being multiplied by the ratio of the average dollar price of the product delivered to Western markets to the average domestic price in rubles of the same product. See Senik-Leygonie (1994).

11 Improving the Performance of Enterprises in Transition Economies

Wing Thye Woo

11.1 Introduction

The essence of Stalinist socialism is the allocation of resources by fiat and the complete ownership of assets by the central government, acting on behalf of the entire population. Stalinist socialism, in short, is defined by the central government centralizing all production decisions and all property rights. The central plan and the state-owned enterprise (SOE) are the ultimate expressions of these two defining characteristics.

All economic reforms in socialist countries can be described as the relaxation in varying degrees of these two centralizations. The usual relaxation of the central plan is the legalization of the sale of above-quota production and the introduction of a profit-sharing scheme between the SOE and the state to enable bonuses to be paid to managers and workers. The usual relaxation of centralized property rights is the legalization of non-state enterprises, i.e., enterprises that are not owned by the entire population.

Loosely speaking, there have been two ways of establishing non-state enterprises. The first way, which is associated with Eastern Europe and Russia, is to place almost equal emphasis on privatizing existing SOEs and promoting the formation of new private enterprises, e.g., individual-owned enterprise partnerships, cooperatives, and joint-stock companies.

The second way, which is associated with China, is to preserve the existing SOEs as much as possible, while allowing the formation of (1) new enterprises that are owned *collectively* by the local community, and (2) new private enterprises. The collective-owned enterprises (COEs) represent *localized socialism* because a significant amount of the shares are jointly owned by the local community, and while workers may hold some of the COEs' shares, these shares are not legally transferable to non-workers. The most numerous and well-known COEs are the rural ones known as the township and village enterprises (TVEs). Until the early 1990s, COEs faced much fewer legal discriminations than private enterprises; e.g., COEs faced lower tax rates and easier registration procedures. The SOEs are in turn preferred over COEs; e.g., SOEs have much easier access to credit from state banks, and it was only from 1987 onward that most COEs were allowed to participate directly in international trade.

When a country like China avoids the privatization of existing SOEs and relies on the growth of the non-state sector to reduce the relative economic importance of the state sector, it should be described as pursuing a gradual strategy of decentralizing property rights. Obviously, localized socialism in the form of COEs represents a lesser extent of decentralized property rights than private enterprises. The Chinese method of establishing non-state enterprises raises two questions that we will attempt to answer. The first question is whether the maintenance of the SOE sector as is would not inhibit private investment in the non-state sector, making the dilution of the role of the state sector more gradual than anticipated. The second question is whether COEs can be as efficient as private enterprises.

The important difference between the decentralization of resource allocation and the decentralization of property rights is that the former necessarily involves the marketization of goods while the latter need not entail the marketization of property rights. For example, many TVEs have transformed themselves into shareholding corporations[1] in the search for a more efficient organizational form, but their shares are legally not transferable. Private enterprises represent the maximum limit of decentralized property rights because their equities are owned by individuals and freely tradeable.

The socialist economic reforms in Eastern Europe and the former Soviet Union (EEFSU) before 1990 can be categorized as decentralization of production within a framework of centralized property rights because the non-state sector was insignificant economically. The post-1984 economic reforms in China can be described as the decentralization of production and the decentralization of property rights. By 1994, the non-state sector in China accounted for about half of gross industrial output. The mass (across-the-board) distribution of property rights in the Czech Republic and Russia in the 1990s and the establishment of legally supervised capital markets for the trading of property rights is the decentralization of property rights carried to the level of normal international practice.

This paper analyzes the issues associated with SOE reform within the above framework of the two centralizations. Section 11.2 reviews the principal defects of the Stalinist economic system. Section 11.3 focuses on the reforms that decentralize resource allocation power away from the central planning agency to the individual SOEs. We will analyze the decentralization of property rights in greater detail because it is a more recent phenomenon in EEFSU and China. Section 11.4 considers the case

---

1. They are sometimes called shareholding cooperatives or shareholding collectives.

for decentralizing property rights, and section 11.5 studies the experiences of EEFSU in doing so. Section 11.6 discusses the rise of localized socialism in China in the form of TVEs as a method of decentralizing property rights. Section 11.7 presents our conclusions.

11.2 Behavior and Performance under Central Planning

The state-owned enterprise in a centrally planned economy was a passive production unit. The state set all the prices and quantities of its inputs and outputs, and the SOE's most important goal was to fulfill its output quota. Profits were of no operational consequence to the enterprise because they were created by the prices set by the planning agency and had to be transferred in their entirety to the supervising branch ministry.

To maximize the probability of achieving the quota, the SOE would constantly lobby its supervising branch ministry to keep its quota from increasing and to obtain additional input allocations. Large inventories of inputs and output were held to ensure that the quota would be met if any negative shocks were to occur. Given the emphasis on the physical volume of output, the SOE had little incentive to improve (or even to maintain) the quality of its products, introduce new product lines, or develop new production techniques.

While the branch ministries had good control over the finances of the SOEs because of the price and quantity controls, they were not able to oversee the technical efficiency of the SOEs adequately. Because of this supervision conundrum, a branch ministry had the perverse incentive to cover up mismanagement within SOEs in order to project a positive image of itself within the government. A branch ministry was, in reality, the chief lobbyist for its SOEs in the policy debates within the government.

The hallmark of branch ministry supervision was rigidity. Rigidity simplifies the ministry's responsibilities to bargaining with the rest of government and with the SOEs over the incremental adjustments to the baseline levels, which in practice meant last period's achieved levels. Baselines pervade every aspect of the economic relationship, e.g., the baseline revenue contribution to the budget, the baseline output quota, the baseline investment allocation, the baseline foreign exchange earnings, and the baseline materials quotient. Not surprisingly, the fear that branch ministries would ratchet the output and revenue baselines upward was another important damper on the SOEs' enthusiasm for increasing production efficiency.

As the primary objective of the baselines was to increase production capacity, the emphasis was on expanding the heavy industries and suppressing the service and light industries. For example, the machine building industry in Russia and the U.S. accounted for one-third and one-tenth of manufacturing production, respectively. The result of this distortion of the production structure was that de-industrialization had to occur when economic liberalization in the 1990s allowed market-generated demand to determine resource allocation.

This bureaucratic rigidity, together with the near-total absence of incentives for SOEs to optimize resource utilization and to innovate, led inevitably to low (negative, in some cases) technical progress, i.e., total factor productivity growth (TFP). This outcome, coupled with the low population growth rates in EEFSU, meant that their economic growth was powered, and limited, by the rate of capital accumulation. Since their production technologies were quite well characterized by the employment of fixed proportions of labor and capital, the result was a decline and then stagnation in output growth (Easterly and Fischer 1994).[2]

11.3 Devolving Operational Autonomy to the SOE

The first policy response to the efficiency crisis in the SOE sector was to introduce elements of a market economy within the existing system of centralized property rights, i.e., experiment with decentralized socialism. The operational autonomy of the SOEs was expanded over time as earlier ones failed to produce the desired levels of efficiency. In the Chinese case, the following sequence of piecemeal SOE reforms were implemented: the right of the enterprise to retain a portion of its profits and dispense it for bonus and welfare expenditure, the right to sell an increasing proportion of output in the free market, the right to introduce new products, the right to raise funds for investments of its own choice, the right to fire workers, and the right to file bankruptcy (the last two rights were never seriously exercised). The surprising consequence of this steady increase in enterprise autonomy in China, and earlier in Eastern Europe and the Soviet Union, was a sharp deterioration in the profitability of the SOEs. Almost half of Chinese SOEs ran operating losses in 1994.

The Polish, Hungarian, and Russian experiences prior to 1990 suggest that enterprise losses under decentralized socialism came from the reduction in the ability of the branch ministries to supervise the firms. The freeing of SOEs from the prices and quantities set by the branch ministries meant that the only information on the financial performance of SOEs came from the SOEs themselves. Since the SOEs now had expenditure autonomy, their managers came under great pressure from

---

2. It is likely that the low degree of capital–labor substitutability in EEFSU was the joint result of the putty–clay characteristic of capital equipment and the non-deviating replication of existing specifications for the convenience of central planning.

the workers to grant increases in direct compensation (wages, bonuses, and various subsidies) and indirect compensation (e.g., housing, recreational, transportation, and dining facilities, and distribution of household goods) that exceeded the growth of labor productivity. The managers generally yielded to such demands because the workers could exert political pressure through the factory's Party secretary, who typically could influence the promotion of the manager; furthermore, any resulting losses would automatically be covered by the state, e.g., by allowing the loss-making SOE to keep the sales taxes it collected.

Even if the salary of the manager were linked to the amount of profits turned over to the state, he could compensate himself by hiding his consumption expenditure (e.g., cars and banquets) as production costs. Hence, the first result of the decentralization reforms was the over-consumption phenomenon, i.e., profits were converted into business expenses. The over-consumption by SOEs directly reduced the revenue of the state and increased inflation to the extent that the state monetized the larger budget deficit. The fiscal crisis of the state meant that infrastructure investments needed to relieve production bottlenecks could not be undertaken, threatening both growth and price stability.

The second result of the decentralization reforms was the appearance of over-investment. SOEs sought to increase future consumption by increasing future output, and that meant increasing current investment. Investment was always undertaken beyond prudential levels because managers recognized that the fruits of successful investment could be captured by the SOE employees through increases in compensation and that the losses of unsuccessful investments would be transferred to the state budget. Given the emphasis on expanding the productive capacity of the economy, and that the decentralized state banks faced the same situation of being able to privatize their profits and to socialize their losses, the explosion of credits added to the inflation.

Both over-consumption and over-investment are the natural consequences of what Kornai (1980) has aptly called "the soft budget constraint." [3] The crux is that the state treasury or central bank had to finance the losses of enterprises because it cannot avoid guaranteeing the financial integrity of activities undertaken under the name of the state. This faith on the part of the SOEs in an eventual bailout by the state is the cause of the large increase in interenterprise arrears whenever a tight credit policy is pursued to reduce inflation. Inter-enterprise arrears allowed the SOEs to continue their operations as usual without the benefit of bank credits. Some governments have repeatedly expanded credit to clear these interenterprise arrears, thus effectively

---

3. Evidence of these two excesses in Chinese SOEs are presented in Fan, Hai, and Woo (forthcoming) and Minami and Hondai (1995).

compromising the credibility of future attempts to restructure SOEs and to maintain price stability.

Even if a hard budget constraint could be imposed on the decentralized SOEs, the fiscal situation is improved only to the extent of the elimination of loss subsidies. This is because the optimal strategy for a decentralized SOE operating under a hard budget constraint is to report profits as close to zero as plausibly possible. The imposition of a hard budget constraint is likely to induce the SOEs to restructure their activities only to the extent that is necessary to eliminate the losses, especially if enterprise personnel have to bear the adjustment costs.

The loss of financial control over SOEs by the branch ministries represented de facto privatization of SOE income streams by SOE employees, particularly by the managers. Joskow, Schmalensee, and Tsukanova (1994) reported that a Russian survey of 13 important industries in 1992 found that almost a third of the enterprises "had been spontaneously privatized" through arrangements such as leasing and transformation into joint-stock companies. This large-scale embezzlement by the managers could well lead to social unrest. Failure to deal with this corruption within the SOEs could erode the political legitimacy of the government. After all, the rallying cry for the Tiananmen demonstrations in 1989 was to reduce inflation and corruption. Thus, it is important to recognize that the SOE system generates both outcomes naturally.

While the financial weakening of SOEs under decentralization reforms is obvious, the effects on production efficiency are less clear. On one hand, one would expect an SOE manager to implement efficiency-enhancing measures, partly in response to the competition from the new non-state firms, and partly in order to generate more surplus that they could divert to themselves. On the other hand, since profits could also be generated by favored access to rationed (low-price) inputs, exemption from taxes, and special retention of foreign exchange earnings, the SOE manager might continue the old habit of seeking favors from the government. The decentralization episodes in Eastern Europe and the Soviet Union did not seem to produce much technical progress in the SOEs.

The evidence from China on technical improvements is mixed. Some studies have found positive TFP growth in SOEs, but one cannot applaud this finding without having to adopt a double standard. The fact is that the TFP growth rate in the SOE sector is at best only half of the TFP growth rate in the TVE sector, 2.4 percent and 4.6 percent, respectively, according to Jefferson, Rawski, and Zheng (JRZ 1992).

Using survey samples, Huang and Meng (1995) and Woo, Hai, Jin, and Fan (WHJF 1994) found the TFP growth rate for SOEs to be, respectively, –4.7 percent in the 1986–90 period, and zero in the 1984–88 period. When WHJF deflated their intermediate inputs in the same way as JRZ, they found the same result, 2.4 percent for TFP growth. However, WHJF found that the JRZ deflation method caused the implicit value-added deflator (VAD) of SOEs in their sample to decline secularly throughout the sample period when the CPI was rising pretty strongly.

Upon examination, the VAD in JRZ and that in Groves, Hong, McMillan, and Naughton (GHMN 1995)—a study that found large positive TFP growth in the 1980–89 period—also declined secularly over their sample periods.[4] Such opposite trends between the CPI and the VAD created by JRZ's and GHMN's deflation methods is troubling because such occurrences are internationally unprecedented.

Naughton (1994) and JRZ (1994) argued that a declining VAD is to be expected when input prices rise more than output prices.[5] But WHJF showed that this relative price movement is not a sufficient condition for a declining VAD. As far as we know, the quadrupling and doubling of oil prices in 1973 and 1978, respectively, did not cause any country's GDP deflator to decline. A declining VAD is also unlikely to be the product of gradual reforms because neither Polish nor Hungarian industrial VAD declined for sustained periods during their pre-1989 gradual reforms.

A declining VAD could be generated when the output price deflator is understated and/or when the intermediate input price deflator is overstated. We know that the increase in the official output price deflator is understated because of the widespread over-reporting of real output (see Woo 1996), but JRZ and GHMN accepted the official output at face value. It appears that JRZ may have overstated their intermediate input deflator, because their VAD declined in the 1980–84 period when it was mostly output prices that were liberalized and most intermediate input prices were kept unchanged.

Recent work by Woo (1996) revealed the following:

1. The ending of the economic incoherence generated by the Cultural Revolution caused a one-time catch-up in the efficiency of SOEs during the 1978–84 period.

2. After that initial rebound, the incremental decentralization measures introduced since 1984 have failed to induce the industrial SOEs to improve their efficiency on a sustained basis.

These results (Woo 1996) reconcile the findings of positive TFP growth in SOEs in the pre-1985 period[6] with the findings of zero TFP growth in the post-1984 period. These findings imply that a study that finds positive

---

4. The declining VAD in GHMN cannot be discerned in the article itself; this facet was revealed in Naughton (1994).
5. See reply by Woo, Fan, Hai, and Jin (1994).
6. Chen et al. (1988), Dollar (1990), Granick (1990), Jefferson (1990), and Minami (1994).

TFP growth in industrial SOEs in the post-1978 period would find zero TFP growth after dropping the 1978–84 period from the estimation.

To recapitulate, the decentralization reforms have led to the following problems:

1. They allowed the SOEs to weaken the fiscal position of the state and to obtain excessive bank credits, hence undermining price stability.

2. They produced social tensions because of the inequitable appropriation of income streams by SOE employees.

3. They induced little, if any, technical progress in the SOEs.

These three problems explain the occurrence of decentralization–recentralization cycles in socialist economies. The Chinese have trenchantly summed up their SOE reform experience as "chaotic upon loosening, and moribund upon tightening (*yi fang jiu luan, yi zhua jiu si*)."

11.4   The Case for Decentralizing the Property Rights of SOEs' Assets

Many transition economies have traced the failure of decentralized socialism to the system of centralized property rights. The state is simply overwhelmed in its monitoring of the management of national assets by SOEs. It would be more efficient to enlist the help of all citizens to monitor the use of the assets, and this is achieved by transferring the property rights of a significant portion of SOE assets to the citizens and allowing these property rights to be freely traded in organized stock exchanges. Concretely, the state introduces company laws, corporatizes the SOEs, distributes part of the shares to the public and the rest to state asset management corporations (SAMCs), and supervises the stock exchanges.

The above conclusion and actions of many transition economies find striking parallels in the experiences of market economies with their SOEs. The international experience is that, in general, SOEs operate inefficiently partly because of the internal rent-seeking motives discussed earlier and partly because of the imposition of non-economic objectives on them by the government.[7] Furthermore, the efficiency of an SOE can be improved when the government focuses significant attention on it, but this improvement in efficiency is seldom sustainable. For instance:

> A number of the SOEs that were judged in *World Development Report 1983* to be well on the road to major and enduring performance improvements thanks to exemplary government reform efforts—for example, the Senegalese bus company, Fertilizer SOEs in Turkey, and manufacturing SOEs in Pakistan—either have improved in performance or have deteriorated.   (Kikeri, Nellis, and Shirley 1992, 17–18)

---

7. See Ehrlich et al. (1994), Megginson, Nash, and van Randenbourgh (1994), Vining and Boardman (1992), and World Bank (1995a).

The decentralized property rights system has three major advantages over the centralized property rights system. The first is that there is now a publicly available indicator of each firm's performance, the price of the firm's equities. The price level and price movement of a firm's equity, when compared to the price levels and price movements of the equities of other firms in the *same* industry, provide unambiguous information to the SAMCs and the firm's board of directors about the competence of the firm's management team. More important, this publicly available indicator of firm performance prevents the SAMCs and the board of directors from becoming apologists for the firm in the manner of the branch ministry under the system of centralized property rights.

The second major advantage of the system of decentralized property rights is that the government budget is now separated from those of the enterprises. In a reversal from decentralized socialism, the state now collects taxes when an enterprise is profitable but is not responsible for the losses of the enterprise. The system of decentralized property rights is a system of hard budget constraints; the firm enjoys financial autonomy but accepts financial independence from the state budget. The firm can still decide how much to pay its workers but it cannot count on the state budget to help out when losses occur. This hardening of the budget constraint is beneficial not only to production efficiency and technical progress but also to price stability. The elimination of a traditional source of inflation undoubtedly enhances the "economic legitimacy" of the state.

The third major advantage of decentralized property rights is that it enhances the political legitimacy of the state by ending an avenue for corruption. Recent news accounts from China revealed that the loss of state assets has reached crisis proportion. In December 1995, the State Administration of State Property (SASP) reported that asset-stripping in the SOE sector "has been about 50 billion yuan [annually] since the early 1980s." [8] This would mean that the cumulative loss of SOE assets in 1983–1992 was equivalent to 24 percent of the original value of fixed assets in the SOE sector in 1992, or 34 percent of the net value of fixed assets in the SOE sector.

In stating the above three advantages of the decentralized property rights system, we are not denying that inadequate supervision of managers by the board of directors, state bailouts of private enterprises, and bribing of state officials by private enterprises also occur in capitalist economies. Such flaws do exist in capitalist economies, especially in those that have extensive economic regulations. Our point is simply that

---

8. "State asset drain must end," *China Daily* December 13, 1995. See also "State toughens stand to protect its possessions," *China Daily* June 2, 1995; "Asset checks can stop fiddles," *China Daily* June 7, 1995; and "Market investigated for losing State assets," *China Daily* June 2, 1995.

these flaws are much more pervasive in countries with centralized property rights. This is why the centralized property rights system self-destructed after 1990.

It is important to emphasize that the decentralization of the property rights of the SOEs has to be accompanied by reforms on other fronts if enterprise restructuring is to proceed smoothly. A national unemployment insurance scheme must be set up, the SOE-based revenue collection system must be replaced by a broad-based tax system, the state banking sector must also be privatized, and the social service functions of the SOEs (e.g., pensions and medical insurance) must be taken over by new institutions.[9]

11.5 The Experience with Decentralizing Property Rights in EEFSU

EEFSU never considered localized socialism as a way of decentralizing property rights. The collapse of their communist governments obviated the political need to create an enterprise form that is different from private enterprise, the dominant enterprise form in the market economies of the world. The standard procedure for decentralizing the property rights of small SOEs is to sell or lease them. For medium and large SOEs, there have been three main methods:

1. mass transfer of SOE assets without preference given to existing SOE personnel (insiders), i.e., outsider privatization;

2. mass transfer of SOE assets primarily to insiders, i.e., insider privatization; and

3. firm-by-firm sale.

The Czech Republic, Russia, and Hungary are respective examples of the above three methods of decentralizing property rights. (Strictly speaking, Hungary started off with the firm-by-firm sale method and then increasingly over time cooperated with management in the privatization process.)

The essence of the mass transfer program is the virtually free distribution of assets to citizens.[10] This can be accomplished by direct distribution of the assets, or indirectly by vouchers, or a combination of both. (Vouchers are distributed to the citizens, who then use these vouchers to bid for shares of SOEs. The valuation of SOEs is thus left to the voucher holders.) In most cases in Russia, the majority of SOE equities was given

---

9. For the case of China, see Wong, Heady, and Woo (1995) and Woo (forthcoming) for detailed suggestions for fiscal system, financial sector, social services, and housing reforms.
10. Lieberman and Nellis (1995) and Lieberman et. al. (1995) are recent excellent case studies of mass privatization.

almost free to the insiders, and voucher holders bid for the remainder of the equities. In the Czech Republic and Estonia, there were no such privileges extended to the insiders; any shares that were not retained by the state were exchanged for vouchers. Obviously, after controlling for the population and geographical size of the country, the transfer of the firms to insiders can take place much faster than the transfer to outsiders.

The firm-by-firm sale strategy of Hungary, by its very nature, is a drawn-out process. Since an important goal is to raise revenue for the state, it requires, at the minimum, valuation (and, maybe, reorganization) of the firm by the state prior to the sale. The Hungarian firm-by-firm sale strategy soon ran out of steam. The privatization program assumed a quick pace only when insiders were given an important role in shaping the privatization.

With hindsight, it is easy to see that the choice of privatization method depended on the distribution of political power among the state, enterprise managers, and worker councils. The hallmark of Hungarian "goulash communism" that began in the early 1960s (to help prevent reoccurrence of a 1956-style revolution against the Soviet Union) was the steady transfer of operational and financial decision-making powers to the managers. By 1990, Hungary was perhaps the most "reformed" of the EEFSU economies, and had the largest proportion of its SOE assets already "spontaneously privatized" by the managers, i.e., it had significant portions of SOE income streams already channeled to the managers. The managers were naturally opposed to "outsider privatization" and, as a delaying tactic, supported the state's desire for orderly transfer of state assets through firm-by-firm sales which require lengthy, extensive pre-sale valuation of assets in each case.

Czechoslovakia implemented central planning with a vengeance after the abortive 1968 uprising against the Soviet Union. So when the non-communists took over the state apparatus in November 1989, they found cowed managers and workers who were not organized to push for their special interests. The Czech reformers were not interested in economic experimentation; they wanted to establish standard international norms of corporate governance as quickly as possible before the insiders could form an effective lobby. In the words of the leading Czech reformer, Vaclav Klaus: "The key task is looking for an owner who will perform post-privatization restructuring, not for a state bureaucrat who will restructure the firm before privatization." [11]

The Russian reformers who assumed power after the failed August 1991 coup had the benefit of learning from the post-1989 reform experiences in Czechoslovakia, Hungary, and Poland. The lesson was clear: powerful managers in Hungary and powerful worker councils in

11. Quote from Hazlett (1995, 31).

Poland had brought to a standstill the states' efforts to enact outsider privatization. Since political power in Russia was about balanced between the reformers and the enterprise insiders, insider privatization was really the only feasible option. Furthermore, insider privatization had the strong (potential) political benefits of increasing the popularity of the Yeltsin government and making an important component of the reform program irreversible.

The Czech Experience with Outsider Privatization

The Czech Republic implemented the mass transfer to the general public through three channels. The first channel was by open auctions of small businesses, and the second channel was by the return of properties confiscated during the communist period. The third and most well-known channel was the distribution of vouchers to citizens who paid a nominal fee to participate in the privatization. Czechs either used these vouchers to bid directly for the shares of medium and large SOEs or exchanged these vouchers for the shares of any combination of the 770 investment privatization funds (IPFs).[12] The shares of the privatized firms and IPFs are traded on the stock exchanges.

The Czech reformers ordered every medium and large SOE to submit a privatization plan within a short time, and invited the public to submit competing privatization plans for the same companies within six months after the deadline for the SOE managers. The Ministry of Privatization, in consultation with other relevant ministries, would pick the winning plan. The effect was that the SOE insiders not only had little time to organize themselves but also became participants competing in the privatization process. Many SOE managers supported voucher privatization initially because they thought that it would lead to such dispersed ownership that individual shareholders would not find it worthwhile to concern themselves with the running of the firms. By the time SOE managers realized that this would not be the outcome, when potential core investors started appearing in the form of investment funds, it was too late for the managers to organize to prevent the impending changes to their privileged positions.

The voucher privatization occurred in two waves. The first wave began in October 1991 and ended in June 1993, and the second wave began in August 1992 and ended in March 1995. In the first wave of privatization, most of the public turned their vouchers over to a small number of investment funds. The seven largest investment funds controlled 45 percent of all voucher points, and the thirteen largest

---

12. "Eastern Europe's capitalism: Who's boss now," *Economist* May 20, 1995, 68.

investment funds controlled 55 percent. This concentration of voucher points in a small number of investment funds is actually desirable because it prevents over-dispersed ownership that leads to the free-rider situation of firm managers being free of supervision and hence able to pursue their own agendas. It is important to note that the concentration of voucher points does not connote concentration of equity ownership, because the ownership of the shares of the investment funds are fairly widely dispersed. Usually, only 5 percent ownership of an investment fund is sufficient to control it.[13]

The disquieting aspect of Czech privatization is that five of the seven largest investment funds are controlled by domestic financial institutions (mainly banks) which are owned at least 35 percent by the SAMC (Fund for National Property) or by other state institutions. Of the bank shares not held by state institutions, a large part is held by investment funds, creating a situation of complicated cross-ownership.[14] The twin phenomena of the influence that the state can exert (through the banks) on the privatized firms, and the cross-ownership among banks and investment funds, have rendered the ownership and control of the privatized firms an ambiguous matter. A return to the old days of firms pursuing non-economic objectives in return for soft budget constraints is a distinct possibility if a non-market-oriented government were elected. The efficiency of corporate governance in the future is hazy:

Whether this banking structure will lead to a German type of arrangement, in which banks relatively effectively monitor corporate performance, or whether the Czech form of bank cross-ownership will allow the banks to avoid any effective external control, in order to resist genuine restructuring and sit parasitically on top of the productive sector, is a question that is still impossible to answer.   (Frydman, Rapaczynski, and Turkewitz 1996)

The Russian Experience with Insider Privatization

In Russia, the workers collective within each state-owned enterprise was given three options (Boycko, Shleifer, and Vishny 1995). The first option gave the workers 25 percent of the shares for free, allowed them to acquire an additional 10 percent cheaply, and sold 5 percent of the shares at a low price to the managers. The second option allowed the workers and managers to buy 51 percent of the shares at 1.7 times the original book value—a very good deal because of the high inflation since 1989. The third option allowed the managers to buy 40 percent of the shares at low prices

---

13. Private communication from Andrzej Rapaczynski, February 1996.
14. Frydman, Rapaczynski, and Turkewitz, in chapter 3 of this volume, note that "...one bank, Investnicni Banka, is in fact 17 percent owned by the funds that it controls."

if they promised not to go bankrupt. In practice, the third option was hardly ever chosen.

The process of choice was very important. It allowed an opportunity for the workers to understand the process of ownership change, and to be an active part of it. In fact, the debate within each factory over which option to choose resulted in an enormous national "school" concerning the market economy. Workers learned the meaning of joint-stock ownership, corporate governance, supervisory boards, share options, secondary-market trading, and other aspects of enterprise ownership. Also, the voting gave an important legitimacy to the process of ownership change, and prevented managers from simply stealing the enterprise. The choice was the workers', and was not imposed from above. Of course, the workers' choice was not unlimited: they still had to select among the three options.

There are many reports that suggest that insider privatization meant manager privatization in a high number of cases. For example:

In Russia's Orel region, 2000 workers at an electronic instrument plant were forced to go on leave while managers illegally purchased the controlling share of the company. In the Vologda region, two-thirds of the shares of a cement plant were registered in the names of the plant director and his mother-in-law. (Waller 1996)

The first empirical evidence on the performance of privatized firms shows that there has been little enterprise restructuring in the short run.[15] It was hence quite natural that Aghion, Blanchard, and Carlin (1996) concluded in their survey essay that insider privatization is not conducive to enterprise restructuring. We think, however, that it is too early to be pessimistic about insider privatization leading to improvements in enterprise performance. The continued generous flow of budget subsidies and bank credits (especially when the central bank was under Viktor Gerashenko) to the privatized enterprises is likely to be the primary reason for the slow enterprise restructuring in Russia. It should be noted that "insider privatization" does not create a new type of private enterprise, as its name may suggest: the owner(s)-operated firm is the oldest and most durable form of firm organization.

In two recent studies on the behavior of investment funds, Frydman, Pistor, and Rapaczynski (forthcoming) found that these outside minority investors have been active shareholders, pushing successfully for enterprise restructuring in a number of cases. Over time, as the insiders sell their shares and as firms issue new stock to raise capital, the investment funds will increase their influence over the running of the firms. The insiders will sell their shares as labor mobility increases, as

---

15. Earle, Estrin, and Leschenko (1995) and Barberis et al. (1995).

the advantages for risk diversification become more apparent, and as they retire. So while the amount of restructuring to date may be disappointing, this state of affairs may not endure because the incentives for change are now in place.

However, one should guard against complacent optimism about the future. There is another drawback to insider privatization that is more serious than the slow pace of enterprise restructuring, a drawback that threatens the commitment to the economic reforms that made privatization possible. The fact is that insider privatization can create gross inequities that could lead to a big political backlash. Insider privatization has made the already privileged workers in efficient, modern enterprises richer by giving them a bigger share of the capital income, and has impoverished the workers of inefficient, technologically backward enterprises by replacing the budget subsidies they have been receiving with ownership claims on what is effectively a rusting scrap heap.

There is a second type of gross inequity. Despite the efforts to make the workers the largest block of shareholders, managers in a significant proportion of the cases have taken control of the firms. Furthermore, given the administrative and legal confusion in post-communist Russia, nomenklatura privatization can reappear on a vast scale under the guise of insider privatization. For example, the highly profitable state gas company (Gazprom) was never really put up for privatization; the bureaucrats simply stole it.

Given the egalitarian emphasis of the immediate past, populist politicians might be able to incite public outrage over the unfair distribution of assets. This social outrage, if led by atavistic elements, could halt, if not reverse partially, the economic reforms. The point is that the main objection against insider privatization is not economic but political. This argues that large SOEs that were stolen by the managers ought to be re-nationalized in order to be re-privatized using the proper official privatization procedures.

The Hungarian Experience with Protracted Privatization

The non-communist government elected in 1990 faced widespread public indignation over the spontaneous privatization that had occurred under goulash communism. The new government immediately established the State Privatization Agency (AVU) to reverse the illegal privatization and enact orderly privatization of state assets. The privatization agency adopted a two-track approach to privatization: a fast track for small state-owned retail and service stores, and a slower track for medium and large SOEs.

The first track (called "Preprivatization") has worked well. Over 10,000 small state-owned stores have been sold, primarily through public auctions.[16]

The second track was necessarily slower because it involved the recovery of state assets and its goal was to raise a substantial amount of revenue for the budget. With the help of prominent (and hence expensive) Western management consulting firms, twenty financially strong enterprises that were deemed to be attractive to foreign investors were put forward for sale (after detailed valuation of their assets and evaluation of their business prospects). The high hopes of the AVU were dashed by the lackadaisical response of the international investment community.

The failure of the First Privatization Program was a heavy blow to the credibility of the government. To cope with the resulting political backlash, the government sought the political support of the managerial lobby by designating 169 key SOEs to remain under state ownership indefinitely. These "immortalized" enterprises were put under the supervision of a newly established SAMC (Av Rt). Over time, the SAMC, in fact, controlled more assets than the State Privatization Agency; three times more in value. The managerial lobby was further wooed by allowing insider privatization (called "Self-Privatization") that sometimes bordered on spontaneous privatization, and giving the managers key roles in designing and implementing the privatization. Specifically,

...the SPA abandoned its plans for centrally-managed privatization and began to cooperate with the management in the decentralized process of ownership transformation. This process, characterized by negotiations among enterprise insiders, potential investors, and the SPA, has led ... to the creation of complicated and confusing property relations....[The] degree to which privatization translates into new corporate governance arrangements is rather unclear. Hungarian companies have developed a number of cross-holdings, in which groups of state companies and banks hold shares in each other, with even the foreign investors usually managing to acquire only minority positions.... As a result, the grip of managers over the enterprises is as strong as ever, and the role of outside ownership appears negligible. (Frydman and Rapaczynski 1994, 158–9)

The lesson from Hungary is that the decision to implement a firm-by-firm sale strategy of privatization to generate state revenue has resulted in a stalled privatization program and little revenue. The privatization program was then revived by allowing what is effectively insider privatization. The Hungarian state has certainly not reversed the spontaneous privatization that happened before 1990; at best, it has slowed the rate of spontaneous privatization since then.

---

16. Lutz and Krueger (1995).

11.6 Decentralizing Property Rights in China: The TVE Phenomenon of Localized Socialism

The foundation for the TVEs was laid during the decade-long Cultural Revolution, when the official emphasis on self-reliance and the break-down of the national distribution system caused the rural communes to expand their non-agricultural activities. These non-agricultural activities of the communes were grouped into production units called TVEs as the commune system began to dissolve in 1979. The concern for rural under-employment led to increasing liberalization of the regulations governing the formation of non-agricultural enterprises, particularly those that were registered as collective-owned. There are three main types of TVEs.

The first TVE form is characterized by tight controls by the local authorities. This tight control over TVEs has come to be known as the Jiangsu Model because of its concentration in three cities in southern Jiangsu province. The movement of skilled labor and differences in pay across TVEs were closely regulated.

The second type of TVE is known as the Zhejiang Model. The local governments in Zhejiang province, although the majority shareholders in many TVEs, normally refrain from intervening in the operational and financial decisions of the TVEs provided that the enterprises make annual contributions to the village funds. These TVEs are essentially "private" in their operations.

The third type is private enterprise masquerading as a TVE. The entire capital of the enterprise is from one individual or a small group, and it pays a fee to the local authority in order to be allowed to call itself a TVE—a charade that is popularly referred to as "wearing a red cap." The main reasons for the desire to disguise the true ownership are lower tax rates, easier approval procedures, less restrictions on the size and operations of the enterprise, and shelter against possible reversal in the political fortunes of the reformers. As the official press described it:

> ... hundreds of thousands of private companies have registered as branches of publicly-owned units on the condition that they pay money to their so-called owners ... [because private companies face] complicated registration procedures, heavy levies and less preferential treatment than State firms [in fund raising and fund use. For example, one] private company had to write 46 receipts of 10,000 yuan each for goods worth 460,000 yuan because non-state firms were only allowed to issue bills under 10,000 yuan. ("Private firms jump to take 'red caps' off," *China Daily* November 4, 1994)

It is commonly believed that the number of red-capped private enterprises is greater than the number of registered private enterprises.

A 1993 survey found that in one county in Hebei province where there were "at least 1000 private businesses, the official number was eight." [17]

It has been suggested that the social service functions (especially housing, health care, and pensions) of the SOE sector have had a significant positive impact on the growth of TVEs.[18] The argument is that the SOEs subsidize the TVEs: SOE workers who resigned, or took early retirement, to accept a job at a TVE have sometimes kept receiving at least part of the social services of the SOE. The problem with this claim is that the areas of China that have the greatest concentration of SOEs, and hence, allegedly, the greatest amount of SOE subsidies to the TVEs, are the areas where TVE growth has been unimpressive, e.g., the northeast provinces. The coastal provinces in central and southern China, which have relatively few SOEs, are the ones that have produced the explosive TVE growth. This negative correlation across provinces between the dominance of SOEs and the growth of TVEs refutes the suggestion that a major reason for the explosive growth of TVEs is indirect subsidies from SOEs. If anything, the negative correlation suggests that the presence of SOEs is detrimental to the development of TVEs. The greater the number of SOEs in a region, the greater is the monopolization by SOEs of local capital and intermediate inputs, and, hence, the more difficult it is for TVEs to expand their operations.

Explaining the Collective Ownership Form of TVEs

By any account, the TVE sector is unusual by international standards. In most countries with rural industry, such as Indonesia, ownership of small enterprises is private, often within a family. By contrast, TVE ownership is collective, at least officially. This has given rise to many debates among academic scholars and policy makers.

Some scholars have argued that collective ownership reflects deep Chinese cultural patterns (Weitzman and Xu 1994). The dominance of private enterprises in rural Taiwan appears to refute this "cooperative culture" hypothesis, however. Other scholars have said that collective ownership is necessary because China lacks a sufficient number of entrepreneurs to develop an economy based on private ownership. Still other scholars have said that collective ownership is an effective way to raise capital funds for rural enterprise and to reduce the principal–agency problem by shortening the supervision distance (Chang and Wang 1994, Che and Qian 1994).

---

17. "Enterprises shake protection cover, " *China Daily*, March 31, 1995.
18. This point was made by Qian (1994) and by Dr. Dongtao Zou of the State Commission of Reforming the Economic System at the conference "Economies in Transition: Comparing Eastern Europe and Asia," July 5–6, 1995, Beijing, China.

We are skeptical of these explanations, at least as a general theory of TVEs. In our opinion, an adequate theory will have to be based on the following three considerations. First, and most obviously, private ownership was basically prohibited in many areas until recently. Therefore, collective ownership of rural industry arose because no other forms of ownership were permitted. Second, TVEs faced lower tax rates and fewer regulations than private enterprises. Third, the collective ownership reflected the low labor mobility in the countryside, largely because of the household registration system. Community ownership was possible because the community members expected to remain in the same place indefinitely, and there was virtually no inward migration.

The Problems with the TVE Ownership Structure

Since the growth of the TVE sector has been so dynamic, does it really matter that its ownership structure is unusual? Why not simply continue along the same path, building on the successful accomplishments to this point? The problem is that the unclear and unusual ownership structure may prove to be a source of future crisis in the rural areas. While things have gone well up until now, mainly because China desperately needed small rural enterprises and there was low rural labor mobility, the future of the TVEs will be hindered if there is no ownership reform in the meantime.

An analogy is helpful. From the 1950s through the 1980s, Yugoslavia fostered a kind of collective ownership of its industrial enterprises, under the label of "social capital." The workers in the enterprise were supposed to govern the social capital. Up to the 1970s, Yugoslavia grew rapidly with this unusual system. Many studies proclaimed the advantages of Yugoslavia's worker–management system, and scholars from around the world praised its achievements. In the 1980s, however, the entire system came crashing down. It turned out that the lack of real owners made an enormous difference. When an economic crisis arrived in the early 1980s, there were no forces to represent the long-term interests of the enterprise. The workers and management continued to pay themselves large incomes and allowed the enterprise capital to be wasted or misused. Few, if any, would now defend the present dismantling of Yugoslavia's syndicalism.

There are five major problems with the collective ownership of Chinese rural enterprises. The first problem is the most obvious. Collective ownership invites political intervention by the local government in the workings of the enterprise. Indeed, many economists praise this political intervention as essential to promoting enterprise formation. But the opposite is also likely: the local government can stifle the healthy development of the enterprise. There are innumerable stories of local officials demanding bribes or personal services from the rural enterprises. Also, good managers are sometimes forced out of rural enterprises by local officials who favor family members or other political favorites. These kinds of intervention have a very long history in China, dating back for centuries.

The famous China historian, John Fairbank (1992), has even claimed that local bureaucratic intervention in rural industries was a major reason why China did not develop a vigorous market economy in past centuries:

> In feudal Europe the merchant class developed in the towns. Since the landed ruling class were settled in their manors upon the land, the European towns could grow up outside the feudal system instead of being integrated in it. Medieval burghers gained their independence by having a separate habitat in these new towns, and new political authority to protect them, in the persons of the kings of nation-states. In China, these conditions were lacking. The early abolition of feudalism and the dependence of the emperor and his officials upon the local gentry left no political power outside the established order to which the merchant could turn for special protection…Between them, the gentry and officials saw to it that the merchants remained under control and contributed to their coffers instead of setting up a separate economy.   (Fairbank 1992, 181–2)

In a sense then, the TVEs reflect a long-standing pattern in Chinese economic history: rural enterprises under the control of local bureaucrats. The risks are the same as in past centuries, as evidenced by the following quotes from recent news reports:

> But ambiguous ownership or property rights in the collective economy coupled with the long standing integration of government administration and enterprises management [have] led to some problems. Among these were incidences where some local officials embezzled or diverted collective enterprise funds or properties to other purposes, and the rights of enterprises or employees were repeatedly infringed upon.   ("Rural firms set 3rd reform wave," *China Daily* February 18, 1994)

> Who really owns township enterprise is a burning question which must be answered. In rural enterprises sponsored by local communities, such as township or villages, the property right belongs to the whole community, but to no individual in particular. As a result, the community leadership randomly interferes with the enterprises internal management, thus preventing the workers themselves from bringing their initiative into full play.   ("Who really owns the township enterprises?" *China Daily* June 6, 1994)

> As China heads toward a market economy, an increasing number of private companies are no longer feeling the need as register as "red cap," or collectively-owned ventures…[because the] difference in preferential treatment between private and public units has been narrowed…. But there is a problem. The collective units are now arguing that private firms could not have developed without their help. As the so-called "owners" of the companies, the State firms usually ask for high compensation for the "divorce" or ask the companies to merge with them. ("Private firms jump to take 'red caps' off," *China Daily* November 4, 1994)

The second problem is that the risks of collective ownership become much greater when mobility in the society increases. With more and more households moving within China, it does not make much sense to make financial investments mainly within one's own community. Currently, when a worker leaves the community, he cannot take his "share" of the TVE with him. It remains within the village, as part of the community property. The result is to limit mobility, and also to increase the risks facing a family if they are forced to move for one reason or another.

The third problem with collective ownership involves the problem of risk diversification. Collective ownership is the opposite of diversification. The community puts its wealth into the enterprises in the community, and workers can end up losing everything—their jobs and their savings. A better strategy, therefore, is for the worker to diversify his risks by investing in financial assets unrelated to his workplace.

The fourth problem with collective ownership is that it limits the scale of operations of the enterprise. Currently, a TVE can grow as a result of new investments by the community (including reinvestment of profits) or through bank loans. It is very difficult, however, to get new outsider investors in the TVE, since the property rights of those outside investors would not be well defined or well protected. The outside investor would also be afraid that the local government would manipulate the profits of the enterprise for the advantage of the community, and against the outside investors. The result of this is that many TVEs will fail to grow to an efficient scale. They will lack the equity investment necessary for growth, and will either rely upon a dangerous level of bank debt or simply remain too small for effective operations.

The fifth main problem with collective ownership is that it prevents a market for managerial control. Suppose that a rural entrepreneur has a good idea for a new enterprise. Perhaps he can convince a township government to support him, but it is possible that he will be unable to do so. In a normal market economy, he would be able to raise his own money to start the business, or would be able to purchase an existing business. Both of these options are currently very difficult in China because of the heavy emphasis on collective ownership. Moreover, because of the collective ownership of TVEs, entrepreneurs only receive a small proportion of the benefits of a successful business that they organize.

Conversely, suppose that an existing enterprise has a bad manager, but one that is favored for political reasons by the local government. This manager will be protected in his job. In a normal market setting, an outside buyer might approach the owners of the business and make a takeover bid, replacing the manager after buying the enterprise. This is nearly impossible with the collective ownership of the TVEs.

These various problems suggest one conclusion: entrepreneurship will not be adequately promoted in the long run unless there is much wider scope for truly private enterprise. With collective ownership, entrepreneurs will not receive adequate compensation, and the marketplace will do a poor job in promoting good entrepreneurs and punishing bad ones.

The TVE as a Transitional Enterprise Form

In addition to the above five problems, there has been a recent development that has pushed the TVEs to "clarify" their property rights. The capacity expansion of many of the coastal TVEs in southern China has forced them to rely increasingly on migrant labor from the poorer provinces. The original inhabitants want to prevent the new residents from having an automatic share in the dividends of the collective-owned enterprises, and so they have corporatized the TVEs and divided the shares among themselves. The fact that the government has not clamped down on what could be the first step in de-collectivizing the TVEs (effective de-collectivization occurs when the shares are legally transferable) has been viewed as implicit approval, and this has accelerated the conversion of TVEs to shareholding cooperatives.

Furthermore, with the further relaxation of discrimination against private ownership since early 1992, many TVEs are taking off their "red caps"—albeit with difficulties in many cases because of demands for "alimony" payments from the local governments. The spurt in investment in TVEs since early 1992 may well be caused by the clearer signal from the authorities that the Stalinist abhorrence toward private ownership will decrease further in the near future. The signal got stronger in November 1993 when, for the first time in the history of the Chinese Communist Party, the Central Committee deemed the clarification of the property rights of the SOEs to be desirable.

11.7 Conclusions

The EEFSU and Chinese experiences show that the marketization of the production of SOEs without the marketization of their property rights destabilizes the economy through inflation and the political situation through corruption. When hard budget constraints are successfully imposed, loss-making SOEs do restructure, but only up to the extent that is necessary to achieve zero profits. However, not only is the maintenance of hard budget constraints on the SOEs a politically difficult task, the financial and technical improvements in the SOEs are generally not sustained in the long run. The fact is that the unsatisfactory performance of the SOEs is due not only to the soft budget constraint but also to the principal–agency problems caused by centralized property rights.

There is now common recognition in EEFSU and China that successful enterprise restructuring requires the decentralization of property rights. The efficient decentralization of property rights involves both the privatization of existing SOEs and the promotion of the non-state sector. In the case of EEFSU, where the state sector dominates the economy in production and employment, the maintenance of the state sector means that a disproportionate amount of inputs will continue to flow there, making it hard for the non-state sector to grow. In the case of China, the surplus labor in the agriculture sector allows the non-state economy to grow without drawing resources from the state sector.

China has now also moved more in the direction of decentralizing the property rights of the SOEs. The corporatization of SOEs, trading of their equities in the Shanghai and Shenzhen stock exchanges, and listing of Chinese SOEs in foreign stock exchanges had begun earlier on an experimental basis. The present greater movement came from the recognition at the 14th Central Committee of the Chinese Communist Party (CPC) in November 1993 that the solution of the SOE problem required reform of the property rights of SOEs.

The above development is, in part, the response to the implosion of the Soviet Union in 1991, which Deng Xiaoping has diagnosed as "committing suicide through inadequate economic reform." It is also clear that there is widespread popular agreement with the CPC's perception that the supervision of enterprises through legal stock exchanges would strengthen the performance of SOEs. This is evidenced in the summer of 1992 from the large inflow of funds into Shenzhen from all over China when the shares of some SOEs were floated there, and from the public demonstrations for more SOE shares to be sold to the public.

There are now 25 property rights exchanges in China where state assets are sold to the public. Reports indicate that there are 150 unofficial property rights exchanges in smaller cities, and the operations of these unofficial exchanges are dependent on the ideological climate. China has not been an exception to absorbing the positive international experience with the system of decentralized property rights.

The quick growth of the TVE sector should not be taken as an indicator of the adequacy of that organizational form. The post-1991 liberalization of restrictions on private enterprises and the increased migration of workers into the southern coastal provinces have induced many TVEs to seek a more efficient organizational form to safeguard the interest of the original inhabitants, raise capital more readily, and protect themselves better from the interference of local officials. The usual new form assumed by the TVEs is the shareholding cooperative.

The fact that there are informal markets for these legally non-transferable shares speaks volumes about popular expectations about the future institutional basis of economic transactions in China. The TVE experience, in short, suggests that localized socialism is not a viable third way to the stark choice between centralized socialism and private property.

However, as the EEFSU experiences show, the establishment of market institutions to enable the efficient functioning of a private property system is not an easy task. It is premature to claim that the Czech Republic's program of outsider privatization has produced core investor groups that have assumed primary responsibility for supervising the privatized firms to pursue profit maximization. Instead, the unanticipated outcome is the cross-holding of each other's shares by investment funds and banks, with the state being the biggest shareholder of the banks—a situation where the state could potentially micromanage the now "private" firms as before 1990. The point here is that it takes a considerable length of time for the state to withdraw from its previous all-encompassing role, even if the state is determined to do so as quickly as possible.

The Hungarian and Russian experiences suggest that insider privatization may be the only politically feasible form of privatization in countries that had implemented decentralization reforms (market socialism) earlier. The fact is that the earlier decentralization reforms had transferred *political* as well as economic power to the managers, enabling them to bargain with the new government. Insider privatization is likely to reduce the ability of activist shareholders to pressure managers to restructure because managers can conveniently justify their inaction under the pretext of protecting employment. In the Russian case, the natural tendency toward slower restructuring was reinforced by the continued easy availability of subsidized credits from the central bank. However discouraging this may seem, we need to bear in mind that there will be natural dilution of the insiders' influence because of the market dynamics associated with the individual ownership of property rights (shares) that are legally tradeable.

As discussed earlier, the biggest drawback to insider privatization may be political rather than economic. When insider privatization is conducted under chaotic conditions, its inherent inequity may be magnified because of massive stealing by powerful managers in contrivance with high-ranking bureaucrats. The resulting resentment over the corruption and gross inequity may bring to power anti-reform groups which would worsen the economic situation.

One important lesson from our analysis is that because the efficiency gains from privatized firms may not appear for a while, the speediest way to improve the performance of the industrial sector is to foster conditions that promote the formation of new private firms. This is akin to the Chinese practice of allowing the growth of TVEs in parallel to the decentralization reforms of the SOE sector. Furthermore, the strong growth of the new firms (and hence of new jobs) will diminish the political difficulties of restructuring the newly privatized enterprises.

The way to improving the performance of enterprises is clear: privatizing existing enterprises to individuals and promoting the establishment of new private enterprises. The key is individual ownership of tradeable property rights. Since there can be no quick results because institutional innovations take time, it is crucial that the privatization be carried out quickly, in as equitable a way as political circumstances would allow.

12

Strategies for Addressing the Social Costs of Market Reforms: Lessons for Transition Economies in East Asia and Eastern Europe

Carol Graham

In the past few years, a great deal of progress has been made in understanding the politics of macroeconomic reform.[1] Fewer advances have been made in understanding the role of compensation, in terms of either its political impact or its effects on poverty reduction. While much of the literature on the politics of adjustment alludes to the critical role of compensation, to date there has been little detailed comparative analysis. The following is a summary of research based on extensive field research in Chile, Bolivia, Peru, Zambia, Senegal, and Poland, as well as a less detailed study in Mexico. This research provides an initial basis for the analysis of the political economy of compensation, safety nets in particular, during reform. In addition, this paper evaluates the applicability of the broader lessons to the transition processes in Eastern Europe and East Asia, with a particular focus on designing safety nets for the countries that have recently embarked on reform in East Asia: China, Viet Nam, and Mongolia.[2]

Broadly defined, safety nets are interventions designed to sustain or enhance the welfare of poor or vulnerable groups at a time of economic transition. While safety nets provide important short-term support, they cannot substitute for basic social services such as health care and

This paper is a summary of the author's recently published book, *Safety Nets, Politics, and the Poor: Transitions to Market Economies* (Graham 1994). The research, conducted while the author was at Brookings, was based on case studies in Latin America, Africa, and Eastern Europe, and was funded by the MacArthur Foundation, the Inter-American Development Bank, and the Swiss Trust Fund of the World Bank. The author gratefully acknowledges this support; the views expressed in the paper, however, are strictly her own.
1. Much of this research was pioneered by Joan Nelson (Nelson 1990). See also Haggard and Kaufmann (1992).
2. The author has no field experience in China, Viet Nam, or Mongolia, and the suggestions for safety net prototypes are drawn from relevant experience of other countries. The suggestions are intended to provide a broad framework for policy discussions rather than present specific detailed programs.

education, or for a consistent macroeconomic framework within which poverty reduction can take place. Some safety net programs, however, can play an important complementary role in poverty reduction by supporting local institutional development. Programs which incorporate the participation of previously marginalized groups, such as non-governmental organizations (NGOs) or neighborhood organizations, can foster cooperation with the state in the design or delivery of social services and provide the poor with more effective channels for demand making.

The success of safety net programs largely hinges on political factors. On the policy front, establishing a consistent macroeconomic framework requires economic adjustments that are often politically difficult to sustain.[3] On the program front, the implementation of safety nets involves the allocation of scarce public resources, which entails political as well as practical choices. Because the poor generally have a weak political voice (i.e., the "old" poor), a government during reform is unlikely to find it politically necessary to provide compensation to this group. In addition, while the poor may bear some of the social costs of adjustment and have the least margin for absorbing negative shocks, often they are not the most negatively affected. An added dilemma is that the poorest and most needy groups are often the most difficult and costly to reach. Thus most governments, for obvious political sustain-ability reasons, will direct the scarce public resources available for compensation to more vocal and organized—if less needy—opponents of reform (the "new" poor).

Yet directing all compensatory resources to vocal opponents of reform is not a particularly cost-effective strategy from a political or from a poverty reduction perspective. Such resources are usually scarce and they are not likely to be sufficient to create good will towards reform among groups who are unlikely to be as well off as they were prior to reform. In some contexts it may be possible to get beyond the traditional old poor/new poor trade-off and create new coalitions for reform by focusing compensatory efforts on groups that traditionally have been marginalized from state benefits. The success of such an approach, however, hinges on the particular political context and relative political weight of the organized opponents of reform vis-à-vis the government.

---

3. An underlying assumption of this paper is that the alternative to making painful but necessary adjustments in most Latin American countries would have resulted in more severe economic crises with worse implications for the poor, and that the resource constraints that those adjustments entailed required a new approach to protecting the poor. For a detailed description of the record of a government that postponed such adjustments by implemen-ting a so-called "heterodox" economic strategy, see Graham (1992). Data on the fate of the poorest sectors during that period is found in *Ajuste y Economia Familiar: 1985–1990* (Instituto Cuanto 1991).

It also hinges on an approach to compensation which relies on the incorporation of beneficiary participation. Such an approach would enhance the political voice, as well as the economic potential, of previously marginalized groups, which is also an important element of poverty reduction. In addition, fast-paced and far-reaching reform, coupled with effective government communication strategies, can provide unique political opportunities for governments to redirect scarce resources to truly needy groups.

Three questions framed this research and analysis. (1) How do the political and institutional contexts affect the nature of safety nets and other compensation and who benefits from them? (2) When and how do safety nets and other forms of compensation affect the political sustainability of reform? (3) When and how can safety nets also contribute to permanent poverty reduction?

As with any attempt to conduct research of a novel and interdisciplinary nature, the analysis has substantial limitations, which stem from the problems inherent to comparing diverse countries and the difficulty of conducting field research, which requires at least minimal data and operational support in a variety of country contexts. Different countries require different safety net approaches, depending on the scope and nature of poverty, the existing institutional structure, and the political context. Nevertheless, several conclusions are presented that are relevant to the implementation of safety nets, as well as to economic reform more generally.

The conclusions about safety nets will have quite different implications for Eastern Europe and East Asia, as the two regions differ vastly in the pace and scope of transitions, their social implications, and public expectations on the social welfare front. For the heavily industrialized economies of Eastern Europe, reform has entailed major output declines and the dismantling of state-owned industrial sectors that provided highly specialized employment for the majority of the workforce. In many cases, short-term safety nets can play an important political as well as social welfare role by helping to protect large numbers of unemployed from major declines in standards of living.

The transition economies of East Asia resemble developing economies with respect to their income levels, proportion of the economy remaining in agriculture, and low level of provision of public social services. For these East Asian countries, reform has created as many, if not more, winners than losers. Significant numbers of poor rural workers have been able to shift to the newly emerging urban private sectors. Because the relative size of the state-owned industrial sector is much smaller than in Eastern Europe, there is far less urgency to dismantling that sector and increasing unemployment, at least in the short term.

Although the populations of these countries were much poorer than those of Eastern Europe prior to reform, and reform created pockets of poverty and new vulnerable groups, social welfare concerns have a longer time horizon and less political urgency than in Eastern Europe. Of prime importance is the creation of viable institutions to provide basic social services and social insurance to the majority of the population.

These differences aside, some of the lessons that emerge after comparing the results of reform efforts, as well as the trade-offs that governments face in trying to address the competing demands of diverse vulnerable groups, are germane to most countries implementing economic reform.

12.1 Safety Nets and Economic Reform: Selected Experiences

Bolivia

Bolivia's Emergency Social Fund (ESF) was the first social fund of its kind, and it attracted a great deal of national and international attention.[4] Enthusiasts of the ESF praise its demand-based approach, its efficiency and transparency, and its rapid results. Critics question the program's ability to alleviate poverty permanently or to target the poorest sectors, and see disadvantages to the program's independent position, outside the public sector. The ESF did not reach those most directly affected by adjustment, the tin miners, and had a disproportionately low reach of the poorest two poverty deciles. The poorest regions benefited least from the ESF in terms of per capita expenditures: the wealthiest of five income levels received $23.97 per capita while the poorest received $9.45. ESF workers represented 6.25 percent and 7.75 percent of workers in income deciles 1 and 2, but represented 13.25 percent, 21.5 percent, and 15.3 percent, respectively, in deciles 3, 4, and 5. By regional standards, however, deciles 3, 4, and 5 in Bolivia are still considered quite poor.[5] A demand-based program that involves beneficiary participation has many advantages. However, the poorest groups are the least likely to have the organizational and administrative skills necessary to present viable proposals and therefore to benefit from such programs as the ESF.

Yet the ESF administered $240 million in its four years of operation. The projects that it created, which ranged from infrastructure such as health posts, schools, and low-income homes to services such as job creation schemes and school lunch programs, benefited over 1 million poor—a substantial number in a population of just under 7 million. Despite relatively weak targeting, the program had a substantial impact

---

4. For a description of several programs modeled on Bolivia's which were set up throughout the region, such as the program in El Salvador, see Graham (1994).
5. For detail, see Graham (1994, ch. 3) and Jorgensen et al. (1992).

on the political sustainability of economic reform and on poverty alleviation. A broader view of poverty reduction, which includes the poor's participation in designing their own solutions as integral to the sustainability and long-term impact of any anti-poverty effort, might place less value on the ability to target the poorest of the poor versus the program's ability to incorporate the participation of disadvantaged groups in the design of their own solutions.

The ESF had a positive political impact by demonstrating that it could work in a transparent and nonpartisan manner, with local governments and NGOs of all political bents, in a country where aid programs were usually influenced by patronage politics. The ESF resulted in an unprecedented collaboration of efforts between NGOs—the groups with the closest ties to the poor—and the state. This allowed the fund to reach the poor in remote communities that had rarely, if ever, seen the state follow through on promises. The ESF also enhanced local governments' capacity by providing them with funds independent of the central government. Due to its demand-based structure, the ESF could not be monopolized by any one political actor at election time: a diversity of actors, from the governing party to local governments and NGOs, could claim credit for ESF projects. As a result, there was no correlation between ESF funds and the outcomes of the 1989 presidential and 1987/1989 municipal elections.[6]

The ESF provided the poor with a means to help themselves, thereby giving them a stake in the ongoing process of economic reform. By doing so it contributed to support for the government—if not for the adjustment program per se—among previously marginalized sectors at a critical time, which enhanced the feasibility of economic reform. Even if the ESF had instead focused its efforts on those who were directly affected by the adjustment program (viz., the tin miners), it is unlikely that it could have eroded their opposition to the government's economic strategy. Meanwhile, the rapid pace of adjustment, coupled with the crash of world tin prices, reduced the political power of the miners' traditionally influential confederation. This does not imply that those who are directly affected by adjustment do not merit compensation,[7] but that most efforts directed at those groups will have a marginal impact on the political sustainability of adjustment.

Senegal and Zambia

The two African countries in the study, Senegal and Zambia, provide an interesting contrast in terms of the impact of political opening on

---

6. For detailed results by district, see Graham (1994, ch. 5).
7. Tin miners were granted relatively generous one-shot severance payments when they were laid off.

sustaining adjustment, reaching the poor, and capacity-building (or lack thereof). In Senegal, adjustment has progressed at a rather slow pace for over a decade, and the political system has remained a relatively stable, if limited, democracy. The first major attempt to compensate the losers from adjustment was the *Delegacion a l'Insertion a le Reinsertion et a l'Emploi* (DIRE), set up in 1987. The DIRE, which was funded by U.S. AID, the World Bank, and the government of Senegal, provided civil servants who had retired voluntarily and university graduates who would previously have taken jobs in the civil service with credits of up to $50,000 to start their own businesses. Due to a lack of training and follow-up, and to the prevalence of clientelistic criteria in the disbursement of loans, the DIRE had a very poor record, both in terms of loan repayment and mortality of enterprises (32 percent). In addition, as the program's budget was administered through the public treasury, approximately $3 million was lost or "filtered" in the process. The beneficiaries were a relatively privileged group, and the projects funded included bookstores and travel agencies in central Dakar. An enormous amount of resources for a country as poor as Senegal were squandered on relatively privileged groups.

This poor record resulted in gradual fading out of the DIRE. Despite the program's original high visibility, its effects on the political sustainability of adjustment were minimal. The program's image was tarnished by clientelism, and the governing party limited its impact on any groups other than its direct beneficiaries. In the end the program did not have any impact on poverty alleviation.

After a wave of civil unrest in February 1988, the government made another attempt to address the social costs of adjustment, and it set up the Agetip program in conjunction with the World Bank. Agetip was influenced by the success of the ESF; it was also set up as an independent agency with a private sector director, in sharp contrast to the DIRE. The Agetip responded to proposals from municipalities for labor-intensive infrastructure projects. In terms of efficiency and number of projects, the Agetip has been remarkably successful[8] and has even been cited as a model for the reform of the Senegalese private sector.

Yet the Agetip is also influenced by the political context in which it operates. There is no debate about reaching the poor and needy groups in Senegal, nor is there any kind of cooperative relationship between the government and the NGOs, which are the only organizations with extensive links to the poor. The Agetip does not use poverty criteria for allocating its projects. In addition, because the opposition boycotted the 1990 municipal elections, the only proposals that the Agetip is funding

---

8. From its inception in 1990 to the end of 1991, the Agetip program implemented over 100 projects and created over 11,000 temporary jobs.

are those from the mayors of the governing party. While in some cases projects do have poverty reduction goals, such as the installation of sewage and water facilities, in others they may be pet projects of the mayor, such as renovating the town hotel. On the other hand, the agency primarily employs unskilled youth.

As the Agetip does not work with NGOs, it has very weak links to the poorest groups. There is a widespread popular perception that the Agetip is "of the system" or a tool of the governing party, and thus its impact on the political sustainability of adjustment, at least among those groups who are not of the governing party, has been limited. Its record on the poverty alleviation front is mixed: it has provided a large number of temporary jobs and some sorely needed infra-structure in poor areas, but the limited nature of beneficiary participation, and particularly of the organizations that are most closely linked to the poor, has limited its potential in terms of both project sustainability and capacity building.

In Senegal, the goal of poverty reduction—and indeed even any debate on poverty—has been subordinate to the interests of politically vocal groups within or linked to the state sector. The slow pace of reform has given these groups much more opportunity to "protect" their privileged positions within the system. The limited nature of political participation, meanwhile, has resulted in a great deal of suspicion of government-sponsored initiatives, limiting the potential impact of the Agetip. This stands in sharp contrast to Bolivia's ESF, which, by working with a variety of political parties and NGOs to reach previously marginalized groups, was able to create support for the reform program.

Zambia provides a sharp contrast to Senegal. While adjustment in Zambia was postponed for years under the UNIP government, and all kinds of state benefits were linked to party membership, the October 31, 1991 elections ushered in dramatic political change. Frederick Chiluba and the Movement for Multi-Party Democracy, which campaigned on a pro-adjustment platform, took over 75 percent of the vote. Upon taking office, the government began to implement a free market economic stra-tegy and publicly stated that reaching the poorest and most vulnerable groups was a priority. Due to the dramatic nature of political change, the groups which traditionally had privileged access to state resources had their influence substantially reduced, allowing the government to focus its efforts on the poorest sector.

The heavy subsidy for the price of maize, which consumed over 15 percent of government revenue, had been the political bête noir for the Kaunda government. Attempts to raise the price resulted repeatedly in food riots and even a coup attempt in 1990. The coupon system, which was in theory to provide cheaper maize to poor groups, had become a tool of the UNIP party, while many of the poor were marginalized from the system and had to pay three to four times the official price of maize on the black market. When the Chiluba government liberalized the price of maize in December 1991, keeping subsidies on roller meal (the coarse grind that only the poorest eat), there was no popular unrest. This was due in large part to the government's explaining the measures to the public, as well as the need to allocate scarce resources for the most vulnerable groups. This contrasted sharply with the Kaunda government, which usually announced measures overnight and was more influenced by entrenched interest groups with a stake in state subsidies. The dramatic nature of political change in Zambia, as well as the pace of reform measures, undermined the influence of these groups, allowing for an increased focus on the poor.

The Micro-Projects Unit (MPU) in Zambia, which is funded by the World Bank and the European Community and is run from the government's National Development Planning Office, is a good example of a program that reaches the needy rather than the privileged. The MPU, also influenced by the success of the ESF, responds to proposals from community organizations, mostly for renovation of existing infrastructure.[9] The program requires a 25 percent community contribution in cash or in labor. It has been successful in revitalizing the self-help spirit in many communities and in reaching remote areas long neglected by the state. The MPU is being expanded substantially under the Chiluba government.

By giving communities a stake in a government poverty alleviation program, the MPU enhances the political sustainability of economic reform, creating a basis of support among previously marginalized but numerically significant groups. In addition, the demand-based nature of the program inherently encourages such groups to exercise their political voice, something unprecedented in the Zambian context, where a one-party state dominated the system for several decades.

Chile

A very different example and model for reaching the poor operates in Chile. Chile had an extensive social welfare structure prior to adjustment; the system was revamped and targeted to the poorest groups during the Pinochet years. Extensive pre-existing programs in

---

9. The proposals must go through local governments to prevent duplication and to ensure that they are in line with local government priorities. To prevent bureaucratic lag, however, the proposals are simultaneously sent directly to the MPU. Thus if a viable proposal seems to be unfairly held up or denied in the local government, the MPU is able to follow up on it.

mother and child nutrition, as well as the public provision of basic health, education, and social security services, were reoriented towards the poorest sectors, and private provision was introduced for those who could afford it. While social spending per capita declined during the adjustment years, it actually increased for the poorest two deciles.[10] Yet many people at the margin lost access to what had been one of the most comprehensive social systems in Latin America. This was not necessarily a positive result, nor is it one that a government that was more responsive to electoral pressure would be able to implement. Yet it proved extremely effective in protecting the poorest sectors during severe economic crisis. The infant mortality rate, for example, not only continued to decline but accelerated in its rate of decline and is one of the lowest in Latin America.

In conjunction with targeting social sector spending, large-scale employment programs were implemented from 1975 to 1987. At the height of the economic crisis in 1982, with unemployment at almost 30 percent, the programs employed up to 13 percent of the workforce. The programs paid one-fourth to one-half the minimum wage, providing a self-targeting mechanism, although critics argue that the subsidy was too low. Implementation at the beginning was haphazard, and labor was often not used productively.

With time, program design was improved, and incorporated some private sector hiring and training. Workers in the private sector-linked programs were often able to find permanent jobs with the same firms. While the programs had several flaws, particularly the authoritarian manner in which they were implemented, even their harshest critics agree that they reduced the potential for social explosion at a time of unprecedented unemployment rates. It is unlikely that a demand-based program could serve as an equally effective means for generating mass-scale employment targeted to the poorest, particularly with the resources available relative to population size. Yet part of the success of Chile's centrally implemented programs is due to its strong administrative capacity rather than to program design.[11]

---

10. For a detailed account, see Graham (1994, ch. 2).
11. In 1987, the programs allocated 5 billion pesos (approximately $20 million) in the government's total social spending budget of 274 billion pesos, and employed approximately 165,000 people or approximately 4 percent of the economically active population. The ESF, meanwhile, had approximately $240 million for its four years of operations, primarily funded by external donors, and on average employed approximately 3,000 or 0.3 percent of the economically active population. For a demand-based program to operate at the scale and speed with which Chile's programs did, it would require substantially more resources, staff, and administrative skill and time. The Mexican Solidarity program, meanwhile, does operate on a much larger scale

The Pinochet regime's protection of the poorest, through a variety of programs, is an example worth noting. Chile's record vis-à-vis its neighbors in protecting the basic health and welfare of the poor during a period of adjustment, and targeting and reaching the very poorest, is indeed remarkable. However, according to other indicators, such as income distribution and per capita consumption, Chile fares less well.

With the 1990 democratic transition, the government of President Aylwin made poverty reduction a major focus of its economic program. The new government also set up a demand-based social fund, the Fund for Solidarity and Social Investment (FOSIS). As line ministries are quite efficient and have extensive coverage in Chile, the FOSIS can work the way that social funds are in theory intended to work: to complement the works of line ministries with outreach programs for the poorest communities and for specific groups. In contrast, in countries such as Bolivia or Senegal, where the public sector is very weak, autonomous and efficient social funds become "catch-all" programs and often get involved in providing services the line ministries ought to be providing.

The FOSIS also seeks to correct the Pinochet government's failure to incorporate any kind of beneficiary participation, as such participation often enhances the sustainability of social programs. This failure, and the authoritarian government's top-down manner, limited the positive political effects of targeting the poorest sectors. Jobs were often withdrawn from shantytowns that were active in political protests. Because the Pinochet regime was free of the constraints faced by most democratic regimes, its lessons on political sustainability are unclear, and its success in targeting the poorest at the expense of middle sectors is unlikely to be replicated easily in most transition economies.

Peru

It is extremely important to note that safety net programs, if poorly implemented, can do more harm than good. They often alienate the potential beneficiaries, as the case of the Peruvian *Programa de Apoyo al Ingreso Temporal* (PAIT) demonstrates. The PAIT program was a public works employment program, modeled on Chile's programs, which was implemented in Lima's shantytowns by the 1985–90 American Popular Revolutionary Alliance (APRA) government. The program provided sorely needed income support as well as some socially useful infrastructure. Yet it was implemented in a top-down and partisan manner, with a great deal of clientelism in hiring as well as constant political

---

than Bolivia's program (discussed below), but rapid and mass-scale employment generation is by no means its primary role. Its budget and staff size are much bigger than those of either the Chilean or Bolivian programs.

manipulation of the workers. PAIT workers were often taken to political rallies to cheer for President Garcia, for example. The program's budget was also manipulated; hiring was drastically increased prior to elections, and then jobs were faded out quietly afterwards, which kept applicants in a constant state of uncertainty.[12] The perception that the program was used as a tool by the governing party ultimately undermined its public image. Most damaging was the program's excessive centralism and top-down implementation, which resulted in its disrupting, duplicating, and undermining the efforts of local self-help groups, which are critical to the survival of the poor in Peru. Its effects ran directly counter to the capacity building that is integral to poverty reduction. Whatever marginal effects the PAIT program had on poverty alleviation were temporary, while the disruption caused to local organizations was often permanent.

Peru's efforts to implement a social fund under the Fujimori government have also been frustrated by the political context. The government announced a program to address the social costs of adjustment when it initiated its reform program in August 1990. Yet no program materialized until a year later, when, under pressure from external donors concerned about the social costs of adjustment, the government announced Foncodes, the National Fund for Social Compensation and Development. The program then took over two years to get off the ground. The primary reason was political: there was no presidential commitment to insulate the program from politics, as there was in the case of the ESF. Indeed, the president insisted on naming the former secretary general of his political movement, who had little managerial experience, as president of the fund. Foncodes' weak administrative capacity and obvious political bent alienated many NGOs and community groups early on. In late 1992, under pressure from external donors, the government appointed a private sector manager for the program, and its operations improved for about a year. In mid-1994, with elections coming up in six months, Fujimori appointed another "loyalist" as head of the fund, and it became a channel for the president's personal reelection campaign.[13] From that point onward, Foncodes' activities ranged from building schools in areas where there were no teachers available to donating computers to villages without electricity.

A major drawback with Foncodes was that it was never perceived as integral to the economic reform program by its main architects. Thus prior to the 1995 electoral campaign, the program was not allocated sufficient priority (or resources in the domestic budget) to demonstrate a government commitment to its credibility and success. Given the institutional autonomy of most social funds, they cannot operate without a

---

12. For detail on enrollments and election results by district, see Graham (1991).
13. For an analysis of the empirical evidence, see Graham and Kane (1995).

high-level executive commitment to insulate them from politics *and* to guarantee them access to sufficient resources. No level of external support or resources can substitute for a domestic political commitment (and allocation of resources) to addressing the social costs of reform. In Peru, when the government did increase the resources going to the social fund, it was blatantly linked to the president's personal campaign for reelection.

Mexico

A program which is gaining increasing national and international attention is Mexico's National Solidarity Program (Pronasol). The program is a Bolivia-style demand-based social fund, but on a much larger scale, in part because the country is so much larger.[14] The ESF channeled $240 million in four years; Pronasol started with a budget of $680 million in 1989 alone and increased to a projected $2.3 billion for 1992.[15] If administrative and infrastructure costs were waived,[16] the ESF would have spent approximately $50 per year on each of its 1.2 million beneficiaries. By the same calculation, Pronasol spent $135 on each of the 17 million people in extreme poverty in Mexico in 1992.[17] Pronasol's highly visible nature, such as its prominent appearance in the president's 1992 annual address to the nation, also suggests that it is having a political impact. Like the ESF, the effects of Pronasol's outreach on groups that had rarely, if ever, received state attention in the past cannot be underestimated.

Pronasol's design was influenced by the ESF and other demand-based social funds, as well as by previous government programs which relied on community initiative in the form of manual labor and food supply. There are 64,000 Solidarity committees nationwide, which are elected locally. In response to popular demands, the committees design projects in collaboration with government staff. Programs range from food support, social services, and infrastructure to credits to various groups such as at-

---

14. For detail on Pronasol, see Graham (1994) and Dresser (1991).

15. It is somewhat difficult to quantify Pronasol's budget accurately, as some money may have been diverted from what would previously have been social sector spending (Dresser 1991, *The New York Times*, November 2, 1992, p. A3).

16. Administrative costs were approximately 5 percent of the total in the case of the ESF.

17. Comparing the resources allocated to these programs is difficult: first, GNP sizes are far from comparable; second, financing sources were different. Bolivia's program was financed primarily from abroad. Only 10 percent of the ESF's budget came from domestic government resources. Mexico's program is financed almost fully from domestic resources. Of the cases in the study, this is comparable only to Chile, which also financed its safety net programs domestically. At their height in 1983, the employment programs alone comprised 1.5 percent of GDP.

risk farmers, indigenous communities, and women. Pronasol supports sectoral ministries by expanding the country's health and education facilities and through scholarship and school meals programs. Finally, Pronasol supports municipal development through municipal and regional solidarity funds.

The wide range and large number of programs make it difficult to make a simple judgment of Pronasol. In addition, it is difficult to separate what may be justified criticisms of the political system—a semi-authoritarian system which, in theory, is in the process of liberalizing—from those of the actual design or content of the program. Ultimately, Pronasol's success as a demand-based program depends on the extent to which the government is committed to allocating resources openly and fairly and to allowing the participation of individuals and organizations of all political bents.

Pronasol's record to date varies depending on the nature of local-level party power structure and the capacity of grass-roots and community organizations. In many regions the program has come into conflict with authoritarian party bosses at the local level, indicating that non-traditional actors have been able to benefit to some extent.[18] While President Salinas demonstrated willingness to let solidarity committees undermine local PRI authorities, he seemed less willing to allow the committees to operate independently in municipalities controlled by the opposition.[19] The extent to which Pronasol is able to reach previously marginalized groups, and can serve as an alternative channel to the PRI, will determine if the program can have the kinds of effects on the economic potential and political voice of the poor that funds like the ESF have had.

Pronasol has been criticized as a populist tool and as a means for President Salinas to build up his personal base of power.[20] The former criticism stems from the president's tactics, such as his very public use of the proceeds from the privatization of the national airline to provide electricity to 500,000 homes in the poorest regions. "Populist" or not, this tactic combined clever salesmanship with the philosophy underlying orthodox economic reform: get the state out of the productive field and into the service provision arena. To the extent that Pronasol is generating support in favor of a new government approach to providing social services *and* for a new channel of communicating with both central and local governments, then the program is contributing to poverty alleviation and institutional development. In the instances where Pronasol

---

18. For detail on these relations, see Fox (1992) and Craig (1992).
19. A case in point is the withholding of benefits from the Tortivales program from 48 Mexico City municipalities where the opposition was particularly active (Dresser 1991). For detail see Fox (1992) and Craig (1992).
20. See Dresser (1991).

is reinforcing traditional clientelistic structures controlled by the PRI, the program's potential to contribute to local capacity building is being severely curtailed.

Poland

A very different experience that demonstrates the political constraints of reaching the poor and vulnerable is the case of Poland. It is also a case that reflects the very difficult structural and political obstacles to reform of social welfare systems in many Eastern European countries. In January 1990, soon after its inauguration, the first non-communist government in Poland launched a dramatic, Bolivia-style stabilization and adjustment program. The program successfully stabilized hyper-inflation. Yet political uncertainty soon stalled structural reforms, as several attempts failed to maintain a coherent government coalition in Parliament. Reforms such as privatization of the financially unviable state industrial conglomerates have been postponed, creating an unsustainable fiscal burden. The longer such reforms are postponed, the greater the public anxiety about their potential social costs. The current social welfare system is financially and operatively unsustainable, and is a major contributor to the rapidly increasing budget deficit. Even prior to the collapse of public finances, the system, which is based on the concept of universal free access to all benefits, was characterized by poor quality of services, unequal access, a growing system of "informal" payments for services, and a skewed incentive structure. Government insolvency, coupled with the need to provide protection for the poor and unemployed (whose numbers will increase in the future), dictates an immediate revamping of the social welfare system to one which provides targeted assistance to the poor.

Proposals considered for reform of the health and social security systems would guarantee basic health care and social security insurance for those who need them, while introducing private providers and a choice of services for those who could afford them. Concurrently, government resources would be targeted to provide a safety net for the increasing numbers of poor and unemployed. Unemployment prior to 1990 in Poland was "hidden" by the maintenance of excess workers on government and industrial payrolls. Open unemployment is now at approximately 12 percent, and in towns or regions that were dependent on insolvent state-owned enterprises (SOEs), it is as high as 30 percent. For political as well as economic reasons, such regions need programs that are more extensive and visible than unemployment insurance. A visible safety net program, such as a social fund or Chilean-style public works program, would be a good means to provide employment and infrastructure at a time when public anxiety about social welfare issues is high. The impetus that demand-based social funds give to municipal development, by encouraging collaboration between non-government and local government institutions, could be very useful in the depressed regions of the country. In such regions local government capacity tends to lag behind that of the rest of the country, yet must confront more extensive social welfare challenges.

Unfortunately, the political debate on the safety net lags far behind the proposals for reform, centering on emotional criticisms of government proposals rather than on any realistic alternatives. As in many countries, vocal and organized opponents of reform, in this case unions and pensioners, dominate the public debate on social welfare issues. At the popular level, meanwhile, there is widespread ignorance and anxiety about future social welfare due to the incoherent debate and to the government's past failure to communicate or explain the ongoing reform process to the public. Populist opposition movements have been quick to capitalize on this anxiety. By the summer of 1992, failure to address adequately the safety net issue and anxiety about the potential social costs of reform led to a series of industrial strikes which virtually paralyzed the government and forced it to make the safety net issue a priority. In September 1992 the government announced two social pacts, one on the future of state enterprises and one on the future of the social safety net, which were to be negotiated with unions and the private sector. The government's attempt to explain proposals to the public and to incorporate popular participation was too little too late, and anti-reformist sentiment dominated both the September 1993 and December 1995 elections, largely due to public anxiety over social welfare issues.

The delivery mechanisms for new forms of social assistance are severely underdeveloped. Elected local governments were only recently constituted, yet they have been given primary responsibility for providing benefits to the poor and unemployed. A host of unresolved issues remain pertaining to the nature of benefits, their financing, who should be eligible, and the delivery of such benefits. Failure to resolve the poverty and safety net issues has eroded support for the economic reform process, and in part explains the victory of the former communists in the December 1995 national elections.

The situation in Poland is far from unique in the region. In other countries, such as Ukraine, public anxiety about social welfare issues has resulted in very delayed reform efforts at much higher social costs. Despite widespread debate about the social costs of reform in the region, there are no examples of countries that have attempted to implement visible safety net programs. In Poland, and in much of Eastern Europe, there is a great deal to be learned from Latin American experiences with social funds and public works programs.

12.2 Lessons from Comparative Experience

Several lessons emerge from the comparative experience which are relevant to policy makers attempting to implement safety nets, as well as to economic reform more generally, in a variety of country contexts. A general conclusion is that safety net programs can reduce poverty and have positive political effects on sustaining economic reform processes. These effects hinge on the programs operating in a transparent manner that incorporates the participation of the poor, thereby enhancing their economic potential *and* political voice. The ability to perform in such a manner on a large scale depends on available resources, the institutional structure, and a commitment from the highest levels to insulate the programs from partisan pressures. Programs must be implemented as an integral part of the macroeconomic reform program, so that successive governments have a stake in their successful implementation and beneficiaries have a stake in the ongoing process of economic transformation. However, these conditions are not always easily attainable.

Two of the conclusions from the comparative studies pertain to the political economy of reform more generally. First, the pace and scope of economic change is a determining factor. Rapid and far-reaching change can actually provide *political* opportunities for reform and for redirecting resources to the poor, as opposed to gradual or stalled economic change, which allows greater opportunities for the opposition to reform to coalesce, and therefore for privileged groups to monopolize the benefits of public social expenditure. Second, communication with the public— particularly but not exclusively pertaining to the social costs of reform— plays a critical role in making economic reform politically feasible and sustainable, and reform of social welfare systems acceptable. In contrast, lack of public understanding of the reform process often leads to heightened public anxiety about its social costs and to short-sighted political behavior; for example, unions trying to maximize short-term benefits as protection against an uncertain future.

Other lessons relate more directly to safety net policy. First, beneficiary participation in the design and implementation of safety net programs enhances their sustainability, both from political and poverty reduction standpoints. Such participation is important if investments in short-term safety net programs are to have a longer term impact on poverty reduction. Yet because participatory demand-based programs often have difficulty reaching the poorest of the poor, such approaches may need to be complemented with separate programs to reach the poorest groups. Authoritarian and clientelist party and local government structures, meanwhile, as in Senegal and Mexico, serve as an additional constraint to the inherent difficulty that demand-based programs have in reaching the poorest sectors.

Second, introducing private sector management techniques and insulating safety net programs from partisan politics have important impacts on the ability of the programs to deliver essential services on the one hand, and to promote an image of transparency and efficiency for public sector operations on the other. This last effect—enhancing the credibility and capacity of the public sector—is an objective of market-oriented reforms in general, and is one way in which safety nets can have positive demonstration effects for the reform process in general. Bolivia's ESF, which stressed private sector management and was implemented in an open political context, is a good example.

Political context obviously makes an enormous difference in the via-bility of these approaches. There is no established link between demo-cracy and reaching the poorest or most needy, however, as even in democracies the poor are usually poor with respect to political voice as well as to resources. Ironically, of the cases covered here, the Pinochet regime had the most success in targeting the poorest, precisely because it did not have the political constraints of having to answer to the more vocal middle sectors that a democratic regime would have.[21] On the other hand, a broader view of poverty reduction, which regards the poor's participation in designing their own solutions as integral to the sustainability and long-term impact of any anti-poverty effort, might place less value on targeting the poorest of the poor and focus on incorporating the participation of disadvantaged groups. Many projects, such as new schools or health posts, also have indirect positive effects for poorer groups who did not participate in their design. Finally, targeting can entail high costs in terms of time and resources.[22] In this light, the success or failure of demand-based programs seems to hinge more on their ability to generate autonomous grass-roots participation than on reaching the poorest among the poor.

---

21. Graham (1994, ch. 2).
22. This raises a question that faces all policy makers attempting to reduce poverty: whether it is better to lift the largest possible number of people at the margin of the poverty line above it, using a straight headcount measure of poverty, or to focus efforts on improving the lot of the poorest, even if the number of people below the poverty line remains the same. Amartya Sen made a major contribution to the measurement of poverty by combining the headcount ratio with the average income shortfall of the poor and the measure of inequality among them (Gini coefficient). Sen's theory and its implications for anti-poverty policy are discussed in Bourguignon and Fields (1990).

The institutional autonomy of such programs, as well as their position within or outside the public sector, is an issue in many countries. On the one hand, autonomy allows for rapid, transparent action that bypasses public sector bureaucratic procedures (which are often costly and time-consuming), reducing administrative costs and directly channeling benefits to the poor. A case pointing to the disadvantages of some government-run programs is the DIRE in Senegal, where $3 million was "lost" in the public sector process. On the other hand, there is the issue of longevity of extra-institutional programs, as neither their budgets nor their operating procedures have any permanent guarantees. To the extent that such programs are considered short-term measures during periods of adjustment or recovery, then institutional autonomy is less of a concern. To the extent that they are considered longer term complements to social sector policies, then it is usually necessary to establish institutional links. Other programs have a hybrid nature: the Agetip in Senegal is a semi-public corporation that is managed as a private sector firm. The successor to the ESF in Bolivia, the Social Investment Fund, remains a separate, autonomous agency that responds to the president but has new formalized links with the sectoral ministries.

Political context also makes an enormous difference in the possibilities for redirecting resources to the poor. Dramatic political change, as in the case of Zambia, or swift implementation of stabilization and adjustment, as in the case of Bolivia, provides unique opportunities for doing so. Less open political systems and stalled economic reform, as in the case of Senegal, give entrenched interest groups greater opportunities to protect their positions. In the cases of Mexico and Senegal, economic change was less sudden than in either Bolivia or Zambia, and political opening was far less straightforward, limiting the potential of programs that in theory were genuinely demand-based. In Mexico, the success of the mass-scale Pronasol hinges on Salinas' commitment to political liberalization and to allowing genuine party competition at the local and central levels. In Senegal, extensive political change seems unlikely in the near future.

In addition to political context, the *nature* of safety net programs is a factor in determining their political as well as anti-poverty impact. Demand-based programs that require community contributions are best suited to creating the sustainable kinds of projects which are key to poverty alleviation, particularly if they become self-sustaining initiatives or enhance local institutional capacity. Centrally implemented public works schemes, however, may be better suited for rapid, mass-scale impact to relieve the social costs of adjustment and for targeting the poorest groups.

Finally, safety nets cannot be expected to substitute for basic service provision nor to make structural changes in asset distribution or ownership structures. Neither can they make up for major adjustment-related trends in real wages or sectoral spending. At best they are useful complements to the activities of weak sectoral ministries and can provide short-term income or employment; they cannot substitute for long-term economic growth. Yet safety net programs such as social funds *can* make revolutionary changes at the local institutional level by incorporating the participation of previously marginalized groups, such as NGOs or neighborhood organizations. This participation may take the form of cooperation with the state in designing or delivering social services and in providing more effective channels for demand making. Ultimately, poverty alleviation initiatives cannot substitute for a broader central-level commitment to poverty alleviation and for functioning line ministries, nor can they operate effectively without a central-level commitment to allow participation of actors of all political bents.

12.3 Safety Net Issues in Asia and Eastern Europe: Lessons for China, Viet Nam, and Mongolia

The above lessons about safety nets will have very different implications in the Eastern European and East Asian contexts.[23] In particular, the lessons about political context have varying degrees of relevance. In the newly democratized and politically fragile contexts of Eastern Europe, addressing safety net issues in the immediate term has particular political salience. In East Asia, where (with the exception of Mongolia) political reform lags far behind economic reform, and economic reforms have entailed much less dislocation of the labor force, there is far less political urgency to safety net issues, and governments can focus more attention on reforming and creating longer term social welfare institutions. In Eastern Europe, in contrast, until short-term social welfare concerns are addressed, it is unlikely that any political consensus will develop on how to reform the region's extensive but financially unsustainable social welfare institutions.

In Eastern Europe, the extent and nature of economic distortions, and the predominance of the state-owned heavy industry sector, left policy makers without realistic alternatives to a "big bang" approach to reform, which included dismantling the unsustainable state-owned industrial sectors. In most countries this entails displacing large numbers of highly specialized workers and significantly increasing poverty and unemployment. In societies which had traditionally espoused egalitarian values

---

23. For a detailed description of the differences in transitions between these two types of economies at the macro-level, see Woo (1994).

and supported an extensive state role in the provision of social welfare, these trends are politically explosive and have brought short-term safety net issues to the fore of the public debate. In addition to short-term safety net issues, these nations must reform their basic social welfare and social insurance systems. These systems, which are based on universal provision of services by the state, are no longer fiscally sustainable. Yet it is unlikely that politically difficult and initially costly reforms of pension and health systems, for example, will be possible until governments are able to alleviate heightened public anxiety over increasing poverty and unemployment and to generate at least minimal societal consensus in favor of reform.

The implementation of short-term safety net programs to protect the poor and/or vulnerable has become as much a political as an economic necessity in many countries. Laid-off and/or soon to be laid-off public sector workers, for example, who tend to be organized in politically powerful trade unions, and pensioners, who also tend to be well organized, have become major political opponents of reform. Their needs dominate the debate on social welfare, often at the expense of attention to poorer, but less vocal groups.[24] As in most of the countries in the comparative study, the most vocal and organized groups are not necessarily the poorest and most vulnerable, which forces difficult choices for resource-strapped governments. Political sustainability as well as poverty concerns will influence these choices.

Many countries in the region should consider the implementation of demand-based safety net programs which could provide short-term employment generation as well as stimulate the development of local and municipal institutions, as was recommended for Poland in the comparative study.[25] This is particularly relevant for depressed industrial regions where private sector development is lagging and local governments are often weak. Where mass unemployment is a particular concern, meanwhile, public works employment programs, as were used in Chile, might be useful supplements to one-shot severance payments, particularly where unemployment insurance systems are not well developed. Finally, while there is much enthusiasm for worker retraining in many countries in the region, training programs have a poor track record in diverse developing and developed economies.[26]

---

24. Families with large numbers of children, for example, tend to be a much higher proportion of the poor than either of these two groups but are rarely organized politically. See Milanovic (forthcoming). In contrast, as Leszek Balcerowicz stated in his presentation describing the situation in Poland at the November conference in Prague, "pensioners have a great deal of time to organize."
25. For another description, see Graham (1995).
26. For detail on the record of training programs, see note 210 in Graham (1994), and Paul (1991).

Younger workers are more likely to get relevant experience and training in the newly emerging private sector. Older workers, meanwhile, could stand to benefit from public works and/or social fund type schemes that provide income support and also contribute to the development of local organizational and institutional capacity.

The main social welfare issues in East Asia differ markedly from those in Eastern Europe. In East Asia the relative size of the state-owned industrial sector is much smaller relative to the overall economy, and the agrarian sector is large and for the most part self-sufficient. Thus the primary concern in the transition has been the development of the private economy, beginning with reform and productivity increases in the agrarian sector. In addition, the East Asian economies began from much lower levels of income and state social service provision. Reforms have created pockets of poverty and increased inequality, particularly in Mongolia, which received large annual subsidies from the Soviet Union and had the most extensive social welfare coverage. Yet in general, reform and the resulting increases in economic growth and agricultural productivity have been welfare-enhancing for the majority of the population, including many of the rural poor.[27]

In all three cases, reforms began in the agricultural sector. Reforms in the state-owned industrial sectors have proceeded at different paces in the three countries, but in all cases they have affected a small percentage of workers that were relatively privileged relative to the rest of the labor force. Finally, of the three countries in the study, only Mongolia has simultaneously introduced large-scale political liberalization and economic reform. Thus the *political* salience of social welfare issues related to reform is much lower in East Asia, particularly in Viet Nam and China, than in most transition economies, which often have new and fragile democratic governments and face major increases in poverty and unemployment at the same time.

Yet in East Asia there is a clear need for effective safety nets for particular vulnerable groups: for example, female-headed households in Mongolia, single and elderly pensioners and the very poor in the rural sector in Viet Nam, and the aging rural population in China. The closing of large SOEs is likely to result in a pool of unemployed workers who will demand government attention. While they are not the poorest groups, in some cases they should be the focus of a part of safety net efforts. More generally, widespread poverty remains the major concern. In part it will be alleviated by sustained growth, but growth must be complemented with more broadly based and equitable social services and social insurance systems, in addition to safety nets for vulnerable

---

27. See Thomas and Wang (1994).

groups. In the longer term, the major social welfare issue is the creation of effective institutions to protect social welfare and provide social insurance for both public and private sectors. While public systems exist in all three countries, they are restricted to a small part of the labor force and are administratively fragmented and financially unsustainable. The minimal coverage of these systems, meanwhile, may mean that the political obstacles to reforming them are far less formidable than in the Eastern European schemes of universal coverage.

China

China began its reform well before Viet Nam and Mongolia. It has experienced more than a decade of strong growth (approximately 10 percent). Poverty levels and trends vary greatly between rural and urban areas, and between different regions of the country. The existing social insurance and assistance systems are designed for a centrally planned economy, cover only a small minority of the workforce, and are ill-suited to the needs of workers in the newly emerging private sector. It is estimated that 13.5 percent of the population is poor, and poverty is increasingly urban.[28] The poor were traditionally thought to be concentrated in specific rural regions of the country. Yet as more evidence on rural and urban poverty emerges, poverty is found to be dispersed more widely than was originally thought. Thus social assistance, which is regionally allocated, is also poorly suited to cope with present trends.[29]

China differs from developing countries at similar per capita income levels in that its welfare indicators, such as infant mortality rates and life expectancy, are similar to those of wealthier middle-income countries. Yet this masks important differences between regions and sectors of the economy. Urban workers in state-owned and collectively owned enterprises have access to reasonably comprehensive systems of social insurance, unemployment insurance, and health care. Even within these systems there is a great deal of variation between regions and enterprises. Rural peasants, meanwhile, do not have access to any kind of comparable system. Social assistance in rural areas is limited and

28. Comparing poverty across countries is difficult at best. This figure uses the World Bank's poverty line of $1 per person per day, using 1985 purchasing power parity (ppp), and household surveys conducted in 1985 and 1990. At a slightly higher poverty line of $1.33 per person per day, 24.34 percent of the Chinese population is poor. The respective figures for 1985 are 11.11 percent and 24.57 percent, showing relatively constant poverty trends. For details see Chen et al. 1994.
29. For a detailed description of poverty trends, see Hussain 1994. See also Riskin 1994.

designed as relief for the destitute, because the rural population is considered to be self-employed. Yet this is not necessarily accurate, as some poor in rural areas have difficulty reaching even subsistence levels, particularly since the breakup of collective farming. Although the development of the urban private sector has had obvious and positive effects on growth, it has also introduced new kinds of social welfare concerns. While the sector has attracted large numbers of rural migrants, there is no system of social or unemployment insurance for those workers. There is growing inequality between different urban occupational groups and between urban and rural areas. Initial reforms of SOEs have made unemployment a concern for the first time.[30] Finally, old-age support is a major issue, particularly for rural families, due to the falling fertility rate, which reduces the base of the traditional, family-based social security system, and to increased migration from rural to urban areas.[31]

The government has made some efforts to reform the social welfare system, beginning with the introduction of unemployment insurance in 1986 and the subsequent introduction of social insurance offices to facilitate workers' entry into the social insurance system.[32] In the early 1990s, a pension reform was introduced which sought to make the pension system a partially accumulating fund with contributions from workers, employers, and the state. Yet these systems remain limited to the state-owned and collectively owned sectors. A more comprehensive reform of the system must incorporate the needs and contributions of the private sector and, equally important, address the needs of the rural poor in a more comprehensive manner.

Rapid economic growth and rising per capita income give China an advantage over most transition economies, because the government can focus on longer term systemic reforms rather than short-term safety net or relief efforts. In addition, as political reform has lagged far behind economic reform, there is not the kind of public debate on safety net or social welfare issues that there would be in a more open political context. While such debate often enhances policy formulation, it also often forces governments to deliver visible improvements to vocal groups—who may not be the neediest—in the immediate term. In contrast to Eastern Europe, in China, as in many developing nations, public expectations of the state social welfare services are low, which gives the government the

---

30. Official urban unemployment is 2.6 percent, but it is as high as 20 percent in some industrial cities (*Financial Times* November 15, 1994).
31. A small percentage of urban retirees do receive pensions (Hussain 1994).
32. There are 3,900 social insurance offices nationwide, which aim to help the newly employed enter the system, transfer benefits for those switching jobs, and help retired workers (Kaiping 1994).

political space to focus on systemic reform rather than on short-term relief. On the other hand, public debate can also increase government accountability and heighten awareness of the situation of particular vulnerable groups, something that will be missing in the Chinese case, at least for the foreseeable future.

The relative lack of immediate safety net concerns does not discount the relevance of some of the lessons from the comparative studies. First, China may experience the political trade-offs common to governments faced with addressing the needs of more visible and potentially vocal, vulnerable groups and those of the less vocal, but more needy, poor. Concentrated urban poverty, for example, is more visible and easily identifiable than rural poverty. It also presents more threat of potential social unrest for governments. Yet the needs of the rural poor are at least as urgent, if not more so. The comparative studies demonstrate the poor returns of concentrating all resources for poverty alleviation on the vocal but less needy, and the political as well as social benefits of reaching marginalized groups with state benefits. In China the government has fewer political obstacles to targeting the poorest groups than would a government in a more open political environment. Second, the particular safety net mechanisms used by other countries, such as mass-scale public works programs, are unlikely to be either necessary or feasible in the general Chinese context of high growth and cheap surplus labor. Yet in some isolated rural areas, or depressed industrial regions where closed SOEs formerly provided the sole source of employment, these mechanisms could provide food or income support for needy groups, as well as useful infrastructure.

In order to address safety net and social insurance issues in China, first and foremost the current policy basis for social assistance, which is regionally based, should be revamped to account for new poverty trends and data. New pockets of poverty, as well as unknown but pre-existing ones, need to be systematically identified. Second, the needs of the marginalized rural poor must be addressed. In the short term, this can be done through social assistance, as in the form of public works programs or other safety net measures noted above, and in the longer term, when financially feasible, through the extension of a social insurance system. By enhancing income and infrastructure in rural areas, such an approach could help to curb excessive migration to urban areas, and possibly also help broaden the base of support for reform. The urban social welfare systems, meanwhile, need to be extended to cover private as well as public sectors, and should be unified under a more central administrative unit to reduce fragmentation between industries and regions. In addition, more administrative coordination between social insurance and social assistance systems is needed; at present it is virtually nonexistent. Finally, in the industrial areas where unemployment is high, or where reform of SOEs is likely to create more unemployment, some sort of short-term social fund or public works programs could be useful in providing assistance to the unemployed. The feasibility of such safety net programs will depend on available resources and extent of demand. Given the large labor surplus, administering such programs could be difficult and should only be considered in areas or regions where employment needs *cannot* be met by the growing private sector. And in all safety net programs, particularly in such a context, wages should be set well below the going market rate to target truly needy workers.

Viet Nam

Viet Nam is similar to China in that it is a rapidly growing economy where developing the private sector is much more critical than dismantling the public sector. Because Viet Nam started off at a much lower per capita income base than China, and is also less industrialized, there is less concern about unemployment resulting from the dismantling of unviable SOEs. As in China, political reform in Viet Nam has lagged behind economic reform, thus reducing the likelihood of public debate or political pressure about social welfare issues. Consequently, the government has the opportunity to focus on creating viable long-term social welfare institutions in addition to addressing some immediate safety net concerns.

Viet Nam began its transition with some advantages that facilitated a quick growth response to reforms. There is a surplus of cheap, skilled labor, which needs some retraining but is far less specialized than the labor forces in Eastern Europe. The country has a high level of educational capital, with a strong basis in primary education. Agrarian reforms were remarkably successful in turning Viet Nam from a rice importer to a major exporter since 1989. There was a rudimentary system of social assistance, with central, provincial, and village or communal level offices, giving the government a starting point from which to build.[33] Finally, Viet Nam discovered oil at the same time that the Russian economy collapsed.

There are also major challenges. Viet Nam's basic health and welfare infrastructure are far more limited than China's. Fifty-one percent of the population is poor, with 80 percent of the population and more than three-quarters of the poor in the agrarian sector.[34] While agrarian reform

---

33. Nhung (1994) and Lich et al. (1994).
34. Twenty-five percent of the population is below the extreme poverty line, defined as having insufficient income to meet basic food needs. See the World

has improved the lot of the majority, there are also pockets of extreme rural poverty. The poorest subsistence farmers, who did not have enough capital, land, or business expertise to take advantage of the reforms, have been hit particularly hard by the weakening of rural cooperatives and the reduction of subsidized inputs such as fertilizer. Poor households lack access to credit and tend not to be beneficiaries of remittances from family workers abroad or in state enterprises. Inequality has increased, both within the rural sector and between the rural and urban areas. There is also concern about poverty among the single elderly and among those employed by faltering SOEs. New problems such as homelessness and child prostitution have also surfaced. Finally, there are particular social welfare concerns resulting from the war: for example, the disabled and orphaned populations are large relative to most societies and have a clear need for immediate social assistance.

The existing social welfare system is geared towards a socialist economy; it is concentrated in the public sector and based on free service provision. A system which does not act as a disincentive to employment or investment must be gradually developed, and private and public schemes need to be consolidated. Extension to the rural areas will likely lag behind due to resource and administrative constraints. However, there are urgent problems in impoverished rural areas that need to be addressed. The levels of social assistance are insignificant: less than 10 percent of the government's social expenditure goes to social relief. The bulk of government social expenditure goes to social insurance for government workers—a small and relatively privileged group. This imbalance and the relative neglect of other social sectors is important to note when considering compensation for laid-off SOE workers, particularly those that are well positioned to find jobs in the private sector. At present most social assistance takes the form of credits or grants for job creation and is targeted in a rather haphazard manner. It should be reallocated as direct assistance for vulnerable groups.[35] In urban areas, particular at-risk groups should be targeted, such as the disabled, single elderly unemployed, and destitute children.

Given the extent of need and existing administrative and resource capacity, safety net mechanisms are likely to be more viable methods to

---

Bank (1995b). See also Nhung (1994) and *Financial Times* December 8, 1994, Special Supplement on Viet Nam.

35. More than 80 percent of the government's social transfers budget is spent on social security for government workers. The poorest 20 percent of the population benefits from only 7 percent of all these expenditures, while 40 percent of government social transfers benefit the top two income deciles (World Bank 1995b). Grants in the job creation schemes are in the form of water buffalo, pigs, seeds, and fertilizer (Van de Walle 1993).

reach the poorest groups than means-tested social assistance programs, which require sophisticated administrative capacity and fairly clear criteria to distinguish the poor from the non-poor. Safety net programs such as public works (for wage or for food), carefully targeted by both location and wage level, could be effective at buffering the income of the rural poor, particularly women, and provide necessary rural infrastructure at the same time. Other groups, such as orphans and the disabled, are easily identifiable and could receive direct income or food support.

In addition, systems to identify and monitor the status of vulnerable groups need to be developed, which will, among other things, require trained social workers. Any strategy should rely on the pre-existing social assistance offices to the extent that it is possible, as well as incorporate the efforts of NGOs and other non-government institutions.[36] Finally, public expenditure needs to be revamped. Public subsidies to higher education or urban hospitals disproportionately benefit wealthier groups, while primary services are underfunded. The poor often cannot obtain adequate health care because of the high cost of drugs (which were free prior to reform) and the decreasing quality of communal health care due to declining salaries and availability of personnel.[37] In this arena, merely shifting expenditures from higher level programs to basic services can have immediate benefits for the poor, even if expenditure increases are not feasible in the short term.

Mongolia

Mongolia differs from China and Viet Nam in that socialist social welfare structures were far more extensive prior to the transition, and there was virtually no private sector role in the economy. What little industry existed was centrally planned and operated; agriculture, meanwhile, was completely cooperative. Although society remained largely rural, and living standards were low, basic services such as health care and education were extensive and publicly provided. An additional and major difference is that Mongolia introduced dramatic political reform just prior to the initiation of economic reforms. While the majority of politicians seem strongly in favor of rapid reform at present, addressing welfare issues may become necessary to sustain support for reform as the social costs become more evident.

Safety net issues are diverse. The disruption of the state distribution system cut off supplies to SOEs, which disrupted production, had negative effects on workers' standards, and reduced the ability of the

---

36. The World Bank is supporting an ongoing effort to establish the routine implementation of a new household living standards survey.
37. Van de Walle (1993).

enterprises to provide the comprehensive social services as they had previously.[38] In rural areas, the breakdown of cooperative agriculture also resulted in a breakdown of the related health and education systems. Primary school enrollment, for example, has fallen significantly in rural areas since the transition. Poverty has increased, with much more significant increases among key vulnerable groups than among the poor in general. While the total number of people below the poverty line increased by 15.2 percent from 1991 to 1994, extreme poverty increased by 56 percent. The total population below the poverty line was 26.5 percent in 1994; 6.2 percent of the population was below the extreme poverty line. This indicates a sharp worsening for certain vulnerable groups, while others have been able to better their situation and even to emerge from poverty.[39]

The clearly vulnerable among the urban population are the unemployed, who lose access to key social services as well as income when they lose their jobs. In rural areas, female-headed households stand out as the most vulnerable group, in part because they fared the worst under the privatization of agriculture.[40] In addition, public resource constraints since the transition resulted in a widespread reduction in the number of daycare centers, making it more difficult for poor mothers to work, and thus they are increasingly dependent on a social welfare system which is in decline. Cost recovery for incidentals such as food was introduced in hospitals and schools with the transition. This has proved preclusive to many poor users, particularly as hospitals and schools which are strapped for resources have been trying to cover operating costs through the charges that they make for incidentals.

The existing social assistance system is limited and rather haphazard. For example, there is no correlation between the poverty levels of regions and the amount of social assistance that they receive.[41] The more remote regions seem to fare worse in general. In addition, social assistance offices are engaged in indirect and poorly targeted activities such as providing interest-free loans to the "poor," without any cost recovery mechanisms. There is a clear need to focus limited resources on the truly vulnerable in the short term. This will entail progress in identifying and monitoring the status of vulnerable groups as well as the provision of direct food or income assistance. The financial and

---

38. Tsend et al. (1994).
39. The most recent and comprehensive estimates of poverty in Mongolia can be found in Subbarao and Ezemenari (1995).
40. How households fared is directly linked to the amount of livestock that they were able to keep. In general women fared poorly on this front. For details see Subbarao and Ezemenari (1995).
41. Subbarao and Ezemenari (1995).

technical assistance of donors will be critical to setting up such systems. Given administrative and resource constraints in the short term, a means-tested social assistance system is unlikely to be viable in Mongolia. Social assistance strategies should therefore operate on a self-selection basis. As women are a critical group, and in many countries are the most active participants of public works programs, low wage public works or food-for-work programs could be effective—as long as wages are set below the going market wage and at least some provision for childcare is made. Where necessary, such programs may also be useful for the urban unemployed until unemployment insurance schemes are financially viable. A demand-based social fund approach, which is increasingly chosen as a safety net mechanism in many countries, is probably not well suited to the Mongolian context, where the population is disperse and partially nomadic.

Given public resource constraints in Mongolia, introducing worker contributions will be key to any viable social insurance system; beyond that there is a great deal of policy choice in terms of what kind of system is chosen. Eventually a public and political debate will be necessary to decide among options such as a fully funded one like Chile's, or a mixed system like that of the United States, or a more public OECD-type scheme. In the social sectors, meanwhile, the use of contributions or user fees in the public health and education systems should be reconsidered, given the preclusive effects such fees seem to have on poor groups, as demonstrated by the already visible declines in primary school enrollment. The rapid pace of political and economic reform in Mongolia and the seemingly high levels of public support for it should facilitate the adoption of far-reaching systemic changes in both arenas.

12.4 Conclusion

Safety net programs can, at times, contribute to both the political sustainability of reform and to permanent poverty reduction. Safety net programs can be a useful tool for incorporating the participation of community organizations, NGOs, and other grass-roots groups in the small-scale initiatives which are rarely in the mandate or reach of sectoral ministries, but are key to self-sustaining development at the local level, and therefore to poverty reduction. It is important that community groups and NGOs are seen to obtain rapid and tangible results from their efforts to present proposals to social fund programs. As a consequence of their successes, more people are inspired to reduce their poverty by organization and self-help methods, and a new political voice is given to previously marginalized groups. Safety net programs such as social funds can also play a new role in facilitating relations between remote or marginalized communities and the formidable bureaucratic structures that characterize the public sectors of most developing countries. Finally, as government-linked institutions introduce the concepts of efficiency, transparency, demand-based allocation, and subcontracting to the provision of social services, safety nets can serve as a basis for more general public sector reform.

The pace and scope of reform are critical in creating or obstructing opportunities for reform in general, and for redirecting resources to the poor in particular. In addition to the pace and scope of change, government communication with the public—particularly but not exclusively related to safety net issues—plays an important role in making economic reform politically feasible. The degree of representation and genuine popular participation that particular governments are willing to allow is a determining factor in the ability of safety net programs to contribute to the political sustainability of reform, in particular to promoting local institutional development and enhancing the political voice of the poor. In the same manner, the programs' impact on poverty reduction will inevitably be linked to a government commitment to making the program function efficiently and transparently, *and* to the broader context for poverty alleviation within which the programs takes place.

It must be emphasized that safety net programs are designed to be important *complements* to mainstream services, and the goals of the programs include developing new institutions and infrastructure, as well as enhancing the income of the poor. In addition, safety net programs operate within a fixed economic parameter: to a large extent their ability to make long-term contributions to poverty alleviation depends on the renewal of growth after reform and therefore on sound macroeconomic management. At the same time, the existence of safety nets may be a critical factor in making reform politically feasible, a prerequisite to attaining this sustained economic growth.

Although safety net issues in East Asia and Eastern Europe contrast sharply, several general lessons can be identified from their experiences during economic transition. In particular, safety net programs should be linked to broader institutional reforms; their benefits should be allocated in a nonpartisan, open manner; and careful consideration should be given to the programs' potential contribution to making the economic transition politically sustainable. How programs are implemented will be a major determinant of their success, regardless of the scale.

While safety net issues are less pressing both from a political and social welfare front in East Asia than they are in Eastern Europe, there is still an immediate need to provide safety nets for particular vulnerable groups. The initial conditions, economic structure, political context, and incomplete nature of the existing social welfare systems give governments in East Asia more flexibility in the design of social welfare policy and institutions for the longer term. The more closed nature of political systems in Viet Nam and China may make targeting the poorest groups more politically feasible. On the other hand, there are no mechanisms of public accountability to pressure for nonpartisan and transparent implementation of social welfare policy.

In Eastern Europe, in contrast, the pressing political nature of safety net issues and the formidable political obstacles to social sector reforms may mean that safety net programs are implemented with no other goal than to enhance the political sustainability of reform at a critical time, i.e., they may fail to complement broader economic reform measures. In East Asia, administrative capacity and availability of resources are the primary constraints. In Eastern Europe, similar constraints are coupled with more difficult structural economic challenges and political pressure to implement policy in the immediate term. There are more opportunities to design and implement effective safety net policies in East Asia, but in Eastern Europe they will be far more critical to the political sustainability of reform.

13 Environmental Protection During the Transition to a Market Economy

Daniel C. Esty

13.1 Introduction

Sustainable development has become the watchword for countries the world over. Government officials almost everywhere acknowledge today the need to protect environmental quality as well as to promote economic growth, recognizing that both contribute to social welfare. The environmental legacy of communist rule in Central and Eastern Europe—cities choked with soot, abandoned waste sites teeming with toxic chemicals, and rivers not only unfit to drink but so corrosive as to be unusable in industrial processes—stands as a stark reminder of the price to be paid in public health and ecological terms for the blind pursuit of economic growth without environmental safeguards. This chapter examines the quest for sustainable development in the context of the transition to a market economy.

The transition from planned to market economies has reshaped environmental conditions in Central and Eastern Europe. Environmental quality has improved in many ways, notably because the transition began with a collapse in industrial production which resulted in a dramatic reduction in pollution. While effective, economic collapse cannot be recommended as a preferred environmental policy. In East Asia, the transition to a market economy has created a vibrant private sector blooming on top of an inefficient and highly polluting state-owned sector. Thus, the transition process in China and Viet Nam has resulted in sharply escalating pollution problems.

Regardless of the starting point, the transition to a market economy presents an extraordinary opportunity for states to establish an economic system that provides incentives for environmental care and a firm foundation for sustainable development. This chapter examines the

I am grateful to Georgie Boge, Sandra Guylay, Tom Ballantine, Mark Weidman, and Ma Zhang for their research assistance.

environmental consequences and issues of the transition process. It identifies common themes affecting environmental quality derived from the experience in Russia, Hungary, Poland, and the Czech Republic that might be applicable in China, Viet Nam, and Mongolia. It also advances some preliminary advice for policy makers on how best to address the environmental challenges that face all emerging market economies and to some extent all developing countries.

13.2   Points of Convergence and of Divergence

The shift from a state-controlled and state-owned economy to a market-driven economic system based on private ownership serves as the common experience. But this point of convergence should not obscure important differences between the transitions in Asia and Europe.

Notably, Russia, Hungary, Poland, and the Czech Republic have undergone dramatic political transformations as well as economic transitions. These countries have begun to develop "modern" civil societies with relatively open political processes, free speech, and opportunities for non-governmental organizations to participate in political decisions. Mongolia's experience has been similar. After the Soviet-backed regime fell, a democratic government emerged that encouraged broad public political involvement at the same time it initiated sweeping economic reforms.

In China and Viet Nam, however, the transformation has been strictly limited to the economic sphere. Beijing and Hanoi, for ideological and cultural reasons, continue to see unsanctioned popular movements as potential threats to their regimes. As will be discussed below, the openness of the political system, as much or more than the market-orientation of the economy, shapes long-term environmental quality. Because the dissimilarities between the European and Asian experiences may overwhelm the similarities, the most apt environmental policy models for China and Viet Nam may be other Asian countries that have undergone rapid economic development.

Beyond the political dimension, the European and Asian economic transitions themselves differ in important respects affecting the environment. In Poland, Hungary, the Czech Republic, and Russia (to a greater or lesser extent), reforms have centered on privatizing state-owned industries. This has meant the closing of many old, inefficient, and heavily polluting factories. Pollution linked to these dirty industries has plummeted. Moreover, the economic discipline of privatization offers the promise of further environmental gains as the European states restructure and rebuild their economies on a base of competition, efficiency, and modern (cleaner) technologies.[1]

In contrast, the transitions in China and Viet Nam have centered on the explosive growth of new private-sector businesses alongside the existing structure of old, inefficient state-owned enterprises. Government-owned heavy industry with outdated technology continues to pollute. Moreover, many of the new private factories, especially the Township and Village Enterprises (TVEs) of China, rely on low-technology production processes or outmoded (but inexpensive) equipment—resulting in relatively high pollution levels. Consequently, East Asian governments face the dual challenge of managing new development, with its attendant increased emissions, while simultaneously trying to mitigate the ongoing pollution of the state-owned sector.

Despite their differences, all of the nations in transition face the common dilemma of how to manage a growing prosperity that gives rise to new consumer demands that in turn create new environmental stresses. Such problems are already evident. For example, Beijing's summer smog has worsened dramatically in the last several years as tens of thousands of new cars have been put on the roads.[2]

The growth in demand for consumer goods and the predictable parallel increase in pollution give added urgency to the task of establishing a coherent environmental policy. No matter how difficult it may be to develop and implement sound environmental programs during the transition process, to change environmental requirements later on will be even more difficult. Once public expectations have been set, and purchases have been made based on assumptions about the level of pollution controls to be required, any drive for tighter standards faces opposition from a huge entrenched interest group.

---

1. An important distinction must be made between environmental improvements in an absolute sense (i.e., lower overall emissions) and gains in a more dynamic sense (i.e., lower emissions per unit of output). The initial gains from economic collapse produced absolute environmental improvements. Further advances will be of the relative type, as expanded production yields higher absolute emissions but lower levels of pollution per unit of GDP due to improved efficiency (see Appendix 13A).

2. China has announced plans to build an affordable "people's car," with a production goal of 1.5 million automobiles per year by 2000. Even if the new cars do incorporate fuel efficiency technologies and pollution controls, as Beijing suggests they will (a claim about which most outside observers are very skeptical), the environmental impact will be enormous. In 1994, there were just seven million cars in all of China, only 10 percent of which were in private hands (*New York Times* September 22, 1994). Thus, the new production, along with some vehicle imports, will likely result in a doubling of the number of cars on Chinese roads by the year 2000 and a doubling again by 2008.

The transition to a market economy presents an extraordinary environmental opportunity. The flux of economic reform should be seen as a rare opening, relatively free of special interest constraints, to align the incentives of the economic system with appropriate environmental values. By eliminating subsidies and introducing the Polluter Pays Principle (i.e., the concept of "cost internalization" for environmental harms) as the centerpiece of environmental policy, governments have a chance to bring market forces to bear in support of sustainable development.

13.3 Central and Eastern Europe's Transition Experience

Environmental degradation played a significant role in launching the political and economic transformation of Eastern and Central Europe. What began as unfocused discontent over acid rain, undrinkable water, and fears of cancer due to toxic exposures eventually mushroomed into a major political force that helped bring down communist governments across the region. For example, some 600,000 people (17 percent of the population at the time) signed a petition in Lithuania in October 1988 opposing the construction of a nuclear power plant. An estimated 5,000 people marched against a planned chemical plant in Yerevan, Armenia, in February 1988. In Hungary, environmentalists garnered over 100,000 signatures in early 1989 on a petition to stop construction of the Nagymaros Dam. Although the timing may be mere coincidence, less than a month after the petition drive the government announced its support for a multi-party political system (Brown 1993).

These unpaid environmental debts are now coming due and adding to the difficulty of the transition process. Indeed, the transition governments in Eastern and Central Europe face disquieting environmental burdens alongside their economic crises. Throughout Eastern Europe, industrial discharges laced with heavy metals, chlorinated organic compounds, and radioactive materials are dumped into water bodies that also serve as local drinking water supplies, rendering much of the region's surface water unfit for human consumption [*Los Angeles Times* July 12, 1991; *International Environmental Reporter Current Report* (*IERCR*) June 2, 1993; *New York Times* November 3, 1994].

Nuclear waste presents a particularly acute problem, especially in the former Soviet Union. More than 10,000 square km of farmland in Ukraine and Belarus remains contaminated as a result of the Chernobyl accident (*Fortune* July 27, 1992). Sadly, cleanup work has largely ceased. Moreover, radioactive exposures may be on the increase because the bankrupt successor states to the Soviet Union can no longer afford to evacuate citizens from the so-called obligatory exclusion zone, nor can they ensure that contaminated food does not reach the market (*Washington Post*

October 29, 1994). Lacking any alternate means of disposal, the Russians have indicated they will probably continue to dump nuclear waste into the Baltic Sea until at least 1997 (*IERCR* November 3, 1993).

These problems have taken a staggering toll on human health in Eastern Europe. Life expectancy is far lower than in the West. The average Russian male's lifespan has dropped from 66 years in 1966 to 59 years in 1995—and is still falling (*New York Times* February 19, 1995; *Los Angeles Times* August 23, 1992). In the heavily contaminated Czech town of Most, the average male life expectancy is 52 years (*Los Angeles Times* December 10, 1989). Although shortcomings in medical care and lifestyle (e.g., poor diet, heavy smoking and drinking) contribute to these public health statistics, environmental factors almost certainly play a role (Hertzman 1995).

The Ill-fated Environmental Past

Although Hungary, Poland, the former Czechoslovakia, and the former Soviet Union had in place "comprehensive" environmental laws and regulations during the communist era, most of the requirements were little more than statements of general principles and mandated outcomes (e.g., "public health shall be protected"). In a few cases, governments enacted more detailed environmental protection packages. For instance, Hungary had a quite thorough Act on the Protection of the Human Environment. But, in general, specific plans for achieving the legislated goals rarely followed.

Although the water and air quality standards suggested in such plans often exceeded those of Western countries (National Trade Data Bank 1993a), the communist governments rarely implemented or enforced their environmental regulations. Government officials formulated economic policies (and, derivatively, environmental policies) with a single goal in mind—increased industrial and agricultural production. As a senior official in the Seminpalatinsk region (the main Soviet nuclear test site until 1989) remarked, "They kept on telling us that it was for the good of the people, the Communist Party, the future. The individual never counted for anything in the system" (*Washington Post* September 7, 1993).

When environmental regulations were enforced, the generally nominal fines levied against state-owned enterprises failed to deter additional pollution. A survey of pollution fees paid by 1,400 Polish manufacturing enterprises during communist rule found that the average fee amounted to 0.6 percent of production costs (*Economist* February 17, 1990). Not surprisingly, industrial facilities frequently elected to pay penalties rather than invest in costly technology to control pollution. Industry officials, with the support of government planning authorities, simply incorporated the penalties into their budgets [Euromoney Central European (Reuter Textline) September 1, 1993]. In addition, government officials routinely granted state-owned enterprises and municipalities "exceptional permission," which amounted to a waiver of established standards. In the former Czechoslovakia, enterprises and municipalities received approximately 2,500 such waivers for ongoing water violations between 1973 and 1990.

Aside from failing to develop or implement environmental laws, the former regimes set the prices of natural resources far below those of international markets. In the energy sector, subsidization not only led to excessive consumption by consumers and industry alike, but provided few incentives for implementation of energy-efficient technologies. In 1990, Hungary, Poland, and the former Czechoslovakia each consumed between four and eight times more energy per unit of GNP than the average OECD member. Even more dramatically, Russian manufacturing companies consumed more than four times as much energy per unit of GNP as their counterparts in the United States (*Fortune* July 27, 1992). Thus, the planned economies suffered inefficiencies that proved both economically and environmentally disastrous.

One exception to this dismal record stands out—the establishment of nature reserves and parks. The communist regimes of Eastern and Central Europe were able to protect natural resources in a way virtually unheard of in the West. The former Soviet Union created 170 nature reserves, extending from the Central Asian desert to the Arctic tundra (*Washington Post* May 31, 1994). The last remnant of the vast primeval forests that once ranged from France to Russia now lies protected within Poland's 11,867-acre Bialowieza National Park (*Los Angeles Times* November 16, 1991). In fact, more than 20 percent of Poland was protected through designation as a national park, national scenic area, nature reserve, and protected landscape area (PAP News Wire March 26, 1993).

The economic pressures of the post-communist era have called into question the long-term viability of these reserves. Moscow and the other new regimes can no longer even afford to retain rangers to protect natural resources from incursions by impoverished neighboring populations— never mind more vigorous ecosystem protection projects. In Russia, for instance, collective farmers residing along the northern border of the Baikalo-Lensky reserve have begun to graze their cattle on park property, an area containing a variety of rare plant species (*Washington Post* May 31, 1994). Market-driven plans for timber production, tourist development, and industry will likely provide additional challenges to the once-protected open spaces.

Promising Changes—and Some Missteps

In the early stages of the transition, the quality of the environment was affected by two key forces pushing in opposite directions. On the one hand, economic collapse reduced the amount of pollution-causing activity. But the accompanying political implosion meant that whatever minimal regulatory structure might have existed also collapsed as bureaucrats went unpaid and often abandoned their positions.

Despite the institutional obstacles, the immediate post-revolution governments made redressing environmental ills a top priority. The environmental zeal that helped spur the revolutions in Central and Eastern Europe carried over, at least initially, into the post-communist era. Although struggling economically, the new regimes sought to revise their environmental statutes and accompanying regulations and to revamp their environmental ministries. The new governments committed themselves to adopting Western (U.S. or European) environmental standards, and they solicited financial support from Western donors to fund new environmental protection systems. Hundreds of millions of dollars worth of environmental projects were launched, funded through local and national sources as well as through bilateral and multilateral assistance.[3]

Without a doubt, ecological and public health conditions have improved in many areas since the fall of communism (*IERCR* June 2, 1994). In Poland, the amount of untreated waste discharges decreased by 40 percent between 1989 and 1993 (PAP News Wire September 30, 1994). In the neighboring Czech Republic, the closure of some plants in northern Bohemia and the installation of filters in others have reduced SO_2 emissions by one-fifth (*Washington Post* August 9, 1994).

The recent reduction in harmful emissions and the improvement in water quality might convey the impression that the transition to market-based economic systems engendered careful plans for pollution prevention and control as part of a strategy to achieve sustainable development. But such is not the case. The environmental advances in large measure represent simply the silver lining in the dark cloud of economic collapse that closed a significant part of Central and Eastern Europe's industrial capacity. For example, by the end of 1994 Poland's economy was producing at only 90 percent of its pre-1989 level. Likewise, in the first five years of its transition, the Czech Republic's economy shrunk by

---

3. The United States committed $1.2 billion in foreign assistance to Central and Eastern Europe between 1990 and 1993. Approximately 7.5 percent of this assistance ($91.4 million) was directed to environmental concerns. In addition, the U.S. Environmental Protection Agency (with support from the European Union) launched a Central European Environmental Center in Budapest to facilitate technology and information exchange with the transition governments.

20 percent (*Los Angeles Times* July 12, 1994). The economic situation is no better in Hungary and even worse in Russia (see Appendix 13A).

In the last couple of years, the harsh economic realities of the transition have prompted many policy makers to reevaluate their environmental commitments. For instance, after an initial burst of environmental enthusiasm, the Hungarian government has been unable to pass a new comprehensive environmental law despite numerous attempts (*IERCR* September 7, 1994). In the Czech Republic, Prime Minister Vaclav Klaus voted against a proposed comprehensive environmental policy, explaining that his devotion to a free market economy left little room for environmental commitments (*BNA International Environment Daily* September 1, 1994). As a result of such attitudes, many of the transitional states have failed to institute anything like the systems for environmental protection they promised in the heady days after the fall of communism.

Russia's environmental efforts have almost completely crumbled in the face of the country's ongoing economic and political crises. Rather than advancing legislation to replace a confusing, contradictory, and generally ineffective regulatory system, the Russian Parliament has chosen instead to retain the old Soviet environmental laws. By thwarting new legislative initiatives and papering over weak laws with cosmetic changes, the Russian Parliament has shifted environmental protection to the back burner.

But the demise of environmental policy reform efforts is not the end of the story. Perhaps ironically, it now seems clear that the most important variable affecting the environment in the transition process is not how well the new government attends to pollution control legislation or to rebuilding its environment ministry but rather how thoroughly and quickly it carries out its economic reforms.

The governments that pursued "shock therapy" found themselves able to align market forces with their pollution-control goals and thus made more rapid economic—and environmental—advances. Poland, for example, ended all energy subsidies by 1990, while Russia continues to subsidize purchases of oil, gas, and coal. As a result, in Russia the economy has fallen faster than emissions, while in Poland emissions have fallen faster than the economy. In Hungary, which, like Poland, pursued a relatively aggressive transition strategy, emissions also fell more rapidly than the economy. (See appendix 13A.)

These data provide important support for the thesis that market forces represent a powerful environmental policy tool. Harnessing market incentives should therefore be the centerpiece of any environmental policy reform undertaken in conjunction with the transition to a market economy.

When the economies of Central and Eastern Europe emerge from their current deep recessions, the critical question will be whether they can sustain lower pollution levels and make further improvement in environmental quality. In the short term, two conflicting forces will shape the outcome to this question. First, pollution levels will rise again as industrial activity and consumer demand pick up. Second, the infusion of new capital and the creation of new manufacturing enterprises will permit the replacement of existing (often highly polluting) equipment with more technologically advanced and (almost always) less-polluting equipment. Whether the first effect, pushing pollution up, will overwhelm the second, holding emissions down, will depend on a variety of factors, notably whether incentives for environmental care remain in place.

13.4 The East Asian Environmental Experience during Transition

The East Asian transition experiences fall into two distinct groups: (1) Mongolia and (2) China and Viet Nam. A former Soviet satellite, Mongolia has undergone the dual political liberalization and economic restructuring that has defined the European transitions, although from a far less developed economic base. In contrast, China's and Viet Nam's political systems remain largely intact, despite an economic revolution that has spawned a thriving private economy alongside the lumbering state sector.

Mongolia: Parallels to Central and Eastern Europe

In Mongolia, the shift to a market economy largely resembles the Central and Eastern European transition. As a Soviet client state, Mongolia depended heavily on Soviet aid, trade, and technology, and it bears Soviet-style environmental scars. Water diversion in the Gobi desert, for example, has destroyed a number of lakes (Chuluun and Oyun 1994; *The Guardian* April 27, 1990). In addition, Mongolia's capital, Ulan Bator, suffers air pollution problems from the low-tech, high-pollution power plants and other industrial facilities built during the Soviet era.

In parallel with the European transition model, Mongolia's economy collapsed when Soviet aid abruptly ended in early 1991. Mongolia's economic transition to a market-oriented economy has been accompanied by the advent of a pluralist government that supports quite open debate over environmental policy. Since 1990, a variety of environmental non-government organizations have emerged, and an environmentally oriented "green" party even held seats in the legislature for a short period (*The Guardian* April 27, 1990).

Mongolia has benefited from significant international assistance during the transition process. The Asian Development Bank (ADB) has financed an effort to develop procedures for assessing environmental impacts. In addition, the U.N. Development Program has a major biodiversity program under way, aimed at Mongolia's extensive wildlife.

Mongolia, however, faces critical challenges. With limited economic prospects, the private economy will likely increase the pressure on the country's tens of thousands of goat and sheep herders to expand the number of animals they graze on a fixed supply of traditionally communal land. If each herder, acting individually to increase profits, adds more animals to his flock, the land could become overgrazed.

Mongolia also faces looming energy and mining-related environmental crises. The collapse of Soviet assistance left Mongolia without a reliable supply of energy. Mongolia has obtained international support for its efforts to develop alternatives such as hydropower on the Egiin River (*Financial Times* August 10, 1992). The Soviet aid cutoff brought most of Mongolia's mining operations to a halt. Power shortages, outdated equipment, distance from markets, lack of technical expertise, and inadequate infrastructure have hampered recent efforts to revive the mining sector (*Mining Journal* March 11, 1994). The marginal profitability of the mines makes it difficult for environmental officials to enforce attention to the inevitable environmental consequences of the extraction process.

China and Viet Nam: Development and Degradation

The economic and environmental consequences of China's and Viet Nam's transition to a market economy differ significantly from those in Mongolia and in Central and Eastern Europe. In China and Viet Nam, economic liberalization, in combination with large amounts of foreign investment, contributed to stunning economic growth since the early and late 1980s, respectively. But the effects of years of rapid economic growth, coupled with inadequate environmental infrastructure, are beginning to take a toll: notably, in the smog in China's major cities, the endemic acid rain in south China, the accumulated industrial and household wastes in Hanoi and Ho Chi Minh City, and the contaminated rivers of both countries. (See Appendix 13B.) For China, and increasingly for Viet Nam, the environmental challenge arises in part from a transition process that has largely ignored the need for regulatory structures as a dimension of a functioning market system and in part from straight development pressures.

Haphazard urbanization stands as a key culprit in the degradation of the East Asian environment. Industries situated in residential areas spew untreated wastes into waterways and noxious fumes into the air.

According to the ADB, less than one-half of all urban solid waste in Viet Nam is even collected. The rest is dumped in rivers, lakes, and other uncontrolled sites, creating public health hazards and contaminating surface water and groundwater (National Trade Data Bank 1993b).

Issues related to fossil fuel burning represent a dire environmental problem, especially in China, which consumed 1.2 billion tons of coal in 1995 for home heating and cooking, industrial use, and electricity generation. Experts forecast that China's annual coal consumption will rise to 1.4 billion tons by 2000 and to 2.4–3.6 billion tons by 2020 (*IERCR* October 7, 1992). Much of this coal is burned at ground level in residential areas, resulting in particulate levels in many parts of China that vastly exceed World Health Organization (WHO) standards (*New York Times* May 25, 1992). In fact, according to the most recent WHO data, seven of the ten most air-polluted cities in the world are in China.

More dramatically, according to the Chinese National Environmental Protection Agency, 27 percent of all deaths in China are due to respiratory diseases (NEPA 1994). Moreover, lung cancer among urban residents in China has increased 19 percent since 1988. These data probably reflect not only outdoor air pollution but also the very high level of indoor air pollution that many Chinese people face due to their use of poorly vented coal ovens for heating and cooking.

Much of China's coal has a high sulfur content and thus contributes to acid rain. In some southern Chinese cities, such as Guangzhou, 90 percent of the rain is acidic (*IERCR* June 16, 1993). In addition, significant SO_2 emissions spill over onto Korea and Japan. China's emissions of greenhouse gases rank the nation behind only the United States. While U.S. emissions are nearly stable, China's CO_2 emissions are growing rapidly (see Appendix 13B). Thus, China is likely to surpass the United States and become the world's largest greenhouse gas emitter early in the next century.

Although the environmental impacts of coal burning are increasingly apparent, the Chinese government's energy policy remains centered on increased coal consumption. From a Chinese perspective, coal is cheap and plentiful. Low-cost Chinese labor makes mining inexpensive, and the coal mines employ a large population in otherwise economically depressed areas.

Arable land in China is disappearing rapidly under pressure for industrial and urban development. One source indicates that acreage devoted to farming has fallen 20 percent since the late 1950s (*New York Times* September 25, 1994). Forests have suffered from similar pressures. Development and war have shrunk Viet Nam's forest cover from 44 percent of the total national land area in 1944 to about 25 percent today (Hanoi interview, July 1995).

In 1993 25.5 billion tons of sewage and industrial waste were discharged into China's rivers, streams, and coastal seas—an amount equivalent to three-fifths of the Yangtze River's annual flow (*New York Times* September 25, 1994). As a result, 80 percent of the river sections running through China's major cities are severely polluted (*IERCR* June 16, 1993). Water pollution problems in Viet Nam have become so bad that one recent analysis concluded that only 30 percent of the Vietnamese rural population has access to safe drinking water (Tho and Xuan 1993).

Despite Beijing's one-child planning policy, population growth continues to plague China. Although down from its high of 1.89 percent annual growth from 1945 to 1985, China's population continues to grow at an annual rate of 1.2 percent today, which translates into an additional 13 million people per year—this adds the equivalent of another Canada to its population every other year (Asian Development Bank 1994). Viet Nam is also experiencing rapid population growth, which puts considerable stress on the nation's limited resources and threatens its environmental future.

Initial Efforts, Significant Shortcomings

China and Viet Nam began to recognize their environmental problems in the early 1990s. In 1991, Viet Nam adopted a 10-year National Plan for the Environment and Sustainable Development, which includes provisions for strengthening environmental institutions, developing urban master plans and zoning laws, stabilizing the population, and developing sustainable energy policies (National Trade Data Bank 1993b). In 1994, China issued a wide-ranging "Agenda 21" program providing a blueprint for the nation's sustainable development and a response to the challenges spelled out at the 1992 Rio Earth Summit. Although ambitious in its scope—the plan covers the full spectrum of environmental issues across all of China—and impressive in the range of interests brought together to create the document—dozens of ministries participated under the coordination of the State Planning Commission and the State Science and Technology Commission and with the support of the U.N. Development Program—China's Agenda 21 provides more of a strategic vision than an action agenda for China's environmental future. The Agenda's "first tranche" lays out nine general priority areas encompassing over 60 projects in institutional development, agriculture, industry, energy, natural resources, pollution, poverty, public health, and desertification. But funding for these projects remains uncertain, as does the commitment to actual implementation.

While the comprehensive national plans reflect a real effort to catalog environmental harms and to develop response strategies, their very breadth undermines their usefulness. The plans fail to set clear priorities and suffer from a distinct lack of specificity. Agenda 21, for example, reads like an encyclopedic wish list, with a project for each ministry and each province. Translating these strategic visions into real policy plans, including implementation and funding schedules, remains incomplete.

A more promising component of China's current environment program is the commitment to develop more sophisticated legal and regulatory structures. The National People's Congress Environment Committee recently launched a major effort, with support from the ADB, to draft new environmental laws and regulations. Viet Nam has also begun to write new environmental laws, but creation of a comprehensive legal infrastructure to support environmental protection has been slow. Rather than borrow from existing models, Viet Nam has tended to develop its own environmental regulatory system "one law at a time" (*Merrill Lynch Investment Update* September 29, 1993). Highlights of this gradual evolution include a 1993 law requiring environmental impact reports and a 1994 "polluter pays" law with a sliding scale of administrative and court-ordered fines (*Vietnam Investment Review* January 3, 1994; *IERCR* February 23, 1994).

Lax enforcement of existing anti-pollution measures in both countries undercuts national standards and discourages industrial entities from investing in cleaner technology. Another stumbling block to coherent environmental protection programs is the tangle of administrative agencies involved in the promulgation and enforcement of standards. Given overall responsibility for the environment in 1992, Viet Nam's Ministry of Science, Technology, and the Environment is intended to serve as the focal point for all environmental issues, but its authority overlaps with that of other national and local government bodies. For instance, up to nine agencies play a role in regulating water use (*Bangkok Post* January 4, 1994). China's National Environmental Protection Agency and local environmental protection bureaus are similarly hampered by ambiguous and conflicting lines of authority as well as a lack of cooperation from powerful economic ministries and state-run enterprises.

Furthermore, while the general nature of the environmental guidelines produced by Beijing and Hanoi allows environmental rules to be adapted to local conditions, this flexibility also opens the door for understaffed and under-funded local authorities to ignore major problems. Many old plants have been "grandfathered" out of new standards, and foreign firms regularly complain that they are held to a higher standard than local businesses, especially state-owned enterprises (*Business Asia* June 17, 1991). Moreover, many Chinese local environmental officials are in the delicate position of financial dependence on the senior party authorities whose businesses are the major polluters.

With the economic power shifting to the provinces in China, Beijing's enforcement authority has further diminished. Local officials often work closely with foreign entrepreneurs to bring new factories and jobs to their regions. Perceiving themselves to be in vigorous competition for these investments with other Chinese provinces (and other developing countries), they frequently indicate a willingness to overlook environmental rules. National officials, apparently recognizing the problems with local enforcement, have organized innovative inspection teams of national-level officials to handle environmental violations in the provinces. Such limited measures, however, are unlikely to result in serious environmental enforcement against powerful polluters.

China announced in 1995 a $10 billion five-year environmental spending program. However, one source estimates that China needs nearly $35 billion simply to retrofit old factories with basic pollution-control equipment (*IERCR* February 10, 1993).

Viet Nam's environmental investments lag behind China's. The entire Vietnamese Environmental Agency has fewer than 200 people in it. Although Hanoi has contributed money to several national-level research studies and to rural water and reforestation programs, environmental projects in Viet Nam depend almost entirely on a trickle of international funding.

The Three Gorges Dam

China's Three Gorges Dam, a massive hydroelectric-power project to be built on the Yangtze River, exemplifies many of the challenges and opportunities facing countries in transition. Under consideration since the early twentieth century, the dam, called by some "the last Stalinist project" because of its immense size, is intended to reduce recurring and costly flooding along the Yangtze River Valley and to provide much-needed hydroelectric power. If completed, the dam will be the largest hydroelectric project in the world, with power production eventually expected to reach 84 billion kilowatt-hours of electricity annually. This figure represents approximately one-eighth of the country's total 1991 electricity output (*IERCR* April 8, 1992). But construction of the dam will displace millions of residents along a 200 km stretch of the river and will flood 100,000 square km of cultivated farmland. It will also destroy some of China's most scenic vistas—a landscape that has inspired poets for centuries.

Of course, the expanded use of hydroelectric power to propel China's industrial growth reflects an important shift away from reliance on coal. According to the State Planning Commission, the dam will obviate the need to burn 40.5 million tons of coal each year. Nonetheless, critics have charged that energy and flood-prevention needs can be met by a series of smaller dams that would protect the scenic gorges and require relocation of far fewer residents. The Chinese National Environmental Protection Agency has expressed concern that soil erosion will increase upstream, causing water quality to deteriorate, and that downstream water will contain less silt, creating less new soil for agriculture. Opponents of the dam also predict that sedimentation upstream will actually increase flooding in that area, dramatically reducing the dam's useful life and impeding navigation on the Yangtze, which remains a key element of China's transport structure.

The Three Gorges project has sparked a remarkable level of internal dissension and open debate in China. An unprecedented one-quarter of the National People's Congress delegates abstained in a key 1992 vote authorizing construction to begin. Officials in areas adversely affected by the dam, including the upstream city of Chongqing, have lobbied against the project's vast scale. The prominence of the project and the deep attachment many Chinese have to the site have spurred the creation of informal non-governmental pressure groups to oppose the project. Although Beijing may see such debate as a threat to its control over the countryside, it is this type of public dialogue that helps to align official environmental policy with genuine public needs.

13.5 Environmental Opportunities and Challenges

The reconstruction of the economic foundation of society undertaken in the transition process offers both environmental opportunities and pitfalls. The biggest mistake that transitional states can make is to conclude that the pressing needs of economic growth must override any immediate consideration of environmental protection. Poorer countries cannot afford as much in the way of environmental spending as richer ones, and countries facing economic crises will not have lavish environmental budgets, but no country should delay all consideration of environmental impacts until some unspecified measure of development has been achieved. While the appropriate level of resources devoted to environmental protection will rise with national income, every country has choices that will optimize environmental protection and maximize social welfare at every stage of development. For example, even the poorest country can site new industrial facilities downwind from population centers.

While some observers have hoped that the emerging market economies could "leapfrog" past the polluting practices of today's industrialized world to cleaner production processes, the fact is that the cleanest technologies are often too expensive for poor countries to adopt immediately. However, while the potential for technology leapfrogging may be limited, there is considerable opportunity for "policy leap-frogging," i.e., learning from the regulatory mistakes of others. Thus, for example, countries need not and should not adopt "command and control" environmental regulatory programs simply because that is what the industrialized countries did.

Countries in transition must incorporate environmental considerations into economic policy making throughout the transition and beyond. Adoption of a "market system" offers no guarantee of improved social welfare. Indeed, crude forms of market economics can result in unregulated market failures and worsened quality of life.

In summary, market economies offer the promise of improved efficiency and greater wealth. This promise cannot be realized, however, without a functioning regulatory structure to "internalize" environmental "externalities" and to create incentives for pollution prevention and control by consumers and producers.

Poland and Russia: Comparative Environmental Results

Market-based incentives have been a key element of Polish environmental reform. Specifically, the country collects fees from polluting enterprises and deposits them in the National Fund for Environmental Protection. Nearly all user fees and fines have been sharply increased since 1989, with the exception of a temporary fee abatement in 1992. Proceeds from the Fund have financed construction of wastewater treatment plants, flue gas desulferization systems, and new fluidized bed combustion facilities at coal-fired plants.

Efforts undertaken by the Ministry of Environmental Protection, Natural Resources, and Forestry to establish a national monitoring system for all essential parameters of the environment and to strengthen the Ministry's ability to impose severe penalties should facilitate enforcement of Poland's environmental laws. In 1991, environmental improvements constituted 1.5 percent of Poland's gross national income. Additional funding for environmental protection has been obtained from an innovative debt-for-environment swap through which outside lenders forgive a portion of the country's debt in exchange for Polish investments in reducing the greenhouse effect, acid rain, and pollution of the Baltic Sea, as well as in maintaining Poland's biodiversity. The United States, for example, has allowed Poland to convert 10 percent of its official debt into zlotys for use on environmental projects.

Poland's achievements stand in stark contrast with the environmental situation in Russia. Inadequate financing and an incompetent bureaucracy have left Russia ill-equipped to carry out much of any environmental program (Peterson 1993). Rampant corruption has further undermined Russia's regulatory infrastructure. Russia's ongoing economic crisis has now sharply narrowed whatever policy options the Russian government might once have had. In fact, it is estimated that strict enforcement of even the existing modest environmental rules could force 80 percent of Russia's factories to close immediately (*U.S. News and World Report* April 13, 1992). In short, Russia's environmental infrastructure has withered in the face of the economic downturn and political disarray that has marked Russia's transition to a market economy.

13.6 General Policy Recommendations

1. Strengthen the rule of law
Without a societal commitment to the rule of law, environmental programs make little sense and are too easily ignored. Thus, legal reform and the creation of an environmental regulatory structure embedded in the rule of law must be at the core of any transition process.

The rule of law has a number of important dimensions. First, property rights must be clear and enforced. The lack of clear property rights results in the over-exploitation of resources (such as excessive grazing on common land in Mongolia) or unchecked pollution. Moreover, an environmental regulatory system without clear laws enforced against all violators inevitably breaks down as those with special connections or with money to pay bribes claim public resources (including clean air and water) as their own. Without consistent enforcement, disregard of the government's environmental program becomes the rule, not the exception.

Another key step toward establishing the rule of law is the elimination of corruption. When enterprises can pay bribes or call on powerful patrons in government for help and thereby avoid penalties for pollution violations, the incentive to invest in pollution abatement is considerably dulled. Another serious consequence of corruption is the disincentive it creates for foreign investment (Francis 1993), because companies find it distasteful (not to mention illegal) to pay bribes and they worry about being competitively disadvantaged when others get preferential treatment.

Transparent (plainly understandable) laws, impartial enforcement of contracts, and clear liability rules are further essential dimensions of the rule of law. In the environmental realm, clarification of liability rules is particularly critical. Uncertainty over potential liability for cleanup costs has led several major foreign companies to shy away from business deals in Central and Eastern Europe. In fact, a 1992 study by the World Bank and the OECD found that environmental liability often ranked above political instability and poor infrastructure as the primary concerns of Western firms considering investments in Central and Eastern Europe. As veterans of numerous regulatory disputes, U.S. firms have been particularly reluctant to invest before environmental laws and regulations—and therefore their exposure—have been clarified. (*Los Angeles Times* August 28, 1994 and July 12, 1991.)

In defining liability at potentially contaminated sites, governments have a variety of options: (1) hold new owners fully responsible for pre-existing environmental hazards and damages; (2) assume public responsibility for most or all environmental liability problems arising from past practices; or (3) address each proposed investment or privatization on an ad hoc basis, with varying degrees of shared responsibility assigned to each party. From an economic growth perspective, option 2, government assumption of responsibility for past pollution, is clearly the preferred policy. Burdening new owners with cleanup responsibilities seriously deters investment. When combined with the uncertainty about how much cleanup might cost, the inhibition on investment can become overwhelming. Ad hoc decision making is not only time-consuming, it also creates uncertainty, which chills investor interest.

2. Align market forces with environmental goals
The capacity to harness market forces for environmental purposes represents the single most important environmental policy opportunity available to economies in transition. Fundamentally, market forces promote efficiency, including efficient resource use, and thus reduced pollution. Governments should therefore adopt the Polluter Pays Principle and use "price signals" to create incentives for environmental care.

Relying on market-based environmental policy instruments, e.g., pollution taxes or charges, effluent fees, tradeable permits, and deposit-refund schemes, can help transitional economies to regulate efficiently and to minimize their reliance on blunt and costly "command and control" regulatory mechanisms. Moreover, the funds generated by fee-based systems can support public investments in environmental protection or other aspects of social development.

Of course, some market mechanisms (e.g., pollution allowance trading systems) require a rather sophisticated regulatory system that most countries in transition will not be able to create. In fact, where administrative structures are weak and the risk of regulatory failure is high, command and control regulations may prove to be the "least social cost" approach to controlling environmental problems. At an early stage in the transition to a modern civil society, governments may well find that simple regulatory approaches aimed at basic public health and ecological goals (e.g., drinkable surface water) are all they can manage.

From an environmental perspective, energy price subsidies represent the most significant market distortion in many countries. Increasing the price of energy positively affects the environment in two ways. Initially, rising energy costs create incentives for energy conservation and the implementation of energy-efficient technologies, both of which reduce energy consumption and attendant pollution. Over time, the adjustment may also bring about a change in the mix of fuels consumed, generally away from highly subsidized and highly polluting coal.

3. Governments must finance environmental protection programs with domestic revenues and not count on international assistance for much help
Reliance on foreign assistance to support environmental programs is a recipe for disappointment or, worse yet, inaction. Western countries have failed to turn many of their funding promises into reality. The unfulfilled U.S. commitment to convert Soviet-made reactors into less dangerous power plants offers just one example of this pattern (*Los Angeles Times* September 4, 1992). Foreign assistance rarely functions as more than a catalyst, spurring increased attention to certain environmental problems. Transitional countries therefore stand a much greater chance of developing viable environmental protection systems if they look to their own economic growth for funding, rather than to promises from international donors and lending organizations.

4. Channeling private financial flows represents a critical point of leverage over the environmental future
Private capital flows dwarf official assistance in most transition countries. China, for example, received foreign aid in 1995 totaling about $3 billion while private foreign investment topped $30 billion. Where and how these private funds are deployed—and specifically what attention is paid to the environmental consequences of private sector development projects—will have a much greater effect on the environmental futures of the transition economies than how World Bank loans or other multilateral or bilateral assistance is spent. Not only are foreign investors an important source of economic growth in all of the countries in transition, foreign companies provide critical access to modern capital equipment, up-to-date pollution control technologies, environmental management strategies, and training in pollution prevention and control.

Creating a business climate attractive to foreign investors is therefore critical. This need not mean, as some suppose, that environmental standards should be set at low levels. To the contrary, multinational enterprises generally prefer to establish facilities that employ the same high environmental standards they follow in their home markets. These companies will usually build facilities with state-of-the-art pollution control technologies so long as this strategy does not competitively disadvantage them in the market place. Such disadvantage arises most prominently where government officials allow other competitors in the local market to violate environmental standards with impunity.

5. Good environmental policy making ultimately depends on public support, which turns on the availability of information and open debate
The environmental harm inflicted on Central and Eastern Europe under the communist regimes persisted for years because of the almost total lack of open dialogue on environmental issues. Environmental policy making requires information about pollution exposures and harms, an ability to assess the risks of harmful effects resulting from various decisions, and the capacity to assess the costs and benefits of policy alternatives. As these regulatory processes are fraught with uncertainty, open discussion of issues, data, analytic methodologies, and policy options facilitates consideration of competing analyses and thus contributes to sound decision making. Non-governmental organizations can play a critical role in alerting the public to the environmental consequences of government actions and by offering alternatives to the established policies.

Ironically, membership in environmental groups in Central and Eastern Europe has fallen since the early 1990s. Yet the role of these organizations has become even more critical; in the absence of broad public interest in environmental matters, they are now virtually the only voices insisting that attention be paid to the environmental aspects of the development process. Although China has recently chartered its first environmental group, "Friend of Nature," and several Vietnamese environmental interests have emerged, public environmental debate remains severely circumscribed in China and Viet Nam. Until a more fulsome environmental dialogue emerges, these nations cannot expect the environmental progress that a more open and competitive policy process encourages.

6. Decentralize regulatory authority to the extent that pollution problems are localized but retain national oversight and central authority over problems that spill across local jurisdictional boundaries
Local decision making about local problems is an important aspect of democracy and argues for decentralizing environmental policy making. But in transition economies with limited policy expertise, central governments will often be better equipped to carry out some aspects of the regulatory process (e.g., technical analyses such as epidemiological studies). Moreover, where problems spill over from one jurisdiction to another, a centralized regulatory regime may be necessary to eliminate any incentive to "externalize" harms.

7. Environmental goals should be pragmatic and flexible
Countries in transition cannot do everything at once. Picking a few key points of emphasis, such as protecting drinking water supplies and eliminating lead from gasoline, often makes more sense than ambitious multi-tiered agendas. Phasing in new requirements over time will minimize costs by reducing the resources devoted to retrofitting pollution controls on existing facilities. Where new factories are being built, it makes sense to require them to meet higher environmental standards. Such a two-tier regulatory structure permits countries to upgrade their environmental performance over time without writing off existing capital investments.

In the early phases of transition, most former command economies in Europe announced their intention to adopt Western environmental standards. A more realistic and credible approach for these countries would entail implementing EU standards over a longer time span of perhaps 20 years. Furthermore, environmental standards should be tailored to local needs and circumstances, so that governments can retain credibility on environmental issues and guard against the public disillusionment, corruption, or regulatory collapse that might stem from a failure to meet overly ambitious targets.

8. Compliance with international environmental agreements will require international support in line with the economic burdens imposed by such agreements
Several current problems are inherently global in scope and must be dealt with on a worldwide scale. But international environmental agreements, such as the Convention on Trade in Endangered Species (CITES), the Montreal Protocol (phasing out the production and use of substances that deplete the ozone layer), the Biodiversity Convention, and the Framework Convention on Climate Change, impose special challenges on resource-strapped economies in transition. The environmental requirements laid out in these agreements reflect the ambitions of the industrialized world to address global environmental harms. However, industrialized nations should acknowledge that resources devoted by the transition governments to comply with international environmental agreements would compromise other development priorities. The industrialized countries should be prepared, therefore, to provide technological and financial assistance to the transition countries to support their compliance programs. Finally, transitional countries should incorporate international environmental considerations into their development planning. Making new capital investments consistent with international obligations is much less expensive than retrofitting later to meet these goals.

13.7 Specific Policy Recommendations

Because the transition governments have achieved varying degrees of success in carrying forward their economic and political restructuring, the most valuable short-term focus for environmental policy makers will differ from country to country. The following discussion provides some preliminary thoughts on what the top priorities might be. Because Poland, Hungary, and the Czech Republic have moved relatively far along the transition path, they are considered as a group. Similarly, China and Viet Nam have important parallels that allow them to be considered together.

Poland, Hungary, and the Czech Republic

Poland, Hungary, and the Czech Republic have eliminated energy subsidies and brought market forces to bear on inefficient state-owned industries. This means that they are now in a position to turn to the more difficult long-term challenges of creating a functioning environmental regulatory structure.

All three countries need to develop stronger environmental protection "capacity." This entails improved data collection programs, the development of environmental "indicators" (which allow environmental progress to be measured and tracked), stronger skills in risk analysis, and a greater capacity for cost–benefit analysis. These countries would also benefit from greater information exchange with other countries so as to obtain the latest thinking on policy tools and strategies.

These "advanced" transition countries should devote the bulk of their environmental energies to the problems of ongoing economic activities as opposed to devoting time and resources to the backlog of problems from the communist era. Of course, some of the most pressing "holdover" problems will require relatively urgent attention because of the threat that they pose to public health or valuable ecosystems.

Ultimately, the environmental prospects depend on the capacity of the governments to attract foreign investment and thereby to modernize their industrial facilities. Obtaining private capital to support investments in environmental infrastructure (e.g., drinking water systems and sewage treatment plants) will also require attention to the investment climate created, which will largely be a function of maintaining the momentum toward the creation of a functioning market economy and modern civil society.

Russia

Russia's capacity to address the environmental legacy of the communist era has been badly hampered by its failure to end all energy subsidies and to put inefficient state-owned enterprises out of business. The hold of organized crime on the Russian economy and the massive degree of corruption that characterizes all Russian governmental activities are further roadblocks to environmental progress.

Russia must undertake serious economic and political restructuring as a prelude to any prospect of environmental progress. Meanwhile, Russia should consider adopting a "federalism" approach to environmental regulation, perhaps resembling the U.S. system with a central environmental agency, regional offices of the federal environmental authorities, and a separate system of state or local environmental authorities.

Mongolia

Mongolia faces unique challenges centered, in particular, on preserving its natural resources. Notably, the nation needs a strategy for managing its grasslands in the face of pressures to increase herd sizes, which could result in over-grazing in a classic "tragedy of the commons." One alternative, but perhaps one that represents too sharp a break with Mongolian tradition, would be to privatize the grazing lands. A second alternative, which would take some sophistication to carry out but which offers real promise, would be to develop a grazing rights allowance system to limit the number of animals to the capacity of the land. Under such a regime, allowances for the optimal number of animals for a particular area might be issued and distributed on a basis deemed fair.

As with the privatization efforts in other countries, a variety of options for distribution of the initial allowances could be considered. For example, all existing herders could be given a fixed number of allowances depending on the size of their existing herd or some other criteria (e.g., a per capita basis). Alternatively, the government could auction the grazing allowances. Finally, the government might choose to distribute the allowances to the traditional community leaders in the countryside, who could use whatever method the local community agrees upon to distribute the allowances. Once an initial distribution is made, herders would be free to trade (buy or sell) their allowances and would be obligated to maintain an allowance for every animal in their flock.

Mongolia's other great asset, its wildlife, is also at risk from the pressures of modernization. Specifically, private entrepreneurs may find it attractive to bring hunting parties to Mongolia and to take animals without regard to the sustainability of particular species or populations.

The government might consider levying a tax on hunting activities. An appropriate fee charged to game hunters coming to Mongolia would maintain a sustainable animal population and provide a source of funds for conservation programs.

China and Viet Nam

China and Viet Nam have the greatest distance to go in establishing functioning environmental regimes to accompany their economic transitions. Neither country has a particularly strong tradition of the rule of law, and thus building a general commitment to compliance with environmental standards will be a challenge. Rampant corruption further dulls the incentive businesses have to obey environmental mandates.

Neither China nor Viet Nam has developed some of the other basic dimensions of a modern state including the capacity for open political debate. Both countries will have a hard time achieving optimal environmental policies unless and until they permit non-government organizations to form and to critique government decisions in the environmental realm. As stressed earlier, environmental problems are so fraught with uncertainty that government policies must be constantly open to challenge from a range of outside interests to ensure that thinking is continually sharpened and better answers displace worse ones.

China and Viet Nam also face environmental problems that arise from the incomplete nature of their economic transformations. Specifically, insofar as neither country has really gone very far in the process of subjecting state-owned enterprises to market disciplines, inefficient production practices continue, with damaging environmental consequences. To further the evolution of their economies (and also their environments), both China and Viet Nam would benefit from eliminating all subsidies, particularly energy subsidies.

13.8 Conclusion

Environmental issues should play a role in government policy choices at all times. The lesson from the experiences of Central and Eastern Europe under communism is that an economic growth-at-any-price attitude leads ultimately to economic and environmental disaster. Facing the Scylla of pressures for economic expansion and the Charybdis of environmental constraints, economies in transition must navigate carefully in their quest for sustainable development. While the transition to a market economy can facilitate simultaneous economic and environmental progress, there is no guarantee that this will occur in the absence of diligent policy efforts.

Appendix 13A   Air Pollution in Central and Eastern Europe during Transition

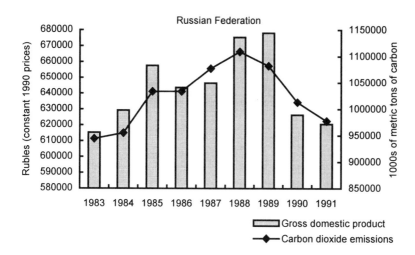

Figure 13A.1
Annual gross domestic product and carbon dioxide emissions in the Russian Federation. Sources: ORNL (1995) and United Nations (1994).

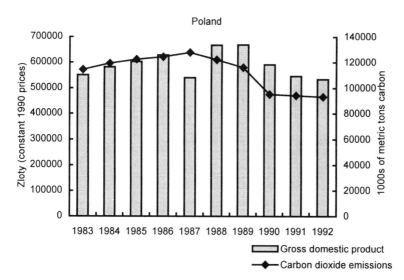

Figure 13A.2
Annual gross domestic product and carbon dioxide emissions in Poland. Note: Poland's 1992 GDP reflects a new system of national accounts. Sources: ORNL (1995), United Nations (1994), and OECD (1994c).

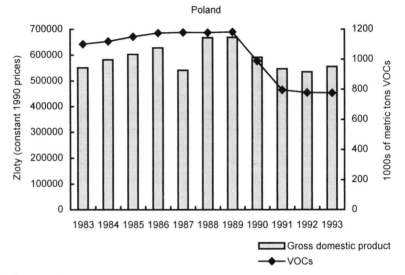

Figure 13A.3
Gross domestic product and volatile organic compound (VOC) emissions in
Poland. Note: 1992 and 1993 GDP data are based on Poland's new national
account system. Sources: OECD (1994c, 1995) and United Nations (1995).

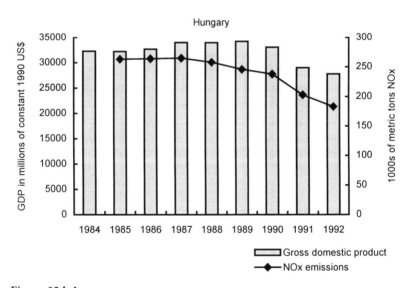

Figure 13A.4
Annual gross domestic product and emissions of nitrogen oxides (NOx) in
Hungary. Source: OECD (1995) and United Nations 1995.

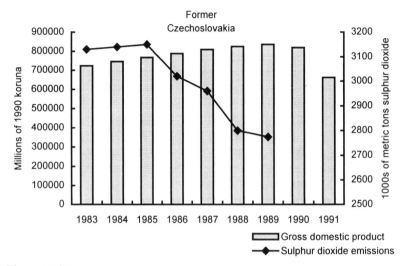

Figure 13A.5
Annual gross domestic product and sulphur dioxide emissions in former Czechoslovakia. Source: OECD (1993b) and United Nations (1994).

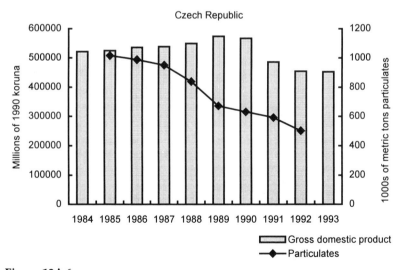

Figure 13A.6
Annual gross domestic product and particulate emissions in the Czech Republic. Note: The Czech Republic's 1992 and 1993 GDP values reflect a new system of national accounts. Sources: OECD (1994c, 1995) and United Nations (1994).

Appendix 13B   Air Pollution in East Asia during Transition

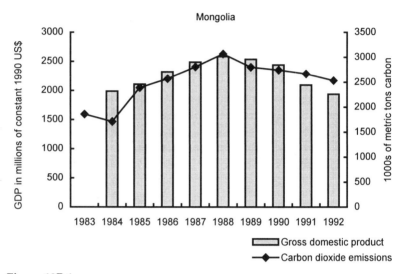

Figure 13B.1
Annual gross domestic product and carbon dioxide emissions in Mongolia.
Source: ORNL (1995) and United Nations (1995).

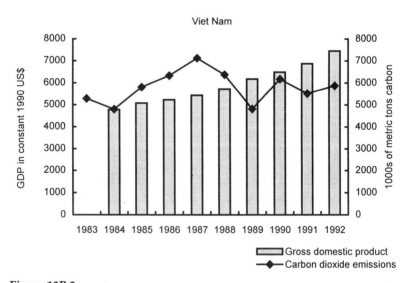

Figure 13B.2
Annual gross domestic product and carbon dioxide emissions in Viet Nam.
Sources: ORNL (1995) and United Nations (1995).

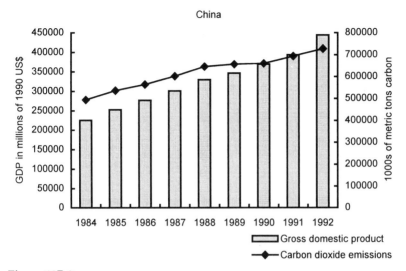

Figure 13B.3
Annual gross domestic product and carbon dioxide emissions in China.
Source: ORNL (1995) and United Nations (1995).

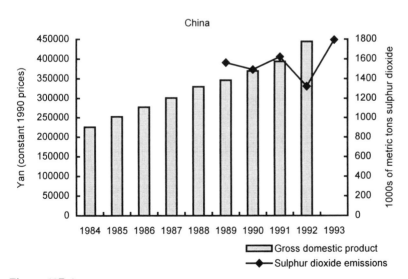

Figure 13B.4
Annual gross domestic product and sulphur dioxide emissions in China.
Sources: ORNL (1995) and United Nations (1995).

Bibliography

Aghion, P., O. Blanchard, and W. Carlin. 1996. The economics of enterprise restructuring in Central and Eastern Europe. In J. Roemer, ed., *Property Relations, Incentives and Welfare*. St. Martin's Press.

Amsden, A. 1994. Why isn't the whole world experimenting with the East Asian model to develop? Review of the East Asian miracle. *World Development* 22(4):627–33.

Antczak, M. Income from the privatisation of state enterprises in Poland, Hungary, and the Czech Republic in 1991–1994. In *Studies and Analyses 80*. CASE Center for Social and Economic Research.

Asian Development Bank. 1994. *National Response Strategy for Global Climate Change: People's Republic of China*. Manila: Asian Development Bank.

Aslund, A. 1995. *How Russia Became A Market Economy*. Washington, D.C.: Brookings Institution.

Balcerowicz, L. 1995. *Socialism, Capitalism, Transformation*. Budapest, London, and New York: Central European University Press.

Balcerowicz, L., and A. Gelb. 1994. Macropolicies in transition to a market economy: a three-year perspective. Paper presented at the Annual World Bank Conference on Development Economics.

Balcerowicz, L., et al. 1981. *Reforma gospodarcza: główne kierunki i sposób realizacji*. (Economic reform: main directions and the method of realization). In: R. Krawczyk, ed., *Reforma gospodarcza—propozycje, tendencje, kierunki dyskusji (Economic Reform—Proposals, Tendencies, Directions of Discussion)*. Warszawa: PWE.

Bandaralage, J.S., and D.T. Nguyen. 1994. The role of foreign direct investment in a transition economy: The case of Vietnam. Griffith University and Institute of Southeast Asian Studies, Australia (unpublished).

Barberis, N., M. Boycko, A. Shleifer, and N. Tsukanova. 1995. How does privatization work? Evidence from the Russian shops. (Manuscript, April.)

Barro, R.J. 1989. A cross-country study of growth, saving, and government. NBER Working Paper Series no. 2855 (February).

Barro, R.J. 1990. Government spending in a simple model of endogenous growth. *Journal of Political Economy* 98:S103–25.

Begg, D. 1991. Economic reform in Czechoslovakia: Should we believe in Santa Klaus? *Economic Policy* 6(2):244–85.

Belka, M., S. Estrin, M.E. Schaffer, and I.J. Singh. 1994. Enterprise adjustment in Poland: Evidence from a survey of 200 private, privatized and state-owned firms. Paper presented at the World Bank Workshop on Enterprise Adjustment in Eastern Europe. Washington, D.C. (September).

Bell, M.W., H.E. Khor, and K. Kochhar. 1993. China at the threshold of a market economy. Occasional paper no. 107. IMF.

Berend, I., and G. Ranki. 1985. *The Hungarian Economy in the Twentieth Century.* Sydney: Croom Helm Ltd.

Berg, A., and J. Sachs. 1992. Structural adjustment and international trade in Eastern Europe: The case of Poland. *Economic Policy*, no. 14.

Birman, I. 1978. From the achieved level. *Soviet Studies* 30(2):152–72.

Biuletyn Statystyczny (Statistical Bulletin). 1994. March and September. Warsaw: GUS.

Biuletyn Statystyczny (Statistical Bulletin). 1996. March. Warsaw: GUS.

Blanchard, O. (forthcoming). *Clarendon Lectures on Transition Economies.* Presented at Oxford University. Oxford: Clarendon Press.

Blanchard, O., S. Commander, and F. Coricelli. 1995. Unemployment and re-structuring in Eastern Europe and Russia. In S. Commander and F. Coricelli, eds., *Unemployment, Restructuring and the Labor Market in Eastern Europe and Russia.* Washington, D.C.: Economic Development Institute (EDI) of the World Bank.

Blaszczyk, B. 1994. The progress of privatization. *MOCT - MOST*, no. 4, 187–211.

Blaszczyk, B., A.S. Bratkowski, and M. Dabrowski. 1995. Macroeconomic trends and policies 1990–1995. Mimeo. Warsaw.

Blaszczyk, B., and M. Dabrowski. 1993. *The Privatization Process in Poland 1989–1992: Expectations, Results and Remaining Dilemmas.* London: CRCE.

Boeri, T. 1993. Labor market flows and the persistence of unemployment in Central and Eastern Europe. Paper presented at the OECD Workshop on the Persistence of Unemployment in CEECs, Paris, September.

Boeri, T. 1995. Unemployment dynamics and labor market policies. In S. Commander and F. Coricelli, eds., *Unemployment, Restructuring and the Labor Market in Eastern Europe and Russia.* Washington, D.C.: Economic Development Institute (EDI) of the World Bank.

Bonin, J., and M. Schaffer. 1994. Banks, firms, bad debts, and bankruptcy in Hungary: 1991–94. Centre for Economic Performance, Working Paper No. 657. London (September).

Bourguignon, F., and G.S. Fields. 1990. Poverty measures and anti-poverty policy. Delta Working Papers. Paris (February).

Boycko, M., A. Shleifer, and R. Vishny. 1995. *Privatizing Russia*. Cambridge, Massachusetts: MIT Press.

Bratkowski, A.S. 1993. The shock of transformation or the transformation of the shock? *Communist Economies and Economic Transformation* 5(1):5–28.

Bratkowski, A.S., et al. 1995. *Fiscal Policy in Poland under Transition*. CASE— Center for Social and Economic Research, Studies & Analyses, no. 49. Warsaw.

Brown, A., B. Ickes, and R. Ryterman. 1994. *The Myth of Monopoly*. World Bank Policy Research Department, Working Paper no. 1331.

Brown, E.F. 1993. In defense of environmental rights in East European constitutions. 1993 University of Chicago Law School Roundtable 191.

Bruno, M. 1993. *Crisis, Stabilization and Economic Reform—Therapy by Consensus*. Oxford: Clarendon Press.

Bruno, M. 1994. Stabilization and reform in Eastern Europe: A preliminary evaluation. In O. Blanchard, K. Froot, and J. Sachs, eds., *The Transition in Eastern Europe*. Chicago: University of Chicago Press.

Burda, M. 1994. Structural change and unemployment in Eastern Europe: Some key issues. Humboldt University Discussion Paper 14.

Cao, Y.Z. 1995. The reform of China's price system. Working Paper no. 3, The Sasakawa Peace Foundation. Tokyo, Japan (April).

Carlin, W., J. Van Reenen, and T. Wolfe. 1994. Enterprise restructuring in the transition: An analytical survey of the case study evidence from Central and Eastern Europe. European Bank for Reconstruction and Development (EBRD), Working Paper no. 14.

Chang, C., and Y. Wang. 1994. The nature of township enterprise. *Journal of Comparative Economics* (December) 19(3):434–52.

Che, J., and Y. Qian. 1994. Boundaries of the firm and governance: Understanding China's township-village enterprises. Stanford University, manuscript.

Chen K., H. Wang, Y. Zheng, G. Jefferson, and T. Rawski. 1988. Productivity change in Chinese industry: 1953–1985. *Journal of Comparative Economics* (December) 12(4):570–91.

Chen, S., G. Datt, and M. Ravaillion. 1994. Is poverty increasing in the developing world? Policy Research Department, The World Bank. Washington, D.C. (March).

Chen, X. 1994. The new pole of the rural reform: Corporate share-holding system. In *China Reform and Development Report 1992–1993: The New Progresses and New Challenges*, pp. 38–52. China Financial and Economic Press.

Cheng, L.K. 1995. Foreign direct investment in China. Paper presented to OECD informal workshop on "Trade and Investment Links between the OECD Countries and China," March 2–3, 1995, Paris.

Collins, P., and F. Nixson. 1992. Management development and economic restructuring in the Mongolian People's Republic: Issues and options. Ulaanbaatar.

Commander, S. et al. 1995. Hungary survey. In Commander, S. and F. Coricelli, eds., *Unemployment, Restructuring and the Labor Market in Eastern Europe and Russia*. Washington, D.C.: Economic Development Institute (EDI) of the World Bank.

Craig, A. 1992. Solidarity: Deconstructing discourse and practice in the politics of concertation. Paper presented to UCSD Workshop, "Mexico's Solidarity Program: A Preliminary Assessment" (February).

Creditanstalt Securities. 1994. *Czech Market Review*. Vienna: Creditanstalt Bankverein.

Czech Statistical Office. 1993. *Statistical Yearbook of the Czech and Slovak Republics*, editions 1990–1993. Prague: Statistical Publications Division.

Czech Statistical Office. 1994. *Economic and Social Indicators of the Czech Republic from 1985 to the 1st Quarter of 1994*. Prague: Statistical Publications Division.

Dabrowski, J.M. 1994. The results of "capital privatization" in Poland. Paper presented at the conference on "Privatization in Poland and East Germany. A Comparison," December 8–9, Warsaw.

Dabrowski, J.M., M. Federowicz, A. Levitas, and J. Szomburg. 1992. *Przebieg procesów prywatyzacyjnych w polskiej gospodarce. I raport z badan: wrzesien-grudzien 1991*. (Progress of privatization processes in Polish economy. First research report: September- December 1991). *Transformacja Gospodarki*, issue no. 23. Gdansk Instytut Badan nad Gospodarka Rynkowa (The Gdansk Institute for Market Economics).

Danzan, D. 1992. Renewal of the financial system. Ulaanbaatar.

Delpla, J., and C. Wyplosz. 1994. Russia's transition: Muddling through. INSEAD Working Paper, 94/60 EPS. Fountainebleau, France.

Dematte, C. 1992. Critical managerial issues in an economic liberalization process. Ulaanbaatar.

Dervis, K. and T. Condon. 1994. Hungary—Partial successes and remaining challenges: The emergence of a "gradualist" success story?" In O. Blanchard, K. Froot, and J. Sachs, eds., *The Transition in Eastern Europe*. Chicago: University of Chicago Press.

Dittus, P. 1994. Corporate governance in Central Europe: The role of banks. Bank for International Settlements, Economic Papers, no. 42. Basel.

Doanh, L.D. 1994. Vietnam economic transition toward a market economy. Hanoi: Central Institute for Economic Management (unpublished).

Dollar, D. 1990. Economic reform and allocative efficiency in China's state-owned industry. *Economic Development and Cultural Change* (October) 39(1):89–105.

Dollar, D. 1993. Vietnam: Successes and failures of macroeconomic stabilization. In B. Ljunggren, ed., *The Challenge of Reform in Indochina*, pp. 203–32. Cambridge, Massachusetts: Harvard University Press.

Dollar, D. 1994. Macroeconomic management and the transition to the market in Vietnam. *Journal of Comparative Economics* 18.

Dollar, D., and J. Litvack. 1994. Macroeconomic performance and poverty reduction. In *Household Welfare and Viet Nam's Transition to a Market Economy.* Washington, D.C.: World Bank (forthcoming).

Drabek, Z., and A. Smith. 1995. Trade performance and trade policy in Central and Eastern Europe. CEPR Discussion Paper no. 1182. London (April).

Dresser, D. 1991. Neopopulist solutions to neoliberal problems: Mexico's National Solidarity Program. Issue Brief no. 3, Center for U.S.–Mexican Studies. University of California, San Diego.

Duiker, W. 1989. *Vietnam Since the Fall of Saigon.* Athens, Ohio: Ohio University Center for International Studies.

Dyba, K., and J. Svejnar. 1994. An overview of recent economic developments in the Czech Republic. CERGE EI Working Paper no. 61. Mimeo.

Dynamika Prywatyzacji (Dynamics of Privatization). 1994. No. 23. *Ministerstwo Przeksztalcen Wlasnosciowych* (Ministry of Ownership Transformation). December. Warszawa.

Dynamika Prywatyzacji (Dynamics of Privatization). 1995. No. 24. *Ministerstwo Przeksztalcen Wlasnosciowych* (Ministry of Ownership Transformation). January. Warszawa.

Dynamika Prywatyzacji (Dynamics of Privatization). 1996. No. 27. *Ministerstwo Przeksztalcen Wlasnosciowych* (Ministry of Ownership Transformation). January. Warszawa.

Earle, J., S. Estrin, and L. Leshchenko. 1995. The effects of ownership on behavior: Is privatization working in Russia? Center for Economic Performance Discussion Paper, London School of Economics. London.

Earle, J.S., R. Frydman, A. Rapaczynski, and J. Turkewitz. 1994. *Small Privatization, The Transformation of Retail Trade and Consumer Services in the Czech Republic, Hungary and Poland.* Budapest, London, and New York: Central European University Press (in cooperation with Oxford University Press).

Easterly, W., and S. Fischer. 1994. The Soviet economic decline: Historical and Republican data. NBER Working Paper no. 4735.

Easterly, W., R. King, R. Levine, and S. Bebelo. 1992. How do national policies affect long-run growth? World Bank Discussion Paper no. 164. Washington, D.C.: World Bank.

Ehrlich, I., G. Gallais-Hamonno, Z. Liu, and R. Lutter. 1994. Productivity growth and firm ownership: An analytical and empirical investigation. *Journal of Political Economy* 102(5):1006–38.

Enkhsaikhan, M. 1992. Some aspects of Mongolian open economic policy. Ulaanbaatar.

Enyedi, G. 1976. *Hungary: An Economic Geography.* Oxford: Westview Press.

European Bank for Reconstruction and Development (EBRD). 1993a. *Annual Economic Outlook*. London: EBRD.

European Bank for Reconstruction and Development. (EBRD). 1993b. *Current Economic Issues*. July. London: EBRD.

European Bank for Reconstruction and Development (EBRD). 1994. *Transition Report*. London: EBRD.

European Bank for Reconstruction and Development (EBRD). 1995. *Transition Report*. London: EBRD.

Faini, R., and R. Portes. 1995. Opportunities outweigh adjustment: The political economy of trade with Central and Eastern Europe. In R. Faini and R. Portes, eds., *European Trade with Eastern Europe: Adjustment and Opprtunities*. London: CEPR.

Fairbank, J. 1987. *The Great Chinese Revolution 1800–1985*. New York: Perennial Library.

Fairbank, J. 1992. *China: A New History*. Cambridge: Harvard University Press.

Fan, G. 1993. Two kinds of reform costs and two approaches to reform (in Chinese). *Economic Research Journal* 1:3–12.

Fan, G., Hai, W., and Woo, W.T. (forthcoming). Decentralized socialism and macro-stability: Lessons from China in the 1980s. In M. Guitan and R. Mundell, eds., *Growth and Inflation in China*. Washington, D.C.: International Monetary Fund.

Fan, Q., and M.E. Schaffer. 1994. Government financial transfers and enterprise adjustments in Russia, with comparisons to Central and Eastern Europe. Discussion Paper no. IDP-141. Washington, D.C.: World Bank.

Finger, J.M., and A. Olechowski. 1987. *The Uruguay Round: A Handbook on the Multilateral Trade Negotiations*. Washington, D.C.: World Bank.

Fishlow, A., and C. Gwin. 1994. Overview: lessons from the East Asian experience. In *Miracle or Design? Lessons from the East Asian Experience*. Policy Essay no. 11. Washington D.C.: Overseas Development Council.

Fox, J. 1992. The difficult transition from clientelism to citizenship, lessons from Mexico. Paper presented to UCSD workshop, "Mexico's Solidarity Program: A Preliminary Assessment" (February).

Francis, D.R. 1993. Officials on the take damage an economy. *Christian Science Monitor*, October 8.

Freeman, R. 1994. What direction for labor market institutions in Eastern and Central Europe? In O. Blanchard, K. Froot, and J. Sachs, eds., *The Transition in Eastern Europe*. Chicago: University of Chicago Press.

Frydman, R., K. Pistor, and A. Rapaczynski. (forthcoming). Exit and voice after mass privatization: The case of Russia. *European Economic Review*.

Frydman, R., K. Pistor, and A. Rapaczynski. (forthcoming). Investing in insider-dominated firms: A study of voucher privatization funds in Russia. In R. Frydman, C. Gray, and A. Rapaczynski, eds., *Corporate Governance in*

Central Europe and Russia. Budapest, London, and New York: Central European University Press (in cooperation with Oxford University Press).

Frydman, R., and A. Rapaczynski. 1994. *Privatization in Eastern Europe; Is the State Withering Away?* Budapest, London, and New York: Central European University Press (in cooperation with Oxford University Press).

Frydman, R., A. Rapaczynski, J. Earle, et al. 1993. *Privatization Process in Central Europe*. Budapest, London, and New York: Central European University Press (in cooperation with Oxford University Press).

Frydman, R., A. Rapaczynski, and J. Turkewitz. 1996. Transition to a private property regime in the Czech Republic and Hungary. See this volume.

Fukasaku, K., D. Wall, and M. Wu. 1994. *China's Long March to an Open Economy*. Development Centre Studies. Paris: OECD.

Gaidar, Y., and K.O. Pohl. 1995. *Russian Reform/International Money*. Cambridge: MIT Press.

Garnaut, R., and Y. Huan. 1995. China's trade reforms and transition: Opportunities and challenges for OECD countries. OECD informal workshop on "Trade and Investment Links between the OECD Countries and China," March 2–3, Paris.

GATT. 1993. *Examen des politiques commerciales, Pologne*, vol. I and vol. II.

Gerschenkron, A. 1962. *Economic Backwardness in Historical Perspective*. Cambridge, Massachusetts: Harvard University Press.

Graham, C. 1991. The APRA government and the urban poor: The PAIT program in Lima's pueblos jovenes. *Journal of Latin American Studies* (February) 23(1):91–130.

Graham, C. 1992. *Peru's APRA: Parties, Politics, and the Elusive Quest for Democracy*. Boulder: Lynne Rienner.

Graham, C. 1994. Mexico's National Solidarity Program in comparative context: Demand-based poverty alleviation programs in Latin America, Africa, and Eastern Europe. In W.A. Cornelius, A.L. Craig, and J. Fox, eds., *Transforming State-Society Relations in Mexico: The National Solidarity Strategy*. San Diego: Center for U.S.–Mexican Studies.

Graham, C. 1994. *Safety Nets, Politics, and the Poor: Transitions to Market Economies*. Washington, D.C.: Brookings Institution.

Graham, C. 1995. Strategies for enhancing the political sustainability of reform in Ukraine. *ESP Discussion Papers*. Washington, D.C.: World Bank (January).

Graham, C., and C. Kane. 1995. Opportunistic government or sustaining reform: Electoral trends and public expenditure patterns in Peru, 1990–95. Mimeo. Washington, D.C.: The Brookings Institution and the World Bank (November).

Granick, D. 1990. *Chinese State Enterprises: A Regional Property Rights Analysis*. Chicago: University of Chicago Press.

Granville, B. 1995. *The Success of Russian Economic Reforms*. Washington, D.C.: Brookings Institution.

Grosfeld, I. 1994. Comparing financial systems: Problems of information and control in economies in transition. Mimeo.

Gross, J. 1979. *The Nazi Occupation of Poland*. Princeton, New Jersey: Princeton University Press.

Groves, T., Y. Hong, J. McMillan, and B. Naughton. 1995. Productivity growth in Chinese state-run industry. In F. Dong, C. Lin, and B. Naughton, eds., *Reform of China's State-Owned Enterprises*. London: Macmillan.

Haggard, S. 1994. Politics and institutions in the World Bank's East Asia. In *Miracle or Design? Lessons from the East Asian Experience*. Policy Essay no. 11. Washington, D.C.: Overseas Development Council.

Haggard, S., and R. Kaufmann. 1992. *The Politics of Adjustment*. Princeton, New Jersey: Princeton University Press.

Ham, J., J. Svejnar, and K. Terrell. 1995. Czech Republic and Slovakia survey. In S. Commander and F. Coricelli, eds., *Unemployment, Restructuring and the Labor Market in Eastern Europe and Russia*. Washington, D.C.: Economic Development Institute (EDI) of the World Bank.

Hamilton, C.B., and L. A. Winters. 1992. Opening up international trade with Eastern Europe. *Economic Policy*, no. 14.

Hamrin, C.L. 1984. Competing 'policy packages' in post-Mao China. *Asian Survey* (May) XXIV(5):487–518.

Handelman, S. 1994. *Comrade Criminal: The Theft of the Second Russian Revolution*. London: Michael Joseph.

Hankiss, E. 1990. *East European Alternatives*. Oxford: Oxford University Press.

Harding, H. 1986. Political stability and succession. In *China's Economy Looks Toward the Year 2000*. Joint Economic Committee, U.S. Congress (May).

Hare, P., and G. Hughes. 1992. Industrial restructuring in Eastern Europe: policies and prospects. *European Economic Review* (April) 36(2-3):670–6.

Hare, P., and Revesz, T. 1992. Hungary's transition to the market: The case against a "big bang." *Economic Policy*, no. 14.

Harrold, P. 1992. China's reform experience to date. World Bank Discussion Paper no. 180. Washington, D.C.: World Bank.

Haughton, J. 1994. Overview of economic reform in Vietnam. In D.O. Dapice, D.H. Perkins, and J. Haughton, eds., *In Search of the Dragon's Trail: Economic Reform in Vietnam* (unpublished).

Havas, A. 1995. Hungarian securities markets. Paper prepared for the CEU Privatization Project.

Hazlett, T. 1995. The Czech miracle. *Reason* (April), 28–35.

Hertzman, C. 1995. *Environment and Health in Central and Eastern Europe, A Report for the Environmental Action Programme for Central and Eastern Europe*. Washington, D.C.: World Bank.

Hsueh, Tien-tun, Li Quian, and Liu Shucheng. 1992. *China's Provincial Statistics*. Boulder: Westview Press.

Huang, Y., and X. Meng. 1995. China's industrial growth and efficiency: A comparison between the state and the TVE sectors. Research School of Pacific Studies. Australian National University, manuscript.

Hussain, A. 1994. Social security in present-day China and its reform. *American Economics Association Papers and Proceedings* 84(2).

Informacja o przebiegu procesów prywatyzacji i o zmianach w strukturze podmiotowej gospodarki w ukladzie terytorialnym w latach 1990–1992 (Information on privatization process and changes in the institutional structure of the economy in 1990–1993 — territorial aspect). 1993. Warszawa: CUP (February).

ING Securities 1994. Czech Republic capital markets. Prague (October).

Inotai, A. 1994. Central and Eastern Europe. In C.R. Henning, E. Hochrietier, and G.C. Hufbauer, eds., *Reviving the European Union*. Washington, D.C.: Institute for International Economics and the Austrian National Bank.

Institute of International Finance (IIF). 1994a. *Czech Republic, Country Report*. Washington, D.C.: IIF (March).

Institute of International Finance (IIF). 1994b. *Hungary, Country Report*. Washington, D.C.: IIF (July).

Instituto Cuanto. 1991. *Ajuste y Economia Familiar: 1985–1990*. Lima.

Jefferson, G. 1990. China's iron and steel industry: Sources of enterprise efficiency and impact of reform. *Journal of Development Economics* (October) 33(2): 329–55.

Jefferson, G., T. Rawski, and Y. Zheng. 1992. Growth, efficiency, and convergence in China's state and collective industry. *Economic Development and Cultural Change* 40(2):239–66.

Jefferson, G., T. Rawski, and Y. Zheng. 1994. Comment on the efficiency and macroeconomic consequences of Chinese enterprise reform by Woo, Fan, Hai and Jin. *China Economic Review* 5(2): 235–41.

Jorgensen, S., M. Grosh, and M. Schacter, eds., 1992. *Bolivia's Answer to Poverty, Economic Crisis, and Adjustment: The Emergency Social Fund*. Washington, D.C.: World Bank.

Joskow, P., R. Schmalensee, and N. Tsukanova. 1994. Competition policy in Russia during and after privatization. *Brookings Papers on Economic Activity: Microeconomics*. Washington, D.C.: Brookings Institution.

Kaiping, J. 1994. Retrospects and prospects of China's reform on social security system. Paper presented to the "Seminar for Social Security Systems in Asian Countries—A Comparison of Problems and Perspectives," March 19–25, 1994, Washington, D.C.

Kaminski, B., A. Winters, and Z.-K. Wang. 1996. Foreign trade in the transition: The international environment and domestic policy. Studies of economies in transformation no. 20. Washington, D.C.: World Bank.

Kaminski, B., A. Winters, and Z.-K. Wang. (forthcoming). Explaining trade reorientation in transition economies. *Economic Policy*, no. 23.

Kaser, M., and E. Radice. 1985. *The Economic History of Europe 1919–1975.* Oxford: Oxford University Press.

Kavran, D. 1992. Government and information technology: Elements of legal background for administrative reform. Ulaanbaatar.

Kikeri, S., J. Nellis, and M. Shirley. 1992. *Privatization: The Lessons of Experience.* Washington, D.C.: World Bank.

Kogut, B. 1996. Direct investment, experimentation, and corporate governanace in transition economies. In R. Frydman, C. Gray, and A. Rapaczynski, eds., *Corporate Governance in Central Europe and Russia* (forthcoming). Budapest, London, and New York: Central European University Press (in cooperation with Oxford University Press).

Kornai, J. 1980. *Economics of Shortage.* New York: North Holland.

Kornai, J. 1990a. *Vision and Reality, Market and State.* New York and London: Routledge.

Kornai, J. 1990b. *The Road to a Free Economy.* New York and London: Norton.

Kornai, J. 1992. *The Socialist System.* Princeton, New Jersey: Princeton University Press.

Kotrba, J. 1994. Czech privatization: Players and winners. Center for Economic Research and Graduate Education – Economics Institute, Working Paper no. 58.

KPMG Management Consulting. 1993. *A Study of the Russian Privatization Process: Changing Enterprise Behavior.* CERT (Heriot-Watt University) and Sovecon. Funded by HM Treasury (U.K.).

Lall, S. 1994. The East Asian miracle: Does the bell toll for industrial strategy? *World Development* 22(4):645–54.

Lardy, N.R. 1992. *Foreign Trade and Economic Reform in China, 1978–1990.* Cambridge, U.K.: Cambridge University Press.

Layard, R., and A. Richter. 1994. Labor market adjustment—the Russian way. In A. Aslund, ed., *Russian Reform at Risk.* London: Pinter.

Lich, T.D., J. Riedel, and N.M. Tu. 1994. Presentation of Viet Nam country paper, Asia Foundation project, "Comparing Transitions in East Asia and Eastern Europe," December 2–3, 1994, Prague.

Lieberman, I., A. Gwing, M. Mejstrik, J. Mukherjee, and P. Fidler. 1995. *Mass Privatization in Central and Eastern Europe and the Former Soviet Union: A Comparative Analysis.* Washington, D.C.: World Bank.

Lieberman, I., and J. Nellis, eds. 1995. *Russia: Creating Private Enterprises and Efficient Markets.* Washington, D.C.: World Bank.

Luo, X. 1990. Ownership and status stratification. In W. Byrd and L. Qingsong, eds., *China's Rural Industry: Structure, Development, and Reform.* Oxford University Press.

Lutz, M.S., and T. Krueger. 1995. Developments and challenge in Hungary. In B. Banerjee, V. Koen, T. Krueger, M.S. Lutz, M. Marrese, and T.O. Saavalainen, eds., *Road Maps of the Transition: The Baltics, the Czech Republic, Hungary and Russia*. International Monetary Fund.

Megginson, W.L., R.C. Nash, and M. van Randenborgh. 1994. The financial and operating performance of newly privatized firms: An international empirical analysis. *Journal of Finance* 49(2):403–52.

Mészáros, K. 1993. Evolution of the Hungarian capital market: The Budapest Stock Exchange. In J. Earle, R. Freedman, and A. Rapaczynski, eds., *Privatization in the Transition to a Market Economy*. New York: Pinter.

Milanovic, B. (forthcoming). *Poverty in the Transition Economies*. World Bank.

Minami, R. 1994. *The Economic Development of China: A Comparison with the Japanese Experience*. New York, N.Y.: St. Martin's Press.

Minami, R., and S. Hondai. 1995. A consequence of enterprise reform in China: Estimation and analysis of the relative income share of labor in the machinery industry. *Journal of Economics* (December) 36(2):125–43.

Mladek, J. 1994. *Czech Privatization Process: Time for Corporate Governance*. Ludwig Boltzmann Institut Zur Analyse Wirtschaftspolitischer Aktivitäten.

Murphy, K.M., A. Schliefer, and R.W. Vishny. 1992. The transition to a market economy: Pitfalls of partial reform. *Quarterly Journal of Economics* 889–906.

National Bank of Hungary. 1994. *Annual Report, editions 1991–1994*. Budapest.

National Environmental Protection Agency (NEPA). 1994. *1993 Report on the State of the Environment in China*. Beijing.

National Trade Data Bank. 1993a. Hungary—environmental issues. *National Trade Data Bank Market Reports*, 17 August.

National Trade Data Bank. 1993b. The Asian development bank's environmental strategy and program for Viet Nam. *National Trade Data Bank Market Reports*, 22 November.

Naughton, B. 1991. Implications of the state monopoly over industry and its relaxation. (Manuscript, January.)

Naughton, B. 1994. What is distinctive about China's economic transition? State enterprise reform and overall system transformation. *Journal of Comparative Economics* (June) 18(3).

Nelson, J. 1990. *Economic Crisis and Policy Choice: The Politics of Adjustment in the Third World*. Princeton, New Jersey: Princeton University Press.

Newman, P., Milgate. M., and J. Eatwell, eds. 1992. *The New Palgrave Dictionary on Money and Finance*. New York: Stockton Press.

Nguyen, D.T., and J.S. Bandara. 1993. Recent development in the Vietnamese economy with special reference to the macroeconomic conditions. Griffith University, Australia (unpublished).

Nhung, L.T. 1994. Country report on social welfare in Viet Nam. Paper presented to the "Seminar for Social Security Problems in Asian Countries—A

Comparison of Problems and Perspectives," March 19–25, 1994, Washington, D.C.

Oak Ridge National Laboratory (ORNL). 1995. Electronic database of carbon international carbon dioxide emissions. Oak Ridge, TN.

Organization of Economic Cooperation and Development (OECD). 1992. *Etudes Economiques de l'OCDE–Pologne*. Paris: OECD.

Organization of Economic Cooperation and Development. (OECD). 1993a. *Economic Surveys: Hungary*. Paris: OECD.

Organization for Economic Cooperation and Development (OECD). 1993b. *OECD Environmental Data Compendium 1993*. Paris: OECD.

Organization of Economic Cooperation and Development. (OECD). 1994a. *Economic Surveys: The Czech and Slovak Republics*. Paris: OECD.

Organization of Economic Cooperation and Development (OECD). 1994b. *Unemployment in Transition Economies: Transient or Persistent?* Paris: OECD.

Organization of Economic Cooperation and Development (OECD). 1994c. *Short-term Economic Indicators Transition Economies 1994*. Paris: OECD.

Organization of Economic Cooperation and Development (OECD). 1995. *OECD Environmental Data Compendium 1995*. Paris: OECD.

Organization of Economic Cooperation and Development–Centre for Cooperation with European Economies in Transition (OECD-CCET). 1994a. *Integrating Emerging Market Economics into the International Trading System*.

Organization of Economic Cooperation and Development–Centre for Cooperation with Economies in Transition (OECD-CCET). 1994b. *Barriers to Trade with the Economies in Transition*.

Pacific Economic Cooperation Council, Pacific Economic Outlook 1996–1997, The Asia Foundation, 1996, p.57.

Panagariya, A. 1993. Unravelling the mysteries of China's foreign trade regime. In D. Greenaway and J. Whalley, eds., *The World Economy*, vol. 16, no. 1. Oxford, U.K. and Cambridge, U.S.A.: Blackwell Ltd.

Paul, G. 1991. Poverty alleviation and social safety net schemes for economies in transition. IMF Research Department Working Paper no. 91/14 (February). Washington, D.C.: International Monetary Fund.

People's Republic of China, National Environmental Protection Agency and State Planning Commission. 1994. *Environmental Action Plan of China 1991–2000*. Beijing.

Peterson, D.J. 1993. *Troubled Lands, The Legacy of Soviet Environmental Destruction*. Boulder, Colorado: Westview Press.

Pinto, B., M. Belka, and S. Krajewski. 1993 Transforming state enterprises in Poland: Evidence on adjustment by manufacturing firms. *Brookings Papers on Economic Activity*, no. 1, 213–55.

Pistor, K., and J. Turkewitz. 1996. Coping with hydra-state ownership after privatization: A comparative study of Hungary, Russia, and the Czech Republic.

In R. Frydman, C. Gray, and A. Rapaczynski, eds., *Corporate Governance in Central Europe and Russia* (forthcoming). Budapest, London, and New York: Central European University Press (in cooperation with Oxford University Press).

Portes, R. 1994. Integrating the Central and East European countries into the International Monetary System. Occasional paper no. 14. London: CEPR.

Qian, Y. 1994. Issues of enterprise reform in China. Center for Economic Policy Research Publication no. 390. Stanford University.

Qian, Y., and Xu, C. 1993. Why China's economic reforms differ: The M-form hierarchy and entry/expansion of the non-state sector. *The Economics of Transition* (June) 1(2):135–70.

Rajewski, Z. 1993. *Produkt krajowy brutto* (Gross domestic product). In L. Zienkowski, ed., *Gospodarka polska w latach 1990–1992*. (Polish Economy 1990–1992). Warsaw.

Riedel, J. 1988. Economic development in East Asia: Doing what comes naturally? In H. Hughes, ed., *Achieving Industrialization in East Asia*, pp. 1–38. Cambridge: Cambridge University Press.

Riedel, J. 1993. Viet Nam: On the trail of the Tigers. *World Economy* 16(4):401–22 (July).

Riedel, J. 1995. A new Taiwanese clone? *Far Eastern Economic Review* November 23, p. 39.

Rieke, W., and Antal, L. 1993. Hungary: Sound money, fiscal problems. In R. Portes, ed., *Economic Transformation in Central Europe, A Progress Report*. London and Brussels: Centre for Economic Policy Research and Office for Official Publications of the European Commission.

Riskin, C. 1994. Chinese rural poverty: marginalized or dispersed. *American Economics Association Papers and Proceedings* 84(2):281–84.

Rocznik Statystyczny (Statistical Yearbook). 1993. Warsaw: GUS.

Rocznik Statystyczny (Statistical Yearbook). 1994. Warsaw: GUS.

Rodrik, D. 1993. Trade and industrial policy reform in developing countries: A review of recent theory and evidence. National Bureau of Economic Research Working Paper no. 4417.

Rodrik, D. 1994a. Foreign trade in Eastern Europe's transition: Early results. In O. Blanchard, K. Froot, and J. Sachs, eds., *The Transition in Eastern Europe*. Chicago, Illinois: University of Chicago Press.

Rodrik, D. 1994b. King Kong meets Godzilla: The World Bank and the East Asian miracle. In *Miracle or Design? Lessons from the East Asian Experience*. Policy Essay no. 11. Washington D.C.: Overseas Development Council.

Rodrik, D. 1995. Overcoming the transformation crisis. H. Siebert, ed. Institut für Weltwirtschaft and der Universität Kiel, J.C.B. Mohr (Paul Siebeck), Tübingen.

Russian Federation. 1995. *Russian Economic Trends*. Various issues. Moscow and London: Whurr Publishers.

Sachs, J., and Woo, W.T. 1994. Structural factors in the economic reforms of China, Eastern Europe and the Former Soviet Union. *Economic Policy* (April) 18:101–45.

Schieve, C. 1995. Experiences and issues of privatization in Taiwan. *Industry of Free China* (January) 83(1):19–34.

Sen, T., and Zhu, G. 1993. A study of out-of-system government revenue of township and village. *Jingji Yanjui (Economic Research Journal)* (September) 9:45–52.

Senik-Leygonie, C. 1994. Industrial restructuring in the CIS. Is Russia going in the right direction? Study prepared for DGII of the Commission of the European Community, January 15, 1994.

Shilling, J.D., and Y. Wang. 1995. *Managing Capital Flows in East Asia*. A regional study by the Office of the Vice President for East Asia and Pacific Region. Washington, D.C.: World Bank.

Sommariva, A.C. 1992. Some lessons for the Mongolian reformers from a comparative analysis in the reform experiences in the Soviet Union, smaller Eastern European Countries and China. Ulaanbaatar.

Standard and Poor. 1994. *Report on Hungarian Capital Markets*.

Stark, D. 1990. Privatization in Hungary: From plan to market or plan to clan. *East European Politics and Societies* 4(2).

Stark, D. 1996. Networks of assets, chains of debt: Recombinant property in Hungary. In R. Frydman, C. Gray, and A. Rapaczynski, eds., *Corporate Governance in Central Europe and Russia* (forthcoming). Budapest, London, and New York: Central European University Press (in cooperation with Oxford University Press).

Subbarao, K., and K. Ezemenari. 1995. Transition, poverty, and social assistance in Mongolia. Unpublished paper (January). Washington, D.C.: Education and Social Policy Department, World Bank.

Svejnar, J. 1993. Czech and Slovak Federal Republic: A solid foundation. In R. Portes, ed., *Economic Transformation in Central Europe*. Luxembourg, European Communities.

Swaan, W. 1990. Price regulation in Hungary, 1968–87: A behavioral-industrial explanation. *Cambridge Journal of Economics* 14:247–65.

Teichova, A. 1974. *An Economic Background to Munich: International Business and Czecholslovakia, 1918–1938*. Cambridge: Cambridge University Press.

Teichova, A. 1988. *The Czechoslovak Economy, 1918–1980*. London and New York: Routledge Press.

Tho, A., and Xuan, L. 1993. Vietnam: Safe water program for rural Vietnam until the year 2000. *Vietnam Investment Review*, October 4.

Thomas, V., and Y. Wang. 1994. Asian socialist and non-socialist transition experiences. Paper presented to The Asia Foundation project, "Comparing Transitions in East Asia and Eastern Europe," December 2–3, 1994, Prague.

Treisman, D. 1995. The politics of soft credit in post Soviet Russia. *Europe–Asia Studies* 47(6):949–76.

Tsend, A., B. Tarvaa, N. Unenburen, E. Tsendjav, and P. Boone. 1994. Mongolia's rapid transition to a democratic market economy. Paper presented to The Asia Foundation project, "Comparing Transitions in East Asia and Eastern Europe," December 2–3, 1994, Prague.

Tseng, W., H.E. Khor, K. Kochhar, D. Mihaljek, and D. Burton. 1994. Economic reform in China. Occasional paper no. 114. International Monetary Fund.

U.S. Department of Commerce. *Historical Statistics of the United States: Colonial Time to 1970*, Series U 207–12, p. 888. Washington, D.C.

UNDP/World Bank. 1994. *Viet Nam: Policies for Transition to an Open Economy.* Country Report 13. February. Washington, D.C.

United Nations. 1994. *Statistical Yearbook Thirty-Ninth Issue.* New York: United Nations.

United Nations. 1995. *Statistical Yearbook Fortieth Issue.* New York: United Nations.

Van de Walle, D. 1993. Poverty, vulnerability, transfers, and safety nets in Viet Nam. Unpublished paper (May). Washington, D.C.: Policy Research Department, World Bank.

Vincentz, V. 1994. External liberalization in a large country: The contribution to the transition process in Russia. Working paper no. 169. München: Ostewropa-Institut.

Vining, A., and A. Boardman. 1992. Ownership vs. competition: Efficiency in public enterprise. *Public Choice* 73:205–39.

Voszka, E. 1993. Spontaneous Privatization in Hungary. In J. Earle, R. Frydman, and A. Rapaczynski, eds., *Privatization in the Transition to a Market Economy.* New York: Pinter Publishers.

Wade, R. 1990. *Governing the Market: Economic Theory and Taiwan's Industrial Policies.* Princeton, New Jersey: Princeton University Press.

Wade, R. 1994. Selective industrial policies in East Asia: Is the East Asian miracle right? In *Miracle or Design? Lessons from the East Asian Experience.* Policy essay no. 11. Washington D.C.: Overseas Development Council.

Wang, C., and Li, X. 1993. The losses of state assets (in Chinese). *Financial and Economic Studies*, vol. 12.

Webster, L. 1992. *Private Sector Manufacturing in Hungary: A Survey of Firms.* Washington, D.C.: The World Bank Industry and Energy Department.

Weitzman, M., and C. Xu, 1994. Chinese township village enterprises as vaguely defined cooperatives. *Journal of Comparative Economics* 18(2):121–45.

Winters, L.A. 1995a. Liberalization of the European steel trade. In R. Faini and R. Portes, eds., *European Union Trade with Eastern Europe.* London: CEPR.

Winters, L.A. 1995b. Trade policy institutions in Central and Eastern Europe: Objectives and outcomes. In L.A. Winters, ed., *Foundations of an Open Economy.* London: CEPR.

Wong, C., Heady, C., and Woo, W.T. 1995. *Fiscal Management and Economic Reform in the People's Republic of China*. Oxford University Press.

Woo, W.T. 1994. The art of reforming centrally planned economies: Comparing China, Poland, and Russia. *Journal of Comparative Economics* (June) 18(3).

Woo, W.T. 1996. Chinese economic growth: Sources and prospects. Working Paper no. 96-08, Economics Department, University of California, Davis (May).

Woo, W.T. (forthcoming) Financial intermediation in China. In O. Bouin, F. Coricelli, and F. Lemoine, eds., *Different Approaches to the Transition to a Market Economy. Economies in Transition*. Paris: Organization for Economic Cooperation and Development.

Woo, W.T., G. Fan, W. Hai, and Y. Jin. 1994. Reply to comment by Jefferson, Rawski and Zheng. *China Economic Review* 5(2): 243–8.

Woo, W.T., Hai, W., Jin, Y., and Fan, G. 1994. How successful has Chinese enterprise reforms been? Pitfalls in opposite biases and focus. *Journal of Comparative Economics* (June) 18(3):410–37.

World Bank and European Bank for Reconstruction and Development. 1993. *Newly-Privatized Russian Enterprises: A Survey* (December). Mimeo.

World Bank and International Monetary Fund. 1990. *Problems and Issues in Structural Adjustment*. Development Committee Series, no. 23. Washington D.C.: World Bank.

World Bank. 1990a. *China: Macroeconomic Stability and Industrial Growth under Decentralized Socialism*. Washington D.C.: World Bank.

World Bank. 1990b. *Viet Nam—Economic Report*. Washington D.C.: World Bank.

World Bank. 1991. *World Development Report 1991: The Challenge of Development*. Oxford University Press.

World Bank. 1992a. *Adjustment Lending and Mobilization of Private and Public Resources for Growth*, Country Economics Department, Policy and Research Series, no. 22. Washington D.C.: World Bank.

World Bank. 1992b. *Russian Economic Reform: Crossing the Threshold of Structural Change*. Washington D.C.: World Bank.

World Bank. 1992c. *Viet Nam. Restructuring Public Finance and Public Enterprises*. Washington D.C.: World Bank.

World Bank. 1993a. *The East Asian Miracle—Economic Growth and Public Policy*. New York: Oxford University Press.

World Bank. 1993b. *The Lessons of East Asia*. a series of papers on country experience. Washington, D.C.: World Bank.

World Bank. 1993c. *Viet Nam: Transition to the Market*. Washington, D.C.: World Bank (September).

World Bank. 1994a. *Poland Growth with Equity Policies for the 1990s*. Report no. 13039-POL. Washington, D.C.: World Bank.

World Bank. 1994b. *Viet Nam Public Sector Management and Private Sector Incentives, An Economic Report.* Report No. 13143-VN. September 26, 1993. Washington, D.C.: World Bank.

World Bank. 1995a. *Bureaucrats in Business: The Economics and Politics of Government Ownership.* Washington, D.C.

World Bank. 1995b. *Viet Nam: Economic Report on Industrialization and Industrial Policy.* Report No. 14645-VN. Washington, D.C.: World Bank (October 17, 1995).

World Bank. 1995c. *Viet Nam: Poverty Assessment and Strategy.* Washington, D.C.: World Bank (January).

World Bank. 1995d. *World Development Report, and World Development Indicators.* New York: Oxford University Press.

World Bank. 1996. From Plan to Market: World Development Report, p. 18. Oxford University Press.

Xiao, G. 1991. State enterprises in China: Dealing with loss-makers. *Transition* (December) 2(11):1–3. World Bank.

Yeats, A. 1987. The escalation of trade barriers. In J.M. Finger and A. Olechowski, eds., *The Uruguay Round: A Handbook on the Multilateral Trade Negotiations.* Washington D.C.: World Bank.

Yeltsin, B. 1994. *The Struggle for Russia.* Times Books.

Zemplinerova, A. et al. 1994. Restructuring of firms in Czech manufacturing: results of the enterprise survey. CERGE Working Paper no. 74, Prague.

Zhang, W., and Yi, G. 1994. China's gradual reform: A historical perspective. China Center for Economic Research, Beijing University (manuscript).

Zhao, R. 1992. Some special phenomena in income distribution during China's transition period. *Economic Research (Jingji Yanjiu)* (in Chinese). Issue 1, pp. 53–63.

Zhong, P., and Hong, T. 1990. *Macroeconomics* (in Chinese). Beijing: Economic Sciences Press.

Zmiany strukturalne grup podmiotów gospodarki narodowej w trzech kwartalach 1994 (The structural changes of the groups of economic subjects in the three quarters of 1994). 1994. Warsaw: GUS. Also May 1996.

Zwass, A. 1984. *The Economies of Eastern Europe in a Time of Change.* Armonk, NY: M.E. Sharpe.

Index